D1563194

Diné dóó Gáamalii

Lyda Conley Series on Trailblazing Indigenous Futures

Farina King

Kiara M. Vigil

Tai S. Edwards

SERIES EDITORS

Diné dóó Gáamalii

Navajo Latter-day Saint
Experiences in the
Twentieth Century

Farina King

University Press of Kansas

Dedicated to Diné dóó Gáamalii family and friends

© 2023 by the
University Press
of Kansas
All rights reserved

Published by the
University Press of
Kansas (Lawrence,
Kansas 66045), which
was organized by
the Kansas Board
of Regents and is
operated and funded
by Emporia State
University, Fort Hays
State University,
Kansas State
University, Pittsburg
State University, the
University of Kansas,
and Wichita State
University.

Library of Congress Cataloging-in-Publication Data

Names: King, Farina, author.

Title: Diné dóó Gáamalii : Navajo Latter-day Saint experiences in
the twentieth century / Farina King.

Other titles: Navajo Latter-day Saint experiences in the twentieth
century

Description: Lawrence, Kansas : University Press of Kansas, 2023.
| Series: Lyda Conley series on trailblazing indigenous futures |
Includes bibliographical references and index.

Identifiers: LCCN 2022061296 (print) | LCCN 2022061297
(ebook)

ISBN 9780700635528 (cloth)

ISBN 9780700635535 (paperback)

ISBN 9780700635542 (ebook)

Subjects: LCSH: Navajo Indians—Religion. | Indian Mormons. |
Church work with Indians—Church of Jesus Christ of Latter-day
Saints—History—20th century. | Church of Jesus Christ of
Latter-day Saints—Missions—Navajo Nation, Arizona, New
Mexico & Utah. | Navajo Indians—Missions. | Navajo Indians—
Ethnic identity. | King, Farina,—Family.

Classification: LCC E99.N3 K444 2023 (print) | LCC E99.N3
(ebook) | DDC 289.3/320899726—dc23/eng/20230103

LC record available at https://lccn.loc.gov/2022061296.

LC ebook record available at https://lccn.loc.gov/2022061297.

British Library Cataloguing-in-Publication Data is available.

Printed in the United States of America

10 9 8 7 6 5 4 3 2 1

The paper used in this publication is acid free and meets the
minimum requirements of the American National Standard for
Permanence of Paper for Printed Library Materials Z39.48-1992.

Contents

List of Images, *vii*

Foreword, *ix*

Acknowledgments, *xv*

Introduction, *1*

1   Diné dóó Gáamalii: Navajo Latter-day Saints, *20*

2   Gáamalii Bina'nitiní: Missionaries, *49*

3   Ólta' Gáamalii: "Mormon School," *84*

4   Sodizin Bá Hooghan: Church, *113*

5   Beyond Diné Bikéyah, *138*

6   Red Power at BYU, *155*

7   Diné dóó Gáamalii Perspectives, *180*

Epilogue, *196*

Appendix: Oral History Interviews and Oral History Sources, *211*

Glossary, *215*

Notes, *219*

Select Bibliography, *275*

Index, *281*

Images

1 JoAnn and Phillip Smiths' wedding, *5*

2 George P. Lee with Phillip and JoAnn Smith, *19*

3 Chinle Latter-day Saint Stake Center, *45*

4 Phillip Smith as missionary with mission companion and mother, *51*

5 Elder Kimo Hanamaikai, *65*

6 Sister missionaries of the Southwest Indian Mission, *67*

7 Lamanite Generation performance, *76*

8 Southwest Indian Mission reunion sign-in table, *82*

9 Arlene Nofchissey Williams and Carnes Burson with Dale Tingey, *110*

10 Farina King with Smith family, *111*

11 Chinle Latter-day Saint Stake gardens, *131*

12 Miriam and Jarrett Chun, *143*

13 Millie Cody with President Spencer W. Kimball, *161*

14 Phillip Smith in Utah, *162*

15 Tribe of Many Feathers in 1964, *167*

16 The court of Miss Indian BYU, 1970–1971, *175*

17 Farina King and Anna Benally, *185*

18 Dennis and Irene Jones with Farina King, *189*

19 Farina King and son holding Cheii (horned toad), *197*

20 Smith family photo in 2019, *208*

Foreword

Over the last five centuries, the Indigenous peoples of North America have had to invest an enormous share of their energy and time in challenging and correcting the multitude of stereotypes and misguided assumptions imposed on them. Meanwhile, over nearly two centuries, the members of the Church of Jesus Christ of Latter-day Saints have had to navigate their way through an obstacle course of misapprehensions, misconceptions, and misinterpretations produced and circulated by "Gentiles." Public understandings of both groups still fail to rest on accuracy, context, and respect.

Publishing a "collective biography" of Diné who are also Latter-day Saints, Farina King has validated the article of faith that I have held for decades: *A historian who tells engaging stories about intrinsically interesting people will have a great advantage when it comes to challenging deeply rooted stereotypes and misconceptions.* Moreover, the opportunity to read *Diné dóó Gáamalii: Navajo Latter-day Saint Experiences in the Twentieth Century* added a new dimension to that long-held belief. An enterprise that corrects *two* well-established structures of misunderstanding, I now realize, will be much more effective than an undertaking that tries to correct only *one* structure at a time. Readers of this book will gain a distinctive understanding, set free of stereotypes and misconceptions, of what it has meant to be Diné and what it has meant to be Latter-day Saint. Even better, King's study of the people who have claimed and occupied *both* those identities provides a graceful and persuasive demonstration of how to move far beyond conventional thinking about the meaning of identity in American life, both past and present.

In one of the finest features of this book, King meets the highest standards for scholarly research and writing, while consistently avoiding the pitfalls of surrendering to academic preoccupations that jeopardize the engagement of audiences beyond the walls of universities and colleges. For historians who aspire to reach wider audiences, this book provides valuable demonstrations of how to ground abstractions and generalizations in compelling stories of lived experience; how to offer full inclusion to the voices of people who have thought hard about their lives; how to select individuals to portray in what I will call "premier parables," or case studies that raise essential questions and provide illuminating answers; and how to keep one's balance while walking on a tightrope above contention and dispute.

Perhaps most important, King is direct in acknowledging her own ties to the world of Diné Latter-day Saints, starting on the very first page of this book: "This book presents the stories of this community as a collective biography, but also through the lens of a historian seeking to understand her own people and family. . . . I trace the entanglement of diverse communities and collective identities that have affected my own experiences and relationships." With this forthright acknowledgment of her engagement with her subject matter, King does not diminish her authority, but deepens it. The presence of the author (which is, after all, the first six letters in "authority") enriches every dimension of this study, as the historian embraces the roles of participant, observer, interpreter, translator, ambassador, and (in a manner that fortunately does *not* bring Gertrude Stein to mind) convenor and discussion leader of a very dynamic salon. If the job of the applied historian means making sense of history, and then figuring out how to live with its legacy, then King is clearly the right person for that particular job. Even better, the stories she tells offer a pair of reminders for her sometimes rattled and divided profession: (1) a faith is not a synonym for complacency—indeed, faith in the value of history has to be tested, before it has meaning; and (2) a resilient sense of community can persist through flare-ups of tension, or to put this differently, a profession that engages in frays together, stays together.

Aligned with those reminders, one of King's particular gifts appears in her treatment of matters that more prosaic researchers might characterize as contradiction or even hypocrisy. Her framework for handling matters of this sort bears a closer resemblance to a recognition of *paradox* than to a condemnation of inconsistency. The Church of Jesus Christ of Latter-day Saints holds various statements and doctrines that exhort its members to respect, welcome, and include "Lamanites," the Church's historic term for Indigenous people. But the willingness and ability to comply with these statements and doctrines have varied considerably. As King writes with her signature frankness, "Many white Latter-day Saints, like other white Americans, have exhibited racism and paternalism toward Native Americans." Yes, non-Indian Mormons were supposed to conduct themselves with grace toward the "Lamanites." And yet every scholar of religious history knows that the relationship between faith and conduct is often a paradox, as believers struggle to put principle into practice. In truth, only the irredeemably naive would expect religious believers to live up to their ideals with consistency. All this book's chapters, but especially chapter 3 on the Indian Student Placement Program, offer invaluable opportunities to reflect on this paradox.

In the same spirit, by reckoning with the paradox that reappears in the history of encounters between Natives and settlers, King makes a significant contribution to current considerations of settler colonialism. Of course, the Church of Jesus Christ of Latter-day Saints was transported to the American West by settlers who were unmistakably intruders in the homelands of Natives. In a world of greater simplicity, we might then argue that the American Indian people—who adopted the beliefs introduced to them by settler-colonial intruders—have also conceded and submitted to the power and authority of the settlers. And yet a strong current of exchange and interaction—intersecting with but not overwhelmed by the more visible current of conflict and violence—runs through the history of the relations between Indigenous people and settlers. Dealing with a variety of Euro-American–introduced religions, a striking number of Indigenous people have found ways to adopt these religions, not on the terms of the settlers but on their own terms. They have even turned the tables of power by finding new and distinctive meanings in those structures of faith. To make this point sharply, assuming that the maintenance of tradition must be a project in purity would do a disservice to the complexity of the minds—and souls—of human beings. Moreover, settlers in westward expansion were hardly unified and homogeneous; after all, the Latter-day Saints who emigrated to Deseret had strong memories of the hostility and persecution they had received from other settlers. Like other Euro-American settler populations, Latter-day Saints have always varied in their attitudes and conduct toward Indigenous communities. The most important determinant of the outcome of this unfathomably complicated encounter has been the actions and reactions of the Indigenous peoples themselves. As King sums this up, "For those who have walked the pathways of Diné and Latter-day Saint beliefs, there is no clear answer of how they connect"; instead, those pathways have led to a multiplicity of destinations.

And yet pathways that diverge also converge, as I am about to testify.

Working with Michael P. Taylor and James R. Swensen, Farina King coauthored an extraordinary book, *Returning Home: Diné Creative Works from the Intermountain Indian School.* The phrase "returning home" in that title carries a distinctive resonance for me. The Intermountain Indian School, "the largest federal Indian boarding school in the United States," was located in my father's hometown: Brigham City, Utah.

My father's parents were Danish Mormons. Although my father left the Church as a young man, he never detached his sense of who he was from his place of origin. There is no question that this had an impact on me. Over the years, I have heard many people make remarks about having "a Catholic sense of guilt" or "an intense Protestant work ethic." Each time I have heard such remarks, I have said to myself, "Then whose sense of guilt do I have, and whose intense work ethic?" Here's my hypothesis: people who cease to be members of a church can still pass on customs and principles to their unchurched children.

My father told my sisters and me a good share of stories from his childhood. We learned, for instance, that our grandmother had theorized her way to a rationale that permitted some aspects of Danishness to overrule Church expectations. In the early twentieth century my father's family was still farming with horses. These horses apparently recognized the special arrangements my grandmother had made with her faith, and at mid-afternoon they paused in their labors and headed to the farmhouse, as the Danes' coffee break also served as the horses' hay break.

A little more than a year before my father's death at age eighty-nine, he was in a hospital, passing the time with a collection of articles I had written. Reading my essay "Haunted America," about violent conflicts between Indigenous people and invaders of their homelands, my father came upon a passage about the Bear River Massacre, a brutal attack on the Shoshone people by the US Army, on January 29, 1863. Here is the passage he read in my essay: "Following the commands of his grandmother, the twelve-year-old Shoshone boy Yeager Timbimboo spent most of the day lying on the snow-covered ground, pretending to be dead. But at a crucial moment, he disobeyed his grandmother, and opened his eyes." And here are the words I quoted from Mae Timbimboo Parry, a Shoshone woman historian who was the granddaughter of Yeager Timbimboo and a lifelong Latter-day Saint:

A soldier came upon him and saw that he was alive and looking round. The military man stood over Yeager, his gun pointing at the young boy's head, ready to fire. The soldier stared at the boy and the boy at the soldier.

The second time the soldier raised his rifle the little boy knew that his time to die was near. The soldier then lowered his gun and raised it again. For some reason he could not complete his task. He took his rifle down and walked away.

In his hospital bed, on the edge of life himself, my father read this passage, looked up at me, and said, "I knew that family."

The Northwestern Band of Shoshone Nation's offices have historically been located in Brigham City and remain in northern Utah. In the late 2010s the Northwestern Band of Shoshone tribal chairman was Darren Parry, the grandson of the woman who told the story I had quoted in my essay, Yeager Timbimboo's great-great-grandson, and an Indigenous person who navigates the pathway where Shoshone and Latter-day Saint identities converge. In recent times, Farina King and other historians invited their friend Darren Parry to attend the annual meeting of the Western History Association.

Here are two opportunities I missed in life. When my father responded to the story from the Bear River Massacre, I should have said to him, "Please tell me about the ties between our family and theirs." And when I introduced myself to Parry, I should have said to him, "My family knew your family."

As Darren Parry's grandmother Mae Timbimboo Parry observed, "No one will ever know what went through the mind" of the soldier who lowered his rifle and walked away. Nor will any of us ever be able to hear that man's name and say that we knew his family. But we do know that the Shoshone people were in an impossible situation as the travelers on the overland trail encroached on their lands from the north, and as Latter-day Saint settlers encroached on their lands from the south. The fact that—almost exactly a half century after the Bear River Massacre—my father was born in that locale is one among millions of the intertwined consequences of the westward exodus of Latter-day Saints into "Lamanite" homelands.

In yet another of those consequences, I now have the privilege of writing this foreword for Farina King's book, in which Diné Latter-day Saints transcend the simple categories of identity that can exercise an undeserved power over human minds. In an era when contests and conflicts over the meaning of history shake the nation, our intertwined life stories make the case for an alternative configuration, in which the past unites us in the present.

Patty Limerick, author of *Legacy of Conquest* and director of the
Applied History Initiative at the University of Colorado, Boulder
February 2023

Acknowledgments

I owe special gratitude and recognition to Jessie Embry for all her invaluable support and collaboration with this research and book from its inception. This book would not have been possible without Jessie, who took me under her wing when she was the associate director of the Charles Redd Center for Western Studies at Brigham Young University. She hired me for the LDS Native American Oral History Project during my senior year as an undergraduate student. Jessie introduced me to the practice and methodology of oral history. I always loved to learn history through stories and interviews, but Jessie taught me what oral history is and how to do it. She provided me with the resources and time to focus on this research. We traveled to the Navajo Nation for oral histories with Latter-day Saint Diné, and we presented together at conferences about Latter-day Saint Native American experiences and histories. I have never met such an exemplary scholar who works so diligently.

The Neal A. Maxwell Institute for Religious Scholarship at Brigham Young University awarded me the Living Faith Author Initiative Grant in 2021, as a Latter-day Saint woman writer, to complete the revisions for this manuscript. The Maxwell Institute also sponsored the Consultation on Latter-day Saint Women in Comparative Perspective, which strengthened my work in Mormon studies. The editors, Miranda Wilcox and Morgan Davis, along with anonymous peer reviewers, went above and beyond to review the manuscript, as did the Charles Redd Center, which also funded the LDS Native American Oral History Project while Jessie served as the associate director.

I am grateful for my parents and their courage and willingness to tell their life stories. My father has faced some painful and hard experiences relating to his personal life and faith, which resurface in the stories. My father and mother continue to inspire me every day, and I am blessed to share their stories with the public through these works.

Thank you to the many Indigenous and Diné Latter-day Saints who shared their stories, which undergird this book. Edwin Tano (Kanaka ʻŌiwi or Native Hawaiian) and Irene Jones (Diné) especially supported the LDS Native American Oral History Project with their time, attention, and connections to Latter-day Saint Diné communities. I express gratitude to Latter-day Saint congregations that permitted me to facilitate conversations about this research with groups of their Diné members, including the Monument Valley Ward, Lukachukai Ward, Franklin Second Ward, and wards of the Page, Arizona, region. I am responsible for this work and interpretation, and I hope that I reflect their incredible lives and experiences well.

I also recognize the many colleagues and friends who have encouraged me to continue with this work. Patricia (Patty) Nelson Limerick showed confidence in me when I was facing serious self-doubts. I was honored to share this study during the Applied History Workshop that Patty hosted at the Center of the American West, University of Colorado–Boulder. Patty arranged for me to present to and receive feedback from many wonderful scholars, including Liza Black, Phil Deloria, Shelly Lowe, and so many others that I wish I could list them all. I am grateful for the position as the Horizon Chair of Native American Ecology and Culture in the University of Oklahoma's Department of Native American Studies (NAS), which supports my research. The NAS Department at the university has connected me with great colleagues, students, and staff, and an exemplary community of learners.

Thank you to my friend, Miriam Chun (Diné), who worked for years on the cover art to best represent this book as Diné dóó Gáamalii. I appreciate the assistance of family and friends, especially Brian King, Braden King, and Michelle Burgess, with reviewing the manuscript and preparing the select bibliography. Many sponsors and colleagues of the workshop and gathering about Indigenous perspectives on the meanings of "Lamanite" have motivated my work in Indigenous Mormon studies, which includes Michael Ing, Monika Crowfoot, Eva Bighorse, Angelo Baca, Daniel Hernandez, J. Spencer Fluhman, Matthew Bowman, W. Paul Reeve, and Barbara Brown, among many others. Organizations such as the Mormon History Association and Global Mormon Studies have also sustained my research and opportunities to network and connect. For this book, I relied on the Brigham Young University Library and Special Collections, the Church History Library, and so many people who have enabled this work.

Thank you to senior editor David Congdon, the University Press of Kansas, and the Lyda Conley Series on Trailblazing Indigenous Futures for supporting this publication. I sustain and commend you and all academic presses for the important services you provide to humanity as avenues to truth telling and healing.

I express my deepest gratitude to my husband, Brian, and our children, Will, Wes, and Luci. I deeply love you and appreciate your patience and support that carries me. Ahéhee'! Walk in Beauty.

Introduction

This narrative begins with my father's story, which shaped my life and relations as Diné dóó Gáamalii—Latter-day Saint and Navajo.[1] In Diné bizaad, the Navajo language, we introduce ourselves by our clans that we inherit. *Bilagáanaa nishłį́. Kinyaa'áanii báshíshchíín. Bilagáanaa dashicheii dóó Tsinaajinii dashinálí.* My mother is of white European-American settler descent, and my father is of the Towering House and Black-Streaked Woods clans. I am born for my father's Diné clans, and I was raised as a Latter-day Saint, since my parents both joined the Church of Jesus Christ of Latter-day Saints as young adults. Because of my background, I take part in Diné dóó Gáamalii communities.

Diné differentiate between Gáamalii (Mormons) and Bilagáana (whites). Linguists who studied Diné bizaad, Robert W. Young and Morgan William, claim that "Gáamalii, and on the western reservation Máamalii, are no doubt Navaho adaptations of the English word Mormon."[2] This book presents stories of the Diné dóó Gáamalii community within a collective biography as interpreted through my own lens as a historian seeking to better understand my own people and family. I trace the entanglements of diverse communities and collective identities between the late twentieth and early twenty-first centuries that have affected my own experiences and relationships.[3] I address how Diné Latter-day Saints, like my father, developed and engaged with a community that faced a flux of challenges, growth, and contradictions in the last half of the twentieth century. Diné dóó Gáamalii communities persisted through tense linkages of different Indigenous and Mormon peoples.

When I was a little girl, in the 1990s, my father stood up and walked to the pulpit from the pew where our family was sitting during a "fast and testimony meeting" at church. He then recounted some of his experiences that I had never heard before. Latter-day Saint congregations throughout the world traditionally include time for sharing testimonies in their sacrament meetings every first Sunday of the month. During fast and testimony meetings, the members of the congregation are invited to publicly speak of their faith. Under the high ceilings of a chapel, I first listened to my dad's conversion story. In moments and conversations, following his public testimonies, I have pieced together his personal journey that led him and our family to join and support the Church of Jesus Christ of Latter-day Saints. Some key themes in my family's experiences form the threads that interweave throughout this book.

Since he was the youngest son, my father's family called him *ashkii yázhí*, little boy. He was born in his family's hogan, a traditional Diné dwelling, behind a rocky ridge not far from the mission site of the Rehoboth Christian Reformed Church in Diné Bikéyah, Navajo country. A nurse midwife from the mission hospital came to the hogan to help deliver him. My father received the names on his birth certificate from the nurse midwife who chose Phillip for his first name after one of the twelve apostles in the New Testament.[4] Lee, the nurse's first name, became his middle name. Although many of his maternal relatives joined the Rehoboth Christian Reformed Church, Phillip's family did not adhere to Christianity at home. His father was a *hataałii*, a Diné healer also known as a "medicine man," who hoped to transfer his knowledge and spiritual practices to Phillip. Schooling exposed Phillip to Christian denominations during his childhood, but he was assigned to or randomly picked a Christian religion in the way a student joins a club at school. The different denominational groups would attract children by offering the most perks such as free food and candy. In junior high school, my dad started to work on a farm in the Teton Valley of Idaho for a Latter-day Saint family during the summers. As a young migrant worker, he developed a close friendship with the farmer, Merle Kunz, and his family. The family invited him to church and to read the Book of Mormon, which my father initially resisted and criticized. When Merle asked my father to read the Book of Mormon, my dad told him to "read *Custer Died for Your Sins* first." I never found out if Merle Kunz read Vine Deloria Jr.'s book, but my father eventually read the Book of Mormon.

The Kunz family convinced my dad, when he was graduating from high school, to apply to Brigham Young University (BYU) after one of his school-teachers also recommended its extensive language programs. Phillip enjoyed learning different languages such as German and Arabic. He enrolled at BYU as a "non-member" of the Church in 1968. He began to believe the Book of Mormon to be another testament of Christ, while studying it for a religion class taught by the dean of General College, Lester Whetten. My dad became convinced from Latter-day Saint teachings that Jesus Christ had come to the Americas, and that Native Americans, including himself, descended from an ancient civilization of Israelite lineage and covenant people—the Lamanites. In 1969, as a BYU student, my father wanted to be baptized in the Church.

His decision to accept the doctrine of the Church drastically changed his relationship with *shinálí hastiin*, my grandfather. When he returned home to Diné Bikéyah to share the news of his conversion, he expected his family to celebrate since he had discovered what he considered to be the truth and happiness in the gospel. Instead of rejoicing with him, his father was outraged and disowned him, forbidding him to return home. Phillip left engulfed with the heartbreak that he might never see his family again for the rest of his life.

My father's conversion to the Latter-day Saint faith followed a series of events that repetitively raised challenges, which begged the question as to why he continued to participate in the Church. I sought to understand what he had to gain from church membership by tracing his experiences and those of other Diné who participated in the Church during the late twentieth century. When my father consciously prepared for his baptism, church officials informed him that he was already baptized. My father then remembered when missionaries of the Church of Jesus Christ of Latter-day Saints took him and other children from the Ramah school's dormitory for Native Americans to a movie in Gallup, New Mexico. They dunked him and some fellow dormitory schoolchildren in water after the movie, but he never understood that the missionaries had baptized them. They simply invited him to an outing. Although he was baptized then, he did not convert to the Latter-day Saint faith until college.

Soon after his conversion, however, certain dynamics at BYU disillusioned my dad. His roommates, fellow Native American students, were members of the Church, for example, but they drank alcohol and broke the school rules. What really frustrated my dad, however, was how white Latter-day Saints discriminated against BYU Native American students in Provo with regard to off-campus housing. While he served as an officer for the Native American student organization, Tribe of Many Feathers (TMF), his primary responsibility involved securing off-campus housing for Native students. He found that many white Latter-day Saints refused to rent to Native students because of stereotypes about Native Americans, including often considering them to be alcoholics. Other forms of racial discrimination also upset my dad during his time at BYU. He remembered, for example, how BYU officials prohibited Native students from dating white people, and they discouraged interracial courtship.

After facing such offenses, my dad transferred to Gonzaga University in the summer of 1969. Although he continued to believe in the Book of Mormon, he was ostracized when he attended church with a Latter-day Saint congregation in Spokane, Washington; everyone in the congregation ignored him even after he tried to introduce himself. Feeling unwelcome, he stopped going to that church and engaged with other denominational groups such as some Jesuits, who invited him to play sports with them. At the end of the term, Merle Kunz called my dad and asked him to help on his farm for a month. During that month in Idaho, Phillip participated in a Latter-day Saint congregation with the Kunz family. Merle encouraged him to serve a mission for the Church, and he offered to assist with the costs. When Phillip hesitated, Merle assured him: "You know the Book of Mormon is true. Jesus is the Christ. That's all you need to know."[5] My dad decided to apply for a mission, attempting to conceal any affiliation with the Navajo Nation in hopes of being sent abroad. Church officials assigned him to the Southwest Indian Mission (SWIM), which primarily encompassed Diné Bikéyah. After his mission, he returned to BYU to finish his undergraduate studies, where he met my mother, JoAnn.

As I discuss how my father joined the Church, some have asked me if he still believes in Diné traditions. Their inquiries often underscore doubts about the authenticity of my family's Diné identity, since people wonder how a Diné could join the Latter-day Saints or any Christian denominational group and remain Diné, although various studies have addressed these similar questions.[6] Families and communities within the Navajo Nation have also questioned and disputed internally and personally the dynamics between religious and ethnic identities. A Diné woman once explained to SWIM president Hal L. Taylor how being Diné was her true religion and "any true Navajo will never be anything but a Navajo, for they are born with their religion in their heart." To this woman and other Diné like my grandfather, when Diné "join other churches, it is only to keep other churches away from them and to become a little more acceptable to other people" such as white Americans.[7] Some Diné have condemned Christian religions altogether, although their relatives might join such denominations. Thomas

The author's parents, JoAnn and Phillip Smith, on their wedding day with Phillip's mother, Johanna Haskeltsie Smith, at the Provo Latter-day Saint Temple in 1974, as displayed in the Smiths' home beside a traditional Diné wedding basket known as ts'aa'. Courtesy of author.

Benally, a Latter-day Saint Chinle Stake high council leader, discussed in 1997 how his sister condemned Christianity: "She gets offended. She says that if the Navajos go back to their traditional ways, they wouldn't have the problems they have now." She blames European colonizers and white American settlers for "disarraying" Diné with religion.[8]

As an adolescent, my father would have agreed with this point while considering his own baptism. In boarding school, he selected a Christian religious affiliation to avoid punishment and retaliation from school officials. He was baptized in exchange for going to the movies. He believes that his heart changed when he converted to the Latter-day Saint faith as a young adult. Referring to other Latter-day Saints, such as his roommates who got drunk on the weekends and Church leaders who forbade him from dating white women, I asked my father how he could have willingly joined the Latter-day Saints. He replied that he "found truth" for himself. Most importantly, Phillip stressed his identity as Diné in conjunction with his church membership. He taught me and my siblings that we are Diné by introducing us to our relatives, kinship, and ancestral homelands in Diné Bikéyah.

DINÉ FOUNDATIONS

This narrative considers how Diné have lived the Latter-day Saint faith while reaffirming their "Navajoness" in the face of challenges and tensions between diverse communities that relate to Diné dóó Gáamalii. I highlight ways that Diné Latter-day Saint converts have developed identities as Diné dóó Gáamalii since the "Kimball Era" or "Lamanite Era." Apostle and Prophet Spencer W. Kimball championed a "Lamanite Cause" in the Church, spearheading an era roughly between 1960 and 1985 that concentrated on preparing Native Americans as Latter-day Saint leaders and exemplars. This book looks within and beyond this time frame, which was integral to Diné Latter-day Saint community building. Latter-day Saint proselytization became most effective among Diné during this period.

Whatever conflicts arose with their families and people due to their conversion and affiliation with the Church, some Diné embraced Latter-day Saint teachings that their people, regarded as the descendants of ancient peoples and the Lamanites in the Book of Mormon, would "blossom as the rose," unify, and contribute to the building of Zion on earth. Some Diné converts have relied on their heritage of *tsodizin dóó sin*, Diné spirituality and ways of life, to understand their mission and potential as Lamanites and Latter-day Saints. Tsodizin dóó sin centers on *hózhǫ́*, roughly translated as beauty, blessing, and harmony, a concept that explains the ways that Diné have perceived and interacted with the world since time immemorial. The Holy People, Diyin Dine'é or Yé'ii, initiate hózhǫ́. Chaos and disharmony stem from failing to sustain hózhǫ́ through ancestral teachings.[9] Diné learn Hózhǫ́ǫ́jí, the Beauty Way, through generations, praying for hózhǫ́ all around them. They evoke beauty through ceremony and speech to "become one with the spirit" and "what the spirits want of [them]."[10]

Hózhǫ́ comes from being spiritually whole and in harmony with the world and all it entails physically and spiritually. To uphold hózhǫ́, Diné seek to respect nature and their fellow beings. Scholar Joel W. Martin explains that "religion was not separated from the rest of life" for many Native Americans, as they "fused spirituality with place and practice to imbue everyday, local realities with the most profound significance."[11] Aligning with this point, Diné did not use a separate word for the institutional concept of "religion" in Diné bizaad, since these spiritual elements constituted an integral part of their lives. Some translators refer to tsodizin dóó sin as "religion" instead of its direct meaning of "prayer and song"—the most common manifestations of spirituality.[12]

Regarding Latter-day Saint teachings and faith, a spectrum of views ranged widely among Diné. A central question has been whether balance and harmony can exist between faith and tradition of Latter-day Saints and Diné.[13] Some Diné became committed members of the Church and believed they had found a new life pathway that fulfilled their Diné traditions and philosophy of Si'ąh Naagháí Bik'eh Hózhǫ́ (SNBH as Diné recently refer to it), translated as "Walk in Beauty" or "live a long life in beauty." In Diné society, "beauty" or hózhǫ́ has represented an ideal of being and environment.[14] Si'ąh Naagháí Bik'eh Hózhǫ́ consists of two parts, male and female, respectively: Si'ąh Naagháí, "Forever Lasting Life of Old Age," and Bik'eh Hózhǫ́, "Road of Beauty." Together, they sustain life and balance.[15]

Gary Witherspoon, a former SWIM missionary of the Church who married a Diné woman and later studied Diné culture and language as an anthropologist, explains that Diné have believed the purpose of life is to become "one [with] the universal beauty, harmony, and happiness described as *są'ah naagháii bik'eh hózhǫ́.*"[16] Diné refer to the sacred directions and mountains in ceremony and everyday life to reinforce SNBH.[17] This central Diné philosophy encompasses a complex code to preserve and restore balance and harmony as people "walk" through four major seasons of life in a cycle of infancy, youth, adulthood, and old age. Walking and journeys have held sacred significance for generations of Diné and Latter-day Saints, and this becomes a central tenet of Diné dóó Gáamalii who seek balance in these overlapping but divergent communities.

Diné Latter-day Saints inherited a legacy of traditional Diné life and spirituality, which enabled some of them to articulate a clear understanding of who they are and their place in the world. Arlene Nofchissey Williams, a Diné singer who attended BYU during the late 1960s, became well known among Latter-day Saint Native Americans for her synthesis of Latter-day Saint hymns, folk music, and Diné chants and prayers in her songs.[18] "I Walk in Beauty," one of her songs on the album *Go My Son* that she did with fellow BYU Native American student Carnes Burson (who is Ute from Fort Duchesne, Utah), is a Diné Latter-day Saint interpretation of hózhǫ́. A part of the song begins:

I walk in beauty.
Yes, I do. Yes, I do.
I talk in beauty.
Yes, I do. Yes, I do.
I sing of beauty,
Just for you and only you.[19]

The song derives its meaning and performance from the Beauty Way Prayer. Williams uses the repetition and vocable sounds from traditional Diné chants, altering only a few action verbs in the verses. The song promotes Diné ancestral teachings and continues to be popular among many Diné Latter-day Saints, as some of them have interpreted hózhǫ́ as walking with Christ in beauty.

During the Kimball era, numerous Diné who were raised with SNBH and other ancestral Diné ways of life joined the Church of Jesus Christ of Latter-day Saints. Under Kimball's vision and leadership, the Church developed intricate programs for Native Americans, including "Lamanite" missions such as the Southwest Indian Mission, Lamanite congregations, Indian seminaries, the Indian Student Placement Program (ISPP), and the BYU Indian Education Program. Kimball's legacy has continued to shape the identity of Latter-day Saint Diné, though they have faced different challenges and experiences over generations in the post-Kimball era.

In 1979, missionaries of the Church knocked on the door of Ernesteen Lynch, a Diné woman who had various affiliations to Christian denominations but was committed to Diné ways of life. Their name tags piqued her interest, including their full inscription of "The Church of Jesus Christ of Latter-day Saints," because Jesus was "the first person [she] really respected, really admired, and really wanted to know in [her] childhood, outside of [her] parents."[20] Although Lynch's father taught her Diné creation songs and oral traditions, her parents insisted that she join a Methodist church and attend its boarding school as a child. She eventually married a Catholic and raised her children in that faith. She later started to attend the Presbyterian Church, but all the Christian churches confused her. As a Diné historian and cultural instructor, Lynch turned to her Diné ancestral teachings for guidance. When missionaries asked if they could visit her, she agreed but warned them: "Don't tell me about your religion. I'm not interested."

The missionaries accepted her terms and began to ask her about Diné worldviews. During one visit, the missionaries explained how they could not find anyone to answer their questions about Diné conceptualizations of God. Lynch told them that, according to Diné, God embodies two beings in the form of man and woman: "He is a great and holy man, and she is a great and holy woman. We symbolize them as our Great Eternal Father and our Great Eternal Mother." Lynch expected to shock the missionaries, hoping that the "persistent young men will go out the door and never return." But, in her words, "they stunned me."

As Lynch and the missionaries compared their teachings, they found more common ground than differences. Lynch decided to join the Church, reflecting on her conversion experience:

> It didn't matter if I had grown up in the Church of Jesus Christ of Latter-day Saints, if I had grown up as a traditional Navajo, or if I had sometime somehow grown up in a society where the two were perfectly inter-twined together. Whatever those societies could have offered in their per-fectness and completeness . . . I had gained all that there in a moment of truth. . . . There is no way that I can separate Navajo from being a member of the Church or of being a member of the Church with Navajo.

Lynch describes a merging and entanglement of her identity as Diné dóó Gáamalii, which stresses an inseparability of the parts that make her whole. I find too often in conversations and dialogues about Native American iden-tities and histories a solid and entrenched dichotomization of the colonized and colonizer as well as the respective separation of Indigenous and white worlds.[21] Some Latter-day Saints have perpetuated these dichotomies that challenge Diné identity, as Diné writer Monika Brown Crowfoot describes in her essay, "The Lamanite Dilemma: Mormonism and Indigeneity": "Many times throughout my childhood, I heard various church members or my parents tell me that we had to choose between being Navajo and being Mormon."[22] I remember hearing similar experiences among various friends, although I could not personally articulate choices that I faced in this way. My parents engrained in my siblings and me an indelible sense of Diné being, while they taught us to follow and live by Latter-day Saint teachings. We knew and recognized being a Latter-day Saint as a life choice. Some of my siblings have decided to distance themselves from the Church but not because of a binary between being Diné or Latter-day Saint.

Assessments and categorizations of various human experiences have often emphasized binaries, especially including Christianity, religion, and spirituality. Because Europeans are those who initially spread Christianity and Euro-Americans are those who introduced Mormonism, such religious affiliations are identified with white colonizers.[23] The oversimplification of the colonizer-colonized divide and two respective worlds, however, obscures the complexities and intricacies of human agency, experiences, and inter-actions.[24] What exists between and within the categories and constructs of colonizers and colonized in the structures and frameworks of colonialism?[25]

Such questions lead to better understanding of Lynch's views and those of other Diné Latter-day Saints, including my family, while considering arguments that Indigenous religious engagement with Euro-Americans is inseparable from colonialism. Scholars have debated approaches to Native American history in terms of colonization and decolonization. Some Indigenous intellectuals, for example, have denounced academic histories of their peoples for perpetuating colonization and demand their decolonization. In *For Indigenous Eyes Only: A Decolonization Handbook*, Waziyatawin Angela Wilson and Michael Yellow Bird define this terminology. Colonization represents the means to "maintain the subjugation or exploitation of Indigenous Peoples, lands, and resources," while decolonization constitutes the "resistance to the forces of colonialism" by breaking "the colonial structure and realizing Indigenous liberation."[26] Christianity and affiliated denominations have historically supported and embodied the colonial structure.[27]

Adherents to the Indigenous decolonizing movements have pursued re-centering Native American and Indigenous studies, underscoring the failures and detriments of Eurocentric and Euro-American research on Native Americans. They often follow postcolonial theories, and some exemplify directions for future scholarship that builds on Indigenous community-centered research. In *Decolonizing Methodologies* (1998), Maori scholar Linda Tuhiwai Smith spearheaded approaches to debunking colonial power relations that academic studies perpetuate. She argues that "governments, states, societies, and institutions," including schools and churches, deny Indigenous "claims to humanity, to having a history, and to all sense of hope" when they continue "to deny the historical formations" of Indigenous deprivation and marginalization due to colonialism. She identifies "decolonization" as an imperative for scholars of Indigenous studies, which requires entering "spaces of resistance and hope" by (re)turning to Indigenous oral traditions, "cultures, languages, and social practices."[28] Since Smith's seminal book, into the early twenty-first century, more historians have traced lived experiences from Indigenous perspectives and epistemologies.[29]

Jeffrey Corntassel, a Cherokee political scientist, and Kanaka Maoli and other Indigenous scholars have emphasized "everyday acts of resurgence" in order to understand resistance and persistence of Indigenous peoples who reinforce their ancestral ties and personal relationships to homelands in sometimes simple but powerful ways through "daily convergences of people, places, and practices."[30]

Part of the decolonizing process of Native American history has included recognizing forms of colonialism in Indigenous-white relations, which has led to various reinterpretations of Diné and "Mormon-Indian" histories.[31] Scholars have identified the Church of Jesus Christ of Latter-day Saints as an imperial institution and perpetuator of colonizing ideologies.[32] Elise Boxer, a Dakota historian from the Sisseton and Wahpeton bands, claims: "Mormon Euroamericans wielded their power to define the racialized 'Other' or 'Lamanities' and further colonized Indigenous peoples in the LDS church." She examines missions among Indigenous communities and programs such as ISPP as "major phases of Mormon Euroamerican colonization." Defining and embracing the terms of colonization and decolonization in historical research have become markers of "decolonizing the mind."[33]

In this study and personal narrative, I engage (more implicitly than explicitly) with the concepts of colonization and decolonization as dynamic processes that involve both social structures and agency of Diné through time. People continue to debate the meanings and impacts of colonialism, especially in the United States, where many Americans lack understandings of Native American histories and experiences.[34] In historian Frederick Cooper's *Colonialism in Question*, he posits that assessing imperialism and colonialism "requires a more searching examination, which in some form is historical."[35] The very terms we use to describe the past, such as "imperialism" and "colonialism," pertain to their own historical developments and evoke various connotations.

These categorizations and frameworks could detract from grasping the actual experiences of historical agents, including those I am trying to understand—Diné dóó Gáamalii. But different studies and arguments have shaped how I view this collective biography, which I lay out partially in this introduction. A major tenet stems from Patricia Nelson Limerick's groundbreaking *The Legacy of Conquest: The Unbroken Past of the American West*, which launched "New Western History" by asserting that "the history of the West is a study of a place undergoing conquest and never fully escaping its consequences."[36] Limerick's work underscores how colonialism and conquest go hand in hand, while illuminating the complexities and convergences of diverse places and peoples such as Diné Bikéyah, Diné, and Latter-day Saints. In her response to anthropologist Patrick Wolfe's articulations of colonialism as "a structure, not an event" that aims to "eliminate the native," Kanaka ʻŌiwi scholar J. Kēhaulani Kauanui adds a crucial point that "indigeneity itself is enduring. . . . Indigenous peoples exist, resist, and persist" even through colonialism and conquest.[37]

Cooper also emphasizes "the ways in which colonized people sought—not entirely without success—to build lives in the crevices of colonial power, deflecting, appropriating, or reinterpreting the teachings and preachings thrust upon them."[38] Anthropologist Jean Comaroff's work reiterates this point in *Body of Power, Spirit of Resistance: The Culture and History of a South African People*, in which she discusses how conversion to Christianity colonized Tshidi Barolong, but they reconstructed a sense of themselves and resisted colonizers by appropriating Christianity.[39] She and John Comaroff also focus on the southern Tswana in a case study of European missionaries' efforts to "colonize [Tswana] consciousness with the axioms and aesthetics of an alien culture." The Comaroffs demonstrate how Tswana have navigated colonialism in different ways by accepting, rejecting, and even "[trying] to recast its intrusive forms in their own image."[40]

Although Native Americans and many diverse peoples may have experienced a colonization of consciousness, these various scholars underline the importance of understanding how peoples have lived and incited change to persevere as Indigenous. These arguments trace two kinds of forces that interplay between Europeans, white Americans, and Indigenous peoples: on the one hand, the structural force of and pressures from colonialism including racialization, and on the other hand, the agency and exertions of self-control by Indigenous peoples. They recognize how Indigenous peoples (re)orient themselves based on the changes they face, and they can direct their own lives. Diné scholar Moroni Benally applies these points in his interpretations of "Indigenous people's faith in a colonizing church" by specifically considering how the Book of Mormon has been used "as both a tool of invasion and replacement, but also, strangely, as an instrument of resistance against the Church itself."[41]

This part of the narrative—identifying and reflecting on colonialism so directly—might make some readers uncomfortable, especially followers of apologetics, but discomfort often indicates learning and growth when confronting complicated histories of Mormonism, racism, and colonialism.[42] I remember feeling very uncomfortable when I first heard arguments that the "Book of Mormon is a tool of colonialism." After a presentation about ISPP for the American Indian Studies Association (AISA) in Tempe, Arizona, which I attended in 2013, a distinguished Native American scholar in the audience asked whether Latter-day Saint converts were "brainwashed."[43] I raised my hand to comment and shared how my father and several of my Native American Latter-day Saint friends consciously believe they are descendants of Lamanites. They believe in the Book of Mormon as "Another Testament of Jesus Christ," and it is a liberating and empowering text to them.[44] I would have argued then, as I do now, that however the Book of Mormon has been (mis)used by others, it may not take away from an individual's faith and personal connection with the sacred text.

In the audience of the AISA presentation that day I also recognized an acquaintance who attended the Papago Ward—a congregation of Native American Latter-day Saints that meets in the Salt River Pima-Maricopa Indian Community.[45] He was visibly troubled, and he approached me and expressed how he did not feel represented in the discourse about ISPP and Native American converts. I later read the following quote from this same individual who joined the Church and participated in ISPP, which helps me understand his angst that day: "The LDS placement program, on the other hand, gave me my free agency. I was always aware of evil influences, but with proper teachings I was able to make choices." To this former ISPP student and convert, ISPP and the Book of Mormon did not brainwash or colonize him but enabled him "to decide for [himself] to live a good life."[46] This memory embodies key inspirations for writing this narrative. Since then, I have not only committed to telling faithful Diné Latter-day Saints' stories but also gained greater appreciation for foundational research and arguments regarding impacts of Mormon colonialism on Indigenous identities. Elise Boxer, for example, expounds in her work that the "Book of Mormon is not just a reflection of Mormon settler colonialism, but has been used to create a discourse that silences Indigenous voices and perspectives regarding their own history as a people on this continent."[47] These different stories and perspectives are not mutually exclusive, and they all need to be heard and understood.

"The value of the story is in the telling," as Cooper stresses.[48] Terms of colonization and decolonization must encapsulate historical narratives and real experiences of diverse Indigenous peoples. Linda Tuhiwai Smith's words complement Cooper's message: "Telling our stories from the past, reclaiming the past, giving testimony to the injustices of the past are all strategies which are commonly employed by indigenous peoples struggling for justice."[49] Indigenous peoples also tell stories to celebrate their pasts and perseverance through struggles. While some Indigenous voices condemn Mormonism in terms of colonization and decolonization, other Indigenous voices share different perspectives of "Mormon-Indian" history. Donald Fixico, a historian of Shawnee, Sac and Fox, Muscogee, and Seminole identity, calls for redressing our approaches to Native American history by considering more than "a narrative of Indian-white relations."[50] Diné debate one another concerning their collective identity and their perception of Diné and Latter-day Saint relations, which this book explores. Most importantly, however, this work reflects the complex intricacies of human lifeways, actions, and worldviews that blur the lines of Indigenous-white settler and colonizer-colonized terminologies.

COMMUNITY

In this book I rely on oral histories to introduce viewpoints of Diné Latter-day Saints who have participated in and contributed to communities with ties to Diné Bikéyah, Diné enclaves off the reservation, and Dinéjí Na'nitin, Diné ancestral teachings. I cannot represent the values and views of all Diné Latter-day Saints, since many Diné experiences and perspectives vary and differ. This work allows me to speak from my personal stories and share the experiences of some from within Diné dóó Gáamalii communities.

Both advocates of the Church and ancestral Diné teachings respectively claim to outline pathways that lead people to happiness. Most Latter-day Saints would explain that "men [and women] are, that they might have joy" not only in this life but also in eternity.[51] Church principles contain extensive beliefs about premortal existence, the purpose of life, salvation, and resurrection. Many Latter-day Saints envision steps to living with God by being baptized, making temple covenants, and following church doctrine.

For some Diné as well as other Native Americans in the late twentieth century, the Church offered them a community that would uphold such ways of life. To develop and sustain that community, they would become involved in missions on the Navajo reservation, known now as the Navajo Nation, and congregations where Diné could worship together. Some Diné youth participated in Indian Seminary programs, and others entered ISPP, also commonly called Placement, where Diné and other Native Americans lived with Latter-day Saint families beyond Diné Bikéyah for their schooling. Some Latter-day Saint Diné then received more training and education in the programs that BYU developed in the 1960s. Diné and Church leaders shared a common goal: to prepare Diné college graduates who would return to the reservation and support communities there. Some Church officials and lay members hoped that the returned graduates would also serve and facilitate congregations and auxiliaries on the reservation, spreading the influence of the Church.

Diné dóó Gáamalii have formed a community that intertwines and hybridizes Diné and Latter-day Saint ways of life. As individuals, Diné Latter-day Saints differ widely in their backgrounds, experiences, and perspectives, yet some of them have committed to sharing core beliefs, values, and practices that underlay their compound identities. Like a double helix, these composite identities consist of merged strands that Diné dóó Gáamalii inherit from Diné, Latter-day Saints of diverse lineages, and various influences. Depending on how this double helix forms and binds, Diné Latter-day Saints determine and navigate their ways through multiple linkages and divisions of worldviews and respective communities. Diné dóó Gáamalii have many of the same strands in these double helix formations of identity, relating to each other as kin. Many of them have gathered as a community in hope of becoming, along with other believers, a people "of one heart and one mind."[52]

Many Diné Latter-day Saints, however, continue to recognize and connect to an overarching Diné sense of peoplehood. In my self-introduction, I referred to Dinéjí Na'nitin, Navajo traditional teachings, of ké, the kinship and clan system, that has defined Diné and our relations to those around us since time immemorial. Diné scholar Lloyd L. Lee explains that "more than three hundred thousand people identify as Diné, and each person has his or her own individual outlook on life, beliefs, and aspirations."[53] Lee focuses on "SNBH, Diné bizaad, ké [relations], kéí [clanship], Níhi Kéyah [Diné land], and Diné baa hane' [Diné history]" as key "markers" of Diné identity, which he characterizes as "open-ended" and fluid.[54] For many Diné dóó Gáamalii, their Diné ancestry and upbringing have remained essential parts of their identity.

Olivia Ben, a Diné Latter-day Saint who moved to Utah County, recognizes how "the basic principles of Navajo culture were instilled in [her]" because she grew up in a "very traditional" home.[55] Because Diné spirituality and identity prove integral to daily life, many Diné begin from an early age to learn where they came from, how to present themselves, and how they relate to the people and world around them. Ben, for example, taught her daughter about her Diné lineage and familial obligations, even though they lived outside of Diné Bikéyah. She understood her identity as intergenerational through ké, kinship: "That's who I am. . . . I feel I am very cultural because I want Courtney [my daughter] to know who she is. . . . She's Native American. She's Diné. She's of the Reed People. That's who she is."[56]

As Ben acknowledges that her daughter knows her clan of the Reed People, I know my clans of the Towering House and Black-Streaked Woods People. We can speak to each other and situate our relations through our clans. Jennifer Denetdale, a Diné historian, asserts that "clan narratives" and "creation narratives" form the basis of Diné history by affecting "Navajo perspectives on the past."[57] The "clan narratives," oral traditions, and sense of spirituality intertwine and guide Diné relationships within society and their natural environment. Ké embodies Diné connections to homeland by representing where Navajo people came from—our origins—which have shaped our ancestors and Diné to this day. For example, the clan of my paternal grandmother, Kinyaa'áanii, Towering House People, derives from Kin Ya'a, the "Towering House" and physical site by Crownpoint in the Navajo Nation. Kin Ya'a lies within Dinétah, the ancestral Diné homeland, where some of the first Diné communities originated near Chaco Canyon and the Ancient Ones. Oral traditions reveal how Asdzáá Nádleehé, Changing Woman, formed and sent the original Diné clans to Dinétah, providing each of the leaders with a *gish*, or cane. The leaders used the gish to search for water on their journey home. One of the leaders leaned to rest against a wall that appeared like a house; therefore, the people named him and his clan Kinyaa'áanii.[58] Diné Ancient Ones embedded origin and kinship stories in specific places like Kin Ya'a to forge their ties to the earth and spaces that Diné continue to know as homeland.[59]

In the late twentieth century, being Diné no longer meant only ké since the US federal government implanted and enforced standards of blood quantum that Diné adopted officially in 1953.[60] Only individuals with a Diné parent and one-quarter of "Navajo blood" can register as a member of the federally recognized Navajo Nation. Forces of colonialism enabled influences such as US government auxiliaries and Christian denominations to penetrate and affect Diné families and communities. Diné have recently added the requirement to identify one's clans for enrollment in the nation, which reconnects tribal membership to k'é. Being Diné remains a collective identity to which many Diné dóó Gáamalii relate and adhere. To some Diné Latter-day Saints, for example, teachings of SNBH and hózhǫ́ have still resonated with them but also signify part of the path to Jesus Christ as their redeemer.

ORAL HISTORIES AND SOURCES

This book traces the experiences and compound identity formation of Diné Latter-day Saints who have shared their oral histories with the Charles Redd Center for Western Studies at BYU and the Church History Department. The Redd Center interviews come from two main parts of what was known as the LDS Native American Oral History Project. The first set began with Jessie Embry's Native American oral history class, which involved several BYU Indigenous students as interviewers who gathered oral histories between 1990 and 1991. Embry later hired me to restart the project as a BYU student between 2007 and 2008. The Church History Department conducted oral history interviews in the Navajo Nation in 1992 and 1997.

Other sources include mission and ward minutes, BYU records, and oral histories with Church leaders. This work is not a comprehensive study of Diné spirituality or of Native American and Latter-day Saint relations, but it reveals relevant Indigenous perspectives and lived experiences, especially from my circle of communities. This narrative is part of my personal journey to understand my composite identity and mixed inheritance of religions, cultures, and ethnicities through the lens of my father, family, and friends. I do not shy away from my proximity to this study but embrace my positionality to share voices of those dear to me. We are Diné dóó Gáamalii, and we can and do speak for ourselves.

The book consists of seven main chapters along with the introduction and epilogue, tracing Mormonism in Diné Bikéyah and Diné Latter-day Saints' perspectives and experiences with the Church and its special programs for Native Americans. This narrative does not focus on a single person's life but rather highlights a life cycle of Diné dóó Gáamalii communities at the end of the twentieth century. These stories do not follow a linear sense of time, as they relate to meanings and significance of Diné dóó Gáamalii. Thus, the chapters align with thematic rather than chronological approaches to key areas of Diné dóó Gáamalii experiences and community life, which include the Southwest Indian Mission, the Indian Student Placement Program, and primarily Diné congregations on and beyond the reservation.

Other than my personal stories, especially relating to my father, two historical figures' actions and involvement appear in and out of this narrative because of their influence on Diné Latter-day Saints. These two individuals are Spencer W. Kimball, the Apostle and Prophet, who championed the causes of Native Americans and minoritized populations in the Church; and George P. Lee, a Diné educator who once represented the success story of Church programs after joining the high leadership echelon of the Church, the First Quorum of the Seventy. Lee later denounced the Church's changing policies and led an apostasy. The epilogue opens questions about Diné dóó Gáamalii identities, especially considering ongoing tensions over resources and sovereignties that affect various communities in and surrounding Diné Bikéyah. I reflect on how Diné Latter-day Saints have developed the double helix of their compound identities and communities.

When some Diné chose to join the Church, many of them asserted that they remained true to themselves and the core values from their Indigenous heritage. They found their own meanings of "Lamanite," in which they sensed pride. Many white Latter-day Saints, like other white Americans, exhibited racism and paternalism toward Native Americans, but some Diné Latter-day Saints sought subtle ways to resist such treatment or to use it to their advantage. Their relationships with white members of the Church have challenged their identity and have pressured them to change. Their conversion, however, also involves appropriation and agency. Many Diné have accepted Mormonism and the Church on their own terms. They could see the world through different views because of their cultural background but also through their conversion to Jesus Christ in the Church. They constructed their own spaces where they could live according to Latter-day Saint teachings while finding harmony with their Diné sense of self-identity, becoming Diné dóó Gáamalii. This historical narrative debuts Indigenous stories of colonial dynamics between Diné, whether they affiliate with the Church or not, and different peoples. Other Native Americans and Indigenous peoples have experienced similar histories and parallel relations with the Church, but I illuminate these specific compound identities from my position as a part of Diné dóó Gáamalii communities.

My father, Ashkii Yázhí, changed drastically during his mission for the Church in the Navajo Nation, as he taught and sought to convert other Diné. He once felt anger and bitterness toward white settlers and the history

George P. Lee giving a statue to Phillip and JoAnn Smith in recognition of their contributions to the "Lamanite Cause," c. 1980. Courtesy of author.

of colonization. He has not excused or denied such histories of violence and darkness that afflicted him and our ancestors, but he began to hope for a future that unified the descendants of the colonizers, colonized, and all those in between whatever categories and identities people assume in the history of US imperialism and expansionism that displaced and dispossessed Indigenous peoples. During Ashkii Yázhí's mission, his father asked to see him, as he lay dying from cancer. Ashkii Yázhí received permission to visit his father at the hospital, where my grandfather told him that he was sorry for casting him out of the family and accepted him as Gáamalii, a Latter-day Saint. They reconciled just before my grandfather died. Ashkii Yázhí is one of the few in his family to actively participate in the Church, but he is still a part of his family. My father decided to be Diné dóó Gáamalii. This book shares the histories of this community and gathering and what that identity means to various people, including my father and family, during the late twentieth century.

CHAPTER ONE

Diné dóó Gáamalii

Navajo Latter-day Saints

In 1948 the Diné Latter-day Saint family of Howela and Ruth Arviso Po-lacca hosted Apostle Spencer W. Kimball in a "trailer-tent under some pines" close to their hogan in Crystal, Navajo Nation, when the church leader specifically requested to recuperate in Diné Bikéyah from his inca-pacitating heart seizures and medical treatments.[1] Ruth Polacca developed an enduring friendship with Kimball during that time and dedicated much of her life to Latter-day Saint missionary work. At a district conference in Toadlena, in 1950, Ruth claimed that "there is something we have told in our Indian traditions, and I've seen this in the Book of Mormon where the Lord would in His own due time reveal his words to our people. This is now at hand."[2] Many Diné dóó Gáamalii in the twentieth century, such as Polacca, believed they were truly the descendants of ancient peoples who met Jesus Christ in the Americas as told in the Book of Mormon. They intertwined their understandings of "Indian traditions," or Diné teachings, and Latter-day Saint doctrine.

Diné teachings center on principles of Si'ah Naagháí Bik'eh Hózhǫ́ (SNBH), "Long Life in Beauty," which represents human journeys through the diurnal processes of the sun, directions of the mountains and earth, and seasons of the year and life cycle. Diné intellectual Roger Begay defines SNBH as "a Holy Path, a spiritual phenomena [sic] relating to all Diné be-ings, in perspective to living a complete life."[3] Diné principles of the Four Sacred Directions and life cycle of SNBH undergird my intergenerational ties with my ancestors and relatives in relation to the Church of Jesus Christ of Latter-day Saints.

According to ancestral teachings, Diné would ask, "Háadish nits'ę́ę́' łee' sitą́?" or "Where are your umbilical cords buried?" This question also means "Where are you from?" Wherever the umbilical cord is buried is the home of the baby since an inseparable connection persists between people and their umbilical cords. Terry Teller, a Diné language and cultural educator, explicates: "A long time ago when a baby was born, the umbilical cords would be buried below the post of the doorway or near the home of the baby symbolizing that that is where the baby's home would be located. Some traditional Navajos still practice this concept to this day."[4] During one of my presentations at the To'Nanees'Dizi chapter, which represents the local government and community of the Navajo Nation in Tuba City, my father was interpreting for me and told everyone that my umbilical cord is buried there to convey to them the purpose of my work and return to Diné Bikéyah. My father delivered me at the hospital in Tuba City when he was working there for the Indian Health Service (IHS).

Although my father has faith in the Church of Jesus Christ of Latter-day Saints, he also continues to honor the ties to home, Diné Bikéyah, where his umbilical cord was buried. Some Diné Latter-day Saints merge and hybridize these teachings of Diné ancestors and the Church, as they carry on an ultimate life goal to pursue happiness. On another trip to Tuba City, I was visiting the Latter-day Saint congregations that meet at the Tuba City Stake Center when I met a Diné elder who confided in me that she buried her grandson's umbilical cord on the grounds of one of the temples built by the Church. She smiled and expressed her greatest hopes that her grandson and family would always be worthy to enter the temple by following Christ.[5] To her and some Diné Latter-day Saints, they began to view the roads to Christ and hózhǫ́ as one and the same, reinforcing SNBH.[6]

In common discourse, there is a clear distinction between "Mormons" and "Indians." Many people treat them as separate groups and identities. They also differentiate them by terms of bicultural and racialized identities such as whites, Anglos, Americans, Native Americans, and tribal nations. This language and approach overlook and neglect the complexities of identities and relationships such as the existence of Latter-day Saint Native Americans and Diné. In my case, they even dismiss my self-identity as a Bilagáana Diné, or white Navajo. I am both Diné and white. I am both Latter-day Saint and Diné. This narrative questions not only how individual worlds and cultures diverged but also how hybrids and descendants of different lineages and multilayered identities have lived and thrived. Hybrids, such as Diné Latter-day Saints, embraced and inherited traits and qualities from multiple distinct groups. Although they chose what they would uphold from this inheritance, various groups of Latter-day Saints and Diné influenced their life courses, and eventually Diné dóó Gáamalii developed as a community. By 1992 as many as forty thousand Diné, or 20 percent of their population, joined the Church of Jesus Christ of Latter-day Saints through baptism.[7] This chapter explores Diné and Latter-day Saint life pathways, respectively, to contextualize a discussion of these diverse worldviews and how Diné Latter-day Saints intertwined them during the late twentieth century.

Some Diné avoided converting to the Church because of dissonances between their Diné background and Latter-day Saint beliefs. They struggled, for example, with popular Latter-day Saint views of Native Americans as both a fallen people and as blessed descendants of the House of Israel. Such impressions of Diné and other Indigenous peoples shaped the infrastructure and processes in American Indian programs of the Church, which altered many Diné lives. Diné converts' faith changed them, but many of them continued to self-identify as Diné in ways similar to how many Indigenous peoples throughout the world have appropriated and claimed different religions as their own.[8] Their faith and church practice diversify what it means to be Diné but do not shatter their overarching sense of Diné peoplehood. In the following part, I introduce Diné teachings of my ancestors, much of which I learned after I reached adulthood. As I have matured, I have realized that I have received these teachings and ways of life in varying degrees since my infancy. For many Diné Latter-day Saint converts of the twentieth century, including my father, they were immersed from an early age in these Diné teachings and traditions.

DINÉ HERITAGE AND CONCEPTS OF SPIRITUALITY

Since time immemorial, Diné have introduced themselves as Ni'hookaa Diyan Diné, We are the Holy Earth People, or as Diné, the People. Diné origin stories describe how the First People, including insects, animals, and masked spirits, ascended a reed through different worlds before reaching and settling in this fourth world, the Glittering World. 'Altsé Hastiin, First Man, and 'Altsé 'Asdzáá, First Woman, came from the first of the worlds, the Black World. They journeyed with the First People through the Yellow World and Blue World. Although different versions of the Diné creation story exist, each of them teaches Diné to value Dinétah and Diné Bikéyah.[9] Diné cultural practices and ceremonies reflect their reverence of the earth and their homelands encircled by the Sacred Mountains.[10]

A Diné elder who directed Navajo studies at Diné College, Andrew Natonabah, stresses that "we should live by the stories given to us long ago." The Holy People created "songs, stories, [and] prayers" that "carries one through old age."[11] Navajos have embedded their stories in songs and other oral forms to preserve their collective identity and history for generations.[12] In their book *A Diné History of Navajoland*, Klara Kelley and Harris Francis classify these oral traditions and ancestral teachings as "empowering stories" that "tell about physical and cultural survival, about a people finding a new relationship to the world around them, often through a victory, however short or partial."[13]

As a premise to many empowering stories, Diné often refer to the Four Sacred Mountains and their correlating cardinal directions. The mountains envelop Diné Bikéyah. Each mountain also directs Diné toward SNBH, or following Diné lifeways, starting from east, to south, to west, to north. The directional mountains represent series of life processes and natural laws including the position of the sun, seasons, and age. Sis Naajiní, Mount Blanca, stands for the East, the direction of the dawn, spring, and infancy. Tsoodził, Mount Taylor, represents the South, daylight, summer, and childhood. Dookʼoʼoosłííd, San Francisco Peaks, is the mountain of the West, where the sun sets, evoking autumn and adulthood. Dibé Nitsaa, Mount Hesperus, the northern mountain, embodies darkness, winter, and old age. Diné poet laureate Luci Tapahonso reiterates these central tenets of ancestral Diné philosophy as she evokes the prayers and songs of the Sacred Mountains in her poetry. Her poem "This Is How They Were Placed for Us" honors Diné Bikéyah and pathways, which are the sources of Diné life, strength, and prosperity through speech, thought, song, and prayer.[14] The earth and land, the mountains in particular, have been the focal points of Diné spirituality. To this day, the land defines Diné identity, although many Diné have converted and joined different denominations.

In a publication from the Rock Point Community School, a Diné language and cultural immersion school, titled *Between Sacred Mountains*, Diné elders teach that "all the answers come from the land itself—sometimes by scientific experiment, sometimes by life experience, sometimes by tradition handed down from the roots of time." They personify the land as "the teacher, and the medicine man, the scientist," while all the people are its pupils. Considering ongoing disagreements and dissonance, they consider how "it is because none of us sees far enough. People living on opposite sides of a mountain rarely see the land the same way until they meet at the top."[15]

My uncle, Albert Smith, used to say that "the mountain is my church." These teachings have helped me understand what he meant by that assertion. The mountains and lands are the living archives and guides of Diné ways of life and knowledge when they connect with physical and metaphysical lessons our people have passed on from one generation to another.

The creation story also entails the beginning of the Diné clan system. In most Diné origin narratives, Yé'ii, Holy People, created the four original clans after slaying monsters and ensuring the safety of their people. They shaped the first clan, Kinyaa'áanii, the Towering House People, from yellow and white corn. Asdzą́ą́ Nádleehé, Changing Woman, a significant Diné deity who personifies SNBH, motherhood, and earth, moved to an island in the West after the creation of the four original clans. Although her husband, the Sun, would visit her, she formed her own people for companionship. From the flakes of her skin, she created four additional clans that traveled to meet and live with the original clans in Dinétah. The Diné clan system continued to grow, which included seventy to eighty clans by the twenty-first century.[16]

To this day, Diné recognize one another by introducing their clans, often before they introduce their given names. As part of the introduction, they say they are "born to" their mother's clan, and then they say they are "born for" their father's clan. Following their maternal lines, they present the clans of their maternal grandfather and paternal grandfather. With that introduction, Diné know where a person came from and how to identify their family. Some Diné use the phrase "Haa dóone'é nílį?" or "What clans are you?" to avoid intimate relations with close relatives.

Similar to many societies, most Diné do not casually speak of their spirituality, worship, ceremonies, and sacred practices. Since Diné beliefs fulfill intricate parts in their everyday lives, Diné culture itself embodies a sacred dimension. According to ancestral teachings and tsodizin dóó sin, things relating to a supreme deity and song, Diné view nature and its creations as sacred, including the mountains, rocks, earth, sky, rivers, plants, and animals.[17] Diné elders, for instance, once commonly taught their children not to disturb mountain rocks to avoid misfortunes, since such actions would upset the Holy People who set the rock formations.[18] Most importantly, Diné youth learned to respect the rocks because of their fundamental belief in hózhǫ́.

Ernie Bulow, an Anglo-American who taught about Diné culture on the reservation, points out that "attaining *hozho*, regaining it when it is lost, perfecting it, is the ultimate goal of Navajo ceremonialism and the center of Navajo philosophy."[19] Since time immemorial, one of the most revered Diné philosophies is Hózhóojik'ehgo Nanitin, teachings of the Beauty Way, and the prayers and ceremonies associated with it. As children, Diné begin to recite the Beauty Way prayers. Although I was raised mostly away from Diné Bikéyah by a white English-speaking mother, my father would sing Diné prayer songs of the Sacred Mountains that he learned from my grandfather and ancestors. For many years, as a child, I did not understand the song and its significance until I began to learn Diné bizaad, the Navajo language. I continue to learn and discern Diné ancestral teachings, some of which have always been with me but take time, guidance, and growth to comprehend.

Although some prayers describe physical relations between the individual and hózhó, Diné understand that hózhó surrounds and enters them when they seek spiritual wholeness and harmony with their world—physically, mentally, and metaphysically. Because of hózhó, Diné treat nature and their fellow beings that the Holy People create and control with great care and reverence. Although my father did not bring me to any of our ancestral ceremonies since his conversion to the Church, he has responded to many of my questions about them with respect and deference. He has explained to me in broad terms that some Diné ceremonies serve to protect hózhó, such as the Beauty Way, while others, including the Blessing Way and Enemy Way, restore it when disharmony and imbalance disrupt the world.[20]

For generations, my Diné ancestors and relatives have believed that the holy songs and ceremonies could heal them. A Diné history and culture instructor, Ernesteen Lynch, recalled that an administrator advised her to consult "a psychologist or psychiatrist." When she hesitated, the administrator suggested a "Navajo diagnostician" who treats an "emotional problem that could become physical." Lynch then met with a female Diné hand trembler who identified her anxieties as a "split" condition between the Diné and "the white man way." The hand trembler cautioned Lynch that she would need to follow either the Diné or "the white man's way," reassuring her, "If you choose Navajo, you can always travel back and forth, but you can't split your identity." When Lynch "chose Navajo," the hand trembler recommended the Blessing Way ceremony to her in order to restore harmony.[21]

As Diné, we possess an enduring legacy of peoplehood, which derives from our ancestral ways of life. Many of our Diné kin have continued to recognize our collective identity despite drastic changes in the world. According to historians Garrick Bailey and Roberta Glenn Bailey, Diné "seldom feel any threat to their social identity. Their sociological and ideological institutions have proved resilient enough to adapt to changes in the most material aspects of Navajo culture and absorb what the people wanted of Anglo-American culture."[22] The Baileys claimed, in the late twentieth century, that Diné never lost their distinct collective identity, but such generalizations risk downplaying Diné struggles with self-identity and sense of peoplehood since contact with Europeans and Euro-Americans. In many cases, Diné faced unrelenting pressures to change for survival but often at the detriment of their sovereignty and community ties.[23] Many Diné, like Lynch, suffered "split identity" crises, for example, although some of them would reemphasize the decision to self-identify as Diné.

DINÉ AND LATTER-DAY SAINT

Euro-American white settler institutions such as schools and churches challenged Diné life pathways and identity as a people, which affected Diné Latter-day Saint converts especially in the mid- to late twentieth century. Despite their religious affiliation with its Euro-American origins of establishment, Diné Latter-day Saints, such as Olivia Ben, reasserted their Diné identity. Ben "was raised very traditional," and "the basic principles of Navajo culture were instilled in [her]," laying the foundations of her self-identity. She focuses on the legacy that she bestows to her daughter, who "knows who she is" as Diné even though "she stands in her all-white school" with different "cliques."[24] When Diné scholar Corey Smallcanyon interviewed Ben in 2008, she was living in Utah Valley in a community of predominantly white American Latter-day Saints. She evokes, however, her ancestral teachings and clan identity, which roots her and her children to Diné Bikéyah.

Nearly two decades before Ben's interview, in 1990, Ernesteen Lynch described herself as "bicultural" because of her engagement with various value systems, specifically Christianity and Diné teachings. While she went to the Methodist church that her parents belonged to and where she attended school, she also participated in Diné ceremonies. She "didn't see anything wrong with going to fire dances. I didn't feel anything wrong with going to blessing ceremonies." Lynch relates Diné spirituality to everyday life practices: "I didn't feel that there was anything less about sleeping in a hogan or helping with the sheep or butchering and doing things in a Navajo way." She conveys how Diné identity does not impose on different people: "We have never asked anybody to become a Navajo. We have never asked anything to be our perception of what life is. Instead of the Navajo worldview being introverted into ourselves, our worldview centers from ourselves and goes out and recognizes distinct characteristics."[25] This point stands in stark contrast to the colonizing forces of many white settler peoples, which pushes assimilation and domination in forms of culture, education, religion, politics, and economy.

While some Diné clearly understand their identity and heritage, anthropologists and historians have offered different explanations of their formation as a people. Some academics have claimed that Diné arrived later than other groups in what became known as the American Southwest, and they have portrayed Diné as relative newcomers who survived and prospered because of their abilities as "cultural borrowers." These studies argue that Diné adapted the cultures of Pueblos and others around them. Diné historian Jennifer Nez Denetdale contends, however, that "such formulations of the Navajo past do not reflect how we see ourselves as a people."[26] In academia, Diné history like other Indigenous histories has lacked Indigenous perspectives.[27] Diné Latter-day Saint viewpoints constitute some of the many diverse Indigenous voices and historical experiences in the twentieth century.

LATTER-DAY SAINT TEACHINGS

In the following section, I will introduce some Latter-day Saint teachings based on my perspective and research to set terms that will reappear throughout this book. I shift between using first and third person because I am navigating my multilayered and intersecting identities as a historian, Diné, and Latter-day Saint. While I explicate Diné and Latter-day Saint ways of life, I acknowledge that many interpretations and articulations exist of these peoples and their respective teachings. This book presents my individual interpretation, which Latter-day Saint scholar Jessie Embry influenced and guided initially as my mentor when she started and supported this project with me during my graduate studies. I am, however, solely responsible for this narrative and its analyses.

My father always said that one of the most significant challenges of his faith was believing Joseph Smith Jr. to be a prophet. He read various studies and some anti-Mormon literature that condemned and decried Joseph

Smith as a fraud. But he also read Smith's own accounts, including details of his "First Vision" when "God the Father and Jesus Christ appeared to Joseph Smith as he prayed in a grove of trees" for guidance.[28] While in this "sacred grove," in 1820, Smith was admonished to not join any church.[29] Smith later received more directions to restore the "true Church of Jesus Christ."[30] My father learned to fast and pray when seeking guidance from his own elders and Diné ancestral ways. In the mountains of Núu-agha-tʉvʉ-pʉ, Ute and Shoshone homelands, while he was a BYU student, my father prayed to know whether Smith was a prophet. He later realized that he was emulating not only his Diné ancestors but also Joseph Smith, who followed "the Epistle of James" to "ask of God."[31] My father sensed an answer that led him and our family on a path to join the Church.

To familiarize all readers with a basic understanding of the Church, there are some points of background that I will highlight especially in relation to Diné culture and peoplehood. Latter-day Saints began to define their pathways with the establishment of the Church of Jesus Christ of Latter-day Saints dating from 1830.[32] Joseph Smith, the founder of the Church, claimed that all the Christian churches confused him while their ministers preached different doctrine and campaigned for converts. After the First Vision, Smith initiated the Restoration of the Church and authority of Christ, which had disappeared with the first generation of apostles and their early converts. Smith and his followers believed that this Restoration prepared the way for the Second Coming of Jesus Christ.[33]

Church doctrine closely follows the teachings of the Old and New Testaments. The Old Testament provides a history of the children of Israel, God's chosen people who promulgate the message of Jehovah throughout the world. According to these beliefs, the same God of Adam, Noah, Abraham, Isaac, Jacob, and Moses came as Jesus Christ to redeem humankind in mortality. Christ offered his life, however, as a sinless sacrifice to overcome Adam's transgression. As a result, he conquered death, and all human beings will be resurrected. With his death and resurrection, most Latter-day Saints believe that Christ fulfilled the law of Moses and introduced the new gospel.

In these teachings of the Church and interpretations of the Old Testament, the House of Israel includes all twelve sons of Jacob. Besides ten of the tribes who disappeared, descendants of the tribe of Joseph left Israel to find their way with divine aid to the Americas. These Israelites included Lehi, a prophet in Jerusalem, who led his and another family across the ocean to this "promised land." The family separated between the followers of Lehi's sons, Laman, Lemuel, and Nephi, respectively, who often fought each other, ultimately leading to the genocide of the Nephites, or descendants of Nephi.[34] Smith claimed that the Nephites maintained a written record, which he translated as the Book of Mormon. Latter-day Saints have applied the book to contemporary life by relating to the scriptures and preaching the gospel of Christ, who briefly visited the people of the Americas after his resurrection.[35] The book contains promises to the Lamanites, descendants of Laman's followers, which church leaders ascribed to Indigenous peoples of the Americas through the twentieth century.

For example, in October 1980 Gene R. Cook of the First Quorum of the Seventy referred to several scriptures to list divine promises to the Lamanites in his talk, "Miracles among the Lamanites," based on his experiences in South America. He considered Indigenous peoples of the region to be Lamanites, and he testified of "spiritual miracles among that people." He witnessed "thousands converted to the Lord" and the development of Church congregations in the forms of wards and stakes. Referring to Latter-day Saint teachings and prophecies, in the Doctrine and Covenants, that "the Lamanites shall blossom as the rose," Cook proclaims: "We have truly seen them 'blossom as the rose' as prophecy has been fulfilled through them. We have literally seen the Lord perform miracles among them by their faith." Cook also reiterates that "the title page of the record their ancestors gave to the world, entitled the Book of Mormon, indicates that the book was 'written to the Lamanites, who are a remnant of the house of Israel.'"[36] Similar to this church leader, most Latter-day Saints studied these prophecies of the Lamanites and equated them with the potential roles of Indigenous peoples of North and South America in the Church throughout the twentieth century.

Joseph Smith taught that Native Americans descended from the Lamanites. While DNA evidence has not substantiated Israelite origins of any Indigenous people in the Western Hemisphere, many Latter-day Saints have believed that some people living in North and South America and the Pacific Islands came from this branch of the House of Israel.[37] From the origins of the Church, whether each Latter-day Saint viewed Native Americans and Indigenous peoples as Lamanites or not, they committed to disseminate the messages of the Book of Mormon throughout the world.

To Latter-day Saints, including the converts of my family, the Book of Mormon and the revelations that Joseph Smith received through his lifetime outline their pathways toward eternal life. The Articles of Faith lay out the first principles that Smith penned when people asked about Latter-day Saint beliefs. First, Latter-day Saints believe in Jesus Christ. After believers acknowledge that Christ can save humankind, they must repent, be baptized, and receive the Holy Ghost. Only those who possess the proper authority, known as the priesthood, can perform these ordinances for them. Church members trust that Joseph Smith received this priesthood authority from John the Baptist and ancient apostles Peter, James, and John. Latter-day Saints consider making covenants in the temple as an essential step toward salvation. They regard temple covenants and ordinances as sacred, rarely discussing the ceremony proceedings except within the temple. These covenants allow them to return to the presence of God, with whom all human beings lived before birth.

Smith and early Church leaders outlined "The Plan of Salvation" in which all humankind lived in a pre-earth life as the spirit children of Heavenly Parents. To become more like their celestial parents required their placement on an earth, which God had prepared for that purpose. They had to receive a physical body and follow the gospel commandments by faith since mortal birth would erase their memory of their premortal life. As part of the plan, Jesus's redemptive atonement would overcome physical death through his resurrection and offer forgiveness of sins by repentance, baptism, the gift of the Holy Ghost, and endurance with faithfulness. At the resurrection, many Latter-day Saints envision that Jesus will judge and place all people in a kingdom of glory based on their earthly lives. Diné converts have often learned and embraced most of these teachings.

DINÉ AND LATTER-DAY SAINT INTERSECTIONS

Diné have struggled to recognize commonalities between Diné and Latter-day Saint pathways because of various cultural incongruencies. They pinpoint differences between their epistemologies, expectations, leadership, human-land relationships, and communication. Diné language and ways of thinking are holistic, constructed by relationships and connections that cycle. Boyé Lafayette De Mente describes this connection of Diné language and philosophy: "The Navajo language attempts to present every concept in its cosmic entirety, showing its precise interrelation with other things. It attempts to reflect the world as it actually is, or is supposed to be—

integrated and harmonious. To achieve this integration and harmony, it is necessary that every word, phrase, and sentence clearly state all of the relationships involved."[38] My father told me that the shape and dimensions of an object determine the usage of terms and language in Diné bizaad. Diné think, understand, and communicate in precise terms that reflect systems of interconnectedness. Expressions and meanings of k'é, kinship, for example, convey layers of relations that symbolize the tight interweaving of Diné society.

Because the Church emerged in an Anglo-based American society and culture, most Latter-day Saints have adhered to a linear and logic-based philosophy. Unlike Diné and many other Native Americans, most Euro-Americans differentiated between the physical and spiritual, or metaphysical, components of life and did not view the world through a circular perspective of relatedness.[39] The family, according to mainstream Euro-American society throughout the twentieth century, primarily referred to the immediate biological relatives in a nuclear family unit. Euro-Americans also used basic vocabulary for family, lacking explicit distinctions between a paternal aunt from a maternal aunt, for instance. Diné acknowledge the lineage and age of their aunts in their terminology. My father, who is a fluent speaker of Diné bizaad, did not teach me and my siblings our ancestral language when we were children, but I have been learning with his support. For example, I call my paternal aunt "shi bízhí" and my maternal aunt "shimá yázhí." In the Navajo language, k'é also represents closer ties between relations. My mother would sometimes become confused when my father introduced one of his cousins as his brother to her, since she did not understand Diné perceptions of family. My father would say: "My cousins are my brothers." The sense of a nuclear family does not exist among Diné who adhere to ancestral teachings.

Most white American Latter-day Saints expected Diné to not only participate but also lead in a church that used different terms and forms of communication. Although many Diné Latter-day Saints attended schools designed by white Americans with directives to assimilate them, ancestral Diné philosophy and habitus have continued to influence them and their relations with the Church.[40] Misunderstandings between Diné Latter-day Saints and white church officials arose in efforts to communicate about leadership and church callings.

The Church ordains men to different priesthoods and offices. Ordained men can exclusively hold particular callings as well. In the general membership, men advance from the Aaronic Priesthood, which used to begin at the age of twelve, to the Melchizedek Priesthood, beginning usually around the age of eighteen, after proving their dedication as Latter-day Saints and manifesting certain maturity. Adult male converts are sometimes given the Aaronic Priesthood after baptism. They usually do not receive the Melchizedek Priesthood until they have been a member for a year.

In Diné communities, select people of different genders, including those who transcend the binary of male and female, could become healers and spiritual leaders.[41] An adolescent would not receive such authority. My father recalled how he had traveled and participated in ceremonies with my grandfather throughout Diné Bikéyah in his youth, preparing to follow his father's footsteps to become a hataałii, a healer. When my father returned home after joining the Church at BYU, he discontinued following his father in ceremonies, which outraged the family. Diné such as my grandfather understood that Diné ways of life, knowledge, and language were only one generation from becoming disconnected, which caused rejections and wariness of Christianity.[42]

Some Diné did not understand the order of priesthood ordination. My father remembered that a respected Diné elder joined the Church when he was sixty-five, but church leaders would not ordain him to the Aaronic Priesthood. This decision offended the man, since he did not see how teenagers who "played in the mud" could have the authority of the priesthood while a convert so respected would be denied the priesthood for a time. Other Diné did not consider the priesthood as powerful as Diné medicine ways, because immature young men possessed it. In Diné traditions and ceremonial practices, Diné restrict the participation and duties of children and youth until they achieve maturity. My father posits that the Church's hesitancy to bestow the priesthood on Diné converts subsided when Gordon B. Hinckley became president of the Church during the mid-1990s and taught that if a man is worthy for baptism, he should receive the priesthood.[43]

Hegemonic Euro-American white settler society assumes a world of capitalism and competition in contrast to Diné society, which was not forced under US jurisdiction until the late nineteenth century. For Euro-Americans, success often meant excelling in school, being hired for well-paying jobs, and receiving high-status promotions. Diné traditionally regarded success in different ways based on community ties. For example, a more respected Diné trait was balance rather than competition.[44] Diné ancestral teachings warn the people about overzealous ambitions for leadership and power such as "doo hwee adaahodzóliʼda" ("do not show off") and "yíní dilyinee jiiná" ("be humble"), which signify humility.[45] Rather than competing to be the leader, most Diné learned to harmonize with others and to be recognized first by the people as humble.

According to former president of the Southwest Indian Mission J. Edwin Baird, this Diné sense of leadership conflicted with his expectations of Native American missionaries and members of the Church. He wrote that the Diné "built-in cultural concept that associates not go faster than the group in their progress . . . seems to be a real hindrance to progress. It is very difficult for them to be different from others."[46] He mistook Diné values of humility and community connectedness for conformity, which stunts personal growth. Anglo-Americans differed in their interpretations of Diné culture and interaction. Anthropologist Alexander Lesser argued that Diné "reveal the same inner Indian feelings about the world and man's place in nature . . . [a] non-competitive attitude, the same disinterest in the American drive for progress and change."[47] When such white American observers consider Diné as "disinterested" in "progress and change," they are only measuring how Diné adopt ideals, principles, and values according to their own standards. Diné have followed their own means of measuring "progress and change," which many white Americans did not detect and esteem because of their perpetual drive to control and eradicate cultural differences. Consequentially, various cultural misunderstandings discouraged missionaries and frustrated Diné who were trying to learn the gospel of the Church.

Another area of tension and difference of perspective is also apparent in views of human-land relationships. Many Americans of European ancestry place a high value on private ownership of land, self-sufficiency, and competition in the free marketplace. For Diné, who follow ancestral teachings, the opposites are often considered strengths. Diné land is cared for jointly, as Ernesteen Lynch stresses: "When we step on that reservation, that whole thing is ours. . . . We all live on it together. It's a very neat feeling. Talk about solid security and identity."[48] Belonging to the land and sharing its resources form the foundation of Diné identity and sense of community, as my family and elders have taught me.[49] Diné have tried to convey that view of place to Anglos, as many Diné call Euro-Americans, since before the Long Walk. In 1864 the US government exiled Diné, including my ancestors, to the desolate reservation of Bosque Redondo, also known as Fort Sumner or Hwééłdi ("The Land of Suffering"), accusing Diné of trespassing on white settlers' properties. In reality, white settlers invaded and seized Diné homelands. In 1868, after many Diné people died walking hundreds of miles to be interned and exposed without proper shelter and sustenance, Diné leaders, including Barboncito, beseeched General William Tecumseh Sherman and the US government to allow Diné to return home where the Creator designated lands for Diné to live and thrive.[50]

With these conflicting focuses on individual progress versus community growth, Euro-Americans and Diné communicated differently throughout the twentieth century. Researchers even exaggerated the differences; for example, Rosalie H. Wax and Robert K. Thomas claim that many Native Americans remain silent compared to whites, who often try to initiate a conversation in an informal social gathering. They underscore how Euro-American and Diné approaches to communication and building rapport often clashed, causing confusion, frustration, and even animosity.[51] Knowing my Diné family and community, these studies sound preposterous to me, since Diné often do not struggle sparking discourse and communicating. These twentieth-century analysts did not comprehend or observe Native American forms of interactions in context, but they epitomized real misunderstandings.

Nonverbal communication, including eye contact, presents another arena of fundamental differences between peoples that affected Diné Latter-day Saint experiences. Jim Dandy, a former Diné educator in Blanding, Utah, remembers when he went on ISPP and attended school in Box Elder County, Utah. He would "look away" from the teacher "because that was something I was taught. Traditionally, they say you shouldn't stare at people."[52] Euro-American instructors reprimanded Diné in similar cases, since they perceived eye contact as a sign of respect and attention—the reverse of ancestral Diné teachings. Such miscommunications bred frustration for both Diné and Euro-Americans, including in interactions that affected Diné Latter-day Saint lives.

Euro-American standards for living also conflicted with some Diné teachings, including those of the Coyote stories. In the late twentieth century, for example, one Diné woman in her mid-thirties struggled to define her core beliefs in relation to the white American society that surrounded her. She no longer followed certain Diné lifeways such as ceremonial practices. Yet Euro-American "modern" living also perplexed her, since it contradicted Diné lessons about the "antics of Coyote, who could never have enough and so lived by deceit and overindulgence." Diné elders and families have educated their youth through storytelling, including the stories of Coyote, who was often mischievous for ignoring Diné mores and taboos but was also regarded as a teacher and creator. For instance, with indoor plumbing, people could "urinate in the homes"—but doing the same thing in Diné culture was a harmful practice introduced by Coyote "to bewitch someone."[53] Euro-Americans considered indoor plumbing a part of civilization and standard for living, but Coyote stories taught Diné that urination in dwelling places was a form of witchcraft. White Americans instructed my grandparents' family to build "outhouses" instead of relieving themselves in a nearby ravine. My father had learned as a child to keep excrement away from the residential areas, and an outhouse violated this practice.[54]

Although white American Latter-day Saints and Diné faced various cultural misunderstandings, Diné inherited knowledge and worldviews that did not contrast so sharply with Latter-day Saint epistemology. My father told me about K'é Hwiindzin, which is one of various Blessing Way teachings, Hózhóojik'ehgo Nanitin. The Blessing Way begins with Ha ahwiinit'i, which translates as "be generous and kind." Diné then learn K'é Hwiindzin, which directs them to "acknowledge and respect kinship and clanship."[55] To some Diné Latter-day Saints, their membership in the Church inducts them into a new clan and form of kinship. Based on my experiences and community connections, which include oral histories, conversations, and interviews, some Latter-day Saint Native Americans have treated "Lamanite" identity as a clan to which they belong. Latter-day Saints see each other as brothers and sisters building Zion, a righteous community. Diné join the family of the Latter-day Saints, while applying the Diné ancestral ideal of K'é Hwiindzin to their growing kinship in the Church.

THE LAMANITE QUESTION

Although my father did not participate in the Placement program, he lived with a white Latter-day family for work and grew close to them during the summers. The Kunz family treated him as kin. Because of their ongoing ties, my parents would occasionally bring our family to visit them in the Teton Valley of eastern Idaho. I began to call some of the Kunz children of my age "cousins." When I was visiting the Kunz family in Victor, Idaho, as a teenager, my family attended a local Latter-day Saint church meeting with them. During the meeting, an elderly woman in the ward approached me to inquire about my background. When I mentioned my father and his connection with the Kunz family, she exclaimed: "Oh! You're one of Merle Kunz's adopted Lamanites!" One of my teenage Kunz "cousins" was standing beside me, and we both instantly looked at each other and tried to withhold our laughter. We both felt it was somehow comical or embarrassing for the elderly woman. In other moments of my life, I have listened in reverence and awe to the testimonies of Indigenous Latter-day Saints, including my father, who have personally identified as (and/or with) Lamanites.

One of the most frequent questions I face, as a Diné Latter-day Saint scholar, is what I think about "Lamanites." The question relates to what I think about various labels and terms such as "Indians," "Native Americans," and "Indigenous." Context and usage of terms matter. Suffice to say, this whole book delves into my complex thoughts and experiences with diverse contexts and meanings of "Lamanite." Although I will refer to several white scholars' debates and assessments in this section, many Native Americans and Indigenous peoples have argued about the meanings and identity of Lamanites. They have expressed their insights, perspectives, and experiences with the term and usage of "Lamanite" in publications, panels, and various forms of media such as websites, podcasts, and films.[56]

Sarah Newcomb, a Tsimshian writer of the First Nation from Metlakatla, Alaska, was raised as a Latter-day Saint but became disillusioned with the Church and appropriations of the term "Lamanite," which inspired her to launch her blog *Lamanite Truth*.[57] In social media, such as Facebook groups, there have been conversations and debates including a Diné man's "Nephite Project," which was created "to begin the building of the New Jerusalem by educating the Lamanites of today about who they really are, and what is expected of them by the Lord, in these latter days."[58] Andrea Hales, a Diné Latter-day Saint and BYU alumna, started an independent podcast series with a corresponding Facebook page titled "Tribe of Testimonies," featuring the stories of Native American Latter-day Saints and "their love of the Savior."[59] Hales identifies Native Americans as the "remnant of the Lamanite people," or "remnants of the Tribe of Israel."[60] Hales once reached out to me about the podcast series, since I have addressed public audiences about my experiences as a Native American Latter-day Saint.

In 2019, for example, I participated in a roundtable at the Mormon History Association conference titled "Indigenous and 'Lamanite' Identities in the Twentieth Century." Kanaka ʻŌiwi (Native Hawaiian) scholar Michael David Kaulana Ing and I later launched a workshop to support Indigenous scholars who address perspectives from their respective communities about the meanings of "Lamanite."[61] The first workshop, in 2022, involved about twenty-four scholars with ties to Indigenous peoples, and we seek to develop an edited volume through these collaborations. In 2021 Arcia Tecun inspired me to organize the workshop and gathering of Indigenous scholars after I read his argument that "Indigenous Mormons shift the cosmology of a hegemonic global Mormon paradigm through 'divine rebellion,' which reimagines Mormonism to better serve 'the Lamanite.'"[62] His work focuses on Latter-day Saint Indigenous lived experiences and understandings of "Lamanite," which sparked my hunger to learn more and turn to my own Diné dóó Gáamalii community with similar questions. Indigenous scholars, such as critical kaupapa Maori scholar Hemopereki Hōani Simon, have also underscored the significance of positionality that the subjectivity and intersectional identity of researchers matter in the approaches and outcomes of scholarship. In his examination of Mormon studies, Simon asserts the need to recognize Indigenous researchers as "the key to explaining our [Indigenous] point of view to the religious and the scholars of religion."[63]

Angelo Baca, a Diné and Hopi filmmaker and advocate for the Bears Ears Inter-Tribal Coalition who has personally faced teachings and appropriations of "Lamanites," trailblazed this work of critical Indigenous Mormon studies in his documentary, *In Laman's Terms: Looking at Lamanite Identity* (2008), which asks, "What is a Lamanite?" and features Indigenous voices from throughout Native America. Baca sheds light on diverse perspectives, backgrounds, and beliefs, from a Latter-day Saint missionary to Indigenous critics of the Church, but they all relate as being Indigenous and part of peoples who have been identified as "Lamanite."[64] Growing up "as a Navajo Mormon," he later asks himself in adulthood: "If Mormons believe that Indigenous people are the 'chosen people,' then why are we continually subjugated and diminished as the literal 'other,' and made to be background characters in a colonial story?" He created his film "to change this dynamic."[65] He later made the award-winning short documentary *Shash Jaa'* (2016) to educate and support the protection of sacred lands of the Bears Ears National Monument, which many white Latter-day Saints of San Juan County have challenged.[66] Baca has worked with scholars in Mormon studies such as Thomas Murphy to continue decolonizing Mormonism and stand for his people in Diné Bikéyah and Native America.[67]

When the debates of the Bears Ears National Monument sparked widespread attention, my parents were living in what is considered San Juan

County—the ground zero of the controversy. Bears Ears is located on contested lands that were recently designated, reduced, and then restored as a national monument.[68] Between 2017 and 2018, I organized a couple of panels in Utah that gathered Diné and White Mesa Ute community members and scholars with various backgrounds and expertise, who each have understood and related directly to Bears Ears as home. Several of them also had some affiliation with the Church.

As Diné dóó Gáamalii, I became concerned with the binary drawn between white Latter-day Saints and Diné in San Juan County, southeastern Utah. White Latter-day Saints are often associated with the colonizers who dispossessed and continue to attempt to erase Indigenous presence and connections to lands they have claimed. On the other hand, Native Americans, including Diné, are stereotyped as romanticized environmentalists and the "ecology Indians" who live as one with nature. The intricacies and complexities of San Juan County resident identities, Native and non-Native American, are commonly overlooked or misunderstood. Latter-day Saint Native Americans are often caught in the crossfire, somewhere in the middle of such dichotomies. Some Native American Latter-day Saints align themselves with fellow (non-Native) Latter-day Saints by turning to the lawmakers and predominantly white church and state authorities in southeastern Utah. Some Native American Latter-day Saints try to avoid the politics altogether, while others openly support recognizing the sacredness of the lands and not treating them as sites only to be torn apart for energy resources. I engaged in dialogues, such as a panel at Brigham Young University held in April 2018 about Indigenous perspectives of Bears Ears, because I know and respect people—both Latter-day Saints and non-Latter-day Saints—from the region of the Bears Ears National Monument as friends and family. I also recognize Bears Ears as a sacred place, not only to my ancestors but also to my people today.

Latter-day Saints are taught to love one another and show tolerance toward different faiths and peoples. To what extent do Latter-day Saints, Native and non-Native American, follow these teachings in relation to those who practice ceremonies and regard areas of Bears Ears as their temples? To many Indigenous peoples, Bears Ears is holy ground, marked with shrines and ceremonies. Similar to how Native Americans do not all relate to and understand Bears Ears in the same ways, there are also major differences in experiences and viewpoints regarding the Church.

In the summer of 2021, *Dialogue: A Journal of Mormon Thought* produced a special issue on "Mormonism and Indigeneity," which included several contributions from Diné and Native American scholars. For this issue, I shared a short story of how my father decided to become a doctor after his mission for the Church, and I organized a roundtable with my husband, Brian King, featuring Native American and Indigenous Latter-day Saint perspectives that challenge the celebratory narratives of Christopher Columbus. One of the most impressive pieces of the issue came from Monika Brown Crowfoot, which she titled "The Lamanite Dilemma: Mormonism and Indigeneity." Crowfoot stresses:

> If God has proclaimed there are no more manner of "-ites," we should believe him. Let us do away with divisive language. I am not a Lamanite. My husband is not a Lamanite. My children are not Lamanites. . . . We are Diné, Oneida, Siksika, Akwesasne, and Anishinaabe, with our own stories and histories passed down from the tender and powerful voices of our elders. We are the Indigenous people of North and South America. We are of the land, living the best we can in harmony with all of God's creations. We live in harmony with our cultural teachings interwoven with our spiritual teachings. We are children of God. We are Indigenous and we are unashamed.[69]

Many Native American and Indigenous peoples like Crowfoot have reclaimed their identities in the throes of colonized spaces and dynamics. Crowfoot addresses how different Latter-day Saints have misused the term "Lamanite" to shame and silence the histories of Indigenous peoples, which she rejects in order to (re)connect with her heritage, culture, and spirituality.

When I was organizing the workshop about Indigenous perspectives on the meanings of "Lamanite," I reached out to several Indigenous public intellectuals, inviting them to participate in the meetings and discussions. The spectrum of responses included extreme opposites and many standpoints in between them. Some individuals refused to even talk about the term "Lamanite" but for very different reasons. One person considered the word too derogatory, while another person believed "Lamanite" identity to be too sacred to discuss and interrogate. Each person came from diverse life experiences, backgrounds, and knowledge, which I respect.

Latter-day Saints do not adhere to any official doctrine regarding the present-day identity of Lamanites or Native Americans. Church authorities encourage members to ponder the words of the prophets and learn the doctrine of Christ by the Holy Spirit. A wide variety of opinions from varying degrees of authoritativeness—but none of them canonical—exists regarding descendants of Lamanites. During the twentieth century, however, many Latter-day Saints equated Native Americans with Lamanites. Latter-day Saint historians Leonard J. Arrington and Davis Bitton examine the paradox of "Indians are Lamanites equivalence." In the nineteenth and twentieth centuries, Euro-American Latter-day Saints often regarded Native Americans as either "noble savages" or the "white man's burden" to "civilize and elevate" through conversion even if Lamanites were "a chosen people."[70] Other analyses of the Book of Mormon have challenged views of Native Americans as Lamanites.[71]

The meaning of "Lamanite" has changed through the twentieth century, according to Latter-day Saint terminology, reflecting variations in the Book of Mormon. In 1975 Lane Johnson wrote an article for the official Church magazine, *Ensign*, in which he defines "Lamanite" as the descendants of Laman, the son of Lehi. In part of the Book of Mormon, "the name Lamanite referred to a religious or political faction whose distinguishing feature was its opposition to the church."[72] The Lamanites represented wickedness and resistance to the gospel of Jesus Christ during those sections beginning in 2 Nephi 5, while Nephites were considered the righteous descendants of Nephi, Laman's younger brother. Later in the scriptures, "Lamanites" became "Nephites" and "Nephites" became "Lamanites." For a time, there existed "no manner of -ites," or such categorizations and divisions of peoples, since "they were in one, the children of Christ, and heirs to the kingdom of God."[73] After generations of peace, the terms reappeared along with contentions and cycles of violence. Both Nephites and Lamanites became wicked, leading to the downfall of the Nephites by the end of the Book of Mormon.[74]

Lane Johnson's definition in the *Ensign* aligns with a common Latter-day Saint attitude during the 1970s, but it alone does not represent wide and diverse historical views of "Lamanite" identity. While many twentieth-century Latter-day Saints accepted that the Book of Mormon presents a history of Native Americans in North America, members of the Church have continued to discuss how many people living in the Americas and beyond relate to these scriptures since the founding of the Church. In 2021, during a devotional address to Latter-day Saints in Oklahoma and Kansas with an emphasis on Native American populations, President Russell M. Nelson reiterated that the Book of Mormon is not a history textbook, as he stressed the truthfulness of its teachings to come unto Christ.[75] At the beginning of the twenty-first century, some scholars questioned the Book of Mormon claims of Native Americans as "Lamanites" and concluded there is no DNA evidence that Native Americans are descendants of Israelites. Other Latter-day Saint scholars debate with those conducting DNA research and reject their conclusions. Both groups, however, could focus more on the shifting definitions of "Lamanite," the name for different peoples in the Book of Mormon, within the Church leadership and lay membership.[76]

Anthropologist Thomas Murphy spoke at the Sunstone conference in July 2022 about his journey over the past twenty years since the 2002 publication of his groundbreaking chapter, "Lamanite Genesis, Genealogy, and Genetics," which stirred the DNA and "Lamanite" controversy. He shared stories of how Church leaders initiated disciplinary action against him because of his studies, which led to his reputation as a "Mormon Galileo" even though he rejected that label.[77] The translation of the Book of Mormon has changed since Murphy's work in the early 2000s. Instead of indicating that all Native Americans are direct descendants of Lamanites, for example, the language was altered to "among" the descendants.[78] Murphy's relationships with Indigenous peoples in the Northwest, outside of Mormon studies, became a focus in his life and work since 2002. He clarified that he was applying what he learned as a "Mormon" to serve and love one another in his work with Indigenous peoples who were reclaiming and perpetuating their ancestral lifeways of canoe journeys, gathering, and sustaining salmon and their homelands and waters.[79]

In 2008 John-Charles Duffy, a scholar of comparative religion, outlined some of the changing views about "Lamanites." He contends that when Joseph Smith presided over the Church between 1830 and 1844, he referred to the "Lamanites" as "our western Tribes of Indians" or "the Indians that now inhabit this country." Smith also identified the ruins in Mesoamerica as belonging to Book of Mormon people. During the migrations of Latter-day Saints in the nineteenth century, Church leaders began to demarcate the peoples of North and South America and the Pacific Islands as descendants of Book of Mormon peoples, although Duffy emphasizes that "Indians of the Intermountain West, being closest to home, received the lion's share of church leaders' attention."[80]

According to Armand Mauss, a Latter-day Saint scholar, church leaders did not encourage missionary work among Native Americans during the first half of the twentieth century. During this period, missionaries were active in the Pacific Islands and Latin America, resulting in a growing number of Latter-day Saint converts in these areas. Scholars already questioned that all Indigenous peoples of the Americas and the Pacific Islands were Lamanites, but many church leaders affiliated them with the Book of Mormon peoples as a missionary tactic. Although Oliver Cowdery, an early Latter-day Saint leader, reported in 1831 about interests of proselytizing among "another tribe of Lamanites. . . . called Navajoes [sic]," the Church did not increase missionary work among Native Americans and Diné until the mid-twentieth century.[81] The most important person to intensify missionary efforts among Indigenous communities in the United States, Spencer W. Kimball, began directing church programs toward Native Americans by the 1950s. While Kimball did not limit his work to Native Americans but spread his "Lamanite" message throughout the Americas and Pacific Islands, he developed a special connection with Diné.[82]

As Kimball and other church leaders reemphasized Native Americans as Lamanite descendants in the late twentieth century, many Latter-day Saints asserted that Native Americans were only part of that lineage. David Kay Flake, an Anglo-American who served in the Southwest Indian Mission from 1958 to 1960, taught on the reservation and served as a counselor to George P. Lee when he was mission president. He stresses that other descendants of Lamanites exist. He criticizes certain Diné who "feel they are the only Lamanites in the world. That's not the truth." He remembers attending General Conference in April 1976 when J. Thomas Fyans, an assistant to the Twelve Apostles of the Church, asked all the Lamanites to stand for a moment. According to Flake, when four to five hundred men stood, "it was just amazing for me to see that."[83]

Flake notices that the focus had shifted from only Native Americans and Diné as Lamanites to the Lamanites of Latin America, claiming: "The criticism leveled at the Church by Elder [George P. Lee] and his followers that the Church has pulled seminary out of the reservation [and] not giving so much attention to the American Indians has failed to realize that the Lamanite people, the people of Central and South America are a lot more productive in the Church than the local Lamanites." White American Latter-day Saints such as Flake continued to stress that Native Americans are not the only Lamanites, which raised some tensions about attention and resources of the Church, which I discuss later in the book.[84] The Church would increasingly support the "Lamanites" who embraced its gospel and membership.

DINÉ AND LAMANITE IDENTITY

The narrative voice and tone of the Book of Mormon often depicts Lamanites as unrighteous people, although there are some exceptions. Scholar Max Perry Mueller recognizes this tone as part of the "narrator's prerogative."[85] A friend who has been a Latter-day Saint bishop, and is also a BYU Native American alumnus and former ISPP student, once told me how he often wondered how Laman and Lemuel would have recorded their own experiences and stories. How would Lamanites such as Abish or King Lamoni record their stories, which Nephite recordkeepers featured in a positive light, unlike their portrayals of Laman and Lemuel? Since Nephites entirely authored the Book of Mormon, some have argued that many Latter-day Saints have read and embraced Nephite interpretations that Lamanites inherited a fallen and degraded state.[86]

Church president Spencer W. Kimball wrote in 1975: "You who are Lamanites remember this: Your Lamanite ancestors were no more rebellious than any of the other branches of the house of Israel. All the seed of Israel fell into apostasy and suffered the long night of spiritual darkness." Instead of focusing on the past, Kimball invited Lamanites to look to the future: "You are a chosen people; you have a brilliant future." He called on "all the Lamanites, the Mexicans, the Polynesians, the Indians, to live the commandments of God and prove themselves worthy of this promised land."[87] Kanaka ʻŌiwi scholar Hokulani Aikau examines the dissonances between Latter-day Saint and Kānaka Maoli understandings of land, known as ʻāinu ("that which feeds"), relating specifically to such Latter-day Saint teachings of a "a chosen people, a promised land."[88] Her work centers on Indigenous perspectives and meanings, acknowledging deep ties of Indigenous peoples to their homelands that precede Latter-day Saint leaders' notions that they must demonstrate their worthiness of the land.

As Armand Mauss reviewed the first set of Latter-day Saint Native American oral histories from the Charles Redd Center, he commented:

> One is struck by how rarely the issue of Lamanite identity is even mentioned, whether in a positive or a negative light. It is [as] though the Indian respondents simply recognized that "Lamanite" is the peculiarly Mormon way of referring to them, but they do not really embrace its fundamental theological implications; or if they do, they evaluate the label with an ambivalence similar to that which white Mormons bring to it.[89]

Mauss discusses some elements of identity from the oral histories and his other sources and reactions to the term "Lamanite." He summarizes that, for some interviewees, the term had "no real 'use' in their lives," "neither troubles them especially nor motivated them." On the other hand, others navigate and connect "both identities, Lamanite and tribal, to enjoy the social benefits of both." Mauss assumes that such balance would be difficult. For another group of Native American Latter-day Saints, the term "Lamanite" is "a claim to special power and status in Mormonism." Mauss applies these analyses of Native American Latter-day Saint oral histories and Lamanite identity only to the context of the twentieth century in the United States.[90]

For many of the individuals represented in the oral history projects of the Redd Center and the Church, Lamanite identity was often not an emphasis. In the 1990s most Diné interviewees referred to themselves as Indians and occasionally Native Americans. In the early 2000s more interviewees called themselves Native American, but those with stronger connections to their tribal nations referred to themselves as Navajo or Diné. The interviewees exhibited mixed reactions to the term "Lamanite." Some referred to themselves by that term throughout the interview. They valued the blessings of the Book of Mormon for Lamanites and felt that the book was written especially for them. Others, however, never used the term and specifically said they did not accept the label of "Lamanite." To many of this group, the Lamanites were the descendants of Laman and Lemuel, unrighteous people in the Book of Mormon, and they did not want to be identified with people who resisted God's commandments. Diné Latter-day Saint Shaynalea Mirabel did not have negative feelings about the term, for example, but she knows that many Native American families no longer participate in the Church because of the scriptures that "talk about them being the bad guys."[91]

When asked if she considered herself a Lamanite, Olivia Ben responded: "I consider myself Diné because of the way I was raised. I never really considered myself a Lamanite; I just always kind of thought that those were the people who were in the Book of Mormon. I remember that being stressed on the Placement Program that we were Lamanites, but I was always like, 'No, I'm an individual and I'm Diné.'" She thought that "Lamanite in general is anyone from the South Pacific, from Mexico, and from Central America. We are in North America."[92] Thomas Benally shared a similar insight when Matthew Heiss, who worked for the Church Historical Department, told him that many of his interviewees did not relate to Lamanites and identified as children of God. Benally, a Diné Latter-day Saint born in 1952,

Chinle Latter-day Saint Stake Center in Navajo Nation, June 2011. Courtesy of author.

agreed and asserted that he was Diné. The term "Lamanite" "didn't click" with him.[93] The Church History Department interviewers specifically asked how people regarded the term and the prophecy in the Doctrine and Covenants that the Lamanites would "blossom as a rose." Virginia Morris Tso Tulley, another Diné Latter-day Saint born in 1961, claimed that she viewed herself as a Lamanite but also primarily as "a child of God."[94]

One of my friends at BYU, Oliver Whaley, a Diné Latter-day Saint, told me how his mission president in West Virginia used to emphasize that he, as the only Native American and Diné, and the mission's "few Tongan and Samoan missionaries [were] special, because they had the blood of Israel." For Whaley, having "a little blood of Israel or not" did not matter. He found that "it comes down to making and keeping covenants." He considered how "Navajo people think of themselves as privileged because they have the Book of Mormon and think they're special or some covenant people. What it comes down to is living the gospel. If you don't, then you're going to miss out." Whaley also could joke about the Lamanite identity. When I asked him how he felt about being called "Oliver the Lamanite," he replied: "It was from a stupid comment." As a BYU freshman, he was the only "non-white" person in his congregation. When he bore his testimony, he wanted to "lighten the mood. . . . I just got up and said, 'I'm Oliver the Lamanite.' It just kind of stuck."[95] On the other hand, Diné such as Shannon Adison positively identified with Lamanites because it meant that "she's a chosen person; she's overcome so much."[96] Diné Latter-day Saint perspectives on the meanings of "Lamanite" and the Book of Mormon vary, which underscores the significance of personal spiritual experiences, thoughts, and interpretations.

AVOIDING "LAMANITES"

The use of and emphasis on the "Lamanite" identity has drastically declined since the 1980s in the Church and among its membership. Many Latter-day Saints now avoid the term outside of its scriptural context in the Book of Mormon. John-Charles Duffy argues that there was "a sharp, immediate decline in Lamanite identification by top-level church leaders" after Spencer W. Kimball died in 1985. By 2000, church leaders were "virtually ignoring" the discussion of Lamanites and focusing on the message of the Church for all people. Minor discussions of Lamanites by some General Authorities and Latter-day Saint apologist scholars continue into the twenty-first century.[97] The "Era of the Lamanites" in the Church faded with the presidency of Kimball. The mission to help the "Lamanites" reach their potential as a promised people was no longer a Church priority at the end of the twentieth century.

As Duffy, Mauss, and George P. Lee have asserted, the Church withdrew the concentration on "Lamanites," especially Native Americans, by the twenty-first century. Mauss argues that the decline in Lamanite emphasis started long before Kimball's death. According to Kimball's son and grandson, who are the authors of a Kimball biography, Kimball had fewer responsibilities that involved the Lamanite and Minority Committee beginning in 1971. As the new Church president, Kimball tried to instruct regional representatives about the importance of addressing the Lamanite populations. Kimball aimed to persuade them that "the Lord certainly had in mind that there should be Lamanite branches, Lamanite stakes, Lamanite missions." Duffy concludes in his study that Kimball could not convince all the Church officials of these priorities. Church leaders eliminated Indian missions and Lamanite youth conferences in the 1970s, then they terminated ISPP and several BYU Indian programs between the 1970s and 1980s.[98]

The Church veered toward other programs that did not specifically benefit Native Americans.

These changes in the relationships between Latter-day Saints and Native Americans reflected a larger historical context of the Church. During the 1960s and 1970s, the Church sought transitions to develop its identity as an international church. In the 1960s Church leaders hired consulting firms who recommended that leaders should no longer serve on the boards of directors for corporations but focus on the expanding Church. Harold B. Lee, Church president from 1972 to 1973, set goals in the early 1960s to correlate all church programs. Following the same objectives as Joseph F. Smith's consolidating programs in the 1900s, the new correlation program called on all organizations to work on a threefold mission of the Church: missionary work, temple work, and perfecting of the saints.[99] The Church centered on the family as a cornerstone. Church leaders asked all families to hold a weekly home evening and provided lesson manuals to steer their discussions. They designed priesthood and auxiliary lessons to match those taught in the home.

This new plan could be dispersed throughout the world and adapted to various cultures. As the leadership started to look beyond the Church stronghold in Utah and the Intermountain West, they also diminished programs that only served people in those areas. BYU limited its enrollment to twenty-five thousand students and remained close to that number into the beginning of the twenty-first century. The Church continued to sponsor schools where institutionalized education was lacking throughout the world, but it paid more attention to high school seminary and college institutes located near public education facilities. A large-scale athletic and recreation program including all-church tournaments was eliminated or transferred to regional levels. Church leaders created a nonprofit health care program from its extensive Intermountain West hospital system. Church officials assigned welfare and health missionaries to areas throughout the world. International programs of the Church replaced the emphasis of Lamanite programs.[100]

While some could argue that the Church marched forward from the 1960s into a large international family-based church, various factors influenced and complicated such changes in Church programs. Whatever the reasons for the shift away from "Lamanite," some Latter-day Saint Native Americans have continued to believe they are the descendants of Lamanites as a "chosen people." In 2022, during a public forum about his book, *The Bear River Massacre: A Shoshone History*, Darren Parry of the Northwestern Band of Shoshone mentioned that he asked Church authorities why they called him and his Native American ancestors "Lamanites" for so long and then suddenly stopped.[101] Since they could not offer him a clear answer, he asserted his identity as Lamanite to them and the listeners of his presentation that day.[102]

CONNECTIONS AND CHALLENGES

Since the mid-twentieth century, some Diné Latter-day Saints have identified connections between Diné teachings of the Walk of Beauty, SNBH, and Latter-day Saint beliefs of the Plan of Salvation. Such understanding requires confronting the views of some Latter-day Saints that Diné and other Indigenous people in North America are God-chosen people but in a fallen state due to the sins of their predecessors. According to many Latter-day Saints with these ideas, the only way that Native Americans could receive the blessings that the scriptures promised to them was to accept the message of the Church and learn to live in a world dominated by white Americans. While they recognized that Native American cultures and spiritual practices contained elements of truth, many white American Latter-day Saints urged Native Americans to overcome the "false traditions" of their ancestors. Latter-day Saints typically considered Native Americans as a chosen people but stressed that they could only reach their full potential within the Church and broader American society by embracing the gospel and abandoning certain Indigenous practices and knowledge. The following chapters show how Diné, and especially converts, responded and influenced that mixed message among them during the late twentieth century. This book explores the history of church programs and the experiences of Diné on their own Latter-day Saint pathways, beginning with the proselytization efforts among Diné and other Native Americans in the southwestern United States.

CHAPTER TWO

Gáamalii Bina'nitiní

Missionaries

My father, Phillip L. Smith, corrected me with a stern grimace when I once stated that he came from Gallup, New Mexico. "I do not come from Gallup," he retorted. "Tséyaaniichii'déé' naashá [I come from Rehoboth, New Mexico]." Tséyaaniichii' or "Termination of Red Streak of Rock" is part of the "checkerboard" of Diné communities that lies at the eastern edge of the border town of Gallup. A part of me wanted to roll my eyes as he said this, especially one day when I stood at the site of the family's homestead and looked down from a hill across the railroad tracks where I could see the Red Rock 10 movie theater and the two Marriott hotel franchises that fall within the jurisdiction of the east side of the city of Gallup. In time, I understood what that demarcation means to my father and my family who live in the Navajo Nation adjacent to the New Mexico town popularized by the song "Route 66" by Nat King Cole in the mid-1940s. The term "border town," in this case, refers to towns that border the Navajo reservation such as Farmington and Gallup, New Mexico, and Flagstaff, Arizona. Tensions and struggles between diverse peoples have shaped the "checkerboard region" for generations. My father's description of his homelands and displacement reflects these divisions:

It's on the eastern side of the Navajo reservation where we spent most of our time [as a family]. We grew up in a place called Bread Springs. Because of land exchanges, we were moved over closer to what they call the checkerboard area. The reservation has been interspaced with private ownership because of the railroad buying up some land for their railroad. We grew up in that area, which is not too far from Gallup, New Mexico, which is on the reservation southeastern side. The area is called Rehoboth. We didn't live right in the community of Rehoboth, which was a Christian Reform community that had a school, and a church, and a hospital. But we lived about maybe three or four miles from there.[1]

Other than indicating the differences between the reservation, the border town of Gallup, and the checkerboard region, my father clarified that he did not affiliate with the Rehoboth Christian Reformed Church community. He was raised with suspicions and distrust of whites and their religions.

During the late nineteenth century, in northwestern New Mexico, the federal government created an "odd- and even-section land ownership pattern" or the "checkerboarding" between primarily railroad companies and Diné as well as whites who gained allotments through the Homestead Act: "Thus, the checkerboard area is a complex mixture—reservation land, land allotted to private Navajos, private Anglo land, land owned by various railroad companies, federal Bureau of Land Management land, and state land."[2] Although part of the "checkerboard" and fraught with border issues, Tséyaaniichii' is a Diné space to my father and family, whereas Gallup is a "border town" under the control of whites who alienate Diné and diverse Indigenous communities. To this day, border towns such as Gallup upset my father and many Diné, sparking movements of "Border Town Justice and Native Liberation."[3]

Border towns also enable convergences of different peoples, religions, and cultures in unexpected ways for those involved.[4] The Church of Jesus Christ of Latter-day Saints, along with other religious denominations, developed strong presences in the border towns and checkerboard region where they based some of their first proselytization efforts among Diné. My father learned of the Church in Gallup from Diné Latter-day Saint seminary students whom he met in the public school. They invited him to seminary and introduced him to the seminary teacher at the Fort Wingate Boarding School, not far from his home in the checkerboard area.[5] Peoples not only attempt to draw borders based on landmarks and ethnicities, but also by religions, spiritual ways of life, and worldviews. Scholar Thomas A. Tweed defines religion as dependent on "crossings and dwellings": "Religions are confluences of organic-cultural flows that intensify joy and confront suffering by drawing on human and superhuman forces to make homes and cross boundaries." He clarifies that religion is "about finding a place and moving across space."[6] This point often pertains to discourse on immigration, but in the case of my father and some of my Diné family and friends, a Latter-day Saint mission shifted boundaries in their homelands.[7]

Phillip Smith with missionary companion and mother Johanna Haskeltsie Smith, c. 1972–1974, in the Southwest Indian Mission. Courtesy of author.

My grandfather, a hataałii or traditional Diné healer known as a "medicine man," taught my dad to value Diné ceremonies and tsodizin dóó sin.[8] Many Diné have explained that they traditionally do not have "religion" in the Euro-American sense of a church or organized institution, but their spirituality intertwines with their ways of life since time immemorial.[9] Despite his immersion in Diné ways of life and his father's disapproval of Christian religions, my dad joined the Church of Jesus Christ of Latter-day Saints as a young adult in 1969. He decided to serve a mission the following year, and the Church assigned him to the Southwest Indian Mission (SWIM), returning him to Diné Bikéyah and Native American communities of the checkerboard area and border towns.[10]

Jimmy N. Benally, one of my father's close Diné friends, also served in SWIM. Considering his connections with Diné community as a missionary, he stressed: "Just being on my own reservation really helped. I could really understand what [Navajos] were going through. It taught me more of my culture and more about my people because I grew up in a border town. I learned more about where I came from and who my people were."[11] Benally implies that his upbringing in a "border town" uprooted him from Diné language and culture. Yet his experiences of service and work in SWIM reconnected him to Diné people, lands, and ancestral ways of life.

Racial and ethnic tensions, particularly between Indigenous and Euro-American populations, have pervaded border towns since their establishment between the late nineteenth and twentieth centuries. Descendants of white settlers have predominantly controlled the schooling and main infrastructures of the border towns at the expense of Indigenous communities.[12] Although Benally was raised on a farm near the San Juan River, Są́ Bitooh or "Old Age River," one of the sacred rivers to the Diné, his mother would not teach him Diné bizaad or let him herd sheep with his relatives.[13] His education from boarding schools, "border town" schools, and the Indian Student Placement Program (ISPP) did not support Diné bizaad and ways of knowing. SWIM not only offered him training in church doctrine and proselytization but also provided him opportunities to get to know his people and their heritage, especially through language and spirituality.

Since the Treaty of 1868, which contains the terms of the Diné return to their homelands, the Navajo Nation, referred to as a "tribe" in many official documents, maintains a reservation with certain boundaries.[14] "Border towns" are near the Navajo reservation, but the federal and local governments deem them nontribal territory and jurisdiction. These border towns lay, however, within Diné Bikéyah according to the immemorial parameters of the Four Sacred Mountains that reflect the cardinal directions from east to north. The mountains and directions interconnect in the cyclical process of Si'ąh Naagháí Bik'eh Hózhǫ́ (SNBH).[15] Diné Bikéyah embodies borderlands in tense flux, as many Diné continue to live by the borders and directions of the Four Sacred Mountains, rather than the reservation. In these spaces, they have faced and interacted with diverse influences that have permeated their homelands, especially Christian religions and missions.

SWIM encompassed Diné Bikéyah and Native American communities in southern Utah, southern Colorado, Arizona, and New Mexico between 1949 and 1972.[16] Although Latter-day Saints have proselytized among many different peoples, they have historically focused on Native American communities whose people they identified as "Lamanites."[17] The Church developed missions for Native American territories and communities to teach the "Lamanites," two of which became known as the Southwest Indian Mission and the Northern Indian Mission.[18]

Under the influence of Spencer W. Kimball and other leaders who championed the "Lamanite Cause," beginning in the 1940s and 1950s, the

Church prioritized penetrating the boundaries of Diné Bikéyah to convert the "Lamanite" descendants.[19] Missionaries faced several challenges in these early years while opening SWIM, which primarily included the distrust and rejection of Diné leaders and communities. The Church then assigned some missionaries to SWIM who could relate with Diné as "Lamanite" and Indigenous. They sent other Native Americans and Pacific Islanders, such as Kānaka Maoli and Māori, from regions with similar settler-colonial historical contexts where the Church already established a presence and following.[20] As more Diné converts joined the Church, church officials placed Diné missionaries like my father and Jimmy Benally on their homelands. Diné called Latter-day Saint missionaries "Gáamalii Bina'nitiní."

With the assistance of Indigenous missionaries, Diné and non-Diné, SWIM grew and fostered a Latter-day Saint community in Diné Bikéyah. SWIM also fueled cultural exchange and confluences of diverse Latter-day Saints, including but not limited to Euro-Americans, Latin Americans, Pacific Islanders, and Native Americans. Missionaries who identified with an Indigenous community affected by settler colonialism found ways to revitalize and reinforce elements of their Indigenous cultures in SWIM. Indigenous missionaries simultaneously deepened and blurred borders in Diné Bikéyah.

Since the early era of the Church in the 1830s, Latter-day Saints claimed to receive revelation for a "mission to the Lamanites" with the belief that the Book of Mormon was "written to the Lamanites, who are a remnant of the house of Israel."[21] In the twentieth century, many Latter-day Saints renewed their efforts to teach the Book of Mormon to Native Americans. Some Euro-American Latter-day Saints described this mission as to become "nursing fathers and nursing mothers" to descendants of the Lamanites. They would prepare a way for Native Americans to "blossom as the rose," become a "pure and delightsome people," and lead in the establishment of Zion.[22] They referred to scriptures, such as Doctrine and Covenants 49:24, which depict Lamanites "blossoming as the rose." Earlier editions of the Book of Mormon included the phrase that Lamanites would become "white and delightsome." The current editions have changed it to "pure and delightsome," presenting this wording as Joseph Smith's original translation. The title page and different phrasing of the scriptures, regarding the Lamanites and their relation to Native Americans, have been debated and revised since Joseph Smith first introduced them. Many Church members interpreted the scriptures literally, fueling racism among Latter-day Saints since they were associating white skin with righteousness. In response, the Church revised some of the wording in such scriptures.[23]

Only six months after he organized the Church, Joseph Smith sent missionaries to evangelize Native Americans in the Indian Territory west of Missouri. The Indian Removal Act of 1830 enforced the removal of various Native American peoples to that region. Few Native Americans converted to the Church, partly because Latter-day Saint missionaries could not receive permission from federal agents. Other Christian missionaries also guarded their proselytizing zones among Indigenous peoples. In addition, many Native Americans were wary of Euro-Americans challenging their ways of life and forcing them to adopt Eurocentric belief systems.[24] One of the first known Native American converts was Lewis Denna, who was described as "a Lamanite of the Oneida nation." He served as an interpreter for Joseph Smith among Potawatomi and later as part of church leadership in the Council of Fifty.[25]

While the early missionaries struggled to spread their message in Indian Territory, they continued to pursue missions to share the Book of Mormon with Native Americans. After Joseph Smith died in 1844, many of his followers moved to the Great Basin under the direction of Brigham Young. Alpheus Cutler, a member of the Council of Fifty, remained in the Midwest to proselytize to the Native Americans but achieved little reception. Latter-day Saints in the Great Basin settled in the homelands of Utes, Shoshones, Paiutes, Goshutes, and diverse Indigenous peoples, straining relations between white Latter-day Saints and Native Americans.[26] The US federal government appointed Brigham Young as an Indian agent, and he pressured Native Americans to adopt agricultural lifestyles based on white Latter-day Saint settler standards and restrictions. With conflicting views and Euro-American encroachment on Indigenous homelands, to say that non-Native Latter-day Saint settlers and Native Americans clashed over limited resources is an understatement.[27]

From 1846 to 1868, Brigham Young led Latter-day Saints, who were predominantly white settlers, from Nauvoo, Illinois, the eastern United States, and northern Europe to what became the state of Utah. As I read histories such as Thomas Alexander's *Brigham Young and the Expansion of the Mormon Faith*, I recoil at the references to lands as "wilderness" and how Young claimed that the "Indians gave the land" to him and Latter-day Saint European-American settlers.[28] What they thought of as "wilderness" has been Indigenous "homelands" since time immemorial. Considering these complicated histories of Latter-day Saints and Native Americans, I am reminded of the mysterious photograph of Brigham Young with a woman, presumably a wife or daughter, sitting next to him with her face rubbed out. Was she his forgotten Native American wife? We might never know, but the image of erasure is seared in my mind.[29] I have been learning from the work of historians such as Jennifer Hale Pulsipher, how Brigham Young and Latter-day Saint mission leaders encouraged intermarriage between early missionaries and Native American women as a strategy to induce Native Americans to "cede land" in regions that are now considered northern Utah and eastern Idaho.[30]

The etched-out face of the woman beside Young aligns with all the efforts to erase the complicated and fraught past of Mormon conquest and colonialism in Indigenous homelands. In 2021 I noticed, in an online "Intermountain Stories" project, for example, how the narrative of "The Provo River Battle" of 1850 relies only on European-American Latter-day Saint sources that framed Timpanogos Utes as "thieves" and how the violence that massacred and forcibly removed these Indigenous peoples from their homelands started because of "a minor theft" on the part of the Timpanogos.[31] The real "theft" and dispossession is inseparable from the white Mormon colonialization of Ute and Indigenous homelands. As historian Jared Farmer argues in *On Zion's Mount*, "paradoxically, the Mormons created their homeland at the expense of the local Indians."[32] These "Indians" have a name they call themselves, and they continue to exist. Mormon colonizers' land grabs among Ute, Shoshone, Goshute, and Paiute people likely affected Diné perception of Latter-day Saints and their religious beliefs and practices, especially as they encroached on Diné spaces, such as Holbrook, Winslow, and Tuba City in Arizona and San Juan County in southern Utah. As I write and focus on Diné Latter-day Saint communities, I realize even more how generations continue to live with soul wounds and without healing, although time passes.[33] The voices, perspectives, public memories, and narratives that people perpetuate can either block or promote such healing, but there have been far more obstructions to healing. After the Treaty of 1868 and the establishment of a Navajo reservation, more Euro-Americans, including white Latter-day Saints, began to encroach on Diné Bikéyah. Tensions marred the first major exchanges between white Latter-day Saints and Diné during the late nineteenth century. Euro-American Latter-day Saints developed settlements, for example, on the disputed lands of the Moenkopi Wash in northern Arizona, the borderlands of Diné and Hopi peoples.

The Navajo-Mormon conflicts culminated when a group of Diné killed the Latter-day Saint leader Lot Smith in 1892. Soon thereafter, federal Indian agents officially expelled the white Latter-day Saint settlers and granted the Moenkopi land and Tuba City to the Diné by 1903.[34]

Some Latter-day Saint traders remained among Diné communities, teaching some Diné about the Church. Lucy and George Bloomfield, for example, introduced the Jumbo family and other Diné to the Latter-day Saint faith when they managed a trading post at Toadlena, Navajo Nation in New Mexico.[35] In 1931 the Bloomfields and Diné Latter-day Saint converts, George and Mary Jumbo, petitioned Church president Heber J. Grant to open a mission among Diné. When George Bloomfield traveled to Salt Lake City for his back surgery in 1942, Mary Jumbo traveled with him and visited President Grant to ask if missionaries could come to the Navajo reservation.[36] Diné, such as the Jumbos, embraced the faith and initiated the mission on the reservation through their exchanges with Latter-day Saints.

Latter-day Saint traders, neighbors from surrounding towns, and Diné requesting Latter-day Saint missionaries faced many obstacles to creating a mission in Diné Bikéyah. The US government and certain religious organizations had determined the presence of various Christian churches on the Navajo reservation, excluding the Church of Jesus Christ of Latter-day Saints. Congress provided a window for other religious groups to enter American Indian reservations by passing the Indian Reorganization Act of 1934.[37] Each Native American tribal nation then had to pass resolutions approving the law. While some historians have questioned Commissioner of Indian Affairs John Collier's motives in championing the Indian Reorganization Act, scholar Peter Iverson explains that Collier's "commitment to cultural pluralism resulted in innovative approaches to education, health care, and religious worship." The Diné struggles and suffering of the Indian New Deal livestock reduction interfered with their concessions to the Reorganization Act, which the Navajo Tribal Council rejected in 1935. According to Iverson, this episode "denied the people a tribal constitution and left a bitter legacy." Iverson argues, however, that these contentions with the Bureau of Indian Affairs and Collier "fostered a greater sense of Navajo nationalism."[38] The US government forced policies of conservation and livestock reduction, which hurt many Diné.[39]

Despite these misgivings, the Church benefited from John Collier's policies, which offered the opportunity for more religious groups to operate on the Navajo reservation. Collier even questioned the Navajo Tribal Council's

1940 decision to ban the Native American Church services and its use of peyote, which Latter-day Saint missionaries had supported with other Christian groups, such as Catholics and Protestants.[40] But he welcomed Christian organizations to send missionaries, establish churches, and offer education and medical services to Diné. Latter-day Saints and Pentecostals "especially gained a large number of new adherents in the years that followed" due to Collier's influence and changing policies.[41]

Ralph William Evans, who ran the Shiprock Trading Post, became the first president of the Navajo-Zuni Mission for Latter-day Saints in 1943.[42] He reiterated a persistent Euro-American Latter-day Saint perspective of Native Americans: "Rather than fight the Lamanites, the Church desires to bring to them a program which if adopted would enlighten them through education and in the gospel of Jesus Christ."[43] He was referring to the violent history of colonialism, in which white Latter-day Saints and Native Americans, especially of the Southwest and Great Basin, clashed over land and resources.[44] The twentieth-century mission represented, to white church leaders, a stark transition to uplift and include "Lamanites," as they called Native Americans, in the Church.

As more Diné became receptive to the Church, "four [unnamed] educated natives" served "as interpreters and part time missionaries" in the Navajo-Zuni mission.[45] One of these "educated natives" could have been Howela Polacca, a Hopi and Diné convert.[46] In July 1946 Polacca addressed the Diné tribal council with Evans to receive approval for a mission on the reservation.[47] Howela and his wife, Ruth Arviso Polacca, befriended and hosted Spencer W. Kimball in 1948 as the apostle recovered from medical issues with his heart.[48] They believed and wholeheartedly supported Kimball, Church leaders, and missionaries.[49] The beginnings of the Southwest Indian Mission stemmed from such relationships between Euro-American and Indigenous Latter-day Saints. During the early years of the mission, most of the missionaries were white married couples. These companionships included the Bloomfields and Albert R. and Gladys Perkins Lyman of Blanding, Utah.[50] Church leaders then developed new boundaries in Diné Bikéyah of a mission and "Lamanites"—First Peoples that embraced the gospel and helped spread it.

Latter-day Saints struggled to forge such borders, as other churches opposed their presence and the Navajo Tribal Council withheld permission for a Latter-day Saint mission on the reservation. James M. Stewart, the federal general superintendent of the Navajo reservation, invited Evans to represent the Church at a gathering of religious leaders in 1946. Evans attended but remained silent, and he later left the meeting because of the negativity toward Latter-day Saints. A reverend, for example, advocated the ban of Latter-day Saints from evangelizing. A preacher in Toadlena, Navajo Nation, New Mexico, also persuaded Stewart that year to warn LDS missionaries not to proselytize since the Church had not received permission from the tribal council.[51] Over the years, different denominational leaders continued to block Latter-day Saint presence in Diné Bikéyah.

After discussions regarding Latter-day Saint requests for a mission, in 1946 the tribal council denied permission because of a split vote. Evans strongly believed that the Navajo Tribal Council chair, Chee Dodge, would have broken the tie in favor of the Church if he had attended the meeting. Evans continued to beseech the tribal council, but he failed to receive a response. When traders cautioned him that the council was planning to vote to remove Latter-day Saints from the reservation, he invited Church General Authorities to frequent the meetings in Window Rock, the Navajo Nation headquarters. Yet the Navajo Tribal Council either tabled or ignored the issue. The council canceled one such meeting, scheduled in January 1947, after Dodge died.[52]

Evans blamed other religious leaders who opposed Latter-day Saints for his issues with the Navajo Tribal Council. He also recognized how the council, as a new entity, was beginning to determine its land and education policies and its relations to the federal government. Other religious sects started to reconcile with the Church. In October 1946 George Albert Smith spoke at an interdenominational meeting, and Evans recalled that the animosity he had felt at the previous meeting disappeared. After the religious meeting, Smith met with Sam Akheah, vice chair of the Navajo Tribal Council.[53]

Evans acknowledged that the Church needed to support Navajo tribal goals to gain the approval of the council. In the late 1940s education featured as a significant issue and priority to the tribal council. Many council members believed that the federal government had failed to fulfill its promises to provide education for all Diné. Twenty-three Diné representatives went to Washington, DC, in 1946, when Chee Dodge specified education as "the gravest concern" to the government officials.[54] Before this meeting, Evans met with various Diné officials and religious leaders to discuss education issues. George Albert Smith presented a resolution to the tribal council in 1947, offering to establish schools and chapels in exchange for a mission on the reservation. The resolution did not reach a vote, and there is no known evidence that anything happened regarding it. Church leaders noted that Sam Ahkeah, then the chair of the Navajo Tribal Council, favored the idea but would not endorse it without the support of his newly appointed tribal attorney, Norman M. Littell.[55]

By April 1947 Evans had served as president of the Navajo-Zuni Mission for four years. Church General Authorities decided to release him and designate S. Eugene Flake as his replacement. Evans asked to stay until the tribal council met in August, but nothing happened at that meeting. Flake then became the next mission president. The mission's name was changed by 1949 to the Southwest Indian Mission with the assignment to proselytize among all Native Americans in Arizona, New Mexico, southern Colorado, and southeastern Utah. The Diné represented the largest Indigenous nation within the mission. Flake requested permission from the tribal council for the mission, but even without it, missionaries continued to work on the reservation. Flake's nephew, David K. Flake, admits that all these missionary efforts were "actually illegal from a technical standpoint."[56] In the early phase of SWIM between the 1940s and 1950s, many Diné did not approve of the Latter-day Saint presence and proselytization on the reservation.

S. Eugene Flake served as mission president until 1951, when Golden R. Buchanan succeeded him. Buchanan had worked with Native Americans in Richfield, Utah, where he represented the General Church Lamanite Committee as the secretary. As other churches continued to condemn Latter-day Saint missionary activities, Diné officials responded by denying opportunities for Latter-day Saints to preach on the reservation under the mission leaderships of Flake and Buchanan. In November 1953 the tribal council prepared to order the missionaries to leave the reservation. Diné leaders then invited Buchanan to a meeting to discuss the matter in Tuba City. The meeting focused on two major complaints against Latter-day Saints: (1) Latter-day Saints baptized children and women without the consent of their husbands and parents, and (2) they imitated and stole Diné stories.

Although some Diné openly contested the mission of the Church on the reservation, several Diné, especially converts, acted as advocates of SWIM in these proceedings. After the public meeting a few tribal council members, including those identified as Maloney, Mr. Goldtooth, and Amos Singer, debated with the Latter-day Saint representatives. According to Spencer W. Kimball, who was present, Goldtooth argued against the mission because "the missionaries had been baptizing people against their will, had been entering their homes without their permission, and had been taking children from the school to proselyte them." In response to Goldtooth's accusations, other Diné at the meeting defended SWIM and the Church. Some Diné school officials denied that missionaries abducted schoolchildren to teach them. A Diné Latter-day Saint with the surname Brody also stood up for the Church by speaking on religious freedom and the number of converts on the reservation.

Kee Kaibetony, another Diné Latter-day Saint who had served with the missionaries, bore witness to the council members against Goldtooth's charges. Kaibetony praised and expressed his pride in the missionaries, since "they made [him] think of Nephi and Lehi, their ancestors." With this support, the Latter-day Saint representatives satisfied most of the council's concerns.[57] Diné Latter-day Saints such as Brody and Kaibetony claimed how SWIM and the church teachings connected them to their Indigenous ancestry. In some cases, individual Latter-day Saints tainted the reputation of the Church, which escalated such debates about the presence of Latter-day Saints in Diné Bikéyah. In another series of tribal council meetings, earlier in the same year of 1953, Diné councilman Sam Gorman referred to "the worst of all" traders whom he identified as "a Mormon at the Salina trading post [who] does everything [Diné community] complain about and over and above, other things."[58] Gorman and other Diné began to associate the negative dealings of this Mormon trader with the Church and Latter-day Saints in general.

Since Buchanan associated the mission challenges with tribal leadership, he encouraged Diné converts to participate in Navajo tribal government and politics. In the March 1955 election, Paul Jones defeated Sam Akheah by three thousand votes. According to mission records, Latter-day Saint voters made the difference. After the election, Diné Latter-day Saints approached Paul Jones and Scott Preston, the vice chair, and the new tribal leaders committed to work with Latter-day Saints. In addition, three to four Diné Latter-day Saints served on the new council, and Buchanan identified twenty-four to twenty-five members of the council who sympathized with the Church.[59]

Relations between Diné, including tribal leaders and community members, and the Church gradually expanded during the late twentieth century. In 1960 the Church produced a public relations movie, *Upon Their Shoulders*, to demonstrate to the Navajo Tribal Council how the Church was serving Diné. Sam Billison, who worked on the council, came to Salt Lake City to view the film in 1960. Spencer W. Kimball showcased the movie to the Navajo Tribal Council in Window Rock that same year. He arrived at the Diné capital "in wonder and with some misgivings and very sober realizing how much was at stake." He lamented: "For fifteen years or more we have been asking for recognition of the Church and its program of proselyting and organizing but to date had been frowned upon and discouraged and efforts have been made many times to get us off the reservation." Kimball and other Church officials hoped that the film would ameliorate the tense relations between the Navajo Nation and SWIM. When Church leaders showed the movie to the council, they received full attention and a positive reception. Kimball considered the opportunity as a blessing and advancement for the mission among Diné.[60] The Church endorsed other multimedia projects, involving Diné Latter-day Saints as the actors and interpreters, to persuade Diné representatives and community members to accept them. Buchanan spearheaded the developments of SWIM under such church public relations and political campaigns.

Some Diné communities continued to distrust Latter-day Saints, demanding the bans on missionaries and traders. For example, during the same year of the 1960 film *Upon Their Shoulders*, Diné communities in the western region of Diné Bikéyah started "to blame the Mormon group, the influx of Mormon missionaries and traders and others whom they think are responsible for this uprising or this program."[61] The "uprising" represented struggles between Diné and Hopi people over jointly occupied reservation lands in northeastern Arizona, known as the Navajo-Hopi Land Dispute.[62] Since many Diné of the area believed "that the Mormon people are the ones who are actually trying to take lands away from the Navajo people," they petitioned for the "removal of these Mormon missionaries and traders."[63] The tribal attorney, Norman M. Littell, traced the origins of these accusations to "three Mormon attorneys [who] are trying to take [lands] away from the Navajo people," and he encouraged Diné to not condemn "the whole Mormon people."[64] Littell named one of the Mormon attorneys, John Sterling Boyden, who told a judge to "send them down the Colorado River to Parker," referring to "all the Navajos who are living on this Executive Order Area" in the disputes.[65] Individual Latter-day Saints, such as Boyden, soured Diné perceptions of the Church, while church leaders sought to salvage and improve relations with Diné and the tribal government.

SWIM LEADERSHIP

After Buchanan, all of the following SWIM presidents had connections to Arizona or had worked with the Church education programs for Native Americans: Alfred Eugene Rohner (1955–1958), Fred A. Turley (1958–1961), John E. Baird (1961–1965), Hal Taylor (1965–1968), and Dale Tingey (1968–1971). SWIM concentrated on Diné along with other southwestern tribal nations. Paul E. Felt left his position as the director of the American Indian Institute and Studies at BYU to become the last SWIM president (1971–1973). Felt proposed to expand the mission to all communities, Native and non-Native American, in the area. He drafted a couple proposals that eliminated SWIM.[66] In 1973 the First Presidency approved his plan to proselytize among all peoples within the mission boundaries.

The Church delegated Felt as the first president of the New Mexico–Arizona Mission, which included those two states and El Paso, Texas. At that time, the Church First Presidency directed that "proselyting languages other than English are not to be neglected."[67] Yet missionaries increasingly used English until they no longer studied Indigenous languages such as Diné bizaad by the twenty-first century. In the summer of 1973, mission leaders stressed their challenges to focus on the "Lamanites" and provide basic church meetings and programs for the American Indian districts.[68] Ken Sekaquaptewa of Hopi and Chinese descent served as a missionary amid these changes from 1974 to 1976. He explained in an interview from 1990: "Basically, it was an Indian mission, and we were only supposed to work with the Indians. Now the mission has changed, and it is all mixed."[69]

The mission later changed to the Arizona Holbrook Mission. In 1978 the Church assigned George P. Lee, a Diné educator, as president of the Arizona Holbrook Mission. During the short interim of his presidency, the mission sponsored "Lamanite" leadership conferences in January and May and a Relief Society conference in June. On June 30, 1978, Lee moved to Salt Lake City and Don C. Hunsaker became the new mission president. That July, the Church reorganized the mission to transfer its branches and districts to the geographical stakes. When Church officials announced that decision in November 1978, the manuscript history recorded that "there was a great spirit of unity and sustaining of mission leaders expressed." The three districts and fourteen of the sixteen branches agreed to the change. The Church postponed the actual transfer to March 1979 to obtain more information about the membership activity in the branches and districts.[70] The mission continued proselytization among Diné, but without the same intensity. Church officials designated Phoenix as the mission headquarters, establishing the Arizona Phoenix Mission in 1984. Ronald L. Singer, a former Diné missionary, believed that the mission lost contact with Diné then.[71]

SWIM MISSIONARY PRACTICES AND CONTACTS

Church leaders on the general and mission levels struggled with ways to introduce the gospel message and teachings of the Church to Diné over the years. As predominantly Euro-Americans, they often used the same strategies of assimilation and colonialism that white Americans in general had adopted during the twentieth century. In their underlying message, they professed to share with Diné the teachings of Jesus Christ and the restoration of the true gospel. They believed their message revealed ancient stories that Diné had heard before, since they considered Diné as descendants of Book of Mormon peoples. The missionaries hoped that these scriptures would resonate with them. Yet they couched their teachings mostly in Euro-American terms, and the missionaries adopted salesmen-like techniques. SWIM usually endorsed the same basic approaches of Latter-day Saint missions in any other part of the world.[72] SWIM leaders and missionaries adapted some aspects to recruit and teach Diné converts specifically. Their efforts to learn the Diné language strengthened their outreach to Diné communities.

SWIM missionaries first needed to find people who would listen to their message. The married missionary couples of the mid-twentieth century met Diné through their trading post business and connections. They also visited people in their homes, and youth in schools when invited. In the 1940s some Diné students asked Latter-day Saint missionaries to teach required religious classes at the Shiprock Indian School. The school officials, however, insisted that the parents must submit such a request rather than the students. Diné Latter-day Saints Mary Jumbo (a former cook at a day school) and Clyde Beyal worked with sixty-five children in Toadlena whose parents permitted them to participate in the Church. All students received some type of mandatory religious instructions then in 1944, and the Latter-day Saint meetings fulfilled that requirement.[73]

Latter-day Saint missionaries introduced official church auxiliary programs in schools, not only to members of the Church but also to nonmember

Diné children. They held Primary weekday classes specifically for children, as well as Sunday schools. The other programs included Cub Scouts and Boy Scouts. In 1947, for example, mission leaders invited Boy Scouts from the Navajo reservation to come to Salt Lake City during the Church's centennial celebration of the Latter-day Saint settlers' arrival in the Salt Lake Valley.[74]

Although the Church found some supporters of its mission in Diné Bikéyah, tensions continued between missionaries and Indigenous communities into the twenty-first century. Some Euro-American missionaries did not show respect to Native Americans and their cultures. Julia Benally, a Diné and White Mountain Apache Latter-day Saint, for example, criticized missionaries in her Indigenous community: "In Whiteriver, [Arizona,] when missionaries come, they treat all the Indians like dirt. They don't like them. They treat them like little kids. Almost every couple missionary that comes to the Rez act like they know it all and they're so holy and pure. Everybody knows all the dirt about them for some reason."[75] I talked to Benally in 2007, while we were attending BYU.

Benally noticed how the missionaries often "went to the store" and "acted like they were on vacation," instead of serving the people. One missionary "treated [her] like dirt," asking her basic-level questions about the Book of Mormon. She added: "It doesn't help either that most of the Mormons in Whiteriver are wild. They have a bad reputation for themselves. That stops missionary work too." She perceived such tensions in terms of race: "The white people didn't want anything to do with us [Indians]." Some white Latter-day Saints refused to visit the nearby reservation.[76] Milli Cody Garrett, a Diné Latter-day Saint, echoed Benally's concerns when she stated: "I think when missionaries go to the reservation that they should be screened."[77] Garrett hoped that Church officials evaluated missionaries for cultural sensitivity and awareness to make sure that missionaries did not hold prejudice against those to whom they would proselytize. SWIM brought diverse peoples together, but the mission also intensified some divisions.[78]

The Church addressed challenges concerning cultural and racial differences between the missionaries and Diné by calling other peoples affiliated with "Lamanites" to serve in SWIM, especially between the 1960s and 1970s. In the mission they identified diverse Native Americans, Polynesians, and Latin Americans as "Lamanite missionaries."[79] According to common Latter-day Saint beliefs, they shared an ancestral history with Diné in the Book of Mormon. Many Latter-day Saints considered Kānaka Maoli

Elder Kimo Hanamaikai, a Kanaka ʻŌiwi missionary for the Southwest Indian Mission, in the Navajo Nation, c. 1972–1974. Courtesy of author.

and Māori, for examples, "Lamanites" by the late nineteenth century.[80] The Church had established missions in both Hawaii and New Zealand among their respective Indigenous communities before SWIM, which prepared the Kānaka Maoli and Maori missionaries who would later serve in Diné Bikéyah.[81] Such diverse Latter-day Saint backgrounds and efforts to relate fellow "Lamanite" missionaries to Diné communities altered methods of proselytization, building an exchange and confluence of Indigenous Latter-day Saints in Diné Bikéyah.

It is possible that General Authorities of the Church believed Lamanites could best convert each other because of this shared sense of heritage and ties to the Book of Mormon. While this assumption could represent the imposition of one group's cultural values and categorizations on other groups, some people imbibed the Lamanite identity and perceived new relations to different ethnicities. Some Latter-day Saint Indigenous Pacific Islanders and Native Americans mirrored this Lamanite identity as a form of Indigenous pride and unity.[82]

The Church does not provide detailed information about how it calls and assigns missionaries to areas, which obscures revelation of its intent to send Indigenous missionaries to Native American–populated regions. Scholars have not determined the exact statistics of the ethnicities of missionaries who proselytized on Native American reservations in missions such as the Northern Indian Mission and SWIM. The SWIM manuscript history, other church documents, newspapers, and interviews, however, present several indicators of the Latter-day Saint Indigenous presence in Diné Bikéyah. In February 1966, for example, a SWIM newsletter reported a count of thirty-eight missionaries of "True Israel" or "Lamanites." These "Lamanite" missionaries included eighteen from Hawaii, five from Samoa, two from New Zealand, one from Alaska, one from Tonga, and four non-Navajo Native Americans.[83]

To some degree, these "Lamanite" missionaries gained Diné trust of Latter-day Saint missions. Many Diné often related better to individuals with "brown skin" than to the white missionaries. They also listened to Diné missionaries who shared their heritage and oftentimes understood their language and culture. Gabriel Cinniginnie, a Diné convert, allowed two missionaries to teach him the gospel of the Church because they were Maori instead of white Americans. He had rejected white missionaries who had tried to visit him before. Cinniginnie explained: "Since these two were Maoris, brown-colored, I decided I'd listen to them. If they had been Anglos, maybe it'd be a different story. Since they were Maoris, I decided I'd go ahead and trust them because they were the same color as my skin."[84] Cinniginnie not only preferred learning about the Latter-day Saint faith from people that he resembled; he also reflected an awareness of white and "brown-colored" racial tensions in the borderlands of Diné Bikéyah.

Zenobia Kapahulehua Iese, a Kanaka ʻŌiwi woman, believed that Diné were receptive to her and other Polynesian missionaries because "we looked like each other. . . . It was easier for us than Anglo missionaries. . . . We related . . . we shared the same history." She was referring to a shared history of colonization, as both Native Americans and Kānaka Maoli have experienced American colonialism. Iese came from Kauai to serve in SWIM between April 1971 and October 1972. The Church assigned both her sisters, Cynthia Kapahulehua and Charlyne Kaulukukui, to missions in Diné Bikéyah, as well as her future husband from Samoa, Tavita Iese. On her mission, Iese recognized similarities in terms of race and Indigenous historical experiences of dispossession, displacement, and assimilationist policies. Diné communities seemed more open to other Diné or brown-colored missionaries such as Polynesians because of these connections.[85]

As young Diné learned and followed Latter-day Saint life pathways,

Charlyne (Kaulukukui) McNeely and fellow sister missionaries in the Southwest Indian Mission, c. 1971–1972. Courtesy of author. A gift from the Charlyne (Kaulukukui) McNeely Southwest Indian Mission photo collection.

Church leaders assumed that sending youth to their own people would improve teaching and converting both the missionaries and their Diné communities. In 1962, for example, the tribal newspaper *Navajo Times* included the story of three young Diné women, Loretta Secody, Susie Little, and Hazel Lewis, who were serving as missionaries.[86] If Diné Latter-day Saints applied for missions between 1950 and 1972, they most likely went to SWIM. Although Ronald L. Singer, a Diné Latter-day Saint, had hoped to go on a Spanish-speaking mission, for example, he expected his mission call to Diné Bikéyah.[87] President Kimball called Rex Lane a "pioneer" because he was "the first full-time Navajo missionary" in the 1950s.[88] Kimball invested a special interest in Lane's mission and corresponded occasionally with him. In one letter, Lane addressed Kimball: "I really enjoy my mission. I am working with the traditional people that don't speak English and use the medicine man."[89] With their understandings of Diné culture and connections to the communities, Diné missionaries such as Lane could facilitate relations between the Church and Diné. Other Diné received assignments as youth missionaries for the summer, or they applied to become full-time missionaries for about two years.

SWIM prerogatives rested on dialogue and engagement between missionaries, including both Diné and non-Diné, and the people. Most missionaries followed directives to teach rather than preach, serving and interacting daily with Diné communities. The missionaries provided direct services to Diné families such as gathering wood and herding sheep, learning Diné ways of life. They often dressed in khaki shirts, tan pants, and ties rather than professional suits as they did in other missions. As a missionary in 1950, Robert Lowell Brown brought a suit for Sundays and tan-colored pants, white shirts, and ties for everyday use.[90] They dressed in less formal attire to appear approachable to the people and to participate in more activities conducive to living on the reservation such as tending to livestock, chopping firewood, hauling water, and traveling on dirt roads.

Many missionaries stayed in hogans without running water and electricity like some of their Diné neighbors. Some Diné, such as Victor Mannie Sr., started to relate to the missionaries after noticing how they "would just get down and dirty with the rest of us." Mannie converted to the Latter-day Saint faith because of missionaries who supported and became a part of the communities in Diné Bikéyah. He remembers: "It didn't matter if we were out herding sheep or we were out there sleeping in sheep skins, they were right there beside us."[91] In addition, missionaries developed welfare services such as quilting, soapmaking, and financial planning in the 1950s.[92] During the 1960s, missionaries used all types of activity-focused proselyting such as Boy Scouts, teen clubs, athletics, and seminary. They sought to teach Native Americans everywhere, as urged by SWIM president John E. Baird, who told them to meet Natives "in jails, on the street, and at campfires."[93] Although the order reflects some derogatory perceptions of Native Americans in lowly contexts, many missionaries followed the directive. In 1949 one of the missionaries emphasized: "Being a missionary can and often does put us into places and doing jobs that we never would have dreamed of in most positions in life. We have all had instances to bear this out. Some of us have been sexton morticians, doctors, veterinarians, nurses, and no one knows what a host of other things."[94]

For the Diné missionaries, some cultural taboos caused difficulties and frustrations. Diné missionaries often served as intermediaries in SWIM because of their knowledge of the language and culture and ties to the community. They could also find themselves caught in the middle of conflicting expectations and roles of Latter-day Saints and Diné kin. For example, some people started to expect Jimmy Benally as a missionary to prepare their dead for funerals and burials. Diné traditionally did not bury their dead and would leave the expired bodies in trees, canyon crevices, or abandoned hogans. When some Diné preferred a funeral and burial for their loved ones, they still adhered to parts of the cultural taboos regarding the dead.[95]

Benally recalled how assisting with these solemnities "really bothered" him, because he had only joined the Church a year before his mission and "still had all these teachings" from his parents and grandparents about avoiding the dead. In 1970 he dug graves and provided funeral services every day for one week in the Tuba City area where a mortuary did not yet exist. Benally chose not to follow the ancestral taboo to serve his people. During his missionary service in that region, he participated in at least sixty-four funerals.[96]

While they prepared funerals and comforted the mourners, missionaries found some opportunities to share their message with more people on the Navajo reservation. When a female pastor died in a fire in Whitehorse, my father and his missionary companion cared for her dead body and conducted the funeral. The pastor's followers then started to attend the Latter-day Saint Whitehorse Branch because of their appreciation and the conversations the funeral generated.[97] My father reconciled his role in burials and funerals, as a missionary, by identifying with Diné who possessed the proper authority to provide necessary community services.[98] SWIM missionaries enabled more exchange and outreach through funeral services, but missionaries had to navigate differences between their faith and cultural backgrounds in such cases.

Once Latter-day Saint missionaries met willing listeners on the reservation, they sought to convey their messages in ways that resonated with Diné. SWIM missionaries featured visual and audio aids to pique people's curiosity, entertain them, and promote their learning. To help with translations, some Diné interpreters tape-recorded missionary messages in Diné bizaad to share with groups at "cottage meetings," a gathering of people in a home to hear a gospel discussion. In one instance, two missionaries held three cottage meetings with groups of about twenty Diné. Although these Diné families had gathered for a "sing" of ancestral Diné ceremonies, they listened to the missionaries and their recordings in Diné bizaad. The missionaries played tapes that a Diné interpreter and Latter-day Saint convert, Clyde Beyal, had recorded. During one of the meetings, an elderly Diné man asked them "whether [they] had as strong 'medicine' (as potent and spiritual speeches) [themselves] as the talk of the recorder had. The story was true as far as he was concerned."[99] This Diné man directly related the translated Latter-day Saint teachings to a Diné sense of spirituality, often translated as "medicine," which represented truth to him.

Missionaries continued to refine their proselytization strategies and prepared more for cultural exchange. In the 1970s, for example, some missionaries used large white sheets as screens on which they projected films or slideshows about topics such as baptism and the "Plan of Salvation," a central Latter-day Saint teaching about the purpose of life. The film slides included captions in Diné bizaad, which the missionaries often read aloud. In such cases, the missionaries did not have to memorize or prepare as much, while also using the language to communicate better with Diné audiences.[100] In addition, the Church published various Diné language learning materials such as *Diné Bizaad Na'nitiníbá*, which served as the SWIM textbook series. Missionaries started with the first levels of the text in the Language Training Center of the Church. In the Level III version of the text, missionaries studied dialogues, vocabulary, grammar, and cultural situations they could expect to encounter among the Diné community.[101]

Diné bizaad, the Navajo language, became a key conduit of exchange in these borderlands. Since many Diné did not speak English fluently during the 1950s, the missionaries started to receive Diné bizaad classes. Unlike other missionaries who typically served for twenty-four months in the United States, SWIM missionaries accepted assignments for thirty months so that they could learn the language. By 1967 they had to pass a formalized language-training program in Diné bizaad before entering their area of service.[102]

The Church experimented with several proselyting methods over the years, creating various formats of lessons for missionaries throughout the world to memorize in 1952 and 1961.[103] The Indian Relations Committee followed church-wide patterns when it issued "Teaching Aids for Lamanite Missionaries" in 1950. According to typical Latter-day Saint mission protocols, the guide instructed the missionaries to focus foremost on "inspiration" and the Spirit instead of strictly the written instructions. These "Lamanite" lessons included several generalizations about Native Americans to develop a few methods to address Native American populations. A passage from one lesson guideline stated: "The best procedure is to take up one subject at a time and gain agreement in concrete terms. This is sometimes hard to do with Indian people but use questions carefully and get them to gain agreement in concrete terms." To demonstrate teaching "in concrete terms," the manual consisted of nineteen lessons rather than the eight lessons in other plans. Golden Buchanan, the secretary of the Indian Relations Committee before he was mission president, encouraged SWIM missionaries to use one-thought sentences when teaching, such as "Joseph Smith was a prophet of God. He was born in New York." The "Lamanite" missionary lessons also emphasized conceptual points more than direct scripture references.[104]

The seventeenth lesson on the Holy Ghost, a member of the Godhead who Latter-day Saints believe gives personal revelation to people, reflected some Native American generalizations of the SWIM manuals. In this part, the guide differentiated between Latter-day Saint views of spiritual divinations and those of Native Americans. The mission manual advised missionaries to proceed with care when teaching about the Holy Ghost, revealing how the LDS authors stereotyped Native Americans as superstitious peoples. The manual authors instructed missionaries to not add to "the many ghosts, superstitions, dreams and hallucinations" they claimed Native Americans believe in, distinguishing the Holy Ghost from evil spirits. The manual includes the following directions, underlining these points of difference in the spirits: "Point out to them that Satan uses all of these things and many others to mislead. You may tell them that they will never see the Holy Ghost but that He will manifest himself to the honest in heart if they will obey the commandments of God." The lesson then directs missionaries to "clinch this lesson," stressing that testimony comes through the Holy Ghost.[105] Since time immemorial, Diné have believed in spirits, who maintain relations with the living. Latter-day Saint teachings, however, emphasized one personal spirit, the Holy Ghost, as a companion and "gift" to believers. Diné traditionally recognized only select individuals in their society with the abilities to communicate and listen to spirits, whom they identified as, among other things, diviners, healers, crystal and star gazers, and hand tremblers.[106]

In 1966 Latter-day Saint apostle Delbert L. Stapley claimed that twenty-six Polynesian missionaries excelled at learning Diné bizaad.[107] The mission encouraged such bilingualism and cultural exchange between Indigenous Pacific Islanders and Diné, which Diné communities acknowledged and commended. The *Navajo Times* featured the story of a Maori missionary in 1964: "Maori Indian Travels 9,000 Miles to Attend Navajo Language

School." Hector Tahu, a fluent Maori speaker and SWIM missionary, drew similarities between the Diné and Maori languages.[108] The article also provided information about SWIM while spotlighting its diverse Indigenous missionaries.

As Indigenous missionaries related more to the people, some of them could also interpret Latter-day Saint concepts better than their non-Diné partners. My father recalls explaining the Plan of Salvation in descriptive Diné terms, because Diné did not share an articulation of the plan in Diné bizaad. He used intricate details such as the "plan" that depicts life before mortality, the period of mortality, and life after death. Most non-Diné missionaries learned and memorized certain key dialogues in Diné bizaad that the Church prepared for them. Several fluent Diné speakers would allow their non-Diné companions to introduce the lesson and present the rehearsed discussion, and then the fluent Diné language–speaking missionaries would address any questions and possibly elaborate on their partners' message.[109]

Besides asking missionaries to study Diné bizaad, Buchanan introduced some new missionary techniques. Some church concepts did not have equivalent terms in Diné, but Buchanan believed that language was adaptable: "If one has a complete command of the language almost any thought can be explained in that language and can be understood by the people. It is a language in which thoughts can be made complete and full by the use of their words and their way of speaking."[110] Christian missionaries among the Diné translated baptism as "water on the head" in Diné bizaad. Latter-day Saints baptize by complete bodily immersion in water, but Latter-day Saint missionaries continued to use the previous Christian translation of baptism. The idea and personage of "God" was also new to Diné, who did not believe in one God but in many deities who represented parts of their origins and daily lives. *Diyin* became the common Diné term for "God," which means "that which is sacred."[111]

In 1958 church leaders prepared another adaption of the regular missionary discussions titled "A Systematic Program for Teaching the Gospel to the Navajo People," which introduced questions and discussions in English and Diné bizaad.[112] Some non-Diné missionaries learned to communicate well in Diné bizaad, which enabled them to connect with more people in Diné Bikéyah. The Latter-day Saint missionary department adopted new discussions again in 1966, which SWIM president Hal Taylor encouraged missionaries to use even in their experimental stage. Many non-Diné missionaries, however, were still hesitant to speak Diné bizaad. John G. Linton, an assistant to Taylor, noted that some missionaries taught at an extremely slow pace, because they wanted to present the Diné discussions carefully.[113]

Non-Diné and Diné missionaries supported one another in these lingual and cultural translation processes. Ronald Singer, a Diné missionary, believed that Diné missionaries contributed to SWIM through their understandings of Diné ways of life, but he only had one fellow Diné companion when he was in the Language Training Mission. Although Singer fluently knew Diné bizaad, he struggled with some Latter-day Saint concepts and terminology. Another missionary in the language training program taught him how to express some of them.[114] Singer assisted his non-Diné companions with comprehending and learning Diné epistemologies and mores. For example, Singer would teach other missionaries how to recognize when someone was not home in the hogan, the traditional Diné dwelling. When he was interacting with other Diné, Singer understood why they avoided certain facial expressions or body language to communicate. He shared his native language and ancestral teachings with his companions.[115]

Lay member Diné Latter-day Saints played a major role in shaping these cultural and conceptual interchanges as intermediaries of languages. Marie Little, a Diné convert, described how missionaries switched between English and Diné bizaad in their lessons to her family during the 1960s. The missionaries knew a little of the Diné language, and her mother could understand some English. Little remembered: "We all helped each other . . . [by] trying to help the missionaries with our language and telling them to say the right words."[116] Little's family were not necessarily official interpreters for the Church, but their everyday engagement and code switching with the missionaries formed a part of the Diné Latter-day Saint discourse in Diné Bikéyah.

Not all Diné missionaries knew their ancestral language fluently, and they learned Diné bizaad on their mission by reconnecting with their communities. Jimmy Benally, for example, struggled in the Language Training Mission Program. He originally hoped to avoid using Diné bizaad. Reflecting on his mission, he pinpointed "phases on [his] mission," including teaching in Diné bizaad, that fortified his faith. In an early phase, he told the First Vision story of Joseph Smith in Diné bizaad and then expressed his personal beliefs for the first time. Benally remembered: "I got through it without any problems in Navajo, and I bore my testimony to her [the person being taught]. I think that's when I was converted. I knew the Church was true with that first lesson." As they served as messengers and interpreters of the gospel, some Diné missionaries developed and embraced their own sense of being Diné dóó Gáamalii—no longer separate identities but a hybrid one.

SWIM returned some Diné young adults to Diné Bikéyah and their ancestral communities after they had migrated elsewhere. Dennis Little, another Diné missionary, also learned Diné bizaad for the first time in SWIM. His family left Diné Bikéyah for his father's military career, which sometimes led them overseas. Little did not live in Diné Bikéyah for an extended period until his mission.[117] For Benally and Little, their experiences as SWIM missionaries strengthened not only their testimony of the Church but also their knowledge of Diné culture and language.

Music and dance became other avenues of cultural exchange and proselytization in SWIM, by which different peoples came together and appreciated one another for their distinct backgrounds. In 1962, for example, diverse missionaries formed an "American Indian and Polynesian" performance show to diffuse local opposition to their work in Lukachukai, Navajo Nation.[118] The mission hosted "Lamanite conferences" to focus primarily on Native Americans and Latter-day Saint evangelization by and for Indigenous peoples. On February 4, 1965, a "Lamanite conference" assembled four hundred people and missionaries that included, among others, the following diverse Indigenous identities: Apache, Shoshone, Ute, Paiute, Alaskan, Hopi, Zuni, Hawaiian, Maori, Samoan, and Tongan. The conference featured songs and music from the various cultures that the missionaries represented. The missionaries prepared and held a "Lamanite talent show" throughout Diné Bikéyah, performing a variety of Indigenous music and dance and involving several languages.[119]

"Perhaps no other race of people loves to sing more than Indians," noted SWIM president Golden Buchanan.[120] His view posed a stereotype, but Buchanan recognized singing as a central expression of spirituality and life among Diné. According to ancestral teachings, Diné sang and chanted their prayers in sacred ceremonies. Many Native Americans shared at least a few cultural components such as the sacredness of singing. To overcome the language and cultural barriers that impeded Diné understanding of Latter-day Saint religious concepts, the missionaries communicated through Indigenous music and cultural performances, particularly those who came from Indigenous communities themselves.

Ernst Clifford Young, a missionary during that time, described how some Pacific Islander missionaries had been professional performers and attracted fans throughout the reservation. In Chinle, more than eight hundred people once attended their show in an old auto shop.[121] The performances "opened up so many doors," as William Keoniana Kelly, a Kanaka 'Ōiwi missionary, recalled. Pacific Islanders such as Kelly starred in the shows. Kelly explained how the missionary strategy worked: "During my mission we were able to do performances all over the mission field to help open up areas for missionaries. A group of us went in, put on a show, and fellowshipped the nonmembers and the members. We left to go to another area and left the missionaries there to work with the nonmembers."[122] The Indigenous dances and music from the Americas and the Pacific intrigued many Diné, and then the missionaries would use the gatherings as an occasion to solicit further discussions about the Latter-day Saint faith and teachings.

Such gatherings prompted missionary work and discussions between missionaries and Indigenous communities. In 1966 the missionaries received forty referrals from nine hundred people who attended their "Polynesian-Indian convention." Missionaries of diverse ethnicities supported this assembly, including three Japanese, one Korean, eleven Native Americans from tribal nations such as the Shoshone, and nine Diné. Some tribal leaders participated in these events, which indicated the ongoing ties between Latter-day Saint communities and Diné politics and leadership.[123] Pacific Islanders represented most nonwhite missionaries. In 1969 another mission "Lamanite" troupe called "Lamanite Singers" began to tour, showcasing Hawaiian, Maori, and Samoan dances such as the Samoan Fire Dance along with Native American parts.[124] The troupe was not affiliated with BYU's Lamanite Generation, which performs to this day under the name Living Legends. For almost two months, Jimmy Benally toured SWIM with a singing group during the early 1970s as a part of his mission service.[125] After Church officials moved the mission base to Holbrook, Arizona, in 1972, the Lamanite show tour continued as an integral part of the mission. SWIM missionaries of diverse backgrounds collaborated to spread LDS teachings and found "investigators" (those interested in learning about the Church) by performing their Indigenous cultures, music, and dances under the banner of "Lamanite" pride and identity.

Although not all Indigenous missionaries embraced a Lamanite identity, some of them understood their mission and related to Diné people through their own interpretations of the Book of Mormon. Iese, for example, did not

Lamanite Generation performance in the Southwest Indian Mission, c. 1971–1972. Courtesy of author. A gift from the Charlyne (Kaulukukui) McNeely Southwest Indian Mission photo collection.

want to label anyone as "Lamanite." While she did not interpret and apply "Lamanite" to Native Americans and Pacific Islanders as many Latter-day Saints did at the time of her mission, she described her mission as strengthening to her testimony of the Book of Mormon. She expressed how "serving among Navajos brought the Book of Mormon to life." Reflecting on when "Christ said, 'Other sheep have I,'" she viewed her missionary role as finding "the other sheep" and gathering disciples of Christ among Diné and Indigenous peoples. Iese would not classify herself or Diné as "Lamanites," but she sensed a kinship with them as a "covenant people" who have faced similar struggles with European-American colonialism as "Natives."[126] As an Indigenous convert, she used Latter-day Saint doctrine to reframe her identity beyond colonial terminology and its implications. She related to Diné and other Indigenous communities by resisting colonization and insisting on their status as First Peoples.

William Keoniana Kelly wanted to serve a mission among Diné after hearing a returned missionary in Hawai'i share his mission experiences. The former SWIM missionary highlighted what he learned while living in the Navajo Nation, including the similarities he noticed between Kānaka

Maoli and Diné. After Kelly received his assignment to SWIM in July 1967, he worked in the mission office for twenty-one months as a mission secretary and assistant to the president. In these official positions, Kelly directed most of his attention to Polynesian, Native American, and "other minority groups like the Hispanic missionaries," because he "felt a kinship" with these diverse missionaries.[127] Like Kelly, many Polynesian missionaries contributed to the proselytizing work through the ties they sensed with fellow Indigenous and historically minoritized peoples. SWIM added another layer to the borderlands of Diné Bikéyah by enabling Latter-day Saint Indigenous encounters and exchanges.[128]

SWIM elders and sisters of diverse backgrounds often initiated the first contact between Diné communities and the Church, building and facilitating Latter-day Saint Indigenous communities and common grounds in Diné Bikéyah. Because the Church made a concerted effort to reach Diné especially through missionary work, Diné developed a distinctive name, "Gáamalii," for Latter-day Saints.[129] They also created a term, *bilasáanaa diwozhí*, "thorny apple" or pineapple, to refer to the Kānaka Maoli missionaries because of their prevalence. Encounters and relationships with Latter-day Saints stimulated such conceptualizations of identities, as Diné and Indigenous cultures shaped articulations and lived experiences of Mormonism.

A SWIM missionary, Sherry Turnblom, recalled that in 1970 church leaders divided the mission into a Diné and an English-speaking area. The missionaries who proselytized among the Diné learned their language. Those working with other tribal nations spoke primarily English. While Turnblom did not learn Diné bizaad, she served in Diné Bikéyah. Diné youth missionaries who had participated in ISPP occasionally translated for her. She referred to a spiritual experience when she felt that the Holy Spirit interpreted for her. The youth missionaries were leading a discussion, and Turnblom would suggest certain topics to them such as the plan of salvation. The youth companions would tell her they had just discussed those subjects in the same order.[130]

The Language Training Center eventually discontinued Diné language lessons since teaching Native Americans became a part of the geographical organized mission. Some missionaries still studied Diné bizaad on their own time to relate to Diné communities. My Diné Latter-day Saint friend Loren Begay remembered a missionary in his hometown of Chinle, Navajo Nation, who exerted the extra effort to learn Diné bizaad. As a teenager, Begay esteemed this missionary and decided that he would like to serve a mission. He claimed: "With the relationship he built with the people, he was a good role model for me."[131]

BAPTISMS

For Latter-day Saints, baptism is a sacred ordinance that shows a person's commitment to become a member and live the teachings of the Church of Jesus Christ of Latter-day Saints. In LDS belief, John the Baptist, who baptized Jesus Christ, restored the authority to perform this ordinance to Joseph Smith and Oliver Cowdery. Latter-day Saint parents usually have their children baptized when they are eight years old. The Church requires someone with ordained authority to baptize people who join after that age, even if converts have been baptized into another church. Latter-day Saints see baptism as a symbol that a convert has symbolically entered a sacred pathway toward eternal life.

While Church leaders launched the new missionary discussions, they also encouraged members to ask their neighbors if they wanted to learn more about the Church and meet the missionaries. As missionaries actively looked for converts, their leaders instructed them to set goals and quotas and not to "waste time" talking to people who were not seriously interested in becoming members. Following this policy, some missionaries blundered under the intense pressure to baptize a certain quota monthly. From 1960 to 1963, for example, several "baseball baptisms" occurred in England. Missionaries invited teenage boys to play the popular American sport, but they could not join the Latter-day Saint baseball leagues unless they were baptized. Although rules prohibited baptizing children without their parents' permission, some young people agreed to baptism to join the Latter-day Saint leagues. Some parents apparently thought they were signing consent-to-participate forms when they were authorizing their children's baptisms.[132]

Similar faults took place in the Southwest Indian Mission. Mission president Baird started a newsletter *Lamanite Israel* that continued through the terms of four mission presidents until 1972. The publication initially explained activities, but later the report included a special category called "Fireball," which listed the hours each team of missionaries worked and the number of convert baptisms each achieved.[133] During the early 1970s my father remembered how the newsletter spotlighted him and his companion for several months in a row as baptism leaders. They even received medallions from their mission president for their achievements. That type of public pressure and recognition led to missionaries baptizing some people without confirming that the converts understood their commitments.[134]

After the Church disbanded SWIM, George P. Lee introduced another newsletter, *Servant Sword*, to increase missionary work on the Navajo reservation. It featured a general message from Lee and his wife, Katherine. In 1976 the newsletter included points for baptisms, teachings, missionary appointments to teach with Latter-day Saints from nearby congregations (known as "splits"), and personal study topics. This Arizona Holbrook Mission newsletter later became titled *Warriors Trump*. One issue, dated May 1977, reported the averages of missionary gospel study, teaching hours, and converts' baptisms.[135]

In one of Rex Lane's mission areas, the SWIM president told him: "You don't have to worry about baptizing the people over there. They have already been baptized." Lane learned that the previous elders offered many services to Diné communities if they allowed the missionaries to baptize them first. This aid included hauling wood and water for the people or transporting them to the trading post and the health clinic.[136] Some Diné Latter-day Saints have told stories of Diné children going to Gallup, New Mexico, for a hamburger and being baptized after receiving a treat. When my father learned about the Church as a young adult and decided to be baptized, he found that his name was already on the church records of baptized members because of such unethical missionary approaches of baptizing Diné children.[137] With these examples, it is no wonder that the Navajo Tribal Council accused Latter-day Saints of "stealing" their children.

Latter-day Saint missionaries expressed the same concerns about these malpractices. A Diné missionary, Lewis Singer, enjoyed the opportunity to "tell people about the Church" in his homelands of Diné Bikéyah. He valued his powerful spiritual experiences during his mission, but he did not baptize many people and explained: "My belief was that if people weren't really converted to the Church, why baptize them?" He added that "when [he] felt like they were really serious and converted, then we baptized the families."[138] Jimmy Benally reflected on the baptisms of his mission: "I would say ninety percent of the kids were baptized to go on Placement rather than baptized into the Church. I learned that on my mission. We always had a quota we had to meet of how many kids we had to go on Placement. As a result, we just went out to fill our quota. We just signed up kids and baptized them to go on Placement."[139]

SWIM also faced challenges because Diné converts tended to view the Church differently than many white American Latter-day Saints who considered the Church as the one and only true church. For many Diné who did not share that sense of institutionalized religion, they would look for positive influences in all places and all faiths. A Diné convert, Eva Price, for example, accredits her sobriety to her contact with Latter-day Saints. She also thanks her experiences in the Native American Church, a hybrid pan-Indigenous Christian religion based on peyote as a vessel of spirituality, which spread among Diné around the same time that LDS presence grew in Diné Bikéyah after World War II.[140]

IMPACTS OF THE SOUTHWEST INDIAN MISSION

Missionaries' memories and perspectives reveal some disconnect and ongoing misunderstandings between Latter-day Saints and Diné. Sherry L. Turnblom, for example, assumed that some of the young Diné teenagers who were serving short-term missions did not understand Latter-day Saint teachings, and she needed to help them. She struggled to find people to teach in Chinle, since she did not speak Diné bizaad. Many people also did not want to let her know that they spoke English. The most common form of proselyting—going door to door—did not lead to much interest in the Church and baptism. Turnblom also remembers that she and her fellow missionaries were evicted from their housing because they were nonrelated people living together. Turnblom was convinced, however, that they were asked to leave because they were not Diné.[141]

Despite the challenges of SWIM, some Diné converts who later became missionaries recognized how the gospel of the Church of Jesus Christ of Latter-day Saints has made a difference in their lives. After serving a mission in Arizona between 1976 and 1978, Ollie Whaley, a white American Latter-day Saint, revisited areas of Diné Bikéyah where he had spent time as a missionary. He met and married Aneta, a Diné Latter-day Saint. The two raised their family in the Latter-day Saint faith in the Navajo Nation, serving and contributing to the growing church congregations there.[142] Some of my family's close friends, including the Whaleys and other Diné who served in SWIM, such as Jimmy and Anna Benally and Marie and Dennis Little, continue their involvement in the Church. The growth of a Latter-day Saint heritage among Diné represents both the roots and the branches of the Church in Diné Bikéyah. Rex Lane's father was a hataałii, known as a "medicine man," but he and Lane's mother joined the Church after Lane became a member. His mother celebrated her one-hundredth birthday in November 2007 when I met and talked with Lane. She had then witnessed at least twenty-six children and grandchildren serve missions for the Church. Matt Begay, one of her missionary grandchildren, credits his grandparents for teaching him the Latter-day Saint faith and his uncle Rex Lane for setting an example by serving a mission. Begay was a missionary in Guam and points to ways in which his mission strengthened his testimony in the Church.[143] The Southwest Indian Mission planted roots among Diné families like the Lanes that fostered the growth of the Church in Diné Bikéyah.

FROM BAPTISM TO MISSION

Although Latter-day Saint representatives stood against the accusations of Goldtooth in 1953 that missionaries baptized Diné children without the consent of their families, such cases occurred into the 1960s. As I mentioned previously, when my father was twelve years old, SWIM missionaries baptized him and at least two other Native American students "without having any lessons or even going to church." The missionaries took the children to a movie in Gallup, "and on the way back to Ramah, [they] stopped at the chapel and were baptized." My father explained that "baptism did not mean anything to us, since we did not know of its significance. And we were not taught anything. After the baptism, we went back to doing nothing except playing around on Sunday or going to the Nazarene church to get candy."[144] He was attending a public school and living in an American Indian dormitory in Ramah, New Mexico, a "border town" that epitomized borderland tensions. Anglo-American Latter-day Saints, Zunis, and Diné have claimed and contested with each other over that space for generations.[145]

My father and other Diné and Indigenous peoples cannot escape the context of borderlands, but some of them have joined the Church and negotiated their own identities in the process. Some of them, such as my father, later developed their Diné Latter-day Saint identity as Gáamalii Bina'nitiní, or missionaries, in the Southwest Indian Mission. He often tells me and our

Southwest Indian Mission sign-in at the mission reunion, April 5, 2019, Orem, Utah. Courtesy of author.

family about life-changing experiences and what he calls "miracles" of his mission, including how he helped deliver a Diné woman's baby in the back of a pickup truck, which inspired him to become a physician.[146] Indigenous Latter-day Saint missionaries both modeled and encouraged development of identities and practices that drew from their ancestral cultures as well as church doctrine. When he was in his twenties, my father consciously decided to live as Diné and Gáamalii, beginning that journey as a mission-ary. While some Indigenous peoples have recognized attempts of Latter-day Saints to introduce their religion to the Diné as another form of colonialism, others have acknowledged Latter-day Saint services, cultural exchanges, and life pathways. My father's stories tell of both experiences.

Most missionaries sought to teach the LDS faith to Diné families and to strengthen church congregations. Some of them also launched and sus-tained an Indigenous network that created reciprocity between Latter-day Saints of diverse backgrounds and Diné communities.[147] In SWIM from

1949 to 1972, Indigenous missionaries blurred and traversed borders in Diné Bikéyah and within the Church by connecting to elements of their own ancestral ways of life. Transnational identification as Indigenous within the global Latter-day Saint community strengthened some of their own cultural integrity, whether they were Diné, Kānaka Maoli, Maori, or other First Peoples.[148]

CHAPTER THREE

Ólta' Gáamalii

"Mormon School"

Ólta' Gáamalii, or "Mormon School," is what Diné people call the Indian Student Placement Program (ISPP), or "Placement," which took place in the late twentieth century. On March 8, 2017, Cal Nez wrote a tribute to his Placement mother: "Thank you for everything you have given me. The true meaning of love. . . . You and dad left an incredible legacy that had impacted many cultures and races throughout the world."[1] Nez, a Diné businessman in the Salt Lake City region, has managed the Former LDS Indian Placement Students Facebook group page.[2] On November 16, 2016, he shared the *Salt Lake Tribune* article "Abuse Case against Mormon Church to Continue in Navajo Court; Attorneys Want LDS Leader Monson to Testify." Earlier in 2016, four Diné former Placement students initiated the lawsuit in the Navajo Nation District Court to sue the Church for sexual abuse in ISPP. The Church challenged the tribal jurisdiction of the Navajo courts, which sought to assess the injuries to former Diné students.[3]

Attorneys Bill Keeler, Craig Vernon, and their affiliates who have worked with numerous cases of Native Americans suing religious denominations for sexual abuse, filed the third lawsuit in June 2016 against the following: the Corporation of the President of the Church of Jesus Christ of Latter-Day Saints, a Utah corporation; the Corporation of the Presiding Bishop of the Church of Latter-Day Saints, a Utah corporation; LDS Family Services, a Utah corporation; and the Church of Jesus Christ of Latter-Day Saints, an unincorporated religious association.[4] One of the lawsuits comes from a brother and sister who suffered and witnessed repetitive abuses in ISPP. They revealed their abuses to program leaders but received no attention "and were placed in homes where they were abused again."[5]

Since Cal Nez maintains the Facebook page and shares his contact information, several journalists have questioned him about his ISPP experiences.

His remarks have been featured in *Atlantic* and *Indian Country Today* articles about the cases and ISPP, in which he defends his positive experiences in the program. Lilly Fowler, a journalist for the *Atlantic*, reached out to Latter-day Saint historians, including Jessie Embry, Matthew Garrett, Elise Boxer, and me, about ISPP. Garrett provided much of the historical background of the educational program that placed nearly fifty thousand Native American youth over the span of about fifty years in predominantly white Latter-day Saint homes where they attended public schools mostly in the United States, but also in Canada.

Nez rallied former Placement students:

> As former placement students, I believe we have an obligation to intervene to bring awareness both positive and negative. I am envisioning a conference in Salt Lake City organized by former placement students to bring awareness to foster healing or continued empowerment. We are grown adults now and reasonably share our experiences on the program. It is unfortunate for humanity to interject such negativity while there are success stories as well. I pray for the victims. I pray for the families.[6]

In response, another former student exclaimed, "I was a success!"[7] To measure ISPP in terms of "success" and "failure" distorts the past; on the other hand, to embrace and assess the complexities of the program allows broader recognition of varied experiences. I seek to understand the context and the options that Diné families and students faced.

While I deplore the abuses and grieve for the victims, I also respect Diné Latter-day Saints who gained and benefited from ISPP and their choices along with their sacrifices and challenges. My cousin, Tyson King, shared his insights with me about his fifth-grade year as a student in the program from 1985 to 1987. He will sometimes attend Latter-day Saint Sunday meetings with his mother, my aunt Phyllis, and he continues to respect the Church and his Placement family. He made a choice to participate in ISPP, asking his mother to register him for the program. He has also decided to sometimes distance himself from the Church and its policies, especially regarding homosexuality, LGBTQ+, and Two-Spirit issues, but he defends his choice and agency.[8] Since the litigation against the Church has ensued, many people have assumed that Tyson was abused in ISPP. Although he does not protest the termination of the program, his response to assertions about his own experiences reveals his frustrations: "These questions continue to surface and [it] has been very detrimental to my psyche. Not that I was abused, but it's a blanketed issue that is tossed over, while I continue to profess and deny any abuse truthfully. In the eyes of many, I am constantly treated like I am a victim, and I am in denial. This is not the case."[9]

"Blanketed" assumptions and interpretations of ISPP shape portrayals of not only Diné experiences but also Latter-day Saints in general. Tom Hartsock of the *Gallup Sun* reported various misread claims, such as misstating George P. Lee as the president of the Church who had ended ISPP. He also stated:

> According to reports, recognized beliefs of LDS members, Native Americans were in two separate groups: the righteous and civilized Nephites (light-skinned), and the idle, savage, and bloodthirsty Lamanites, cursed by God with a skin of blackness and became loathsome. (See verse in 2 Nephi 5:21, Book of Mormon.) Both fled Israel in 600 B.C. With that belief as a starting point, it becomes easier to understand the abuse that came after, even towards children as young as eight, and both male and female.[10]

These descriptions misinterpret many Latter-day Saint beliefs and perspectives, although it is impossible to deny that some self-identifying Latter-day Saints have espoused such distorted understandings of scriptures. Nephites and Lamanites come from the same family and heritage, and they belonged to the family of Lehi when they left Israel. Lamanites also repetitively joined and converted to the following of Christ, becoming more righteous than Nephites in certain episodes of the Book of Mormon. While Nephite civilization collapsed due to the people's wickedness and falling away from God, the Book of Mormon contains promises of prosperity specifically for Lamanites and their descendants whom many Latter-day Saints have considered to be Native Americans.

Several scholars, reporters, and community members have decried the racist undertones of Church leaders that equate "whiteness" with righteousness. For example, Church president Spencer W. Kimball declared: "These young [Native American] members of the Church are changing to whiteness and delightsomeness."[11] Yet such language often resonated with Diné as figurative, although there are exceptions and variations to their interpretations and lived experiences. Of many diverse Diné viewpoints, my father never expected to become white by joining the Church, and he never wanted to be lighter skinned. Although my father never participated as a student in ISPP, his insights about joining the Church are similar to those of Diné Placement student Dan Smith, who said: "I began to feel good about myself and happy that I was born an Indian."[12] Smith was born Diné, and he would live as a Diné even though he converted to the Latter-day Saint faith and some people might perceive him as "whiter" for it.

The Church envisioned a pathway for Diné converts that targeted steps for personal growth in spirituality and knowledge. Since Latter-day Saints have believed that "whatever principle of intelligence we attain unto in this life, it will rise with us in the resurrection," education as a form of improving minds represents a spiritual goal.[13] Latter-day Saint leaders also insisted that children must receive a positive education to excel in the secular world. But how did different people define "education," and who controlled the education of their children? The emphasis on education resonated with Diné, since reservation schools had been notoriously deficient throughout the twentieth century. Latter-day Saint interests in educational opportunities aligned with Diné concerns, which the metaphor of the "ladder of education" epitomizes. Many Diné believe that Hastiin Ch'ilhaajiní, "Man of the Black Weeds Place" or Chief Manuelito, advised his posterity before he passed away in the late 1800s: "My grandchild, the whites have many things which we Navajos need. But we cannot get them. . . . My grandchild, education is the ladder. Tell our people to take it."[14] Yet to what extent did Diné, including Diné students, shape that "ladder of education" and the future of their children, as white Latter-day Saints and other non-Diné sought to control and dominate Diné schooling?

This chapter first refers to how Diné navigated schooling, which often separated children from their respective communities and families. Although Diné and other ISPP students may have come from similar backgrounds, each student had distinct experiences in the program. Instead of indexing or categorizing their experiences as negative/positive or good/bad, I consider the spectrum and variety of Diné experiences on their own terms. Diné called ISPP Ólta' Gáamalii ("Mormon school"), since the program arranged for Native American youth, who were mostly but not exclusively Diné, to live in Latter-day Saint homes off tribal reservations during the school year throughout the second half of the twentieth century.[15] Since my father never "went on Placement," as they say, I have mostly drawn from the stories of Diné Latter-day Saints that they shared with the Redd Center or from other Latter-day Saint oral histories.

DINÉ EDUCATION

While Manuelito spoke about the importance of education, for many years some Diné rejected the plan to attend schools. As World War II ended, however, the Navajo Tribal Council passed a resolution demanding better schools for Diné children. First, the tribal leaders pointed out that only 6,000 of 20,000 Diné of school age (six to eighteen years old) could access schools. Even for those children, they faced long distances, overcrowded schools, and poor-quality instruction. As a strategy of survival, some tribal leaders began to repeat what white American officials had drilled in them: "that education like the white man's is needed to learn better farming, to learn how to improve livestock, to learn to improve health, and to learn trades." Following such priorities, twenty-three Diné representatives traveled to Washington, DC, in 1946 to entreat Congress to pass legislation obligating the federal government to provide the schools promised in the Treaty of 1868.[16]

Although this lobbying gained attention, many Diné communities still lacked nearby schools. As schools were being built, the federal government's "Special Navajo Program" (1946–1959) offered students vocational training in various boarding schools off the reservation, such as the Intermountain Indian Boarding School in Brigham City, Utah. Intermountain opened specifically for Diné students in the 1950s and became one of the largest federal Indian boarding schools in the United States before it became an intertribal school in 1974.[17] BIA officials were convinced that to be successful, Diné needed to leave the reservation. Some studies of Diné education contended that Native Americans must be "acculturated" into mainstream society. Diné leaders disagreed and insisted on more adequate schools near the students' homes. In 1953 the Hopi-Navajo Long Range Rehabilitation Act led to more on-reservation boarding schools and then to the development of a Navajo public school system.[18]

Latter-day Saint leaders reached out to the tribal council through a concerted effort to provide Diné with access to functional and well-equipped schools, including an offer in 1947 to support on-reservation boarding schools.[19] Individual white Latter-day Saints attempted to start schools for Native children in the Southwest. In the late 1940s, Albert and Gladys Lyman opened a school in Blanding called Holti (referring to "school" in Diné bizaad). They defined their mission in American Indian education to "raise their [students'] standards, educate them, find better employment, arrange to help them with their economic needs, care for their sick, bury their dead, and [help] in every other way that a neglected people needed the loving hand and guidance of an interested friend to be their benefactor."[20] The Church officially built and dedicated a school in Tohatchi, Navajo Nation, in January 1951. Clyde Beyal, a Diné convert known as a "pioneer" to fellow LDS Diné, welcomed two thousand visitors to the school at its opening reception.[21]

Latter-day Saints also found opportunities to offer religion classes at "Navajo day" and boarding schools where Diné students attended. In the nineteenth century, Latter-day Saints provided private religious schools in Utah communities, to be replaced by public schools in the 1880s. The Church continued some weekday instruction through religion classes for elementary students, but those were eventually cancelled. Church officials then developed a seminary program for high school students beginning in 1912 and an institute program for college-aged students in 1926. The seminary program for Native Americans adapted those previous programs.

Latter-day Saints conducted youth seminaries at several boarding schools, but one of the most active was at the Intermountain Indian Boarding School.[22] That program worked well, since many Latter-day Saints lived in the surrounding community of Brigham City. Seminaries became a significant proselytizing system, since nearly all of the boarding schools required the Native students to take some type of Christian instruction. School administrators often required parents to select the religious classes their children would attend, but many students chose a program based on which one provided the best food or music. My father remembers, for example, that he and several of his siblings were drawn to Latter-day Saint activities at the Ramah school Indian dormitory when that group provided treats and gifts, especially during holidays such as Christmas. When Damon James attended Intermountain in the late 1960s, he often went to the church that appealed the most to him and his friends. James remembers Brigham City as a "Mormon town" and how the prophet of the Church told the locals to "tolerate" the Native American students. Despite these petitions from church leaders, James described how white Latter-day Saints in Brigham City treated students based on "seeing color" and racial discrimination. James was baptized in the Church, but he claims that Christian religion did not matter to him as he followed different interests in his school years. He focused more on the festive activities and presents that the Church offered instead of its doctrine.[23]

THE INDIAN STUDENT PLACEMENT PROGRAM

For many scholars, ISPP is the prime example of Mormon colonization of Native American peoples.[24] It represents a clear instance of Latter-day Saints removing young children from their kin and cultural settings, pressuring them to live in another society during the twentieth century. For these scholars, the Church's "solution" paralleled the federal boarding schools where school employees forced Diné to speak English, cut their hair, and conform to Euro-American definitions of whiteness. Some Diné agree with that assessment and, using principles of decolonization, recognize that their culture and identity were suppressed or belittled. Since this realization, some of them are returning to their ancestral ways of life. But other Diné saw Placement as a path for them to access schooling and learn the gospel with Latter-day Saints, valuing lessons from their experiences in Placement that they passed on to their children. Many Diné Latter-day Saints grapple with both perspectives, recognizing the suffering of separation from their families and cultures and the opportunities of their journey.[25]

Beginnings of the Placement Program

ISPP's origins are traced to a young Diné woman, Helen Rose John Hall, who came to Richfield, Utah, to harvest sugar beets with her family as migrant laborers in the postwar era. When Helen was about six years old, her family hid her from the agents of federal Indian boarding schools who removed Diné children with or without their families' consent.[26] She eventually attended the Tuba City Boarding School for about five years until she was twelve years old, when her family expected her to end her schooling. In 1947 Helen thought of a plan to continue her schooling by living with a local LDS family in Richfield.

Despite her father's misgivings about "Bilagaanas' education" and lacking financial support, Helen reached out to a Latter-day Saint family in the Richfield community.[27] She beseeched Amy Avery, telling her, "I want to pitch a tent in your backyard to stay in."[28] In one of her letters to Amy, Helen expressed the appeal of learning about the Book of Mormon as couched in her desire to return to school and "to understand more," although her father "says, no, I will not go to school."[29] Helen's determination inspired Amy to call Golden Buchanan, who was a local Church leader in the stake presidency and Latter-day Saint "Lamanite affairs." After consulting with

Spencer W. Kimball about Helen's request to stay in Richfield, Buchanan received instructions from the apostle "to take [Helen] as a daughter and sister [into the Buchanan home]."[30] Golden's wife, Thelma, hesitated, struggling with her negative perceptions of Native Americans that had influenced her since childhood. Under pressure from her husband and Kimball, she eventually agreed to host Helen, who worked to earn the trust of the family over the years "and remained close [with them] throughout their lives."[31] Under Kimball's leadership, Buchanan and other Latter-day Saints such as Miles and Celia Jensen set the precedent for the official ISPP by initially recruiting students from the Navajo Nation to live with families in Utah for the school year.[32] ISPP began because a young Diné woman convinced LDS leaders and community members in Richfield with her assertion: "I want to stay and go to school."[33]

An Official Church Program

In 1954 Church leaders advanced the experiment in central Utah to an official Church program, considering its development in education and retention of Latter-day Saint Native American youth. The Church registered ISPP as a foster care program with the state of Utah and later with other states including California, Idaho, Washington, and Arizona. Since the Relief Society already operated a social service program, Church leaders placed ISPP under its authority. Along with Miles Jensen, the Church assigned other social workers to work with the students, their Diné families, and their Placement families. Over the years more students participated in the program: in 1957 there were 307 students; 324 in 1961; and 987 in 1965. By 1967 a past director of ISPP, Clarence R. Bishop, noted that three-fourths of the more than fifteen hundred ISPP students were Diné.[34]

The program peaked in 1970 with about five thousand students, until the Church slashed ISPP in half by the late 1970s, and approximately twenty-five hundred students were enrolled through 1984. Church officials then reduced the program again, and by 1992 only 350 to 400 students were involved. ISPP continued to operate until 1996, when Church leaders decided to discontinue the program once all those who were enrolled graduated from high school.[35] Sociologist Armand L. Mauss argues that "the program seems simply to have died a natural death" following demands and growth of public education for Diné and Native Americans that would enable students to stay with their own families, and the Church began redirecting its resources based on "cost-benefit assessments" of ISPP.[36] The last graduation of an ISPP student happened in 2000. Over the years, an estimated seventy thousand students participated in ISPP. [37]

The reasons for the closure of ISPP vary, but several factors played important roles, including expenses. ISPP director Clarence Bishop concluded that "the Church was finding it necessary to extend their financial resources to serve Native Americans and other Lamanite members in a more general way."[38] Changes in legislation also jeopardized the program. In 1978 Congress passed the Indian Child Welfare Act (ICWA), which seeks to prevent public and private groups from removing Native Americans from their kin and tribal nations. While some scholars identify this law as the beginning of the end of ISPP, the program continued for almost twenty more years. Government officials treated it as an exception, because parents consented to it and the students returned home during the summers. Some Placement parents indicate that ISPP ended in California because state law forbade placing Native students in non-Native American homes.[39]

The Navajo Tribal Council began to challenge programs like ISPP by fortifying opposition to separating Diné children from their homes and cultures. Major issues erupted as well when a non-ISPP group wanted to bring Diné students to the St. George, Washington County, School District in Utah and exempt them from paying out-of-state tuition, comparable to the arrangement made with ISPP. The case went to court, and the ruling mandated that all students whose parents were not residents should pay tuition. The Church was not willing to require that added fiscal responsibility for ISPP participants.[40]

The end of ISPP coalesced with the termination of the "Lamanite Cause," an era that Spencer W. Kimball's leadership defined through the numerous programs that Mauss describes as "the 'conveyor belt' of the Mormon education and socialization process," or what historian Matthew Garrett calls "making Lamanites."[41] ISPP, Indian seminaries, and BYU Indian programs all faced the chopping block in the late twentieth century, as Kimball could no longer sustain them. Ezra Taft Benson became the Prophet and President of the Church in 1985, and he was known as a vocal conservative.[42] He held political appointments before his church presidency as US secretary of agriculture, and he endorsed the John Birch Society, which was notorious for conservative and racist leanings.[43] As a conservative Republican politician, he would have been familiar with the movements in Utah and on the national level for termination of Indigenous sovereignty and efforts to integrate and assimilate Native Americans.[44] While scholars have examined LDS Indian education programs as assimilationist systems, the same programs also served as platforms for empowerment for some Native Americans and required resources and attention from the Church, which conservatives such as Benson sought to reduce by the 1980s.

Diné Student Views of Placement

Latter-day Saint Diné remember ISPP from different perspectives, but many feel ambivalent. They acknowledge that Placement provided benefits to its participants, but it also exacted a cost in Diné family relations. Jacqueline Keeler, a Diné and Yankton Dakota scholar and journalist, has publicly condemned the program for creating a rift in her Diné family by distancing part of her kin from their ancestral culture and identity.[45] Some interviewees from the Redd Center oral histories describe their time on Placement as an uplifting educational and spiritual experience. For others, Placement was a living nightmare. I have met Diné former Placement students with either or both perspectives of that time in their lives. Several interviewees or narrators have seemingly contradictory insights from Placement, because they stayed with different host families and had dramatically distinct experiences. In response to assessment questions about ISPP, Bishop pointed to students who graduated from high school, went to college, and became leaders in their communities. Many Placement students also served missions for the Church, married in the temple, and raised their children in the Church. Bishop acknowledged: "If the goal of the program was to provide an educational opportunity for Indian students, it surely did that." He continued, however, on another note: "What the student, foster families, and parents at home did with that opportunity may or may not be considered a success—depending on the individual situation."[46] Bishop's evaluation and emphasis on "the individual situation" points to how Latter-day Saint Diné could see the opportunities ISPP provided but also mourn the toll and broader context.

Before I continue to relay these diverse and complicated Diné experiences of Placement, I want to reiterate how important positionality and standpoint are to understanding these narratives by sharing part of my path to learning about Placement. There was only one time I had to walk out of a classroom, because I did not know what would happen if I stayed one more minute. Another student in the class who had been frustrating me with her condescending attitude of how her life experiences trumped anything we were learning from the instructor started to dominate the class conversation by sharing her story of "Othering" based on our class reading of Edward Said's *Orientalism*.[47] She was talking about how she was complacent in the cleaning of Native American children being prepared for ISPP. They deloused and showered the children before they were placed in LDS host families. She said that "this experience epitomized Othering. We othered those children."

At that moment, I was triggered, thinking of my cousins, who are brothers to me, and how they had experienced the Placement program. There was so much I could not say in the limited time of the class meeting. And did I want to try explaining it to this individual who spoke so definitively? Some people rush in with their opinions and perspectives, ready to judge and tell us what experiences mean. Did they stop to think about the families who made the decision to send their children to those programs, or children like my cousins who constantly live with those experiences and memories? Do they know the children and their families, and have they asked them directly about their experiences and perspectives? How have they tried to directly reconcile with them?

Even if people are testifying to what they witnessed, they need to listen to the actual families and try to understand what they faced. My cousin was a little boy when my parents visited him in his Placement home. He begged my parents to take him home, but they wouldn't do it. I know that my parents regret that choice to this day. They thought they were doing what was best for my cousin. These memories are so painful. It reminds me of the time I pressed my father trying to understand how his own parents dropped him off at an Indian boarding school. How can any parent take their child to the boarding school? I was angry and frustrated, trying to make sense of it. My father, sensing the implications of my hard-pressed questions, blurted: "My mother loved me. They [his family and parents] loved me." I then reflected on what choices they had, which were fewer than the choices available to me. There is always a choice, but some choices are limited and pressing as life and death. Listening to Placement stories calls for this kind of empathy, considering what choices Diné students and their families had in a world marred by colonialism, including its destructive systems and structures.

The following stories from the Redd Center oral histories, some of which I facilitated, reveal mixed reactions to ISPP. As with the Southwest Indian

Mission, people have viewed ISPP either as a vehicle of colonialism or as a merging of Latter-day Saint and Diné pathways. I have focused on sacrifices and learning experiences, while emphasizing the dilemmas that Diné students faced on Placement.

Family Sacrifices

Leaving her family was especially hard for Eileen Quintana, who slept with her mother on a sheepskin even when she grew older. Despite this closeness, Quintana recognized that her mother had few options regarding the schooling and upbringing of her children. Her father passed away when she was five years old, and her mother "was left to take care of three children with hardly anything." The LDS missionaries offered to help her and checked on their family. As a result, her mother "really ended up seeing their goodness and appreciating some of the qualities that the [missionaries] showed. Through time, she decided that maybe we would be better to see the bigger world from that program than what she could show us."[48] Her mother agreed to send her children on Placement.

Knowing what was best for her children and seeing them leave stirred conflicting emotions. Quintana recalled that she never saw her mother cry except when she left for her third year in ISPP. On the morning of her departure, she awoke to find that her mother had left the hogan. She then spied her mother in the shade house crying. Quintana stresses: "I think that image stayed with me for many years. Even though my mother had not shown me the tears right out, there were times when she did show that. She knew it was important for me to go out, to learn some of these things that she was not able to show me."[49]

Quintana later assessed that the sacrifice was not worth the loss. She perceived the efforts to remove Diné children from their homes as colonialism, and she made a conscious decision to decolonize and return to the ancestral beliefs and practices of her family. Although she no longer lived on the reservation when I interviewed her in 2008, she recognized a need for Native American families to teach their children. She helps facilitate that by working with the Title VI program that encourages bilingual and Native American–centered education in a Utah school district.[50]

Other Redd Center interviewees continued on a Latter-day Saint pathway and practiced that faith. They still recognized that Placement demanded family sacrifices. Brenda Beyal's mother joined the Church and sent her children on ISPP because it was an "opportunity for her children to learn the gospel and also to gain an education." Looking back, she reflected on her mother's decision: "I think it was twofold for her. At that time, my mom was a single mom, and she got a lot of flak from a lot of people, because she sent her children on Placement." Regardless of what others in her community assumed, Beyal's mother and grandparents told her, "Go and learn. Go and glean what you can. Bring the very best back with you. We're sending you, because we love you." As a result, Beyal recognized a purpose for her time away from her family and homeland. She claims that "we were sent for the right reasons. I don't think I had a problem with wanting to be white; I just knew that the white people had something to offer, and I was willing to take what I could."[51]

Julius Ray Chavez also found educational advantages from ISPP, even if it meant leaving his family. His mother had been baptized as a child, but she did not raise her children in the Church. When he was in the fourth grade, his mother registered him for ISPP. When the children were boarding the bus, he clung to his grandmother, but she told him: "'You have to go. . . . I didn't get an education, but for you this has got to happen.' With firm resolve, she pushed me on that bus, and I was gone." Although he lived with Placement families, Chavez remembered his grandmother and her influence on him. Diné value ké, family, and kin, which included extended relatives in a tight-knit network. ISPP separated children not only from their parents and siblings but also from the larger community of their kin. Like many other Placement students, Chavez became frustrated by the adjustment each school year of going back and forth between his Placement family and Diné family on the reservation. Each time he left his grandparents to return to school, he wanted to hold on to them.[52]

Cultural Restraints

Placement students were not only removed from their families but also isolated from their culture. As a consequence, some students suffered from cultural disconnections and misunderstandings as their Diné background often jarred against new social settings. While some Diné claimed to accept being acculturated to a white society, balancing different cultural backgrounds, other students resented the restraints on their culture.

Diné families sometimes helped their children who went on Placement preserve Native American culture. While Chavez's grandmother told him not to mention Diné ancestral teachings and ceremonies while he was on Placement, he absorbed Diné beliefs when he returned home. He continued to embrace his Diné identity because his parents and grandparents prepared him by teaching him Diné ways of life and being. While he missed some ceremonies in Diné Bikéyah during Placement, he learned them at later times.[53]

Ellouise Paredes's parents raised her with a deep respect for Diné culture and ancestral values. Her mother only spoke Diné bizaad, and her father was a hataałii, a Diné healer. Although she remained on Placement until she graduated from high school, Paredes remembers the difficulties of being cut off from Diné culture during the school year. Church leaders planned ISPP to immerse the students in Anglo-American culture and society. Placement arguably did not punish Diné students for speaking their language or practicing Diné traditions to the extent that Indian boarding schools did, but ISPP intertwined their ways of life with white American culture by removing the youth from Diné influences. Paredes, for example, struggled to find ways to communicate with her parents during the school year. Her parents did not write her letters since they only spoke Diné bizaad. While she enjoyed gathering with other Placement students once a month, she was frustrated that no one would speak Diné bizaad with her.[54]

Paredes's Placement mother also shocked her by cutting her hair. To Diné, hair symbolizes life and blessings, and the longer the hair, the longer the life and greater sign of respect to the Holy People.[55] Diné usually cut their hair only when they are mourning. While Paredes understood the cultural significance of her hair, her Placement mother thought of a haircut in terms of hygiene and appearance.[56]

Audrey Boone, another former Placement student, noticed, during the 1990s, that allowing youth to go on Placement only as teenagers helped counter some of these cultural misunderstandings. She preferred enabling "Indian kids [to] stay longer with their natural parents" because "they can gain that foundation of their culture into their lives." At the same time, she recognized Placement as part of larger hegemonic systems to "integrate Indian students into the Anglo schooling."[57]

"Apples"

Frequently, fellow Diné referred to Placement students as "apples" or bilasáana—"red on the outside but white on the inside." Placement students also felt this derision from other Native Americans who condemned the program and its affiliates. They did not completely fit into dominating white society, but when they returned home to Diné Bikéyah they sometimes strained to (re)connect with their Diné community. Some students endured how white LDS Placement families held onto stereotypes about the "poor Indian" people. Since some Placement students entered the program with head lice, the standard procedure required all new students to bathe and receive treatment for lice as soon as they arrived. My family friend Jimmy Benally remembered: "The first thing they did [when we arrived at a reception center] was they bathed, scrubbed us down and put this stuff in our hair to kill all the lice." He was shocked, because "we never had lice in our family." When he arrived at his foster home, "the first thing we did . . . was they scrubbed us."[58] While attending a SWIM reunion in 2013, Jimmy openly repeated this story as a joke, chuckling at how he went through several cleanings on his first day of the Placement program even after his Diné family washed him. In this context of sharing his story, Jimmy applied humor and laughter to expose challenges and mistreatment he faced as a Placement student.[59]

Although Jimmy gave the Placement family a letter from his mother that described their farm and two cars, his foster parents believed that he did not understand hygiene or manners because of his background. During his first dinner with his host family, they explained in minute details what they were eating. Benally was left-handed, but his foster mother thought he was imitating his foster brother who was using his left hand to eat while his right hand was in a cast. The Placement family treated Jimmy as if he had never eaten at a table before.[60]

Moving back and forth between the Placement program and Diné homes spurred more complications for Diné youth during such a foundational stage in their growth and self-identity. Audrey Boone realized how she was assuming different experiences and perspectives of class. For example, when she returned to her Diné family from ISPP, she recalled that her sister would touch the new clothes her foster parents had purchased for her, gawking and uttering, "Rich." Boone did not consider the clothes or herself as "rich," but she knew they did not come from a thrift store. She sensed a class divide festering between her and her Diné family because they perceived wealth differently after she participated in Placement.[61]

Jimmy Benally, like other ISPP students who appraised the program, stressed how students could escape the reservation's challenges (like alcoholism) while on Placement, but the struggles remained when they re-turned home in the summer.[62] Placement did not erase the social issues with which Diné and people in general have wrestled, but it prepared some individual students to overcome them. For some students, Placement even exposed them to alcohol, as Maybell Begay White remembers how some Placement students distributed alcoholic drinks after a youth gathering.[63] ISPP did not make student participants immune to issues that teenagers face in their journey of self-discovery and independence.

Placement students were often the only Diné in the school, so it was common for them to feel isolated and alone. Chavez was the only Diné in his classes, and his foster mother encouraged him to complete extra work. She later told him that the school wanted to place him in a slower class, but she had refused. Chavez bemoans that "I always had to in little ways prove myself even to the community who I was and what I was." To impress his Placement community, he became active in music at his high school and served as president of the seminary.[64]

Helena Hogue became ashamed of her Diné family and did not want to return home in the summer. In addition, her fluency in Diné bizaad waned in Placement. Hogue reconciled these inner tensions and later reconnected with her Diné family but only after much effort and pain.[65] For Irene Jones, ISPP also exacerbated discord in her familial relationships. Her stepfather, for example, insisted that she and her sister use peyote. After her sister re-fused and asserted that her "alliance and her commitments were going to be to the LDS Church," he demanded them "to leave and never come back." ISPP also strained Jones's relationship with her mother over the following ten years, as her mother "would hardly ever speak" to her. The dilemma still vexes Jones, since she had embraced Latter-day Saint beliefs that families are forever but continues to face difficulties with some of her relatives.[66]

The choices and experiences of some Diné Latter-day Saints convinced them to live away from the reservation. Benjamin and Anthony Gardner's mother went on ISPP and married a white American missionary who served in her area. Her foster dad was their father's mission president. For a while, the family lived in Flagstaff, Arizona, on the edge of Diné Bikéyah by Dookʼoʼoosłííd, the Sacred Mountain of the West also known as the San Francisco Peaks. But their mother was uncomfortable when her family in-vited her to Diné ceremonies. Their mother envisioned a crossroads: "She learned for herself and from her family's experience that her family couldn't find a compromise between living traditional Navajo values and living the

LDS gospel. The ones that tried to do both would always end up falling back to the Navajo traditions that they used to have. So, she left the reservation."[67] She decided to diverge from her Diné family's path, pursuing a new road. For some Diné Placement students, they grappled with their Latter-day Saint faith and their Diné ancestral teachings, while other Placement students saw the two teachings as intertwined. Prestine Ann Kelly, for example, expressed gratitude for both her Diné and Placement families, recognizing how she gained "the foundation on the reservation to be successful in a new culture and [having] learned to love diversity and to be accepting of all peoples."[68]

Placement Host Family Lottery

Some Placement students came to a home where they became part of the family. They stayed from the time they were eight until they graduated from high school. Some relationships between students and host families continued after the program. The foster parents sent them on missions and to college and continue to be grandparents to the students' children. Yet, for various reasons, some students moved from family to family, sometimes every year or even after part of a year. This situation put stress on the students who were not only away from their own homes but also did not feel accepted by the host family. Wallace Brown, who participated in ISPP in 1953, lived with four host families before he was fourteen years old. At that point, he returned to his own family on the reservation. While he learned something from each family, he had to adapt to different backgrounds, communities, stages of life, and livelihood. He went from a host family with a small business in central Utah to an older couple in southern Utah to a family in Salt Lake Valley to a dairy farm in northern Utah.[69]

As a ten-year-old, Helena Hogue felt homesick when she first went on Placement, but she enjoyed living with her first family. Her Diné mother then asked her to come home after the first year and sent her to a boarding school. She missed the academic support of her foster mother, a teacher, and she looked forward to returning to ISPP two years later. She received a new host family, however, with a foster mother who was an immigrant and spoke little English. The parents were also young and had very small children who could not relate to Hogue, which presented its own challenges. After four years, she requested a change. Her third Placement family was not active in the Church, and Hogue missed the religious experience. She was grateful for a Young Women's leader who encouraged her to attend church.[70]

Elouise Thinn Goatson envied her husband's Placement experience: "Very few had really good foster families like my husband. He stayed with them for the whole ten years." Unlike her husband's stable situation, Goatson was "being shuffled through" Placement as a sixteen-year-old, which she described with disdain: "It was very unpleasant, so that wasn't a good thing." After attending a boarding school until the last two years of high school, she forged a fresh experience. For her, the boarding school was "not something that you really want to chat about" because of students' hardships, but "the Placement Program was not all in the best situation either." In her first year, she moved between three different host families. The first was a young couple who used her as a babysitter. The second was a family with many children who left her feeling that they just wanted to fulfill a duty. The third family, however, "had a full understanding of what it meant to have a foster child in the home." Goatson articulates a purpose of Placement, which her third family exemplified: "The objective of the whole thing was to educate [Native American youth] and to be able to have them understand the religion. It was to be familiar with what the Mormon religion entails. They [the third family] were willing to take the time to work with me," unlike the other families. If she had not met her third family during her first year of ISPP, she "would have never gone back."[71] Students often needed to cohabitate with Placement siblings, with whom they sometimes did or did not bond. Matches between Placement students and families resembled the lottery, since compatibility varied in such relations depending on sheer luck of circumstances at times.

Testimony

While ISPP publications underscored education as the main reason for the program, the foster families hoped that the students would gain a testimony that the Church provided a necessary pathway to happiness through Jesus Christ. Many foster families agreed to participate in the program because they believed the Book of Mormon gave them a responsibility to help Native Americans gain a knowledge of the gospel. Many of them thought that Diné students should maintain their language and parts of their culture. But the most harmful effects of Placement stemmed from widespread beliefs among white Latter-day Saints, including Placement families, that all or at least some of Diné ancestral teachings and ways of life were detrimental and necessary to avoid.[72]

For many of the Redd Center interviewees who participated in ISPP, gaining a testimony of Christ was an essential part of their experience living in a Latter-day Saint Placement home. The interviewees, for the most part, were Diné who attended church, lived the Church standards, and believed that the Church reveals a true pathway to their salvation. Those experiences are not a comprehensive or even representative sample, and their narrative may not be true of most Placement students. But their stories underline a dimension of Diné dóó Gáamalii that is often missed when the focus only turns to frameworks of colonialism and other all-encompassing terms of Diné and LDS relations.[73]

Diné Placement students entered the program with varying family backgrounds and experiences that influenced their perceptions of the Church. Patty Tauchin Etcitty always remembers her Diné family teachings of hózhǫ́, prayer, and spirituality. Her father instilled in her "that a home is where you are together as a family, even if it is under a tree." She explicitly asserts that her Diné family "had family home evening without even knowing it," which centered on "telling stories and discussing Navajo philosophies."[74] Victor Mannie Sr., on the other hand, was another former Diné Placement student who did not have an upbringing with such family home evenings. He was baptized when he was eight years old and then went on Placement. His father had joined the Church after living with a family, and Mannie assumed that Latter-day Saints influenced his father. However, his father had not followed or instituted typical LDS home worship such as family home evening. Mannie learned about these kinds of practices in Church only when he went on Placement, during which he formed a testimony of the gospel.

Mannie chose to return home after middle school since the high school near his parents' home could provide a respectable education. He reflects on Placement and his Church membership, emphasizing inconsistencies:

We went on the Placement Program for a number of years. During the Placement Program, that's where we learned a lot more. [It was] where we were taught about the religion and this part about what the Church really meant when you gain a testimony about the plan of salvation and all the different parts of holding the priesthood. We pretty much lived a life of "in the Church off and on" always through our lives.[75]

His testimony of Christ grew, but his journey mirrors ongoing movements and vicissitudes of religious life that Diné Placement students faced.

Unlike many first-generation Diné LDS converts, Emery Bowman was born into a family with a Latter-day Saint background. His grandmother was baptized and, according to Bowman, was a faithful member for years until "she felt that she was going away from Indian tradition, so she went back to the Navajo teachings." Bowman recalls that his grandmother "always considered herself a Mormon. She thought the Church was good for our family." His mother was also baptized and combined Latter-day Saint and Diné beliefs. As a single mother, she sent her children on Placement, which "scattered" his brothers and sisters.[76]

When Bowman went on Placement at eleven years old, he knew more about Diné ancestral knowledge than Latter-day Saint teachings. He stayed on the program for nine years and lived five years with one family and four years with another family. His brother had lived earlier with his first host family, and they were supporting his brother on a mission when Bowman arrived in 1977. He appreciated that this family encouraged him to adhere to Diné traditions and language. At one point, he resented the Church's references to his special mission as a Lamanite. Eventually, he intertwined his grandfather's teachings to enjoy the journey on Placement and his foster father's guidance in the LDS faith. Diné prioritized respecting and listening to their elders, as in Bowman's case with his grandfather. He read the Book of Mormon and focused on his host family's gospel teachings. He shared those concerns as a student representative, "basically a psychologist," with other ISPP students who struggled in their new environments. He encouraged them to also read the Book of Mormon and to find a testimony of the gospel.[77]

Educational Value

Some interviewees believed ISPP's greatest advantage was that it gave them a Euro-American education, which was not accessible in every part of the reservation at the time, especially before the twenty-first century. Former Placement student Brenda Beyal stresses, however, why she would not send her daughter on such a program: "I think the Placement Program served its purpose. I think our generation has enough opportunities and their generation has enough opportunities. We, as parents, have enough opportunities and enough tools in our little parent tool bag to raise our children in the gospel and raise our children to value education. I think that time [of Place-ment] is passed."[78] Beyal's comments indicate generational shifts between the late twentieth and early twenty-first centuries, as she became a parent with confidence in her family's access to church and schooling. Beyal has taught Diné and Native American culture and knowledge to not only her own children but also many youth as an educator. In 2022 she led the Native American Curriculum Initiative with the BYU ARTS Partnership and the Utah Division of Arts and Museums, training teachers in Utah to respect-fully feature Indigenous artists and their work in their lessons.[79]

Helen Hogue believes that ISPP prepared her to become a good relative: "If I hadn't had it, I don't think I would have been where I am today or have the things that I've been blessed with." She reflects on the alcoholism that plagued her family, especially her parents, accrediting the Church and ISPP for pulling her through life. Her family looks to her for help and guidance because of her experience on Placement. Hogue's husband also went on Placement, and they have raised their children as members of the Church. Like Beyal, however, Hogue would not enroll her children in Placement. She elaborates on her reasoning:

> Because I have been on Placement. It did me good. I think it is my own responsibility now to teach them. I've been taught how to better my life. For me to have gone on Placement means that I need to teach my children what I've been taught. I need to see how they are going to turn out from what I've been taught. I don't want to have somebody else raise my chil-dren. I have to put into use what I've been taught and give it to them.[80]

Some Placement students, as Hogue reveals, acknowledged a need for Place-ment in their personal context, but they viewed the program as a temporary form of support that was no longer necessary and would be detrimental in their present family circumstances.

ISPP officials conceptualized the program to teach students valuable skills to navigate challenges and secure their livelihoods. Some Placement students became convinced that the program prepared Diné for success, which they often measured by professional development, careers, and mar-ried family life. Considering Diné who returned to the Navajo Nation after Placement, Victor Mannie defines "success" in various ways. He also ac-knowledges the debates about the program's impacts on Diné and other Native Americans: "We hear over and over that the Placement Program was good and acted for the benefit of Native Americans at that time, but its function did not carry on like they wanted [it] to. But I feel that it did a lot of good for a lot of Native Americans, especially Navajos that went on this program."[81]

Mannie celebrated how Placement introduced students to "a different way of life, a different religion," and the program "helped a lot of families" come to an awareness of "things that are happening out there in the world that a lot of students would never have seen if they had never been on the Placement Program." Mannie recognizes that "a lot of people say [Placement] didn't help" Native American students, but he presents a counterargument that "it provided a lot of doors to be opened for a lot of the Native Americans I see on the Navajo Nation." For example, he highlights that "there's a lot of former Placement students that are in the government that are more outgoing because this program was enacted."[82] One of the most prominent identifiers of success that Mannie highlights is that some students found their voice, becoming "more open, more vocal," as Diné youth on Placement. In 2019, while visiting a predominantly Diné LDS congregation in Diné Bikéyah, I heard about a special presentation at the Fort Wingate Branch that featured and celebrated former Placement students and their stories.[83] Some Placement students, such as Mannie and the individuals who participated in the Fort Wingate Branch event, learned that their experiences and insights matter, and they could be leaders, advocates, and activists for their people and communities in the world.

REFLECTIONS ON PLACEMENT

The Church's guidelines for ISPP are as follows:

> The objective of the Placement Program is to provide educational, spiritual, social, and cultural opportunities in non-Indian community life for Latter-day Saint Indian children. It is felt that through the exemplary living of select Latter-day Saint families, these Indian youth will be motivated to use their experiences now and later for the benefit of themselves and their people. . . . The Program exists primarily for the leadership development it affords the Indian children.

The statement added that short-term goals were overcoming "poverty and deprivation of individual children," but "long-term educational goals, leading to the general development of Indian people for generations yet unborn cannot be sacrificed in the interest of immediate welfare assistance."[84] Church officials claimed to design ISPP to empower Native American youth to lead in their contemporary communities such that their lives would shape the many generations ahead. Decades after she initiated ISPP, Helen John Hall ruminated on the impacts of the program: "It brought Anglos and Indians together and made us assist each other. Thousands of Indian youth have received educations and spiritual training. Thousands of Anglos have learned to understand and love Indians."[85] Helen stresses the reciprocity of ISPP that she personally observed and experienced, which most people overlook. Placement, for better or worse, was an exchange between different peoples too often overly dichotomized as white settlers and Native Americans who learned from each other. This learning process, in turn, changed each of them.

In sharing their experiences, many of them in personal conversations with me, Diné oral history narrators provided insights into what happened on the ground as primarily white Latter-day Saints sought to apply the stated ISPP goals. Some Diné Latter-day Saints have simultaneously celebrated and criticized ISPP. While full-fledged opponents of ISPP condemn most if not all components of the program, many people hesitate to label Placement as definitely good or bad, including Placement students themselves and their families, as well as observant scholars. Emily Benedek, for example, the author of *Beyond the Four Corners of the World: A Navajo Woman's Journal*, commends the story of Ella Bedonie who was born in 1952 and later went on ISPP but also sustained her Diné ancestral teachings.[86]

Bedonie recalled her first experiences with the Latter-day Saint missionaries. A middle-aged white couple came to her home and described the plan of salvation with a flannel board showing "a diagram of the heavens." Bedonie decided to enter the Placement program when she saw a sign about it at the Tuba City Boarding School she was attending. She explains that, in those early postwar years, "Navajo families consider it a good opportunity for their children to have experience in the white world and a chance for a better education." Bedonie, like other Placement students, compared her experiences with Indian boarding schools, which they viewed as worse than Placement in terms of traumatizing and challenging Diné youth.

When she went on Placement for the fifth grade, Bedonie did not cry at her departure as she had when she left for boarding school. Latter-day Saint expressions of hope and optimism for Native Americans touched her as she developed trust in her Placement family. Although she noticed similarities between Diné understandings of the four worlds and Latter-day Saint teachings of life after death, Bedonie did not ever "become totally Mormon." After growing up and getting married, she knew that she could not live without Diné ancestral teachings. She was relieved to tell her husband that she was leaving the Church, and he understood her decision. For most of her life, she did not connect with the Church except through her Placement parents, who continued to love her and stayed in touch after she returned to the reservation. Her Placement family continued to support her, including her foster father's contributions of thousands of dollars to help cover the medical expenses for her cancer treatments. Bedonie felt that some Diné were "brainwashed" to accept Latter-day Saint teachings, but she also recognized her own "good experience" with Placement that extended her family ties.

Placement was a part of the Latter-day Saint Indian education track that connected Diné youth to LDS communities and families while supporting and developing their membership in the Church. The Church's Indian education programs sought to develop a rising generation of Indigenous leaders and faithful Latter-day Saints who could sustain their people through the gospel. Although Church members consider Placement in spiritual and religious terms, all the people involved, such as students, families, and Church officials, also envisioned Placement as honing the skills to compete in a national labor market and achieving material gains.

A white Latter-day Saint trader's wife and missionary on the Navajo reservation, Lucy Bloomfield, wrote "Lamanite Song of Thanks," perpetuating a message that the gospel opened Diné eyes to their true identity and potential as children of God and followers of Christ. Bloomfield disguises her own voice as a Native American convert, which is a form of misappropriation. Her song lyrics follow:

> From our eyes the scales are falling
> Truth from error is discerned
> Now the Lord sends us true gospel
> That for ages we have yearned.
> Now the "Great White Father" help us
> Now our Book has been restored.
> Telling us we are of Israel
> And of Jesus Christ our Lord.
> Help us now to heed this message

Arlene Nofchissey Williams and Carnes Burson with Dale Tingey in a Latter-day Saint church, c. early 2000s. Courtesy of author.

Help our hearts to understand.
Help us now to claim our birthright
Here upon our "Promised Land."[87]

Many Diné Latter-day Saints sang Bloomfield's song, and some actual Native American converts' beliefs aligned with the lyrics. Adolph June Jr. attributed the beginnings of his faith in the gospel of Jesus Christ to his upbringing with ancestral Diné teachings. For example, his father exemplified prayer and singing to deities in Hózhǫ́ǫ́jí, the Blessing Way ceremony, along with recognition of "the sacredness of things in our environment." According to June, these "traditional values" developed his curiosity "to learn what the real truth was, and if there was a living God and how the whole universe was created."[88]

Diné Latter-day Saint youth learned Bloomfield's song at the Intermountain Indian Boarding School where the Church established a major Indian seminary program for Diné youth.[89] Considering the context of Diné Intermountain boarding school students rehearsing this song, the lyrics epitomized a condescending common white settler's concept that Native Americans needed the aid of white Christians to be redeemed.[90] The "Lamanite's" gratitude reflected white Christians' mentality, those of Latter-day Saints like Bloomfield in this case, who viewed themselves as leading Native Americans into the light of a true knowledge of their "Great White Father." White Latter-day Saints who were involved with their Church's Indian education programs often exhibited strong colonizer forms of paternalism and maternalism, which affected some Placement students.

The theme song of the Indian seminary filmstrip series *Tom Trails*, "Go, My Son," complicates understanding of these Indian education programs. The lyrics summarize the Church's hope for ISPP and illuminate how some Diné dóó Gáamalii live through the entanglements of their different affiliated cultures. Arlene Nofchissey Williams and Carnes Burson, a young Diné woman and Ute man, respectively, wrote this song for a BYU performing group, Lamanite Generation, to rally Latter-day Saint Native Americans to the cause of the Church in Indian education. It rapidly became popular throughout the Indian program and beyond in general circles. Echoing the words of Diné leader Manuelito, they wrote:

Go, my son,
Go and climb a ladder
Go, my son.
Go, and earn your feather.
Go, my son,
Make your people proud of you.
Go, my son,
Get an education.
Go, my son,
Learn a good vocation.
And climb my son.
Lift your people up with you.[91]

P. Jane Hafen, a Latter-day Saint Taos Pueblo scholar, stressed how Williams and Burson "employed both popular and traditional musical styles without sacrificing Native American values of tribal recognition and community."[92] Nofchissey and Burson convey Indigenous values of kinship and peoplehood with a repetitive song that follows traditional Diné verse forms. The address to a "son" represents all familial relations. The song also demonstrates how Nofchissey learned to combine both types of backgrounds from her Church education and Diné upbringing. For some Diné Latter-day Saints, ISPP embodied the hope of this kind of balance between the teachings of Jesus Christ and Diné.

During one of my visits to my parents while they lived in Monument Valley, Navajo Nation, a respected local Church leader had stopped by and showed interest in my studies of Diné Latter-day Saint experiences. He was a former missionary in Diné Bikéyah and remembers when his mission president, George P. Lee, would tell him and fellow missionaries that they "need to put every red-faced child on that bus" to Placement.[93] Church officials upheld Lee as a success story of the Placement program at the time, since he became one of the first Diné and Native American General Authorities. But this former missionary and local area leader knew that Lee's directions about Placement contradicted Church social workers, who instructed missionaries to only enroll baptized Diné youth with strong connections to the Church.

After his mission, he later married a Diné woman who had participated in Placement. His wife started the Placement program when she was only eight years old, and she would cry herself to sleep almost every night in her longing for home. Her foster brothers also molested her, intensifying her trauma and suffering. He not only knew of the abuses that his wife endured as a Placement student, but he remembers how one of his hardest missionary experiences was when he accompanied social workers to inform a Diné family that a foster father had sexually abused their daughter who would then be transferred. He discovered that the Church followed formal processes for addressing such dire situations.

As he continued to serve in different capacities for the Church in the Navajo Nation, including as a bishop, he learned of more cases of sexual abuse and trauma that affected Diné Latter-day Saints. As Church leaders and members ask him about ongoing litigation against the Church for sexual abuse that happened during Placement, he feels reluctant to call Placement "good or bad." As a missionary, some Diné children begged him to go on Placement. Diné Latter-day Saints, such as Yvonne Martin Bigman, assert that "the LDS missionaries came and rescued me" because they helped her enter the Placement program.[94]

Shinaaí, my older brother as I would say in Diné bizaad, Tyson was one of those Diné children who pleaded with his mother to start Placement. He appreciates how the Church halted the program, and he acknowledges

Farina King with her sister Emmalani (Smith) Longenecker, aunt Phyllis Smith, cousin Tyson King, and husband Brian King, 2007, in Gallup, New Mexico. Courtesy of author.

the abuses that happened to some Placement students. But he also wants acknowledgment of his story and experience in the 1980s that does not diminish any other Placement student's lived experience:

> The notion, or the idea that being a part of the program was thought of by many as a part to assimilate, or basically try to "turn me into an Anglo American." I am constantly being asked if while I was on the program I was treated like days of old when Navajo children were taken to boarding schools. Were you told not to speak your Native Tongue? Were you told not to mention any of your Navajo Culture? Were you forced to only read of the Bible? These were many questions that I have always been asked when I mention that I was on the Placement Program while I was growing up. I will continue to defend that it was never the case. In fact, the family I was placed with, literally every day, they would ask about my culture. They would ask me how to pronounce certain words. They would ask me about my culture all the time. Never once did they ever not allow me to call my mom or any of my family. I called my mom every Sunday, and I had an Uncle who visited me quite frequently while he was on travel for work as well.

While one of the requirements was to attend the LDS church regularly and seek guidance through the membership, it was never a task rather, it was something I desired to do.[95]

Tyson and many Diné Latter-day Saints seek to define themselves and their own experiences rather than only being judged in overgeneralizations.

Sexual abuse and fallout of the Placement program stem from various factors, but especially from the violence of settler colonialism that forced the subjugation and dispossession of many Indigenous peoples. Voices of resistance, resilience, and strength rise out of these struggles, injustices, and pain to illuminate hope and ways of healing and reconciliation. Sarah Newcomb, my Tsimshian friend of the First Nation from Metlakatla, Alaska, who decided to no longer participate in the Church after being raised as a Latter-day Saint, has told me that we need to listen to "many voices" with compassion.[96] These voices include those that cry out for justice from their suffering and those for recognition of their faith and joy even through difficult circumstances. When a Diné LDS friend revealed to me that his mother was abused as a Placement student, I was shocked that he and his family were still active in the Church. My friend, his mother, and their family sought justice and truth about the abuses that happened during Placement, and they continue to believe in the teachings of the Book of Mormon and the Church. His story and perspective taught me that even families debate the impacts of the Church and Placement, and criticism and praise for both are not mutually exclusive.

Many Diné Latter-day Saints have clung to their cherished communities and extended families because they were taught to return to them as part of the Church's goals of sharing the gospel and leading their people. Yet their Church education changed them by introducing white settler culture and values into their lives, sometimes alienating them from their Indigenous families. The next step in the life path for many Diné Latter-day Saints was a growing sense of community, which they experienced by becoming more involved in Diné and Native American congregations on and off the reservation.

CHAPTER FOUR

Sodizin Bá Hooghan
Church

*Dóó ákogo éiyá díí sodizin bá hooghan éí shinaʼnitin bee ábiiʼdiilyaago índa
ataaʼ biyiʼjįʼ binaanish íishjání íidoolį́į́ł.*

*And if it so be that the church is built upon my gospel then will the Father
show forth his own works in it.*

—3 Nephi 27:10, The Book of Mormon

As I recall some of my earliest memories of going to church, the Window
Rock Ward in St. Michaels, Navajo Nation, comes to mind. On Sundays
I wore my best dresses and entered the white-painted church with a dark
brown panel on the front and a white steeple on top. In Diné bizaad, Diné
call the area Tsʼithootso, a place "that extends out in yellow and green" or
simply "green meadow," referring to the yellow blossoms and grasses that
grow in the summer.[1] I remember greeting friends and smiling faces at
church, and even finding a way to escape outside under the shade of the few
trees within the fence of the church grounds to play with one of my peers,
Darrell. Romero and Laura Brown, Darrell's parents, were among the familiar faces to me since they lived close to the church and regularly attended
the local congregation. Although my family moved away from Window
Rock while I was still a child, my family returned and visited the Browns on
occasion. Darrell and I grew up and started our own respective families, but
I have contacted the Brown family over the years, especially seeking their
insights when working on this book.

My husband, Brian King, interviewed Romero Brown, who told him:
"Since Farina is part Navajo, ask her why the Navajo's hogans or home doors
are facing east. The scripture in St. Matthew explains that 'as the sun cometh
out of the east, so will the son of man be.'" Romero "noticed that the main
doors of the temples were facing east" when he first entered the temple.[2] He

recognized connections with Diné sacred symbols, practices, and ancestral teachings as he learned more about the Church of Jesus Christ of Latter-day Saints and its gospel of Christ. The significance of the Four Directions stood out to him, which he could understand as both Diné and Latter-day Saint in parallel and intersecting ways.

Latter-day Saints, including Diné converts, view church attendance as an essential part of their pathway to the temple, because it provides them the opportunity to take the sacrament, learn and understand gospel teachings, and gain support with their spiritual aspirations in their local communities. According to their beliefs, the sacrament enables them to renew baptismal covenants and remember the atoning sacrifice of their Lord and Savior, Jesus Christ, by partaking worthily of the bread and water, which represent Jesus's flesh and blood. But the chapel is more than a place to worship. It is a place to socialize and to strengthen a community of faith through interaction. It is a place to learn and teach the principles of the gospel. It is an opportunity for members to serve one another. Since the Church operates by lay ministry, members alternate in responding to "callings" from hierarchical leaders to function as the preachers, the teachers, the clerks, the administrators, and the volunteers, to describe just a few positions.

As I shared previously, my father's baptism did not adhere to general expectations and guidelines of the Church, and he did not even realize the deeper meanings of his baptism until later in his life. Frankie Gilmore had a similar experience, which fed his bitterness toward the Church for many years. He was "baptized after one punch and cookie session," and he then entered the Placement program with little understanding of the Church. Once he started going to church, the local leaders humiliated him for struggling with basic gospel questions by requiring him to attend classes with smaller children.[3] Diné Latter-day Saints often live through distinct experiences of common rites of passage for all members of the Church such as baptism and temple work. Several of my Diné cousins, for example, hesitated to be baptized because of their fear of being immersed in water. They did not know how to swim, and they did not often immerse themselves in deep water. Access to pools and large baths for swimming and immersion in water are less common in Diné Bikéyah, which has a predominantly arid and desert climate.

One of my cousins, Flora, mustered the courage to be baptized, especially from the friends and community that connected with her in the Fort Wingate Branch. After her own baptism, she prepared to enter the temple to do what Latter-day Saints call "baptisms for the dead," which involves being baptized by immersion as a proxy for ancestors and the deceased who never were baptized in their lifetime. "Temple work" refers to these ordinances for the dead. Flora again faced her fear of immersion in water at the temple. In one of the most sacred spaces to Latter-day Saints, Flora sought to overcome her feelings of dread and mistrust. An onslaught of doubts and questions racked her. Could she trust the skinny young man who was baptizing her? Would he hold her steady and pull her up before she drowned?

As I have pondered my cousin's experiences with baptism, I realize the significance of relationality and mutual understandings among Diné Latter-day Saint communities, which wards and branches have offered them in the Navajo Nation. Some of Flora's friends and family from her home congregation were able to enter the temple with her, reassuring her and sensing her specific challenges. One of her daughters and other Diné relatives have also shared her anxieties about immersion in water. After her first time participating in baptisms for the dead, Flora could then support them if they also decided to confront this fear of being baptized. It is important to recognize this discomfort and actual threat for some Diné when they take this leap of faith to be baptized and to become a member of a Latter-day Saint congregation.

DINÉ WARDS AND BRANCHES

For the Church and SWIM leaders, the next step after placing missionaries on the reservation was to form congregations where the newly baptized Diné could worship. This chapter explores the formation and development of these congregations and growing Diné LDS communities. The Diné congregational units were like other Latter-day Saint congregations in areas that recently opened to the Church, but unique contexts related to the relationship between the Church and the Navajo Nation and Diné culture distinguished them. After addressing some of these general comparisons, this chapter features several LDS Diné congregations in Diné Bikéyah.

The SWIM president and the General Authorities formed predominantly Diné congregations to serve converts on the reservation. By the late 1960s the mission consisted of fifty-seven branches and seventeen districts.[4] In 1974 there were seventy-seven congregations on the Navajo reservation.[5] According to the general policy of the Church, each branch had geographical boundaries, which allowed congregations on the reservation to include Diné and non-Diné members who lived and worked in the area. Diné Latter-day Saints worked with Church leaders and other members to forge their own spaces and boundaries, marking their communities in Diné Bikéyah. The congregational unit, a ward or branch, served as the basis for the community while the meeting place such as a chapel represented the space of the community. These Diné LDS spaces and communities mutually fostered each other. The church buildings strengthened Diné Latter-day Saint communities by providing them with space, and the communities built and maintained the church buildings and their other spaces.

MEETING PLACES

In some areas, including Native American reservations, government restrictions limit the expansion and building of churches. In Diné Bikéyah, the first meetings of Latter-day Saints often took place in hogans and trading posts. They involved missionary-led programs rather than official branches. For example, in April 1949, missionaries held a children's primary Sunday school in the hogan of Richard Thomas, a "good Navajo member." During one meeting, fourteen of Thomas's eighteen children and six adults attended and crowded in his hogan. A missionary recalled that the children were unreceptive until a young lamb in the hogan started bleating along with the singing. The lamb sparked outbursts of laughter, then everyone listened to the church lesson. Thomas interpreted for the missionaries because most of his family did not know English.[6]

Rudy Begay, a Diné convert, told me how the few Diné Latter-day Saints sat on large logs in the back room of a trading post for their meetings in Shiprock.[7] George and Lucy Bloomfield hosted gatherings in their trading post in Toadlena. The Babbitt brothers, although they were not Latter-day Saints, allowed some meetings in their trading post in Tuba City during the 1940s. Donald Smouse, a Latter-day Saint trader in Borrego Pass, built a small chapel on his trading post property that was dedicated in 1959. In 1945 a trader in Crystal told the missionaries they could not live on his land or hold meetings there; in 1959 the same situation occurred in Leupp. The owner of Sunrise Trading Post, who was Latter-day Saint himself, asked the LDS elders to leave his property because Diné leaders had warned him that they would boycott his business if the missionaries continued church activities there.[8]

The Church saw trading posts and other buildings that they did not own as temporary meeting places. A consistent goal was to own property and build chapels. When Latter-day Saints petitioned the Navajo Nation for Church-owned venues on the reservation, some tribal officials resisted the idea of LDS congregations just as they had opposed SWIM. A major concern was landownership, which had been complicated since the designation of the reservation. While the US federal government holds tribal lands in trust, the Diné tribal government also authorizes the land use.[9] The Church recognized this land regulation in 1946, when SWIM president Ralph W. Evans and Apostle Spencer W. Kimball listed privately owned lands on the reservation as possible locations for meetinghouses. Since the status of some of these lands were unclear, missionary Albert R. Lyman had recommended to Evans in 1945 that Latter-day Saints only congregate in homes until the Church received permission to construct chapels.[10] Latter-day Saints struggled to coordinate building chapels on the reservation.

World War II delayed the first attempts to build LDS churches on the reservation because construction materials at that time were scarce. After the war, the reluctance of the Navajo Tribal Council to grant permission for land use continued to hinder building plans. During the early postwar period, the tribal council was petitioning the federal government to expand the reservation. The council delegates worried that the government would question their land claims if they allowed external groups to use the land for nontribal purposes. In 1950 Church leaders complained that "the [tribal council] ha[s] evaded the issues of chapels on the reservation now for many years."[11] By 1965, however, new leaders on the council were willing to approve chapel construction depending on available permits or leases, which Church leaders celebrated as a major turning point.

The approval of the tribal council did not eliminate all the challenges to developing a Diné Latter-day Saint space on the reservation. Diné have traditionally made decisions by consensus rather than allowing only their leaders to determine policy. In the Church, members are asked to sustain leaders and teachers as they receive callings from their "presiding authorities"; however, such votes rarely show negative responses. Mission leaders did not recognize the irony when they criticized how Diné communities sought "a complete unity before they move ahead."[12] Once the tribal council approved a church building, the local Navajo chapter had to make the final decision on whether the nearby residents agreed to a church for Latter-day Saints. Tense relationships between some Diné and local Latter-day Saints could interfere with settling such agreements. For example, when SWIM president S. Eugene Flake asked for a chapel in Shiprock, some local Diné blamed the Latter-day Saints for pushing them off the land and saw no reason to share their area. Others accused the Latter-day Saints of not allowing their children to attend a school in Kirtland, New Mexico. Some Diné countered these claims by describing how Latter-day Saints had improved their living conditions. Without a unanimous voice, however, Diné withheld permission for a chapel.[13]

The Chinle Ward exemplifies how the Church obtained permission to build a chapel on the reservation. In 1959 a Latter-day Saint named Ernst Clifford Young moved to Chʼínílį (Chinle) when a Latter-day Saint congregation did not exist in the area. The Young family came from a long line of Latter-day Saints and wanted to network with other members of the Church. After searching, Young found a few people who had a Latter-day Saint background, including two Diné. When his wife June joined him in 1960, she started a Relief Society in their home. Mission president Hal Taylor authorized the elders to form a branch and called Young as the Chinle Branch president in August 1960. The congregation continued to meet in the Young home until attendance at the meetings increased to twenty-seven members and then to ninety.

The branch then rented a four-room building to accommodate the growing congregation. When the building was demolished the branch met in the tribal chapter house for Sunday meetings and weekday youth seminary. The branch later used the Bureau of Indian Affairs auditorium. Members of the branch consolidated all their meetings in the morning, since they shared the BIA building with a Baptist congregation that used the facilities in the afternoon.

While the branch grew in Chinle, the members still struggled to find a meeting place. Church leaders purchased a site for a building, but the Navajo Tribal Advisory Board would not approve construction for twelve years. Assistance eventually came from Walker Norcross, who was then president of the Chinle chapter. Norcross told the Church leaders to stay home while he presented the petition to the chapter. Some Diné representatives continued to resist the move, and the vice chair opposed the chapel. The Latter-day Saints of the branch united in fasting and prayer, asking God for the chapter to approve their petition. In 1965 they believed that their prayers were answered when the chapter sanctioned the Chinle chapel, and SWIM president Hal Taylor dedicated the building in 1966.[14]

Chinle Church officials recorded in a general history of the congregation: "This past week has climaxed a more than four-year struggle to have our chapel site approved by the tribe. The site was approved by the tribe December 1, 1964, but the papers hit one bottle neck after the other." When the presiding bishopric finally received the resolution on April 1, 1965, there was "much rejoicing of both Indian and non-Indian members of the Branch."[15]

By the 1970s the mission leaders had developed a way to work directly with the chapters to receive permission to build chapels. This approach included first asking an influential Native American Church leader to request time on the chapter agenda. All Latter-day Saints in the area would attend the meeting, during which a Diné representative would present on behalf of the local congregation. The guidelines emphasized that the Church was a guest on the reservation and should engage in a cordial discussion with no arguments. The meeting would start with a prayer, according to Church guidelines, and then focus on the wholesome activities the Church provided and the constitutional right for freedom of religion. The speakers would often stress how Latter-day Saints "believe that the Indian people are a choice and favored people in the eyes of God and that they will become a great people."

Church leaders also encouraged Diné missionaries, including those who had served full-time or shorter youth mission assignments, and ISPP students to share their testimonies of the Church. They highlighted notable stories of Diné Placement students, such as Nora Begay, who became Miss Indian America, and Bahe Billy, who earned a doctoral degree in agronomy. Diné Latter-day Saints paved the way for the establishment of Church meeting places as they did for the Southwest Indian Mission.

Securing a physical building constitutes only part of congregational life. Wherever a congregation meets, it sponsors activities that unify the members as a community. Besides a Sunday meeting that includes sacrament and talks, Latter-day Saints participate in separate programs for children, teenagers, and adults. While the types of activities have changed over the years, the programs have emphasized community service. The manuscript histories of the congregations on the reservation refer to programs that existed throughout the Church. From the 1920s to the 1960s, most wards organized various activities, which could have included a program every night of the week. Latter-day Saints held dances, sponsored Boy Scout troops, encouraged father-daughter dates, arranged basketball tournaments, and celebrated holidays like Easter, Christmas, and Halloween with parties. Diné congregations on the reservation listed these same activities along with service missionary and construction work on local Latter-day Saint chapels. Some aspects of activities stemmed directly from a Diné context such as the Relief Society bazaar's Navajo tacos.

SHADOW LEADERSHIP

When the Church extends to a new area, Church officials may create a branch that depends on another ward or branch for assistance with leadership and organization. As the branch grows and the members learn more about Church procedure, the congregation becomes independent, and more people are available for staffing, administrating, and teaching positions. On the Navajo reservation, Church authorities followed a slightly different approach. To train Diné Latter-day Saint leaders, Spencer W. Kimball and Golden Buchanan used what they referred to as "shadow leadership," an approach that aligned with a colonial paternalistic assumption that Diné needed supervised training in their positions, unlike most other Latter-day Saint leaders. Buchanan and Church officials intended for Native Americans to sense "responsibility" in their local congregations, but they assigned missionaries or "Anglo" Latter-day Saints "who had been in the Church a long time" to support each Native American priesthood leader even if the "assistant" would "have to do 90 percent of the work."[16] A white American woman and the Chinle Stake primary president, Winna B. Kalauli, described in 1991 how this policy affected Diné Latter-day Saints: "The general feeling when you have an Anglo and Lamanite [is] a Lamanite will step back and they will let the Anglos take the lead." Because she believed in this tendency, she tried to be "really careful" and "to hold back because I don't want to dominate."[17]

Former SWIM president Dale Tingey referred to Kimball, who "insisted on having the Native Americans participate rather than let the Anglos assume the leadership positions and do most of the teaching. He and President Tuttle . . . would always say: 'We want participation, Dale, not perfection.'"[18]

Kimball felt that when Church leaders focused on encouraging Diné to participate in Church functions, rather than meeting a "perfect" standard, more Diné would embrace the Church and lifeways to follow Christ. The histories of several congregations illustrate the varying experiences in Diné wards and branches and how Diné Latter-day Saints shaped their community spaces. Some of the branches lasted a short period of time while others have remained. The branches varied in size and activities. The two cases presented here, the Lee Branch, or later known as the Window Rock Ward, and the Tuba City Ward, trace the formation of two strong congregations that continue to gather Diné Latter-day Saints. Church records and oral histories provide rich resources in reconstructing their histories.

LEE BRANCH AND WINDOW ROCK WARD, ST. MICHAELS

The same congregation of my early childhood memories, the Window Rock Ward, is one of the strongest wards in Diné Bikéyah. It meets in St. Michaels, the area of Window Rock and the headquarters of the Navajo Nation. Diné call the landmark "window" in the towering sandstone formations Tséghá-hoodzání or the "Perforated Rock," which signifies the region. Diné have told stories of ałk'idą́ą́ or long ago, when the Wind pitied the people because a vicious snake was terrorizing and turning them into stone. The Wind created the hole in a large rock wall with its breath, through which the people chased and exiled the snake.[19] Tségháhoodzání still stands as a symbol of Diné peoplehood, ingenuity, and blessing.

Not far from Tségháhoodzání, a Latter-day Saint trader, Lester Lee, owned a trading post across the street from the St. Michael Indian School. The area of Ts'ihootso, or "Green Meadow," became known as St. Michaels because of the Catholic mission that Mother Katharine Drexel started at the turn of the twentieth century. Drexel founded the Sisters of the Blessed Sacrament, and Pope John Paul II canonized her as a saint in 2000. Beginning in 1902, Franciscan missionaries opened the Catholic school for Diné youth with the support of local Diné and funding from Mother Drexel.[20] Lee held a ninety-nine-year lease on the land of his trading post, which he donated to the Church of Jesus Christ of Latter-day Saints.[21] In 1950 the Church initiated the building of a chapel on the donated land through the service and work of local Latter-day Saints for a branch. To honor Lester Lee, Church leaders named the branch after him.

An official branch was organized in 1960, and the branch supported service missionaries who worked on an $80,000 expansion to the meetinghouse in 1963. Church leaders called several Diné Latter-day Saints to serve as the "labor missionaries." They completed 20 percent of the construction, and SWIM president Edwin Baird praised their work: "Navajos can help show the Church and the tribe that we mean business. Your lives and testimonies will go into this building, and it will belong to you." Baird recognized the building as the first of its kind in the mission and as the fourth meetinghouse constructed on the reservation in four years. Since the chapel was larger than other buildings, Diné Latter-day Saints from various wards and branches throughout the region attended meetings there.[22]

The new addition was completed in 1965. According to Church policy at that time, the Church had to pay completely for a building and its construction before its dedication. Since the branch had not finished fundraising its required percentage of the construction cost, General Authority A. Theodore Tuttle did not dedicate the building until October 13, 1968. With much anticipation, 120 people came to the dedication instead of the usual ten to fifty members who attended the regular Sunday meetings.[23]

The Lee Branch continued as part of SWIM until 1972, when it was transferred to a geographical stake, the Arizona Snowflake Stake. Ernesteen Lynch remembered that when she was baptized in 1979, she "joined the neatest church," which had been renamed the Window Rock Ward. She had since attended many wards but emphasized that "your first ward as a convert always seems to be the most special." To her, what made it so extraordinary was "we had half Navajos and half Anglos, but we were not Navajos on one side and Anglos on the other side." At the time, she noticed that the "bishop was a Samoan . . . he was not white. His wife was white." She describes the ward as a "true community": "Whenever there was a potluck, we were all there. When somebody came, we welcomed them to the church. We always shook hands with everybody and talked to everybody that came just visiting. It was . . . a really solid group of people."[24]

Reflecting on my family's time in the Window Rock Ward between 1989 and 1990, my mother, JoAnn Smith, appreciated visiting teaching and how a friend in the ward helped her prepare for delivering her baby at the Fort Defiance hospital by advising her about the hospital protocol. My mother also reminisces about times when the ward gathered and members would share fun stories. She recalls how one member, Leroy Gishi, could make everyone laugh by telling stories of his mission when he froze his pillowcases to sleep at night because of the extreme heat. The ward hosted dances and other family events, which our family attended.

My mother served as a counselor in the ward Primary Presidency, and my father, Phillip Smith, taught Sunday School in Diné bizaad. My parents had six children at the time, and my mother was pregnant with her seventh child who was born in 1990. My older brother was a freshman in high school and started seminary in the ward, which posed certain challenges for my family. He was the only seminary student as one of the few active Latter-day Saint teenagers in the area, and the seminary instructor often did not come to their scheduled meetings. The younger children in our family played and became friends with other children in the ward. The ward provided a community and home for my family when we lived in Window Rock, especially since we resided far from our extended family and struggled sometimes to relate with other Diné in the region because of our mixed ancestry and religious background.[25]

Shaela Willie Avery, a Diné Latter-day Saint who was raised attending the Window Rock Ward, acknowledges exemplary Diné Latter-day Saints for sustaining the ward. She mentions one ward member who was educated through ISPP and had endured tragedies, such as losing her husband and a child as an adult. Despite these challenges, Avery noticed that this fellow congregant "stayed close to the Church and stuck with it. I see her reach out to other people and help them. It is her going out and showing that love to others and showing them how, 'Yes, this can be a part of our lives' that really helps people come back [to the Church]."[26] Members of the ward showed dedication toward one another in their interactions at church and home. Laura Brown, who left the Church for a while with her husband Romero after the excommunication of George P. Lee, felt that same closeness. She had dreamed of seeing her deceased son, who told her: "Thank you for your prayers and thank the Deschines [a family in the Window Rock Ward]." Brown believes that her son recognized the Deschines because of their service with family history in the ward.[27] The Window Rock Ward fostered family history and temple work as other Latter-day Saint congregations did, which bonded the Diné Latter-day Saint community.

When historian Jessie Embry and I were researching and conducting oral histories with Diné Latter-day Saints in the early 2000s, I visited the Window Rock Ward, which was predominately Diné. In the sacrament meeting that I attended, a Diné woman, Rose McCabe, spoke about her conversion to the Church. The second speaker, Shelby Willie, Shaela Avery's younger sister, gave her "farewell" talk before leaving for a mission to Guatemala. After her talk, a group of friends joined her in singing a spiritual song as part of the service. The young women were all dressed in traditional Diné clothing such as the biil, or Diné rug dress, and moccasins. The bishop was Shelby's father, Jerome Willie, who concluded the meeting by sharing his testimony of the Latter-day Saint faith. All the speakers on that Sunday con-textualized their experiences and conversion to the Latter-day Saint faith as Diné raised on the reservation. They cared for livestock like many Diné, and their connection to Diné Bikéyah people and culture shaped their outlook on the world and their personal decision to affiliate with and serve in the Church.

After the sacrament meeting, I attended a Relief Society session, during which the instructor applied ancestral Diné teachings. She wrote Diné terms of "Hweʼodlą́" on the blackboard with "Hajoobaʼahwunidzin," "Jijooba," and "Hahajoobáʼi," which she associated with gospel principles of faith, hope, charity, and humility. Between and after church meetings, I conversed with several of the members about their children and families. In one meeting I sat next to an elderly mother and grandmother of the Tulley family who spoke only Diné bizaad. According to Diné custom, I greeted her respect-fully as shímá sání, "my grandmother," and introduced myself in Diné bizaad. The Church has provided a space for such community-building among Diné Latter-day Saints. Diné dóó Gáamalii call each other "brother" and "sister," as do most members of the Church, but we also recognize that we are kʼé, or kin, through our clans and ties to Diné heritage.

The Window Rock Ward has evolved since its founding in the 1960s. In 1992 the president of the Chinle Stake, Edwin I. Tano, considered Window Rock one of the strongest wards in the stake while some other congrega-tions were "barely hanging on." The Window Rock Ward attendance ranged from 165 to 180 members in the 1990s.[28] During the early 2000s, when I visited the ward, the congregation had recently sent its young adults to serve missions abroad, and attendance primarily comprised Diné members with a minority of white members. A Diné bishop presided, and Romero Brown served as one of the first Diné stake presidents.

Some members believed that the ward would continue to grow and as-sume an important role in Diné Bikéyah. David Flake, a white American Latter-day Saint who served in the Window Rock Ward bishopric, wished for a stake center in the area. Stake president Romero Brown also clung to that hope. He envisioned that one day the Church would open a temple—a

House of the Lord dedicated to sacred purposes through which the most devout members of the Church may enter—in the Navajo Nation which has yet to come to pass. Diné Latter-day Saints built a fortress community of the Latter-day Saint faith among Native Americans from the small Lee Branch, weathering many obstacles and trials that Diné congregants continue to face. Diné heritage and culture supported the foundation for the ward and its members, unifying them.

TO'NANEES'DIZI

A Diné elder, Robert Begay, once told me why Diné call my birthplace To'Nanees'Dizi: "It means there is a stream of water in all directions. So, that's how it is here [in Tuba City]. If you take a pole seven feet deep, you'll dig into some kind of underground river. It's just water in all directions here. So, that's why it's called To'Nanees'Dizi."[29] The term "To'Nanees'Dizi" translates as "tangled waters," referring to the springs that Begay delineated to me. To'Nanees'Dizi, also known as Tuba City, is a hub for Diné and Hopi peoples with one of the largest populations in the Navajo Nation.

Histories of land disputes have affected To'Nanees'Dizi and its communities. Some white Latter-day Saint settlers entered and began to live in the area, beginning in the 1850s, but the US federal government forced them to leave by 1903.[30] Hopi and Diné have vied for influence and land claims for generations, resulting in forced Diné relocations that devastated their families and fueled mineral extraction in the region during the late twentieth century.[31] In a meeting with the Navajo Tribal Council in 1961, Walter Wolf revealed how some Diné remembered the origins of the Navajo-Hopi Land Dispute: "This problem in Moencopi started about 1876 when Jacob Hamblin led a group of Mormons into that country and made a settlement there. Apparently, some Hopis . . . migrated into this area and sought the protection of the Mormon settlers in the area."[32] After the expulsion of LDS settlers, their early presence remains visible through a trading post and a few names carved into some rock edifices of the landscape. According to a Navajo Nation report from 1996, however, Latter-day Saints represented one of the largest religious groups in To'Nanees'Dizi with an estimated twelve hundred members.[33]

Some Diné Latter-day Saints drew connections between their lives in the twentieth century and those of earlier Latter-day Saint settlers from the nineteenth century. Some of these connections even startled them. Virginia Butler, a Diné Latter-day Saint, for example, recalls her sister's frightening experience babysitting overnight for a bishop who lived near what was then a Latter-day Saint chapel and a cemetery of the LDS settlers. In the middle of the night, her sister suddenly awakened to see "a little pioneer girl with blonde hair standing in front of her." Unsettled by the apparition, her sister refused to return to babysit for that family, but Butler interprets the incident as evidence that "we have a lot of rich history here as far as pioneers go."[34] Although the appearance of the "pioneer girl" upset her sister, Butler recognized it as a sign that Latter-day Saint presence remains in To'Nanees'Dizi through generations.

In the twentieth century SWIM's initial missionary couples, Albert R. and Gladys Lyman and George and Lucy Bloomfield, proselytized in Tuba City. They taught and converted people in the area but struggled to secure a place to worship. The Lymans started to hold meetings in the Babbitt trading post. Lyman later reported to the mission president, Ralph Evans, that the missionaries arranged gatherings at members' homes because they did not have permission from the Diné tribal government to host other meetings.

The Latter-day Saint missionaries viewed the Hopi as more receptive to their message. In 1949 the Bloomfields rented a house to serve as a chapel in the Hopi village of Moenkopi. Two years later the mission organized a branch for both Hopi and Diné congregants. The Church then leased property in the village and built a chapel there in 1953, and the branch eventually paid a portion of its construction. Apostle Spencer W. Kimball later dedicated a new church building, which the Church completed in 1965.[35]

Some Diné Latter-day Saints from Tuba City remember attending church in the Hopi village. As a missionary, Ray Pooley proselytized several months in the area and recalls that "almost seventy-five percent of the people in Moenkopi were members of the Church," and many Hopi were baptized. When he and his wife moved to Tuba City for work, however, very few members participated consistently in the local Latter-day Saint congregation. Furthermore, Church officials divided the area membership into two branches: a Hopi and non-Native American branch and a Diné branch. Pooley noticed that the ward grew as students returned from ISPP and more members moved to the region.[36]

When the Hopi Tribe decided not to renew the lease for the Church in Moenkopi, Church officials began to search for another place to build a chapel.[37] In the 1940s they identified private lands they could possibly buy, including the Babbitt property of traders in Tuba City. The Babbitts were Catholics who had given some land to their church. They were friends of Harvey Gardner, the stake president in Page, Arizona, and he had frequently asked if they would sell land to the Church. After a heavy snowstorm that partly destroyed one of the Babbitts' business buildings in Flagstaff, Gardner's company repaired the building. When the Babbitts asked how they could repay him, Gardner arranged for the Church to buy some of their land to construct a stake center in Tuba City.[38]

Building a chapel required a heavy financial sacrifice for the local Native American members. When my dad was bishop of the Tuba City Ward in the 1980s, the Church required local members to raise 10 percent of the chapel construction costs. Recognizing socioeconomic disparities on the reservation, Church officials asked Latter-day Saints in Tuba City to provide for 6 percent of the expenses. My dad remembers that they tried to fundraise primarily through "a variety of bake sales and yard sales." Despite these efforts, the Tuba City members did not raise enough money by the deadline the Church had set to begin construction. My dad recounts that "then a true miracle happened": "We were short $3,000, and we had been fasting and praying. There was a missionary couple who had served there named the Cannons. They sold some land, and they wrote a letter addressed to the 'Bishop of the Tuba City Ward' . . . [and] sent money to be used on behalf of the ward. The money was the exact amount that we needed to proceed with the chapel."[39] My father has shared this experience with me and others as an example of a test and blessing of faith. Such experiences form composites of his testimony and conviction of the Church and its gospel. Other Diné Latter-day Saints also acknowledged this miracle, such as Lillie Pooley, who remembers that having a stake center "was a joy. It was something that we really all prayed for."[40] These "miracle" moments reinforced a collective sense of discipleship and a community of believers among Diné Latter-day Saints in To'Nanees'Dizi.

In 2012 two wards met in the chapel in To'Nanees'Dizi. Most of the members attending were Diné. One elderly Hopi woman attended the Tuba City First Ward when Embry and I visited the ward. After I asked one congregant why fewer Hopi attended, he simply replied that they no longer wanted to. Another member heard that Church officials once considered organizing three wards in Tuba City because half of the town had been baptized. The Tuba City Second Ward estimated having three to five thousand members on the rolls, but fewer than two hundred people attended the meetings. As a result, the few "active" members carried a heavy load for the congregation. Virginia Butler, for example, began to worry when the bishop asked her to accept a fifth calling, a type of service assignment and position, in the ward.[41]

Rex Black of the Tuba City First Ward became increasingly involved in the Church and embraced his priesthood callings when he realized that non-Diné Latter-day Saints no longer came into the area to assume such leadership roles. Black and other Diné congregants considered callings more seriously when they had the opportunity to fulfill them and learn from the experiences of leadership and service.[42]

Lack of activity and service had continued to challenge the Tuba City wards. When my dad served as a bishop there were fifteen hundred members in his ward, but only 0.01 percent of them did their home teaching (when church members visit and help fellow members of the same congregation).[43] The stake president advised him to contact the "inactive" members to ask if they would like to be removed from the membership rolls. None of the inactive members that he reached wanted to be excluded from the ward register. Frustrated, my dad described families that had participated in ISPP and "were doing well as far as the world is concerned," but they did not interact with the Church and congregation. He worried that "their children were not being taught the gospel." He claimed that the inactive members would often suffer when their youth lost direction, "acting out and getting involved in alcohol," substance abuse, and premarital "sexual activities." My dad thought the answer to their distress was the need to raise their families with gospel teachings and values.[44]

Some Diné Latter-day Saints appreciate that many of the programs in the Tuba City wards are standard throughout the Church. Liz Nez is "grateful that no matter where I go in this Church it is the same. We teach the same; we preach the same; we testify of the same things."[45] Charlene Manygoats agrees that "no matter what branch, what ward you go to in another town in another state we are all studying the same gospel principles."[46] Nez and Manygoats, like other committed Diné Latter-day Saints, find affirmation in being part of a larger community and network of Latter-day Saints throughout the world.

Service and participation in worldwide Church programs resonated with Manygoats, who referred specifically to how her calling with Young Women inspired her to attend church. She avoided the Church for a while, but she started to become more engaged with her local congregation as a Young

Women's program leader. Manygoats reflects on her experiences with the Young Women's program: "I was able to find myself through the different values and the different activities." As the Relief Society president in 2012, she focused on caring for the "sisters" of the ward and teaching them the importance of visiting teaching. Manygoats noticed how her service in various church programs strengthened her own sense of being and purpose. Virginia Butler acknowledged how her faith grew through her church callings as the ward primary president, stake primary president, area seminary instructor, and coordinator of youth programs such as Boy Scouts. Although her career as an emergency medical technician demanded much of her energy, she felt blessed to devote time to these roles in her congregation since she learned the scriptures more herself while serving youth.[47]

Some common church activities such as reenactments of the Latter-day Saint pioneer trek conveyed mixed, ironic, and distasteful messages for Native American congregations. A teenager in the Franklin Second Ward, a Native American ward in Provo, Utah, responded incredulously when invited to a pioneer trek with fellow Native American youth: "What do you want us to do? Attack the wagon train?" In the Tuba City Latter-day Saint community, Liz and Harlan Nez decided to participate as the "ma and pa" for a pioneer trek reenactment to show how the pioneers overcame their obstacles and to teach Diné youth that they could do the same. Liz wanted to directly assist the youth during the trek, but the adults could only watch them. She compared that experience to "how Heavenly Father and Jesus Christ are. They see us struggling, but we have to overcome it and say, 'Yes, I did that. I can do it.'" Her husband Harlan learned about the importance of commitment, remembering: "For a long time I used to wonder why the pioneers did what they did." The trek reenactment taught him "it was because of their faith and their belief that they would be willing even to sacrifice their lives for what was right." He stated that "sometimes, I was not that committed. I realized that I needed to be that committed. I needed to be willing to sacrifice my life for the truth—for the gospel—because it is really worth it."[48]

To most Latter-day Saints, including Diné dóó Gáamalii, entering the temple symbolizes serious commitment to the Church and the gospel it teaches. Members of the Tuba City area were assigned to attend the Snowflake Temple, a three-hour drive, but the temples in Monticello, Mesa, and St. George were within three hours on the road as well. For Liz Nez, temple attendance brought her closer to God: "It is where I commune with

Heavenly Father the most and renew my covenants and remind myself that I am going to stay true and that I want to go back to the celestial kingdom."[49] Diné Latter-day Saints such as Liz Nez viewed church and temple service as opportunities for blessings that enriched their lives and future.

In 2009 the Tuba City Stake developed a gardening program to help members of the Church be more self-sufficient and to interest inactive and non-members. The ward gardens added to the spaces where the Diné Latter-day Saint community grew. Stake president Larry Justice, a white business owner in Tuba City, helped arrange for missionary married couples to grow area gardens. Ruth Littlefield and her husband, for example, received their mission call in February 2012, sending them to the Navajo Nation by the following month. They came with a recreational vehicle for their lodging, and the Church provided hookups. Littlefield believed that "the garden program was truly inspired by Larry Justice. . . . It has helped activate people." The program had eleven hundred gardens and twenty missionary couples in 2012. Liz Nez also praised the program: "It has brought a lot of people coming and looking at things. The garden is just like a testimony" because the people can watch both grow.[50] In 2013 the *New York Times* featured these LDS gardening projects in an article, "Some Find Path to Navajo Roots through Mormon Church," which asserted: "In a land troubled by dysfunction and despair, a growing number of Navajos have been turning to the Mormon Church."[51] My parents worked with missionary couples in Monument Valley to start their own garden, growing corn, flowers, squash, and various vegetables they shared with Diné community, as well as their relatives. Community members often complimented them on their garden, and it became a sign of welcome in the area. Some Diné embraced many of the Church programs such as youth programs and gardening to enliven their families and people.

When Jessie Embry and I attended the Tuba City wards in April 2012, Edwin Tano, the past stake president of both the Chinle and Tuba City stakes, arranged for us to interview some of the leaders in the wards. We attended the sacrament meeting in the Tuba City Second Ward. I attended all the classes for that ward, including a Sunday School class in Diné Bizaad instructed by Ray Mitchell, a former bishop in Tuba City. Mitchell taught about how the scriptures can restore hózhǫ, using Navajo language to explain church doctrine. All the meetings used a format and order of service very similar to other wards that I have attended. A member of the bishopric

Chinle Latter-day Saint Stake gardens, 2011, Navajo Nation. Courtesy of author.

invited the congregation to bear testimony, and I stood and spoke of my family's experiences in the area when my father, Phillip Smith, served as the bishop. When I was an infant, my father and fellow Diné Latter-day Saints labored, fasted, and prayed that the Church would build a chapel for them. As an adult, I returned to To'Nanees'Dizi to find how Diné Latter-day Saints have developed a gathering place where they continue to grow.

CH'ÍNÍLĮ́

One of the other first stakes in the Navajo Nation is centered in Ch'ínílĮ́, or Chinle, which translates as "where the water flows out," since water flows from the nearby Tséyi' or Canyon de Chelly.[52] Water carved the sandstone cliffs of Tséyi', "the place within the rocks," shaping spires and fertile grounds of the canyons that people have cultivated and sustained over generations for millennia. By the late nineteenth century, Diné returned to Tséyi' and developed the surrounding town of Ch'ínílĮ́ after the destruction and forced removal of the Long Walk era. Latter-day Saint presence did not grow noticeably in the area until the second half of the twentieth century through the Southwest Indian Mission.

During the existence of SWIM, the congregations within the Navajo Nation were assigned to its jurisdiction. The mission presidents organized the branches into districts that created a second level of administrative leadership, and white American leaders usually presided over these districts. For example, after serving as the branch president in Chinle, Ernst Young was called as the district leader for the Central Navajo District. According to Young, the goal of the district was to promote the Church among Diné. Young recalled: "We worked with as many Navajos as we could."[53]

In 1965 the Church divided the Central Navajo District and created the Chinle District with thirteen hundred members and six small branches. When church authorities first called Young as a district president, Apostle Boyd K. Packer told him to establish a stake in five years. Young privately questioned this goal, predicting that it would be at least twenty-five years before Chinle and the surrounding area could support a stake. Stakes require a committed Latter-day Saint membership, which includes a number of priesthood leaders. Chinle became a stake headquarters in thirty-five years.

After the Church changed SWIM into a geographical mission in 1971, the branches were assigned to nearby stakes that extended beyond the Navajo Nation. Church leaders like Spencer W. Kimball hoped that the Church would eventually establish five stakes within SWIM boundaries, in Kayenta, Chinle, Tuba City, Polacca, and Page. Harvey Gardner explained how a stake was finally organized in Chinle. He had suggested a stake to the Church leaders several times, but authorities like Apostle Packer insisted that a stake required a greater number of priesthood holders.[54]

As a regional representative with jurisdiction over several stakes that bordered the Navajo Nation, Gardner and stake presidents from Blanding, Page, Gallup, Holbrook, and Winslow asked General Authority H. Burke Peterson for a Navajo stake in 1990. The stake presidents promised that they would "shepherd the new stake" and "train and strengthen leaders." They believed that "there is a feeling of readiness that we perceive throughout the reservation," especially given an increased number of returned missionaries. Winslow Stake president Dale Patton also described how Diné responded better to Native American leadership and how predominantly Anglo-American stakes struggled to serve Diné congregations because of physical and cultural distance.[55]

In response to this letter from area stake presidents, the General Authorities agreed to create the Chinle Stake in 1990. The initial boundaries covered 25,000 square miles on the Navajo Nation and 10,000 square miles on the Hopi Reservation, and they included twelve wards and branches.[56] The stake had only 149 Melchizedek Priesthood holders, but its records showed ten thousand baptized members.[57] While the stake was created shortly after George P. Lee's excommunication, most Diné and local Latter-day Saints did not dwell on the possible connections between the two events. Church officials called Edwin Tano, a Kanaka ʻŌiwi (Native Hawaiian) former SWIM elder, as the first Chinle Stake president. Tano spoke Diné bizaad, lived in Diné Bikéyah, and was married to a Diné woman. Tano remembers that "I spoke my mind" when he received the calling: "The day of the Lamanite people to be hand-fed, patted on their heads and constantly reminded that they were a chosen people had to come to an end if they would even expect to rise to their true stature." Tano felt that many Diné Latter-day Saints had "mimicked, copied, parodied, all of the good things of the gospel," but they were only going "through the motions" without understanding the basic doctrine.[58]

Some Diné Latter-day Saints perceived the formation of the Chinle Stake as a watershed moment, reinforcing Diné participation and authority over their own congregations. James Lee Dandy from Blanding believed that many "Lamanites will get involved" because they "feel inside that this is their stake." Ruby Whitesinger Benally of Ganado, who served in the Stake Relief Society Presidency in 1997, claims: "I feel more of our own identity, more of a cohesion" with the creation of the stake.[59] With their shared backgrounds and identities as Diné Latter-day Saints, the members of the Chinle Stake would unite and persist in their faith.[60] William Numkena, a Hopi man who served as the stake patriarch, considered the stake "a step upward, one step higher from when the mission field was opened up here [in Chinle]." Numkena thought that "if the members understood what we are working for, I am sure they would work a lot harder to reactivate their members."[61]

Mitchell Davis Kapuni Kalauli, bishop of the Tuba City Ward in 1992, recalled being a missionary in the area during the 1960s. The branches were so small that the Primary children went to seminary, which normally only high school students attended. Since Chinle had become a stake center, he had seen the Church grow in numbers and leadership. More members were worthy of attending the temple and found ways to go more often. More leaders and auxiliaries fully staffed wards. Kalauli believed that when leadership was "local," the stake "flourish[ed]."

Kalauli remembered, however, the early hardships of the stake. Although there were 2,000 members on record, only 225 attended meetings in Tuba City. Many Diné youth were baptized for ISPP or other reasons, for example, but they discontinued their participation in the Church. Members turned to the bishop rather than to assigned home teachers for help, and active members had to assume a lot of the responsibility.[62] Some miscommunication between stake and branch leaderships caused several unexpected cancellations of activities.[63] Dan K. Smith, a Diné Latter-day Saint convert and a member of the stake, first viewed the stake boundaries as too large, but he soon became convinced that the expansive boundaries provided necessary experiences for Native American members to become more independent and confident in the Church. While he appreciated the help that Native American congregations received from other stakes, as a branch president twice, a counselor, and a district president, he felt that Diné Latter-day Saints needed less assistance from non–Native American members. He also described how some Diné resented that the stake president was not a Diné elder from the region.[64]

Despite such challenges, the Church became an extension and support of family for faithful Diné Latter-day Saints. Doug Roe, the high councilor assigned to the Steamboat Branch, praised a Diné branch president, Peter Lee Yazzie, for his commitment and diligence that sustained the branch. Yazzie worked with the missionaries and other Latter-day Saints to continue branch activities and meetings, inviting members to return to church. He did not lose hope even when his family were the only ones present at some church meetings.[65]

By the 1990s, numerous Diné Latter-day Saints of the Chinle Stake served in their congregations and were willing to sacrifice for their faith. More active members accepted callings, paid tithing, and served missions. Local members contributed to the missionaries' expenses, building the familial feelings of support. In 1997 Tano reflected on the Chinle Stake: "I am learning that the Lord has his hand in the work by the growth and changes in people and the progress we are making in our building construction projects and in the parcels of land we have requested from the local chapters upon which we will eventually build legitimate LDS chapels."[66] In 1995 Diné Latter-day Saints not only sustained the Chinle Stake through their devotion but could then celebrate the creation of the Tuba City Stake, the second stake on the Navajo reservation.

The mutual relationship between space and community continues to influence Diné Latter-day Saint congregations as they persist and grow. Diné Latter-day Saints prioritize a meeting place, such as chapels, where they feel at home and build their community. In 2013 I visited the Lukachukai Ward of the Chinle Stake when the ward was meeting on the Diné College campus in Tsaile. The bishop at the time, Ralph Begay, and other local members explained to me how the ward had been trying to open their own chapel for decades. Most of the Navajos on the ward membership rolls did not attend church regularly, and so the ward lacked the required participant numbers to request a chapel. Many of the inactive members told Church leaders that they did not go to church because the congregation did not have their own chapel.

Church leaders in the area then started a petition, receiving over a hundred signatures by which Diné members promised to attend meetings if the Church constructed a chapel for the ward. A local representative in the Navajo Tribal Council supported the Latter-day Saint requests for building a church in Tsaile. After much praying and fasting of the congregation, the Navajo Nation's tribal government granted the Church permission to build the chapel, and its construction was scheduled for some time between 2013 and 2014. As of 2023 the chapel stands in Tsaile where Latter-day Saints gather from the area. In 2022 I talked with the former stake president, Romero Brown, about the Tsaile chapel. He told me how a local Diné man, who was not a Latter-day Saint, allowed for the use and building of the church on his land as long as he could access a hitching post on the grounds for his horse when he rode to the site.[67] The Lukachukai Ward, like most congregations in the Navajo Nation, has created their own space where they nurture their community and expand Diné Latter-day Saint networks.

Over the years, wards and stakes in the Navajo Nation have provided a place for Diné members of the Church to worship and serve one another. During the late twentieth century, church leaders overcame difficulties in earning trust and permission to open chapels on the Navajo reservation with the support of Diné congregations. The wards and branches have functioned much the same as other Latter-day Saint congregations, regardless of their distinct cultural and geographical concerns. Yet the increased migrations of Diné Latter-day Saints away from Diné Bikéyah presented other challenges. The Church responded initially by creating specialized units for Diné and other Native American members who lived away from their ancestral homelands, but church leaders later dissolved most of these "Lamanite" wards and branches by the twenty-first century. Only a few of these off-reservation congregations designated for Native Americans have remained into the twenty-first century, which the next chapter examines.

The histories of Native American congregations demonstrate how Diné Latter-day Saints have formed communities centered in spaces of the Church. Community was the key to following the pathway to eternal happiness, *hool'aahgo il' hózhǫ* in Diné bizaad, since Diné Latter-day Saints, like other converts of the Church, believed that they needed to support one another to build Zion and one day return to their heavenly parents.

Beginning in 2020, the outbreaks of COVID-19 in Diné Bikéyah tested Diné Latter-day Saint communities, as the Navajo Nation faced some of the direst circumstances of the pandemic. My parents continued to attend the Monument Valley Ward, but Diné congregations began to meet only online and moved their meetings to virtual spaces. Many Navajos live with health and socioeconomic disparities and lack access to clean running water on the reservation, which fueled the rapid spread and devastation of COVID-19 to a point where 2,500 Diné per 100,000 residents were infected in the Navajo Nation by May 2020.[68]

The Church of Jesus Christ of Latter-day Saints responded with various initiatives, which local Diné Latter-day Saints supported. These programs and efforts included partnerships with farmers to provide sheep and supplies to Navajos; Operation Firewood Rescue to prepare and deliver firewood from fallen trees after a storm on the Wasatch front of northern Utah; and coordination between Church members, leaders, tribal government, area health services, and full-time missionaries to launch and sustain humanitarian projects.[69] The Tuba City Stake center became "a sewing center for fabricating masks and hospital gowns."[70] My parents would share photos of themselves with ward members and volunteers, helping package and distribute donated food and supplies to the Diné community around them.

Diné Latter-day Saints also mourned with those who lost their livelihoods and loved ones. President Ollie Whaley of the Tuba City Stake expressed the sorrows of their Latter-day Saint community when they held a graveside service for a thirty-one-year-old member of their stake after the coronavirus caused his death: "It was a very sad thing." As president of the Chinle Stake at the time, Romero Brown asserted that in the face of such suffering and hardship: "many of our people are evaluating their lives and renewing their commitment to the gospel."[71] Diné dóó Gáamalii have rallied and persevered in faith together even when forced to remain physically distant during such unprecedented challenges. My father, as a Diné physician practicing in the middle of the pandemic hotspots, held onto his faith more than ever, reassuring me when his sister, my aunt Florence, died of COVID-19 in May 2020 that we will see her again. Wards and congregations have reminded many Diné Latter-day Saints that all people are family.

CHAPTER FIVE

Beyond Diné Bikéyah

Although I have focused primarily on congregations in Diné Bikéyah, Diné, like many other Native Americans, have relocated to cities and different areas for schooling, employment, and various reasons. Many of them have settled in communities near their homelands, and others headed to distant urban centers. Some Diné Latter-day Saints, for example, moved to Utah for wage-earning work opportunities and proximity to other Latter-day Saints. In cities with a strong Native American presence, church leaders have occasionally organized branches and wards specifically for Native Americans. These congregations follow the pattern of other specialized units in the Church, but with a few differences.

This chapter examines various dynamics of Native American wards and branches beyond Diné Bikéyah that include Diné members by delving into the history of a specific Native American ward, known as the Franklin Second Ward, in Provo, Utah. Border-town spaces adjacent to the Navajo Nation but technically off the reservation also present complicated contexts for Diné Latter-day Saint experiences, which require attention in future discourses and studies. My family has lived in or near border towns, which shaped one of my relative's perceptions that white Latter-day Saints "love the Lamanites, but they hate the Indians."[1] Border towns embody ongoing tensions between Native and non-Native communities and populations while they serve as hubs of entanglements between many different peoples who come together.

Although the Franklin Second Ward stems from unique origins as a former BYU Lamanite ward, as they were called, its history shows many of the same concerns that other Native American and specialized units have faced over the years. Some Native American Latter-day Saints have viewed separate ethnic or Native American wards as a form of colonialism and segregation, while others have regarded them as a way of preserving and bolstering Native American cultures in the Church. Diné Latter-day Saints have debated whether to support Native American specialized units beyond Diné Bikéyah. Some of them consider such units a "crutch" that limits Native Americans. Other Diné Latter-day Saints see them as necessary to fellowship and involve Native Americans in congregations. Despite such ongoing debates, Diné Latter-day Saint communities have grown outside of Diné Bikéyah in Native American congregational units, forming a space and presence based on their common heritage and experiences as Indigenous peoples.

As some church leaders questioned the organization of separate language and ethnic congregations, a debate intensified among the Quorum of the Twelve in 1966. Although Spencer W. Kimball rarely recorded details of quorum meetings in his journal, he once wrote: "I was so vigorous in my protestation [against eliminating ethnic branches] that the President did not take a vote on it." The quorum later referred the matter to the Indian and Minority Group Committee, which Kimball chaired. While Kimball did not receive complete support from the committee, they tabled the issue.[2] Golden Buchanan, who worked with the committee, explained that "there are those on the committee that think everything should be integrated."[3] In 1972 the Church also distributed a letter asking stakes to provide service opportunities for Latter-day Saints from underrepresented ethnic backgrounds within their wards. Some stake leaders interpreted the letter to mean that they should dissolve ethnic units; others asked to create new units.[4]

Church leaders introduced the Basic Unit Plan in 1977, a simplified church structure for small units, because of the growing concern for Native Americans who belonged to small and specialized congregations.[5] In 1980 Kimball presented the plan in an address titled "Aid Minorities" to regional and stake leaders: "We can no longer merely teach and preach to [minorities], but we must establish the Church among them."[6]

As Church authorities have formed and dissolved specialized units, confusion and alienation often spread among members of the respective units. In the early twenty-first century, the designated church leaders look at each case individually and adhere to the same procedure required when geographical wards and stakes petition to change their boundaries. The stake president, sometimes with recommendations from area leaders, applies to the boundary committee with information about the total membership, total men holding the Melchizedek Priesthood, and a proposed meeting place. A member of the Presidency of the Seventy who oversees the stake's area presidency recommends applications in the United States. The proposed change then proceeds to the First Presidency of the Church, who makes the final decision.[7]

FEDERAL GOVERNMENT INDIAN POLICY OF RELOCATION

As the Church focused on specialized units following World War II, the US government shifted its policy on ethnic and racial relations from separatism to integration. The federal government couched integration of Native Americans in terms of relocation, assimilation, and conformity to white American dominant society. In 1943 federal officials conducted studies that showed poor economic and educational opportunities on Native American reservations.[8] The investigators of this study placed responsibility for some of these terrible conditions on the Bureau of Indian Affairs and federal policies. American politicians began to claim that the Indian Reorganization Act had not improved tribal governance on the reservations. "Terminationist" legislators such as Utah senator Arthur V. Watkins devised plans to terminate the treaty-based relationship between the federal government and tribal nations, threatening Indigenous sovereignty and self-determination.[9]

Watkins and his followers contended that the federal government should treat Native Americans the same as other Americans, rather than wards of the government, by absorbing them as full citizens of the United States. But their "termination" policies and efforts primarily targeted the recognition and claims of Indigenous peoples as sovereign nations, especially Indigenous rights to their homelands under terms of treaties. In 1953 Congress passed a resolution declaring that tribal nations would be "freed from Federal supervision and control" if they approved termination.[10] Most tribal nations, including the Navajo Nation, did not approve the resolution and law. This policy started to change in 1961 when the federal government stopped emphasizing the program, which hurt tribal nations especially in Utah where Watkins piloted termination among Southern Paiutes.[11] Although I do not delve further into the background of Watkins and terminationist policies in this book, it is important to note that Watkins identified strongly as a Latter-day Saint, which raises questions about the influences of the Church and his interpretations of the Book of Mormon on his politics—which in turn affected Native Americans throughout the United States.[12] President Richard Nixon called for the end of the policy by 1970 and presented a new policy of "self-determination without termination."[13] This new strategy was "to strengthen the Indian's sense of autonomy without threatening his community."[14]

Nixon's idea of self-determination started in the 1950s just after the termination law passed with the Indian Relocation Act of 1956, which opened "job training centers" in major cities and paid for Native Americans to move to those areas.[15] As a result, an increasing number of Diné and other Native Americans relocated to cities like Los Angeles, Cleveland, Denver, Seattle, Dallas, Salt Lake City, and Chicago.[16] These newcomers often felt misplaced and lonely in their new surroundings.[17] Along with other churches, Latter-day Saint leaders established a special congregation in Southern California to address these feelings of displacement, which some Diné dóó Gáamalii attended. The Manuscript History of the Indian Branch, organized in Los Angeles on August 20, 1961, summarized that the branch was "to provide the Lamanite members of the Church with an opportunity to become active in an organized unit of the Church, to mingle with their own people, to serve in positions of responsibility, to grow in the gospel, and to have an opportunity to socialize and progress under the influence of the Church."[18] According to the Church records, in 1962, a married Diné couple, Shirley Hastine Yazzie and David J. Willie, attended the Los Angeles Indian Branch.[19] Several Native American congregations developed to sustain Native American Latter-day Saints, including Diné converts, which reflected intertribal community building and networking in cities since the relocation policies of the early postwar era.[20]

DEBATES ABOUT OFF-RESERVATION NATIVE AMERICAN WARDS

While Diné and non-Diné Latter-day Saints primarily debated about off-reservation Native American specialized units in terms of being either a "support" or a "crutch," some Diné appreciated how the separate wards provided an opportunity to serve and to be served in the Church. Diné Latter-day Saints have valued how Native American congregations encouraged the use of Diné bizaad (Navajo language), although the units conducted most of their work in English. I recognized the use of Diné bizaad when I attended the Franklin Second Ward in 2012. In Native American congregations, Native American Latter-day Saints also shared a mutual support in their religious and spiritual pathways. Audrey Boone remembers that "it was a neat experience to be in a group together where we were striving to help one another as Indian people in the Church." She adds that "it was good to see the Lamanites. We were trying to unite and strengthen one another as a group."[21] For Boone, she acknowledged not only fellow Native Americans in the Church but also what she believed were fellow descendants of "Lamanites" who mustered strength in their unity and gathering.

When Ernesteen Lynch struggled to fit into her geographical ward, she turned to a Native American ward. She felt people looked down on her in the non–Native American ward because she "was Lamanite, a single mother, and head of household." While members told her they loved and cared for her, their outreach often came in paternalistic and condescending forms. They treated her as if she was "not unique, distinctive, and special, but almost freaky, a negative connotation rather than a positive connotation." She enjoyed the Alma Ward, a Native American congregational unit, because everyone understood their Diné background and identity. The members of her previous ward judged her, and they belittled her and nonwhite members by telling them they "aren't doing it right" or properly living the gospel. Lynch stressed that geographical wards needed more "mutual understanding and respect." That respect did not develop after "one session of having somebody come in and talk about their Navajo experience in the Church. It takes a lot of listening and talking back. It takes a real focused effort to get that mutual respect going."[22] She believed that mutual respect was more feasible in a Native American congregation.

Although some Diné Latter-day Saints have found refuge and strength in Native American wards and branches off and on the reservation, they also referred to some setbacks and conflicts when congregations separate Native Americans from other non-Native members. Diné Latter-day Saint Arnold Yazzie recalls how tensions escalated when church authorities divided a stake along the border of the Navajo Nation and Farmington, New Mexico, region into separate wards: "All the Anglos had to go to Kirtland and all the Navajos stayed in Shiprock." Latter-day Saints in the area, such as Yazzie, perceived this reorganization of the stake as segregation, which disrupted families with "mixed marriages" of Anglo and Diné. Yazzie considered this separation of Anglo and Diné congregations a "mistake." He noted that "people even left the Church because of segregating people."[23]

As more Diné converged with many diverse peoples in different places, some of them likened Native American congregational units to racial or ethnic segregation. While living in Orem, Utah, one of my lifelong friends, Miriam Chun, expressed her decision not to join the Franklin Second Ward,

Miriam and Jarrett Chun, 2006, in Provo, Utah during an ice-skating activity with the Tribe of Many Feathers, the Native American student organization of Brigham Young University. Courtesy of author.

a nearby Native American congregation, in terms of inclusion and openness. Miriam and her husband, Jarrett, who is Kanaka ʻŌiwi (Native Hawaiian), "don't have a problem with the Lamanite ward," but they preferred to attend church based on geographical boundaries rather than cultural or ethnic designation.[24] Miriam respected that some members of the Native American ward "have a lot of pride in their culture," but they sometimes "exclude other cultures." Miriam added: "In the Church, they tell you to invite anyone in the Church, and it shouldn't have to be something distinguishing through skin color or ethnicity." She and Jarrett believe that they fulfill a Church calling to invite and welcome all peoples to a congregation regardless of race, ethnicity, and tribal affiliation by attending their geographical ward instead of the Native American ward. She frames this perspective by acknowledging that she and Jarrett can also meet and introduce different peoples to their respective cultures in a congregation: "It's just we would rather be more open than exclude ourselves."[25]

Some Diné Latter-day Saints reasoned that Native American specialized units limited Native American members by separating them from other Latter-day Saints in their neighborhoods and discouraging them from reaching out to diverse peoples. Although few off-reservation Native American congregations still exist, considering such criticism, the remaining units such as the Franklin Second Ward in Provo have established a presence and space for Diné Latter-day Saints who live away from Diné Bikéyah and Diné dóó Gáamalii communities.

THE FRANKLIN SECOND WARD: A NATIVE AMERICAN WARD IN PROVO, UTAH

Between 2011 and 2012, I attended the Franklin Second Ward of the Provo South Stake. As a Diné, I had the opportunity to participate in one of the last Latter-day Saint congregations designated for Native Americans. I remember one Sunday when the stake president, A. LeGrand Richards, stood before the ward Relief Society and asked the women in attendance if they had any questions for him. A member of the ward Relief Society presidency made a comment instead. Her voice quivered with emotion and tears filled her eyes when she told Richards how grateful she was that he "took in" the ward. She had been inactive from church service for seventeen years before she attended the ward, and she expressed how she probably would have remained inactive if not for the Native American ward that the stake president reorganized as a part of his area. Richards explained to the women in response how the ward fulfilled a promise from his patriarchal blessing.

Richards's patriarch told him that he would serve the "sons and daughters of Lehi." Most Latter-day Saints receive their patriarchal blessing in their youth, which they consider as a form of personal revelation and divine guidance in their lives. Richards believed that his role in organizing and working with the ward answered this part of his blessing. He also sensed that Native American Latter-day Saints in Utah County struggled to participate in their respective congregations. Richards told the women that he supported the Franklin Second Ward so that "none [of the Native American Latter-day Saints] fall through the cracks." The culture and ancestry that Native American Latter-day Saints shared strengthened their faith and participation in the Church especially away from their ancestral homelands and tribal nations. If the members of the Native American ward "step up to the plate" by working and running the ward functions and activities, according to Richards and other supporters of the ward, Native American Latter-day Saints of Utah County can gather as a congregation and encourage one another in the gospel.[26]

This brief history of the Franklin Second Ward highlights dynamics of specialized Native American wards that Diné Latter-day Saints have experienced. Several Native American student wards started on the BYU campus. One ward, the BYU 144th Ward, included many ethnic groups, including Latin Americans, Polynesians, African Americans, Asians, and anyone who felt different from the white majority at BYU. Unlike most BYU wards, Provo community members could also attend the BYU 144th Ward. Chauma Kee-Jansen, who is Diné and an enrolled member of the Assiniboine-Sioux Tribe, attended the BYU 144th Ward, which shaped how she started to identify with people of color. She remembers that the ward members "all came from families that had a culture different from the mainstream Mormon culture," describing how they bonded: "We were people of color on a big campus, where you feel like you were getting lost in the shuffle and in the crowds, and you were just trying to find your footing and your place . . . you were trying to figure out how to find your voice as well, as a person of color in the world."[27] Kee-Jansen found "comfort" and support in the BYU 144th Ward, because she and fellow congregants related to one another as people of color in a predominantly white church university and space.

In the 1990s Church leaders invited nonstudents to become part of the North Park Fifth Ward, a new congregational unit for Native American families in the North Park Stake. A Diné Latter-day Saint, April Yazzie, participated in the North Park Fifth Ward, which she remembers as "a big family." For April, church activities resembled family reunions: "We all knew each other. We always took care of each other. We'd always feed each other a lot. That's probably my favorite thing was when we got together because your parents have memories and then the kids just go off and run."[28]

This Native American congregational family wanted to stay together when Church officials dissolved the North Park Fifth Ward in 2005. In a sacrament meeting, stake leaders announced that they disbanded the ward without forewarning the congregation. Taran K. Chun (Wahiawā native and Kanaka ʻŌiwi), a counselor to Bishop Alvin Watchman (Diné), recalled how Watchman declared at a bishopric meeting on March 20, 2005: "Today, we are being released."[29]

The news of the ward's closure shocked most congregants such as the Young Men's president, Alan Groves (Northern Ute and Hopi). The ward had held the Priesthood Executive Committee (PEC) meeting that morning for all ward priesthood leaders, but only he and the bishopric attended it. When Groves proposed plans for future activities, the bishopric told him about some releases that day. Since Watchman had served as the bishop for ten years, Groves assumed that the stake would release him.

At the beginning of the sacrament meeting, the stake president announced that Church leaders dissolved the ward. The stake clerks then distributed letters informing the members about their new wards. Groves remembered the bewilderment and the tears, sensing that "for a lot of people it was a monumental time of their lives."[30] The decision to disband the ward disheartened Groves, for example, because the Young Men's program was growing. A Diné member of the ward, Brenda Beyal, remembers the "shock" and disappointment in response to the notification: "I don't think it was handled as well as it could have been handled. I think there were a lot of loose ends that were left."[31] Taran Chun worried about the future repercussions: "I remember vividly pacing back and forth in Bishop Watchman's office thinking of all the families I felt would fall by the wayside not having the opportunity to receive the blessings of this cultural ward."[32] Chun's concerns echoed worries that Latter-day Saint Native Americans could "fall through the cracks" in other congregations.

Even if they felt hurt and questioned the decision to dissolve the North Park Fifth Ward, most members followed the directions of their church leaders. Chun, as well as most of the ward, concluded: "In the end, I knew that if the direction came from the First Presidency of the Church, it came from the Lord, and I accepted the reality of this decision under the faith that I had in the inspired leadership of our church."[33]

Several Latter-day Saint Native Americans of the North Park Fifth Ward continued to attend church and worship with their Native American family congregation. They used whatever venues they could in the Church to bypass the official decision to dissolve the Native American congregational unit. The ward respected the leadership of the Church, but the members wanted to preserve their ward family. Former ward members immediately devised plans to petition for the reinstatement of the ward in another Provo stake.[34] Chun approached A. LeGrand Richards in hopes that he would accept the ward in his stake. Richards expressed his sympathy, but he pointed out that the Church was eliminating specialized wards without language requirements. Chun and his wife, a Diné woman named Nizhoni, followed Richards's advice to attend their geographical ward and accepted callings in their new ward, but they still sensed "an emptiness and longing . . . to be with our former ward members, those of our culture and faith."[35]

The Chuns were not the only ones struggling to part with the Native American congregation in Provo. Three former bishops of the North Park Fifth Ward met with Merrill J. Bateman, a General Authority of the Church and former president of BYU. Bateman inquired about the effectiveness of church programs such as the ones for the youth in the ward, and he wondered if a local stake president "would be willing to adopt [the Native American ward] into his stake." Chun thought of his previous conversation with Richards and referred Bateman to him. Bateman then called Richards and discussed the members' concerns.[36]

In reviewing the situation, Richards agreed to work with Chun and other leaders of the former North Park Fifth Ward. He invited former North Park Fifth Ward members, including Brenda and Anthony Beyal, to a taco party. When Brenda met Richards, he reassured her about the reorganization of the Native American ward. Brenda asked him: "Is this from the Lord?" He then looked at Brenda "right in the eyes and said, 'Yes, Sister Beyal. This comes from the Lord.'" This affirmation "quieted [her] fears," because Brenda needed to know that this effort did not stem from "a group of people trying to maneuver the Church."[37] Brenda touched on an internal conflict that most of the former North Park Fifth members faced during this ordeal.

Devout Latter-day Saints learn to obey and heed their church leaders. As dedicated Latter-day Saints, Brenda and other members of the North Park Fifth Ward felt obligated to follow their leaders who decided to dissolve their ward. Yet they deeply desired to maintain their Native American family ward. Past members of the ward wrote letters to Church officials requesting a new Native American ward. They also fasted and prayed together for their congregation. Because of their determination and faith, they believe that Church authorities reorganized the congregation as the Franklin Second Ward only a few months after they had dissolved the North Park Fifth Ward.[38]

Several factors influenced the determination and unity that the Franklin Second Ward members mustered to sustain the ward. Such factors include a common sense of identity as "Lamanites," or as a chosen people with great potential; the Native American and Native Hawaiian Latter-day Saint network that supported members in various ways, both spiritual and temporal, as in job searches; and the efforts in family history and temple work. Native American members sometimes connected with kinship relations in the ward. Since members could choose to attend the Franklin Second Ward or their geographical ward, some families participated in multiple congregations. Individuals of the same family unit could decide to attend different wards. While I attended the Franklin Second Ward, I met a Diné woman who went with her children to their geographical ward, but she also participated in the Native American ward. Another ward member's teenage sons preferred their geographical ward youth program. In both cases, the youth gradually started to attend church with their parents in the Native American congregation.[39]

In retrospect, most members of the Franklin Second Ward consider that their struggles to preserve the ward strengthened their congregation. Chun believed that eliminating the ward had "humbled" the members and "reminded them of the great privilege and opportunity that was theirs to meet as a Native American Ward." Both members who had been attending the ward regularly and those who only came occasionally realized the need to commit and maintain the ward. Chun noted that about 130 members attended the North Park Fifth Ward before church officials disbanded it. After its establishment, the Franklin Second Ward averaged an attendance of 220 members within a few years. Attendance for monthly temple trips increased from five to thirty people. More teenagers participated in the ward over time. Members of the Franklin Second Ward served as missionaries and developed family history work.[40]

A former non-Native stake clerk, Randy King, praised the way that the first bishop, Anthony Beyal, interviewed potential members to ensure that they were willing to contribute to the ward.[41] Richards regarded the ward as equal to other congregations in the stake, and he called ward members to serve in stake leadership positions. After stressing that only one stake leader came from the North Park Fifth Ward, Brenda Beyal noticed: "Now, the stake Young Men's President is from our ward. . . . We have two high councilors from our ward. We have the stake Young Women's camp leader director from our ward. I'm in the Young Women's [stake] Presidency. . . . We're in equal partnership in this stake."[42] The ward members recognized that involvement in the stake unit protected the congregation from future threats of disbandment. The Franklin Second Ward fit well in the Provo South Stake, which included other diverse and specialized congregations, including Spanish and American Sign Language. President Richards celebrated diversity in the Church as well, which Latter-day Saint Native Americans of the Franklin Second Ward appreciated.

As Dakota scholar Elise Boxer of the Sisseton and Wahpeton bands has addressed in her study of Mormon conquest and its impacts on Indigenous peoples, Latter-day Saint celebrations of Pioneer Day perpetuate legacies of settler colonialism. Boxer emphasizes how ongoing LDS narratives and festivities of this holiday romanticize the violent dispossession of Indigenous homelands at the hands of Euro-American Latter-day Saint settlers who claimed the lands for themselves in what became Utah.[43] The Provo South Stake's celebration of Pioneer Day evoked this fraught past and its erasure, as stake leaders tried to include the Franklin Second Ward in the stake activities.

The annual stake celebration of Pioneer Day on July 24 exposed both the Franklin Second Ward and Provo South Stake general members to different perspectives on the meanings of the holiday, developing an exchange and relationship between the ward and the stake. Some Franklin Second Ward members hesitated initially to participate in the Pioneer Day commemoration. Alan Groves, for example, questioned and bemoaned such an event that praised Euro-American Latter-day Saints for coming and dispossessing his Indigenous ancestors and people of their lands. President Richards invited a drum group from the ward to the 2007 celebration to promote stake unity, but the drum group and most members of the Franklin Second Ward did not attend the gathering.

The following year, a Native American member on the high council appealed to the Franklin Second Ward to attend the stake Pioneer Day event. He also asked the ward drum circle to sing, and the group accepted the invitation. As a part of the drum group, Groves was impressed by how many people showed interest and support of the group at the stake gathering. A stake leader acknowledged the drum group and announced that they would sing some Native American songs, encouraging people to watch and listen. After singing a few songs, the drum group leader welcomed everyone to participate. The group taught some round dances and songs to the audience. From this experience, Groves recognized the Pioneer Day celebration as "a chance for our ward, our stake, to get together as a whole."[44] LDS Native Americans in the Franklin Second Ward, including many Diné members, began to see Pioneer Day as an opportunity to teach about Native American cultures and histories, which challenged common narratives and misunderstandings. In several pioneer stories and depictions that underlay Pioneer Day, Native Americans appear as aggressors and threats, or merely part of the "wild" environment, which white Latter-day Saint pioneers must survive and tame. By disrupting such misrepresentations of Native Americans, in the Pioneer Day event and other instances, the Franklin Second Ward reeducates descendants of white Latter-day Saint settlers and reminds them that Indigenous peoples are still here.

COMMON IDENTITIES

Some Latter-day Saint Native Americans viewed a Native American ward off the reservation as a way to support missionary work and provide role models for Native American youth. Chun emphasized how some Native Americans returned to church after years of inactivity. He recognized "a renewed spirit of missionary work within the ward," less gossip and more fellowship, higher efforts in "home and visiting teaching," more "service projects and activities," and sacrament meetings "filled with the Spirit."[45] Native American and Indigenous Latter-day Saints developed a common identity as part of the Franklin Second Ward, which they believed would offer them a comfortable and welcoming environment to grow in the Church.

I sensed this common identity as a member of the ward between 2011 and 2012. Although I blend in as "white passing" in predominantly Euro-American congregations, I was excited to attend a local family ward for Native Americans with many Diné Latter-day Saints. I enjoyed listening to regular references to Diné Bikéyah, places that are familiar to me. In a sacrament meeting, for example, some young women recalled singing Diné songs together during the stake girls' camp. One young woman described her grandmother singing praises to God in Diné bizaad, and then she started singing more in church. She told the congregation how these songs helped her feel the spirit and relate to the role of music in Diné spirituality. In some sacrament meetings, I also shared my experiences with my Diné family and culture that ward members understood.

Although the Church no longer refers to Indigenous peoples of the Americas and Pacific as "Lamanites," some members of the ward grew up identifying with the descendants of ancient peoples from the Book of Mormon, and they have received strength and assurance from that belief. While I attended the ward, I served as a youth Sunday school instructor, teaching from Church manuals and scriptures. I remember hearing a mother of one of the teenagers in my class who is Mexican and married to a Diné man address the youth Sunday School class since she was their previous instructor: "You are direct descendants of the House of Israel despite whatever anyone else tells you." She asserted that they have a responsibility to bring the gospel to "the reservation."[46] Her words of admonition and testimony appeared as an anachronism in several respects. Her reference to Latter-day Saint Native Americans as "Lamanites" was similar to the language of the Kimball era. Although most of the youth have only lived in Provo and Orem, Utah, she expected them to "return" to Native American reservations to share the gospel with their kin.

Native Americans have not been the only ones who have attended the Franklin Second Ward. Some Native Hawaiians, Polynesians, and Latin Americans among other diverse members have also attended the ward who self-identify with Native American as "Lamanites."[47] Some Euro-Americans have joined the ward to serve and attend church with Native Americans, including former missionary couples that served in the Navajo Nation. Most white members of the ward believed in what has been called the "Lamanite cause" since Kimball's leadership in the Church. Native American Latter-day Saints also sought the opportunity to serve one another in the ward. I recall how a Native American member who worked at Utah Valley University recruited, trained, and offered jobs to fellow Native Americans in the ward. Ward members met through social networks and created a Utah County Native American network, which offered them opportunities to participate in cultural events and activities such as powwows and Native American business fairs.

Native American and Indigenous Latter-day Saints considered family history resources as another benefit of the ward. During my time in the congregation, a Kanaka ʻŌiwi Latter-day Saint, Kaleiwahine Kim, led a proactive program of Indigenous family history, holding regular meetings, tutorials, and trainings with various new technologies and approaches to family history such as how to use digital tools, resources, and blogs. Diné Latter-day Saint scholar Corey Smallcanyon taught a Diné genealogy class for beginners to help ward members learn about their ancestors and complete temple work. Smallcanyon provided information on how to access tribal census rolls and other advice for Diné genealogy and family history. Through these classes, I met distant relatives who could collaborate with me on family history. The Franklin Second Ward brought Diné family together in an enclave of Latter-day Saint Native Americans beyond Diné Bikéyah.

DINÉ IN INTERTRIBAL NATIVE AMERICAN CONGREGATIONS

Intertribal congregations have provided avenues for Diné to worship with other Native Americans in areas away from the refuge of the Four Sacred Mountains that demarcate Diné Bikéyah. Besides the wards and branches discussed in this chapter, the Church of Jesus Christ of Latter-day Saints has also organized Native American congregations near different Native American schools. For example, Diné could join Latter-day Saint Native American congregations while attending the Intermountain Indian Boarding School in Brigham City, Utah, before its closure in 1984. Some Diné students attended church with fellow Native Americans in Richfield, Utah, where the federal government established a dorm for Native Americans to attend the local high schools in Sevier County. The Church dissolved these Native American student congregations.

Besides the Franklin Second Ward, the Papago Ward in the Salt River Pima-Maricopa Indian Community near Phoenix, Arizona, takes pride in claiming to be the longest-continuing Latter-day Saint Native American congregation.[48] The Papago Ward is open to any Native American in the Phoenix area, and I visited the congregation and met several of the ward members while I lived in Mesa during my graduate studies at Arizona State University. According to members of the ward, between 2012 and 2014 the Papago Ward represented approximately fifty different tribal nations. Some Diné Latter-day Saints have attended the Papago Ward, including Thomas Tsinnijinnie, who served as the bishop in 2013 when I met him.[49] During my time in Mesa, I held a workshop about Native American family history, inviting members of the Papago Ward. I emphasized the importance of oral history in understanding Native American family histories. Although the Papago Ward members came from many different Native American backgrounds and communities, they related to each other by seeking to know their respective Indigenous heritage and families.

In recent years the Church has developed Native American oral history programs to support family history. In 2019 two nonprofit organizations with ties to the Church, FamilySearch and American Indian Services (AIS), recruited four college students to pilot an oral history program in the Navajo Nation.[50] Most of the students came from Diné families and returned to Diné Bikéyah to record their own family histories. Hailee Roberts was an undergraduate student at the University of Utah during the pilot oral history program. She is a Diné woman of the Bitter Water and Edge Water clans who was born and raised in Salt Lake City.[51] She became the team lead for the project, exemplifying how the program strengthens connections between Diné off and on the reservation. Roberts described what this work with oral history means to her: "I was able to take the time away from my current reality and instead go down and find out my own family history and traditions. . . . We were able to figure out who we are and know where our roots come from."[52]

The experiences of Roberts and fellow students in this pilot program reveal how Diné Latter-day Saints from off-reservation backgrounds can sustain relationships with kin and community in the Navajo Nation. A Diné student at BYU, Sheiyenne Baloo, who identified as a Latter-day Saint, reflects on the intergenerational linkages from participating in the oral history program: "Being able to make a name become real through pictures or conversations with existing family members who knew your ancestors intimately is a spiritual experience, and it makes you appreciate and recognize them."[53] Baloo came to better know her Diné relatives of the past and present through the combined work of oral history and family history that the Church sponsored. Church officials and partners such as AIS considered the pilot program of 2019 as a beginning for larger programs that could extend beyond Diné Bikéyah, involving more Native Americans of diverse tribal nations.[54]

In some off-reservation Native American congregations, I met fellow Diné Latter-day Saints such as Tsinnijinnie who are my relations. My father is born for the Tsinaajinii clan, which is the namesake and clan of Tsinnijinnie. In both the Franklin Second and Papago Wards, I not only formed kinship relations with Native American Latter-day Saints in the sense of a "ward family" but also connected with Diné relatives in urban areas. Native American specialized units have furthered the growth and presence of Diné Latter-day Saint communities beyond Diné Bikéyah by providing common ground for Latter-day Saint Native Americans despite the integration and dissolution of most ethnic-based wards. For a time in the late twentieth century, Brigham Young University also offered some spaces where Diné Latter-day Saints met and formed "Lamanite" communities with fellow Native American and Indigenous Latter-day Saints.

CHAPTER SIX

Red Power at BYU

This chapter traces Diné experiences of my father and close friends that he met in his young adulthood at Brigham Young University. BYU expanded the horizons and contacts of Diné Latter-day Saints as they grew into adulthood and extended their families with diverse Native and non-Native peoples. A collective of Diné youth unified with other Indigenous Latter-day Saints at BYU, embracing Red Power on their own terms as BYU launched one of the largest Native American university programs in North America during the late twentieth century.

NATIVE AMERICAN BYU STUDENTS IN THE CIVIL RIGHTS ERA

In 1970 the BYU newspaper, the *Daily Universe*, featured a story on how Gilbert Frazier and other Native American students represented Red Power by pursuing college degrees at BYU.[1] Frazier, "a 37-year-old Sioux," planned to apply his BYU studies to advancing American Indian initiatives and "community action programs." He found support from special Native American educational facilities, curriculum, faculty, staff, and, in his words, "the sense of unity with other Indians."[2] Hundreds of Native Americans attended BYU as Apostle and Prophet Spencer W. Kimball championed "Lamanites" and their future in the Church of Jesus Christ of Latter-day Saints during the civil rights era.[3] Latter-day Saints, including church leaders and lay members, continued to distinguish Native Americans as descendants of Lamanites from the Book of Mormon.

By developing and defending an expansive system of "Lamanite" programs and services, Kimball influenced the lives of many Native Americans before his Church presidency in 1973 until he passed away in 1985. By the early 1940s, he dedicated much of his ministry to "the Indians in all the world."[4] BYU Native American students, such as Jeanie Sekaquaptewa

Groves (Hopi), recognized how "the Lamanite was a really big push" during Kimball's leadership. BYU created and sustained active Native student programs that marked the university as "a recognized national leader in the education of American Indians."[5] While Groves attended BYU, she sensed a major emphasis on Native American recruitment, retention, and matriculation, which enabled graduates to serve their communities through their professions and vocations.[6] Adrian L. Smith decided to attend BYU in 1970 because of the large Native American student population. She wanted "to see a nationwide representation of Indians being and living at one school—just like one large tribe," and she found "a group familiarity with the over 500 American Indian students" at BYU.[7] Some Native students applied the term "Lamanite" to identify this "one large tribe."

The Church Indian Committee, including authorities such as Kimball, Matthew Cowley, and Delbert L. Stapley, envisioned BYU as "the world center for Indian cultural study and education." They believed that Native American graduates "would become a leaven" by encouraging "other young people to go on into higher learning."[8] BYU Indian Education in the 1960s and 1970s aimed to prepare Native American LDS emissaries for Indigenous communities. Considering this context, I address the complicated relationships that Native youth, including Diné like my father, developed with BYU leadership, faculty, staff, fellow students, and other Native Americans.[9]

BYU claimed the largest Native American student population of any university with nearly six hundred Native enrollees by 1970.[10] Many Native students were Latter-day Saint converts who had participated in the Indian Student Placement Program (ISPP), which arranged foster homes with LDS families for them during the school years before college.[11] My father, Phillip Smith, was among some of the BYU Native American students who never "went on Placement." My father felt that ISPP alumni sometimes excluded him for that reason.[12] For example, some other students labeled him as a "rez boy," and they doubted that he would graduate and find gainful employment. Vickie Washburn Cox, who is Comanche and Choctaw, resented the "stereotype" that all Native American LDS youth participated in ISPP. As a BYU Native American student, she often had to address questions about a program in which she never participated.[13]

Since many Native American students attended BYU, their experiences varied widely. Some students engaged with the National Indian Youth Council (NIYC), the American Indian Movement (AIM), and other related forms of activism, while many others avoided and were offended by such groups. Some Native Americans criticized fellow students and former ISPP participants for mimicking whites and abandoning their people.[14] In the early 1970s BYU officials expelled Victor Selam, who identified with the tribal nations of Warm Springs, Yakima, and Nez Perce, after he defied the school standards that forbade male students from growing long hair. He also encouraged other male students to respect traditional Indigenous cultures by not cutting their hair.[15] Selam demanded: "How will Indians rise up if they sit back, quote prophecy, and do nothing like some people at B.Y.U.?"[16] Whether BYU Native students agreed to participate in such activism or not, they often advocated for their respective communities and sought actions in the interest of their people that aligned with the Red Power movement.

Stanley Snake of the Ponca Nation, a BYU student and former president of the NIYC, latched onto "a new awakening of Indians all over North and South America" in 1972. He urged Native American youth at BYU and beyond "to complete their education and then help their tribe improve its conditions."[17] Some church leaders encouraged Snake and other BYU Indian students with the common motif of "get an education" and "lift your people up with you."[18] Kimball implied this concept of uplift when he told BYU Indian students in 1975: "Your Lord has permitted you to walk through the dark chasms of your ancestor's making, but has patiently waited for your awakening, and now smiles on your florescence, and points the way to your glorious future as sons and daughters of God."[19] Ideologies of racial uplift had historically characterized diverse religious rhetoric, affecting various Christian denominations and African American and Native American followers. Of the different scholarly analyses on the impacts of this uplift notion, one study demonstrated how some communities applied uplift as a "source of [racial] identity."[20] Some Latter-day Saint Native American students related likewise to uplift. Kimball's message of a Lamanite "awakening" reinforced Snake's key points, emboldening him and other students to embrace their identities as Native Americans.[21] During the 1960s and 1970s, some LDS Native youth unified to stand with their respective communities, while believing that they were part of revitalizing an exceptional race: Lamanites, the lineage of Lehi and Abraham.[22]

Several former missionaries, including Natives and non-Natives, who proselytized in Native American communities started the Tribe of Many Feathers (TMF) at BYU in the 1950s, which eventually consisted of over a hundred members by the 1970s. TMF, the Native American student club, operated an elaborate network with academic programs, housing, campus standards, and events such as the annual Indian Week.[23] Many Native students paid TMF membership dues and participated in club-sponsored dances, parties, sports teams (both on and off campus), and a radio program called "Proudly We Stand."[24] TMF officially started the Miss Indian BYU Pageant by the mid-1960s to select a representative, which followed the general trend of Miss Indian pageants that occurred throughout the country.[25] Some TMF members, including Miss Indian BYU, advocated for Native American rights and Indigenous cultures despite ongoing tensions in Latter-day Saint and Native American relations.

Although some BYU students like Snake became involved in the NIYC, AIM activists often viewed Latter-day Saint Natives as "apples" (bilasáana in Diné bizaad). They believed that LDS Natives rejected their Indigenous identity and people. Vickie Comes Out Bird (Mandan-Hidatsa) recalled how Indian activists "would refer to [Latter-day Saint Native Americans] as 'Apple Indians,' you're red on the outside but white on the inside and you're not really an Indian." As Miss Indian BYU 1972, she responded in defense: "I didn't agree with that because at that point in my life I was more proud than I ever had been if I was on the reservation."[26] I examine struggles over BYU Native American representation and activism through the gendered perspectives of TMF members such as Miss Indian BYU and male student officials. TMF members, many of whom were Diné, shared goals with AIM and Red Power mobilizations, but they strategized and pursued those common efforts in their own ways—shaping their own communities and support mechanisms especially by gender—to promote Indigenous peoples and their rights.

While some scholars have described BYU Native student experiences in terms of binaries and the clash of two worlds defined by race, I trace how these young Natives linked diverse communities.[27] I assess not only their decisions as individuals but also as representatives of multiple groups that affiliated along intersecting lines of indigeneity, race, gender, ethnicity, and religion.[28] They sometimes bridged different communities by centering on the overlaps between them, although such connections could be tense and fragile. In some cases they prioritized certain communities and identities, and they may have adhered to dominant social constructs of race and ethnicity. They acted in the context of Latter-day Saint entanglements with settler colonialism. The ISPP and BYU education stemmed from the historical hegemony of the United States and descendants of Euro-American settlers that displaced and dispossessed Native Americans, but those programs affected Native youth in diverse and sometimes unexpected ways.[29] Twentieth-century Native Americans, including generations of BYU students, made choices to not only survive but thrive in the aftermath and perpetual cycles of violent colonialism and power dynamics. Some BYU students decided to join the Church with faith and empowerment to enrich their people and families.

The Church built its headquarters on the homelands of Utes, Shoshones, and other Indigenous peoples, engulfing white Latter-day Saint settlers, Native Americans, and Native Latter-day Saint converts in conflicts and "violence over the land" during the nineteenth century.[30] Efforts to assimilate Native Americans and terminate tribal status continued in the twentieth century, involving forms of schooling and education.[31] In the case of some Native Americans, however, BYU educational programs strengthened the students' tribal and Indigenous connections and identities. Diné have overwhelmingly represented the majority of Native American students at BYU since the second half of the twentieth century. In the 1973–1974 BYU academic year, for example, Diné ranked as the largest population of Native Americans with a count of 280 students. The second major tribal representation of twenty-six students came from the Oceti Sakowin Oyate, which consist of several tribal nations related as the People of Seven Council Fires (known as Sioux nations).[32] BYU Native students created and fostered their own communities, which remain as Latter-day Saint Native American networks spanning vast distances and generations, especially in the Navajo Nation. BYU tracked "more than 1,500 Indian alumni (not just graduates) over a forty-year period" before 1992.[33] In 2017 the establishment of the BYU Native American alumni chapter embodied these ongoing networks. Patrick Willie, a Diné Latter-day Saint, performed a hoop dance that he choreographed to "Go, My Son" at the first official meeting of the chapter. "Go, My Son" has served as a BYU Native American theme song since the advent of "Red Power at BYU," calling Diné and Native youth to higher education for the benefit of their people.

Comes Out Bird first heard Arlene Nofchissey Williams (Diné) and Carnes Burson (Ute) performing their song "Go, My Son" during an assembly at her boarding school in South Dakota. As a sophomore in high school, she did not consider college until the "words to that song just touched [her] heart." Recognizing Williams and Burson as Native students, she desired to emulate them. Despite opposition and ridicule from her family and community, she joined the Church the following year. The church standards aligned with her commitments to sobriety and chastity.[34] Bird later sang "Go, My Son" with Williams and Burson, who became her close friends at BYU. The song became not only "a national anthem of Indian students in college work" but also a melody of hope for many Native American young men and women.[35]

During the late twentieth century, the song linked Latter-day Saint and Native American common initiatives in a message to motivate Native American youth to attend BYU. Williams told Comes Out Bird that "'Go, My Son' is in the Book of Mormon," referring to how scriptures inspired the lyrics.[36] The song also memorializes the legacy of Manuelito, a Diné leader who persevered through the Long Walk—the removal of Diné from their homelands to the internment of Hwééłdi, Fort Sumner and Bosque Redondo, between 1864 and 1868.[37] Navajos credit Hastiin Ch'ilhaajiní, or Manuelito, for advising his posterity to seek education, which he compared to a ladder to climb.[38] The song became an underlying motif for BYU's multicultural performance group, Lamanite Generation, later known as Living Legends, and Miss Indian BYU often sang the song in their shows.[39]

Royce Flandro, director of the BYU Indian Education Department in 1966, traveled with the "BYU Lamanite Entertainment Group" throughout different American Indian reservations. The group sang "Go, My Son" as part of its effort to "persuade students to go on Placement and families to host the children," which bolstered BYU Indian programs by pipelining ISPP graduates to the college.[40] The lyrics repeated the message that Native Americans needed to "get an education" and "learn a good vocation" to advance and uplift their people.[41] BYU Native American students have harmonized in chorus to "Go, My Son" over generations, epitomizing an Indigenous community that intertwines Latter-day Saint and intertribal values.[42]

My father never performed in Lamanite Generation as a BYU student, but he wanted his children to know and respect "Go, My Son" and its message. My parents taught us "Go, My Son" instead of "The Cougar Song," unlike most other BYU alumni. Before I learned a word in Diné bizaad, the language of my Diné ancestors, I could sing and make the hand signs of that song. My siblings and I were born into a "Lamanite" world and were connected to past and ongoing dynamics of Latter-day Saint and Native American relations that the song embodies. My decision to attend BYU relieved my parents, and I followed in my father's footsteps by joining TMF.

This personal background inspired me to explore the histories of Native Americans and Diné at BYU, including my father's. I have pursued

Miss Indian BYU 1975 Millie Cody giving an elk skin with the lyrics of the song, "Go, My Son," to President Spencer W. Kimball of the Church of Jesus Christ of Latter-day Saints. Courtesy of L. Tom Perry Special Collections, University Archives, Harold B. Lee Library, Brigham Young University.

understanding what it means to not only be Diné but also Native American as a Latter-day Saint by seeking diverse perspectives and oral histories of LDS Native Americans who connected at BYU. This study of BYU Native American students, who became representatives and activists in the 1960s and 1970s, is a part of my continuous journey. Some scholars may consider such autoethnographic writing too subjective and biased, but I embrace my voice and closeness to the people, my friends and family, in this narrative to (re)claim and share our stories. BYU Native students did not just walk between "two worlds," as most scholars portray their experiences. They, and many different Native Americans, walk through many worlds that overlap, correlate, and conflict.[43] Their abilities to navigate and possibly intercon-nect some, if not all, various communities feature in this chapter, which extends beyond only Diné experiences.

As I listened to the stories of my father and other BYU Native American alumni, I began to decipher a hidden and forgotten history of LDS Native youth in the late twentieth century.[44] Some Latter-day Saint Native students stood against the grain at BYU and beyond the school, supporting Red

Phillip L. Smith, the author's father, in Utah, c. 1970–1971. Courtesy of author.

Power through the NIYC—a national student organization dedicated to Native rights. Other BYU Natives found subtler ways, specifically under the surveillance of Church-school authorities, to participate in Indigenous revitalization and resurgence as well as intertribal coalition building through a collective "Lamanite" identity. "Go, My Son" and BYU Indian programs directed Native Americans to complete college studies and pursue careers that would serve their communities, including the Navajo Nation for Diné students, but Native students related in different ways to Indigenous representation and activism. Various groups, inside and outside of Indigenous communities, contested and debated the meanings of "uplift" and approaches that Native Americans should follow for the well-being of their people and future.

To combat social injustice and support Indigenous communities, some TMF members and BYU Native alumni, especially men, became directly involved with Native youth initiatives during the civil rights era. Melvin "Mel" Daris Thom of the Walker River Paiute acted, for example, as TMF president and continued to lead regional and national Native youth organizations after he graduated from BYU in 1961.[45] Thom served as TMF president for three years while studying civil engineering at BYU.[46] Dan Edwards, a fellow TMF member and a Yurok alumnus, described Thom as a "brilliant organizer."[47] From 1959 to 1960 Thom served as president of the Southwest Regional Indian Youth Council. In August 1961 he became the first president of the NIYC, defining its purpose: "With the belief that we can serve a realistic need, the National Indian Youth Council dedicated its activities and projects to attaining a greater future for our Indian people." He asserted that Indians "are going to remain Indian people for a long time to the future, with every right to that identity."[48] Some Latter-day Saint Native Americans and TMF members like Thom led Native activists with pride in their heritage and futurity.[49]

During his first year at BYU, my father befriended Stanley Snake, who involved him in the NIYC. Shizhéé, Phillip Smith, remembered how Snake was a bold "non-traditional" student in his thirties with a hunched back due to kyphosis. The taunts and ridicule that he had faced in his youth toughened Snake.[50] His older brother, Clyde Warrior (Ponca), cofounded the NIYC. In 1968 Snake served on the NIYC board, and he later became its president in 1972.[51] Smith first met Snake and Thom at the Gallup Indian Center in New Mexico before he graduated high school.

In the autumn sometime between 1969 and 1970 Smith traveled with Snake to several gatherings, including a NIYC national meeting at the University of Oklahoma (OU) in Norman.[52] The discussions focused on the issues and needs in Indian country such as combating alcoholism and poverty. Some Native students petitioned to abolish the "Little Red" mascot at OU to "preserve our ethnic identity" with dignity. They charged that "Little Red will never feed hungry Indian children; Little Red will never help more Indian students come to OU."[53] After the meeting, however, some attendees distributed alcohol, became intoxicated, and ignited a fire on campus. Smith left when people began drinking, but he later heard about the incident and how OU banned the NIYC.

Smith began to doubt the organization when he observed that the same people who vowed to oppose alcoholism later became drunk themselves. Many AIM activists also disappointed him because of their addictions to substances and sex.[54] In 1968 Thom expressed empathy, understanding the prevalence and ramifications of alcoholism, in a eulogy for the past NIYC president, Clyde Warrior: "Warrior 'died of alcoholism,' cirrhosis of the liver, as so many of our brothers fall. It's a sad thing that this has become almost an honorable way for an Indian to die. Because when an Indian drinks, he's a free man. . . . They will keep on dying until people recognize them and respect them for what they are."[55]

As Smith reflected on civil rights movements, efforts to address poverty, alcoholism, and poor health resonated with him. Poverty and race were inseparable for many minoritized populations since socioeconomic status and race intertwined. The Poor People's Campaign brought many diverse and marginalized peoples, including Native Americans, together to fight for their human rights in demonstrations between 1967 and 1968, which reverberated in "America's War on Poverty."[56] Issues of socioeconomic disparities and injustices offered a common platform across racial and ethnic divides, which appealed to some BYU Native students like Smith by enabling them to interact with different communities.

As I mentioned before, my dad demanded that his Latter-day Saint friend Merle Kunz read one of his favorite books and inspirations, *Custer Died for Your Sins*, soon after its publication in 1969 when Kunz invited him to read the Book of Mormon.[57] Kunz also encouraged my dad to attend BYU where he read and was converted by the Book of Mormon. My dad accepted the Church as a BYU student after taking a Book of Mormon class for non-members as taught by Dean of the General College Lester Whetten. As a BYU freshman and sophomore, my dad continued to support Red Power and pride in Native identity by standing with Diné and other Natives as they confronted legacies of colonialism.

Most of the BYU Native students were Diné like my father, but the other half of the students came from over seventy different tribal nations.[58] From 1967 into the 1970s, the Indian Mission program, ISPP, and BYU Indian Education collaborated and met monthly with Kimball "to plan [their] concerted efforts to build up the people."[59] Missions such as the Southwest Indian Mission and Northern Indian Mission reached out to Indigenous peoples by introducing them to the Church and organizing congregations among them.[60] Missionaries worked with members and recent converts to recruit students for ISPP. Church authorities and many foster parents encouraged ISPP graduates to continue their education at BYU. Many church officials, Placement families, and students envisioned that Native graduates would gain the skills they needed to work among their respective communities and serve their people as Latter-day Saint ambassadors.

Native students entered BYU programs that white church officials initiated in the 1950s to address the so-called Indian problem, which referred to socioeconomic disparities of Native Americans.[61] During the Termination Era of the 1950s, church authorities engaged with renewed efforts to integrate Native Americans through schooling and legislation to dissolve tribal status and relocate Native Americans to cities.[62] Academic Vice President Earl C. Crockett, who helped establish the BYU Office of Indian Affairs in 1961, believed "knowledge of the Lamanite people set forth in the Book of Mormon and the Doctrine and Covenants, together with the continued emphasis on redeeming these great people," spurred Church leaders to expand the Indian programs.[63]

In 1956 the first known Native American student graduated from BYU. Native American students received "special consideration for admission."[64] The enrollment of Native Americans increased from forty-three students in 1963 to 535 students in 1971.[65] BYU director of Indian affairs Paul Felt expected a larger enrollment, since there were ten thousand Indian seminary students and seventeen hundred ISPP students by 1966.[66] Jim L. Dandy, a Diné man who graduated from BYU in 1974, reminisced about the Indian program, since many Native students came together: "Everybody took care and helped one another. When one person got in trouble or one person had a need, we used to help each other a lot."[67] Alumni passed on their nostalgia to their children, who sometimes became second-generation BYU Native students, like Jeremy Begay who is Diné. Begay's parents told him about BYU's past "huge Indian program" with "lots of Native Americans": "They call it the good old days."[68]

During its heyday in 1970, TMF began to regularly disseminate a newsletter, the *Eagle's Eye*, which provided an "outlet for the literary and intellectual talents" of students and a forum on Indian affairs.[69] In one of the first newsletters, Richard "Dick" Neztsosie, a Diné student, addressed the Red Power protests at Plymouth Rock: "Thinking about this made me reconsider, where do I stand in relation to groups like these? Where do most of us stand?" He noted how different peoples were upholding "the image of whatever race, tribe, or group they belong to," "developing nationalism," and launching movements such as Black Power and Red Power. While some of the ideas and efforts to "retain identity" resonated with Neztsosie, he disagreed with Red Power "tactics" such as the protests. His response represented a composite of Latter-day Saint and Native American perspectives. He recognized the issues that Red Power exposed, but he turned to Church teachings for guidance.[70] A couple decades after he wrote the article at BYU, Neztsosie reflected on how his feelings toward the Church and his confidence developed: "Once I did learn about the church and the gospel, the confusions and uncertainties that I felt were not as much an issue as they were at one time. I felt more at peace, more at ease with who I was and what I was."[71]

BYU Native students defined their presence and collective identity in relation to the campus community and larger national groups such as the NIYC. In 1971 TMF hosted discussions about Native American identity, leadership, relations with national organizations, and "the Indian standing."[72] Paralleling the spread of pan-Indianism on the national level, some Native students gained a stronger sense of "Lamanite" identity when they participated in TMF. Claralynn West (White Mountain Apache), Miss Indian BYU 1973–1974, exclaimed: "I caught myself imagining the olden ways, yet now I feel like Lamanite." She envisioned speaking with Geronimo and historic Apache leaders about "the medicine of truth; The strength for our people, to become one tribe, to be unified, and beat to one drum the dreams of our hearts; To see the richness of our true culture, to be thankful, yet humble enough to see our weaknesses, and strong enough to be Lamanite."[73]

Many Native students like West embraced Kimball's words and the "Lamanite Cause" as empowering, and they wanted to spread those messages. Some BYU students appropriated the Lamanite identity as a form of Indigenous pride, using "Lamanite" as a conduit for their unity and advocacy instead of joining AIM. Native Americans who identified themselves as Lamanites turned to prophesies in the scriptures and official Church discourse that foretold how "the Lamanites shall blossom as the rose."[74] As part of their convictions, they would receive the promises to their lineage by fulfilling their mission to serve and build Zion, bringing together followers of Jesus Christ.[75]

For some BYU Native students who held these beliefs, they also continued

Members of the Tribe of Many Feathers at Brigham Young University, 1964, including Chester Yazzie, Sandy Romero, Thorton William (*front row*); and Grace Yazzi, Helen Jones, Frances Cashnerl, and Cleo Jackson (*back row*). Courtesy of L. Tom Perry Special Collections, University Archives, Harold B. Lee Library, Brigham Young University.

to resist assimilation and detribalization by advocating for Indigenous cultures and communities through public performance, dance, and song. The club sponsored a program of Native American dances as early as 1959 and 1960. In 1961 Robert F. Gwilliam, an advisor to Native students in the BYU Indian Education Program, recommended that a dance program become an annual event as "a source of pride and satisfaction to the Indian students on campus"; they could fundraise for the club and the student performers.[76] The BYU Lamanite Generation started in 1971 as a traveling troupe that students of Native American, Polynesian, and Latin American descent auditioned to join.[77] This group provided an opportunity for students affiliated with "Lamanite" identity to practice together in rehearsals and share their respective cultures through music and dance.[78] As a part of Lamanite Generation in the 1970s, Ken Sekaquaptewa (Hopi) found that "Lamanite culture is interrelated," comparing Indigenous peoples of the Americas and Pacific Islands.[79] Native students in the group performed dances from intertribal powwows such as the fancy dance and hoop dance, while different Indigenous communities attended their shows.

By the 1970s Indian Week became an annual tradition that celebrated Native students and cultural exchange at BYU. During Indian Week, performances, guest appearances, lectures, banquets, and competitions spotlighted American Indian education and cultures. The keynote speakers represented Native American communities. In 1972, for example, Miss Indian America Louise Edmo (Shoshone-Bannock) encouraged BYU students to "be loyal to oneself, tribe, and to the American Indians" and "to improve the Indian cause." Edmo rallied Native youth to protect and uphold their homelands, cultures, heritage, and education. She recognized AIM with some ambivalence like Neztsosie and other BYU Native students: "I don't agree with their tactics, but their ideas are great, and they are the ones who make the Indian known."[80]

With deep suspicion of AIM and activism in general, BYU president Ernest L. Wilkinson (1951–1971) monitored and reprimanded anyone on campus if he perceived deviations from sanctioned conformity.[81] Wilkinson and BYU officials banned TMF for the 1966–1967 school year after some students in the club "had conducted some clandestine activities in the mountains east of the University with one of its powwows."[82] TMF held a powwow in the mountains after Director Felt forbade Native American dances during Indian Week in 1966. Felt worried that the "traditional Indian customs" and dances "left something to be spiritually desired," and he and other school officials also tried to squash any student opposition.[83]

American Indian students led by their peer Howard Rainer (Taos and Tewa) organized the powwow to take place on campus when they were told to halt their preparations and actions because "the Brethren disapproved of such Indian dances."[84] Rainer asked school officials if he could talk directly with the brethren, or Church leaders, to explain what the dances signified to Indigenous peoples, but they rebuffed such efforts. He started to organize protests and gather a following among BYU Native students to demand a powwow, threatening to cancel or boycott the upcoming Indian Week on campus. Students divided over the controversy; some students rallied with Rainer, while others accepted the dancing prohibition to avoid conflict. Wilkinson met with Rainer and planned his expulsion from BYU.

Rainer started reaching out to Native American communities outside of

BYU in preparation for a protest on campus when BYU professor of psychology Robert Bennion advised him to halt the demonstration.[85] Bennion informed Rainer that Kimball would contact Wilkinson with an order to apologize and allow the dances. Soon after this exchange, Wilkinson called Rainer to meet him and reinstated him at BYU, telling him: "I was told to apologize to you." Rainer remembered that "Wilkinson never apologized for anything! But he apologized to me that way."[86] School officials noted how the dance ban "caused a great deal of animosity among the gradually increasing numbers of Indians that we had on the campus at that time." Faculty and staff struggled "to keep [Native students] from becoming a part of the militant Indian uprising that was emerging throughout the nation." Flandro feared that some students left BYU because of these issues with TMF.[87] Rainer described the incident as "chaos," emphasizing how it separated and antagonized the students.[88] He led the "resistance" to fight for powwows and tribal identity on campus before the contentions deescalated.

The powwow ban and controversy of 1966 underscored that "BYU was losing 50% of all the Indians that enrolled at the University," motivating the administration to reinforce the Indian Education programs. Flandro and other school officials sought "to provide outlets," such as the *Eagle's Eye* and other resources, to discourage "clandestine powwows and other activities, both on and off campus, particularly in the mountains."[89] Rainer and other students worked to reinstall TMF, which Wilkinson allowed to reorganize through the Associated Students of BYU by 1967. Club members wrote a new constitution and bylaws, and George P. Lee (Diné) became TMF president. Flandro recalled that Lee was a "humble Navajo" who "led in a rather dictatorial way but at least a way that was supportive of the University policy and for the best good of Indian students."[90] Native youth like Lee were regarded as the more complacent students, but school and Church officials commended their obedience.

In 1969 AIM activists contacted my dad, Phillip Smith, seeking TMF support to establish a chapter in Utah "since BYU had all the Native students."[91] When AIM came to BYU to recruit students, they asked Howard Rainer to enlist, but he declined: "They didn't need me, and I didn't need them."[92] Although they did not join AIM, Rainer and other BYU students followed Indian affairs and movements that involved the organization. After the occupation of Wounded Knee by AIM and Oglala Lakota that began in 1973, Rainer addressed the issues: "What is so sad is that it takes a Wounded Knee to wake up everyone that what is happening is happening because decent social conditions, fairness, equality and mutual respect, have not existed for many Indians throughout their entire existence." He empathized with AIM and Wounded Knee through a rallying call: "LET'S NOT BURY OUR HEARTS IN WOUNDED KNEE, BUT CURE THE DISEASE ONCE AND FOR ALL!!"[93] The "disease" or "Indian problem" were terms that Native youth used to decry the social injustices, socioeconomic disparities, and racism that afflicted their peoples and communities.

BYU officials watched TMF and Native American students closely into the 1970s. In a campus memorandum from October 15, 1970, BYU Dean of Students J. Elliot Cameron introduced a policy that "no student organization which would be exclusively for the purpose of the Indian student (red power, etc.) should be considered without the express approval of Dean Whetten." Cameron explained that this direction stemmed from the university efforts to block BYU Native American students from "[organizing] groups separate and apart from the Tribe of Many Feathers." He referred to how "Polynesian students have been attempting to organize," which could motivate Native American students to follow their initiatives.[94]

Wilkinson rebuked Smith, who was TMF president in 1970, for resembling an "activist" and associating with the NIYC.[95] To the chagrin of Wilkinson, in 1969 Smith and other BYU Native students wore red armbands to demonstrate against the underrepresentation of Native American football players during a BYU game against the San Jose State University Spartans. Jerry Garrett, the news editor of the *Daily Universe*, inadvertently inspired the protest by his "tongue-in-cheek" satire in the newspaper. His fabricated script, titled "Lost Dialogue," begins with a BYU student asking another student why he is wearing a red armband. The student explains that "we're starting a demonstration against San Jose State" because "they discriminate" against Indians.[96] Garrett used this discourse about BYU students wearing red armbands to parody San Jose State students and others who wore black armbands to demonstrate against BYU and its affiliated athletics.

The black armbands became a symbol to denounce BYU and the Church's racist policies of banning Blacks from the priesthood and from temple endowment and sealing ordinances.[97] As BYU students and supporters "'[grew] weary' of protests charging BYU with racism," they started to dismiss the criticism against them by arguing that diverse Native American students attended BYU more than any other school. Representing BYU, Dean of the College of Physical Education Milton Hartvigsen addressed the Western Athletic Conference: "If we're racist because we only have half a dozen Negroes, then other schools are racist because they don't have enough Indians."[98]

In 1968 twenty-one Black San Jose football players boycotted a game against BYU at San Jose State University, which left the stadium nearly empty "except for a hundred or so heavily armed guards." There were numerous security issues, including bomb threats received by the BYU team. The unrest intensified in 1969 after the University of Wyoming's coach barred fourteen Black players from the football team for planning to wear black armbands in protest of the Black priesthood and temple ban and racism in the Church. In the game that followed, some fans threw debris at BYU players. In Laramie, protestors "picketed and interrupted" Latter-day Saint meetings and services, and they encircled the BYU team's hotel.[99]

In 1969, as BYU prepared for a rematch with the San Jose Spartans in Provo, the Associated Press circulated news among major outlets in the Southwest and Intermountain West regions that two to three hundred BYU students planned to wear red armbands to the football game. A part of the press release included:

> A BYU faculty representative to a Western Athletic Conference meeting in Denver, Dean Milton Hartvigsen, issued a statement saying there are 279 American Indian students on the BYU campus. "Should some of the other schools in the Western Athletic Conference be branded as racist because they have almost no Indians in their student bodies?" he asked. He pointed out that San Jose has no Indians. "The idea has caught on," he said. "The time is really ripe for something, because the students are despondent over the crazy charges being thrown at them."[100]

My father and other BYU Native students acted to support Native American civil rights and causes but incidentally challenged the Black civil rights causes and efforts. Larry Echo Hawk (Pawnee), the only Native American football player in the game, "was not pleased" when dozens of Native and non-Native BYU students stood together wearing red armbands at the game. After the event, Wilkinson met with my father, reprimanding him that these actions were "not becoming of the Lord's university" and they cannot treat others with that disrespect even if they disagreed with them.[101] Wilkinson framed such actions as contrary to the school's honor code. My father did not contest the president then, but he decided to transfer to another school not long after this meeting. Censorship, conflicting directives and initiatives for racial causes, and racism and discrimination confused him and distanced him from BYU at least for a temporary period.

While protests and condemnation of the Black temple and priesthood ban and other related racial church practices broke out during BYU sporting events between the late 1960s and 1970s, some Latter-day Saint Native Americans began to settle and articulate their beliefs about the Church through these contentions. Before Ken Sekaquaptewa enrolled at BYU, he first attended Arizona State University (ASU) where debates about Latter-day Saints intensified during a basketball game with BYU in the late 1960s. Some of Sekaquaptewa's friends started to ask him about the Church, having considered his religious affiliation. Sekaquaptewa questioned his own beliefs, wondering whether he should continue to associate with the Church: "If I'm a member of the church, what do I believe? Do I believe strongly enough that I'm going to support it? If I am, then I better be active; if I'm not, I better not get involved.'" After he studied more about the gospel, he decided to serve a mission for the Church and later transferred to BYU.[102] By considering the controversies of the Church and racial issues, some BYU Native students came to define and understand their own identity as Latter-day Saint Native Americans.

Some AIM activists targeted BYU Native students such as Miss Indian BYU and the Lamanite Generation, accusing them of being fake Indians. Vickie Bird described how AIM disapproved of the Church: "They didn't like what [Latter-day Saints] were doing with Placement by taking the kids off the reservation and trying to Americanize them and teach them the white man's ways."[103] AIM demonstrated in Salt Lake City, publicly denouncing the Church in 1973 and 1974.[104] Some Native Americans taunted Bird and other BYU students when they traveled with the Lamanite Generation and Lamanitettes during that time. The Lamanitettes were a dance group consisting of only Native American female students.

Bird, who participated in both the Lamanitettes and Lamanite Generation, remembered how "AIM people" interrupted their shows: "Sometimes they would yell during our performance or make themselves moan so that we knew they were there. They were making comments about us. . . . It was kind of scary because some of them were very adamant about what they believed." In one case, some Native Americans in the audience berated Bird by comparing her to "a stripper out there" after her solo dance to the theme song of *The Good, the Bad, and the Ugly* (1966). They also chided the entire Lamanite Generation: "You're Indians, and you shouldn't be portrayed that way."[105] The troupe "did modern numbers along with traditional numbers," which upset some Native American crowds.

Some BYU Natives like Vickie Cox did not know any traditional Native American dances or songs. The rare occasion that she wore her "native dress" was when she signed "Go, My Son" as Miss Indian BYU (1968–1969) for the Lamanite Generation. She danced to the song "Cherokee Nation" with the Lamanitettes, which memorialized and mourned the Trail of Tears, forced removal, and suffering of the Cherokee.[106] The song also symbolized the resurgence of tribal identity, ending with the line: "Cherokee nation will return."[107] Although Cox and BYU Native groups danced to contemporary music and styles, they sought to honor and advocate for Native causes and experiences through their performances.

As a BYU Native representative, Cox knew that "we were doing something more than performing a show"; they were (re)building relations between Native communities and the Church. The director of the Lamanite Generation, Janie Thompson, arranged tours to Native American reservations, high schools, and communities, including areas where Latter-day Saint missionaries were banned.[108] AIM and other Native groups sometimes resisted such efforts, questioning the motives and roles of BYU students and their leaders. These tensions illuminate, however, the intricacies of Indigenous representation in Latter-day Saint Native American experiences. Dustin Tahmahkera, a Comanche scholar of critical media, assesses analytical dichotomies in *Tribal Television*: "To question sitcoms' representations as stereotypes/not stereotypes, positive/negative, or accurate/inaccurate sets up noteworthy but very limited analysis."[109] Binaries limit understanding of complicated experiences and representations of Native American identity, which include BYU Native students like Miss Indian BYU in the civil rights era.

When the Miss Indian BYU pageant began, other Indigenous communities and organizations had already established similar competitions to select Native American women as representatives. Although Europeans and Euro-Americans had appropriated roles and images of Indian princesses in settler colonialism, some forms of Indian "royalty" developed that celebrated Indigenous peoplehood, sovereignty, identities, cultures, and homelands. Pan-Indian traditions such as intertribal powwows and pageantry brought peoples from different tribal nations together to collaborate, set standards for the pageant candidates, and accept common public figures. Jeanie Sekaquaptewa Groves, Miss Indian BYU 1968, remembered that the pageant designated "a good example of an LDS Native American, an LDS Lamanite that was active and could represent the Church as well as the Indian." She felt that "others had representatives and we needed to bring ourselves up to that level because the stereotypes about Indians are so predominant."[110] The judges of the Miss Indian BYU Pageant evaluated the contestants' knowledge of their Native American heritage and their ability to uphold moral values. The winner served as an ambassador who bridged diverse communities, including the Church, BYU, and Native Americans across the country.

Many BYU Native students struggled to connect diverging communities of Latter-day Saints and Native Americans in the context of Red Power, AIM, and the civil rights movement. Activists of the "Red Power and Indian Militant movement" refused to recognize Nora Mae Begay (Diné) as a representative of "the true Indian," since she was a "product" of ISPP. Begay became Miss Indian America XVIII after holding the Miss Indian BYU title (1970–1971). Begay propagated the platform "that cooperation and unity between the different people of the world as well as among the many Indian tribes will result in a better future for all of us."[111] Tensions underlay her conceptualizations of individual and collective identity. Begay appreciated how ISPP taught her "that a person should be regarded as an individual and not as a member of a group," but she continued to emphasize group identity by linking communities as the title bearer of Miss Indian pageants.[112]

Begay perpetuated common messages that resembled Red Power when she told BYU Natives "to 'never be ashamed of your heritage, your people, and your parents. Always be proud you are an Indian and always stand up for what you believe.'" Like other BYU students, she rejected AIM tactics such as "militancy, claiming that it destroys the Indian heritage."[113] While she promoted the strategy of "cooperation and unity," other Natives regarded such approaches as passive and complacent. Vickie Bird noticed how Begay "made a lot of Indians angry" because of her advocacy for the Church.[114] Begay also disparaged some fellow BYU Native students like my father, Phillip Smith. He remembered how she accused him of "not being Navajo" because of his fairer skin. Smith joked with a fellow TMF member by imitating Begay's traditional presentations. When she showed "the rug" after a Diné weaving demonstration, they exclaimed: "Behold, the rug!"[115]

Smith also recalled how some male Native American students teased female students like Begay by changing the lyrics of "Go, My Son" and singing: "Go, my daughter. Go and get a husband."[116] Native American Latter-day

The court of Miss Indian BYU, 1970–1971, including Nora Begay and her attendants Betty Henderson (*left*) and Beverly Ketcher (*right*). Courtesy of L. Tom Perry Special Collections, University Archives, Harold B. Lee Library, Brigham Young University.

Saint women faced the same pressures as other Latter-day Saint women to prioritize marriage, childbearing, and family before college degrees and careers.[117] As these examples reveal, perceptions of race and gender affected how Native American students judged and interacted with one another. BYU Native communities experienced flux and tensions, as Begay, Smith, and other students navigated various influences and conceptualizations of Indigenous identity that entangled race, gender, religion, culture, and generation.

In 1976 Begay warned Miss Indian BYU candidates to expect and "overcome the negative criticisms of your people." She told them that they would "represent all tribes, and Indians outside BYU will look at you as a representative of all students at BYU."[118] Such advice pertained directly to Vickie Bird, who followed Begay as Miss Indian BYU. Begay's reign tainted Bird's opportunities in the Miss Indian America Pageant. Reflecting on her experiences as a contestant in the national Indian pageant, Bird noted that Begay "spoke so much about the Church that I think in some ways it was good but in some ways it wasn't as if she was representing all of Indians. It was like she was more representing Mormon Indians. A lot of the Indian population didn't feel like she was really for them." Begay "set this precedent" for BYU Native students, which disadvantaged Bird in her efforts to represent diverse Indigenous communities as Miss Indian America. Although some Natives scrutinized her and BYU Native students for their LDS affiliation, Bird was honored to share her heritage and faith as Miss Indian BYU.[119]

Mildred Cody Garrett (Diné and Ute), Miss Indian BYU 1974–1975, expressed gratitude: "The Lord surely loved us to let us have the color of skin that we have and have all the memories that we have of our grandparents and our great grandparents."[120] Garrett celebrated her race (represented by skin color) in terms of Latter-day Saint belief and Indigenous ancestry. Jeanie Groves articulated this intersection of the Church and Indigenous ancestral teachings: "Both promote all the good things in life or the good things that you should do. They may go about it in a different way." What Garrett, Groves, and my father, among other former BYU Native students, stressed was the efforts to "influence others' lives for the better" through the compound lifeways they forged between the 1960s and 1970s.[121]

"MULTICULTURAL" BYU

After the height of Native student participation in the early 1970s, BYU Indian programs diminished as officials claimed to support more minority and "multicultural" (primarily nonwhite) students. Native American enrollment dropped drastically to fewer than two hundred students by 1986.[122] Officials clumped the Indian Education Department, the center of BYU Native programs, with the Multicultural Education Department before eliminating it in 1985.[123] Janice White Clemmer (Wasco-Shawnee-Delaware), a BYU alumna and former employee in the Native American studies and multicultural programs, claimed that many school affiliates started to accuse the university of "favoring American Indians over other racial minority groups." They scrutinized all the programs and resources, including the Native American studies degree.[124] Church authorities became more concerned about correlation and "managing diversity in the international Church," relying on standards of uniformity and inclusiveness as other ethnic groups joined the Church in larger numbers.[125]

Officials redirected several of the Indian Education programs toward other minority students, emphasizing "inclusivity" and "multiculturalism" instead of "Lamanites" and American Indians.[126] These redefined efforts, however, stifled an opportunity for the university to lead in Native American studies and student support. They also erased the programs and perpetuated the obscurity of the histories and memories of BYU Native representation and activism.[127] In the early twenty-first century, Jeremy Begay noticed only a few Native students at BYU: "None of them had a common bond other than skin color."[128] The stories and experiences of shizhéé (my father) and other BYU Native alumni (re)connect these histories and Indigenous presence and community at BYU. On March 23, 2017, more than a hundred alumni supported initiating a Native American alumni chapter, including Howard Rainer, me, and others who stood for remembering and fortifying this community of Latter-day Saint Native Americans.

Rainer also called for action, demanding that BYU (re)commit dedication to Native American students and studies throughout the campus. He had previously cited Alma in the Book of Mormon, who stressed "the restoration of many thousands of the Lamanites to the knowledge of the truth" and how the Lord's power would preserve their "future generations."[129] Cynthia Connell, the BYU Native American alumni chapter president at the time, reiterated this scripture and then added: "The Lord sees us as one united flock with a unified mission to establish Zion."[130] Connell referred to how divisions not only fall along lines of whites and Native Americans but also threaten communities internally, such as generations of LDS Native Americans who attended BYU and formed a group identity of "Lamanites."

A prominent BYU Native American alumnus, Larry Echo Hawk, led and advocated for Native American rights as the assistant secretary of Indian affairs (2009–2012) and in other roles. In 2012 he accepted an assignment to one of the highest echelons of Church leadership, becoming the second

Latter-day Saint Native American general authority since the excommunication of George P. Lee. Echo Hawk addressed Latter-day Saints throughout the country, and I heard him speak to a Native American gathering with many Diné attendees in Flagstaff during the summer of 2013. He referred to Kimball's influence on him, which he has repeated in his public discourses. Echo Hawk was impressed by Kimball's speech titled "This Is My Vision," in which he told BYU Native American students that he dreamed of Lamanites as "lawyers" and "as heads of cities and of states and in elective office." Echo Hawk interpreted the message as "a challenge from a prophet of God: 'Get an education. Be a lawyer. Use your education to help your people.'" He "carried an excerpt from that talk in [his] scriptures" to study and reread it as a personal blessing and guidance.[131]

Echo Hawk related to Kimball's vision, not only as a "Lamanite" but also as a Pawnee. He and other BYU Native students connected to Red Power by answering a call to "get an education," which gathered and shaped a community. Whether everyone in their community has self-identified with "Lamanite" or not, they have sought to cement their unity through the intertwining of Latter-day Saint and Native American teachings that they have woven based on their diverse backgrounds and experiences. They have recognized the contributions and efforts of past BYU students who directed their education through representation and activism to serve Native American communities and their tribal nations. Diné such as my father, and later my siblings and I, related to the BYU motto to "Go Out and Learn, Return to Serve," like many other BYU Native students that we met. In some ways I exist because of the university. My parents met at BYU and dated only a little after my father remembers attending a "Lamanite ward" where they told the students to only date people of the same race or fellow Native Americans.

I remember back at BYU during my undergraduate days when a Diné friend told me that he would support me if I decided to raise my voice about some troubling affairs and issues happening at BYU with Native Americans. In 2020, more than ten years later, I became more willing to speak about related concerns because I still see them. I did not speak then because of fear. Like many Native American students, I was just trying to get by, traversing the challenges of college and young adult life. Many Native American students are affected by the impacts of socioeconomic disadvantages, disparities, perpetuated racist systems and structures, and pressures to "uplift" their peoples.

But now I am trying to build coalitions with underrepresented and marginalized students and alumni affiliated with BYU. The university is taking some initiatives, and I hope they do things right and in the best ways possible. When I found out in 2020 that there was no Native American representative on a committee organized to address race and inequality, I decided that it was time to speak up and do the best I could to support the committee and efforts to make a difference. I launched a petition to request that a Native American representative be included in the BYU committee of race, equity, and belonging, which was granted soon after the committee members were announced. The petition was part of efforts to build coalitions and bring diverse peoples of all walks of life together in mutual respect and better understanding of our interconnectedness, emphasizing abilities to navigate and bridge various communities.[132]

Whatever affiliations with institutions of higher learning and education, I hope that people consider what they can do to support and encourage healing and equality wherever they are. I am trying to do that with the various communities, organizations, and institutions to which I am connected, as I seek to walk in beauty. On this long road and journey, every step matters. Hózhǫ́ó naasháa doo. My father and BYU Native American alumni have inspired me by their examples of seeking truth and supporting civil and human rights.

CHAPTER SEVEN

Diné dóó Gáamalii Perspectives

This chapter reflects on the growth and dynamics of Diné Latter-day Saint communities in the late twentieth century to the present and the challenges that Diné experience as they come to understand their identities as both Diné and Latter-day Saint. Diné dóó Gáamalii have defined their identities on their own terms based on their experiences, perspectives, and understandings of being. Diné people take different approaches to balancing what it means to be Diné and Latter-day Saint in practice and everyday life, both inside and outside church spaces.

DINÉ LATTER-DAY SAINTS AND CULTURE

In *Weaving Women's Lives: Three Generations in a Navajo Family*, anthropologist Louise Lamphere features the intergenerational ties of a Diné grandmother, mother, and daughter who all became involved with the Church. Like many Diné, their interactions with the Church affected each of them in various ways that mix positive and negative experiences. Eva Price, the grandmother, wrestled with alcoholism but overcame it because of the "interconnected influences" of her family and faith in both the Church of Jesus Christ of Latter-day Saints and the Native American Church. Her daughter, Carole Cadman, was baptized as a Latter-day Saint and participated in the Indian Student Placement Program for three years. Cadman's daughter, Valerie Darwin, was part of ISPP for only two days in junior high school; she quit the program because she longed for home. Although Lamphere rarely mentions the Church in her book, these brief examples show that, while the Church programs helped Price with her alcoholism and Cadman with her schooling, the Church was also "deeply transformative and led to new dilemmas and conflicts, pulling the family apart."[1]

Price, Cadman, and Darwin might not even self-identify as Latter-day

Saints, but they exemplify how many Diné have navigated and intermingled such diverse cultures and teachings. Some Latter-day Saints are wary of syncretism.[2] Church leaders have encouraged converts from ethnic groups to maintain parts of their culture that align with the church teachings while asking them to avoid practices that are inharmonious with the doctrine of the Church. As Dieter F. Uchtdorf, a member of the First Presidency and a convert from Germany, explained in 2008: "We members of this Church speak many languages, and we come from many cultures, but we share the same blessings of the gospel. This is truly a universal Church, with members spread across the nations of the earth proclaiming the universal message of the gospel of Jesus Christ to all, irrespective of language, race, or ethnic roots."[3]

Church authorities have hoped that believers will first abide by the teachings of Latter-day Saints, and then follow the congruent aspects of their respective cultures. Even though Price gained strength to overcome alcoholism by participating in the Church of Jesus Christ of Latter-day Saints and the Native American Church, including peyote ceremonies, many Latter-day Saint leaders probably would question the benefits of the Native American Church. For Price to be considered a devout and practicing, or "active," Latter-day Saint, most LDS leaders would expect her to renounce the Native American Church. Many Diné, in contrast, have followed a syncretic approach, combining what individual Diné see as the best of all worlds.[4] This different worldview helps explain why there were many baptized Diné on the reservation but very few who participated fully in the Church during the twentieth century. The Diné converts who became devout Latter-day Saints have faced conflicts when they have rejected some of their Diné ancestral teachings.

Considering oral histories from the LDS Native American Oral History Project and the Church's History Department, Diné Latter-day Saints expressed mixed reactions to how they relate Diné and LDS beliefs and practices. Some of them saw similarities between their beliefs and Church teachings, while others questioned their compatibility. For some Diné Latter-day Saint converts, they believed that the Church introduced them to the whole truth, which added to their knowledge from their Diné ancestors. Laura Brown, a Diné convert, remembers that her mother had "a really hard time letting go of [Diné] ceremonies and spiritual traditional things until she went through the temple for my grandmother, her mother." After those experiences, her mother said that "the Church has everything," and then her mother no longer wanted to continue participating in Diné ceremonies.[5] Laura implied that her mother finally understood that the Church fulfilled all the teachings and practices her mother needed, which prompted her to turn away from Diné ceremonies and spiritual practices.

As some perceive differences between Latter-day Saint and ancestral Diné lifeways, Diné Latter-day Saints vary in how they apply LDS and Diné teachings in their lives. Some of them believe they can participate in Diné spiritual practices; others believe that Diné ancestral rituals oppose or invalidate Church teachings. Some Diné Latter-day Saints will avoid Diné rituals but participate in social activities around them. However, others believe they should not participate in such social activities because they worry about confusing their beliefs and devotion to Christianity.

Hal L. Taylor, the president of the Southwest Indian Mission from 1965 to 1968, thought that many Diné had a "blindness or inability" to fully comprehend, embrace, and live according to the gospel that the Church upheld. He assumed "that every move that they make is associated somehow with their old traditional and pagan ways. We come along with a completely different concept of life and expect them to change over to our way of life when we find that it is difficult even for our own people to live the Gospel like they ought to."[6] Taylor clearly disparaged Diné beliefs as "pagan," but he also recognized the magnitude of the change that Latter-day Saints expected of Diné converts.

Taylor recounted a striking experience to James D. Mathews in a letter dated August 15, 1967. At the time Mathews was writing his master's thesis about Diné reactions to Church teachings based on their cultural background. Taylor had once asked a Diné woman who was baptized why she was not active in the Church; he cited her response in the letter, which described how changing religious beliefs was more than just following a different set of precepts. In the introduction of this book, I quoted this anonymous Diné woman, who underscores how "true Navajo" is an innate identity of religiosity and spirituality. She also claims that Diné only associate with churches on superficial levels, because being Diné is "their religion in their heart."[7] This idea of a "true Navajo" reminds me of a close relative who joined the Church and once confided in me that he would drive within hearing distance of Diné ceremonies just to listen. He always knew and acknowledged the power of Diné ceremonies, even if he stopped talking about that faith openly with Latter-day Saint peers and family. He could never tell his own spouse about these inner beliefs since she might condemn him for (re)turning to Diné traditions. Since the examples that follow are selective, showing a wide variety of beliefs, they should not be considered representative of a monolithic Diné dóó Gáamalii experience.

CEREMONIES AND CULTURES

Diné convert Betty Henderson attended "squaw dances," as they were called in English, "because this is where my family gets together—something like a family reunion."[8] But she considered such events mainly family gatherings and focused less on religious components. She claims that "in the past, medicine men had a place in my life, but now I recognize that they didn't hold the priesthood."[9] The priesthood represented true spiritual authority and power to Henderson and many LDS converts. Kenneth Nabahe, a Diné Latter-day Saint, did not believe in the "sings" and ceremonies involving the ritual creation of sandpaintings. He focused on the "artistic values" at such events, comparing them to how Euro-Americans visit museums.[10] He asserts that "this Church has given me a sense of destiny and purpose. It has given me direction."[11] Nabahe's conversion to the Church redirected him toward ceremonies taught and officiated by Latter-day Saints, while he began to view Diné sandpainting as art instead of ceremony.

Susie Little shared similar sentiments to those of Henderson and Nabahe, self-identifying as a "new Navaho generation." Her membership in the Church marked her initiation into this new generation of Diné Latter-day Saints. Little thought this new generation "no longer felt the need for the Navaho religious traditions." Speaking personally, she explained: "Because the Church was able to fulfill my needs." However, Little clarifies that being Diné remains an integral part of her identity: "As for preserving my Navaho identity, I am proud to be a Navaho and feel this is important, but I would first consider myself LDS—a child of God."[12] Several Diné Latter-day Saints have articulated this sense of order to their multifaceted identity, which places being Latter-day Saint first. Like Little, they might consider being Latter-day Saint to correlate with understanding their identity as a child of God. Yet Latter-day Saints learn that all people are children of God. Adhering to the LDS faith would align with such beliefs in common humanity and relations as children of Heavenly Father, as Latter-day Saints often call God.

The Redd Center Native American oral history narrators exhibited mixed feelings about how much of their Diné ancestral culture they could maintain and in what forms. A few of them talked about cooking Diné foods. Even fewer discussed dancing and attending powwows. For those who were married with children, of the thirty-nine narrators in the 150 oral histories, twenty-five focused on teaching their children LDS values. Fourteen of them emphasized and taught their children values and traditions that were specific to their tribal nations.

Many of the Diné Latter-day Saint narrators seemed apprehensive toward participating in Diné ancestral ceremonies. Helena Hogue, a Diné woman, refused when her parents asked her to be involved in a "sing" or ceremony. She confirmed that she knew "there are some good things in that, but I just don't feel right about it."[13] James (known as Jim) Dandy tried to navigate a middle ground as Diné dóó Gáamalii. When he talked with oral historian Jessie Embry in 1990, he told her that he enjoyed going to the sings but did not participate in the ceremonies: "The sings keep in contact with what my tradition means and to know a little bit about my culture. But that doesn't mean that I go to and participate in the actual performances that they have." Since Diné spirituality and culture intertwined, he acknowledged how some people see conflicts between Diné and LDS beliefs.[14] Dandy shared how he engaged more with Diné ceremonies in his autobiography, *Navajo Tradition, Mormon Life*, which was published in 2012.[15]

Julius Ray Chavez experienced a clash between different lifeways, being drawn simultaneously to both Diné and Latter-day Saint teachings. He feared that people would judge him as "bouncing in between." However, he asserted that only God knew the intents of his heart.[16] Alexia Lopez, another Diné convert, doubted the existence of a middle ground for Diné dóó Gáamalii, because European-American culture dominated in the Church.[17] As Diné joined the Church, they introduced Diné culture to LDS spaces and circles. Although Jimmy N. Benally and his wife Anna emphasized Latter-day Saint teachings and claimed to not "dwell" on Diné traditions, they taught their children some Diné dances, songs, and ancestral practices, which they often shared with their school and church communities in Provo, Utah.[18] I will never forget when Anna Benally showed me her father's moccasins, known as kélchí in Diné bizaad, and told me how he wore them during Diné ceremonies such as Yéii' bicheii dances.[19] She cared and held onto her father's kélchí, teaching me and others about the significance of Diné life and spiritual ways.

Some Diné Latter-day Saints struggled to balance the teachings of their Diné ancestors and those of the Church, although they often respected both

Farina (Smith) King with Anna Benally, 2006, Provo, Utah. Courtesy of author.

of them. While Ernesteen Lynch was working on a master's degree in history at Brigham Young University, she described a point in her life where she felt emotionally ill. She decided to consult with a Diné ancestral healer, known as hataałii or medicine man, and she asked for a Diné ceremonial blessing. The hataałii told her that her suffering stemmed from attempting to live in two cultures—like walking along a fence with a foot on either side. She would not find healing until she settled on one side of the fence. At the time, Lynch was not a Latter-day Saint; the hataałii was only referring to her life in the Diné world and the Euro-American world.[20] When Lynch later joined the Church of Jesus Christ of Latter-day Saints, she found that her dilemma continued. She commented at a symposium about Diné culture that her children had probably seen her use corn pollen more often than they had seen her reading her scriptures.[21]

Olivia Ben participated in ISPP and remembered a meeting with members of the First Presidency in 1991, when she was a junior in high school. She recounts that Gordon B. Hinckley and Thomas S. Monson told her and fellow Native American youth to keep their culture alive. She attends the Native American ward in Provo, because her daughter appreciates not being the only brown-skinned person in the congregation. She planned for her daughter's Diné puberty ceremony, Kinaaldá, so that she could learn from her aunts, matriarchs, and relations what it means to be a Diné woman. Olivia explained what being Diné Latter-day Saint means to her: "I feel that the Church and culture go hand in hand. Because I was raised very traditional, the basic principles of Navajo culture were instilled in me. That's who I am. With the Church, I just bring what's best out of my culture and just make it much better."[22] Olivia viewed her conversion as a uniting of the best of Diné and LDS teachings and spirituality.

While Jim Dandy sought to avoid cultural conflicts, he considered how Latter-day Saints questioned and frowned on "the superstitious things that we do." He pointed out that some Diné Latter-day Saints returned to ancestral teachings, such as his uncle "who was very strong in the Church not too long ago." His uncle "turned to a medicine man" after he became sick.[23] In 1990 Edwin Tano became the first stake president in the Chinle Stake, composed largely of Diné members. Recognizing the social pressure to participate in Diné ceremonies known as "sings," Tano advised members of the stake to attend community socials and sustain friendships but to not take part in the Diné ceremonies.[24]

Anthony Beyal, who served as the first bishop of the Franklin Second Ward in Provo, identifies as both Latter-day Saint and Diné, but "most of [his] beliefs and values are in the Mormon Church." He considers his faith in the Church as a way "that we can better ourselves. I know that, and I have a conviction of that." He provides some background about his upbringing: "I don't deal heavily in the [Diné] culture. My mom and dad steered us away from that, but I could have delved into the cultural side, the religious side of the Navajos and prayers. They taught me a little bit about what's good from it and what to avoid and not do."[25] Anthony's parents introduced him to Diné lifeway teachings, but they also filtered his connections with Diné traditional forms of spiritual practices.[26] Some Diné families limited their own children's understandings of Diné ceremonies and culture, which often directed their progeny to embrace Christian denominations such as the Church of Jesus Christ of Latter-day Saints.

Anthony cautioned a Diné Latter-day Saint woman who once asked him how she could "get to know the spiritual side of Navajos." In his counsel to her, he differentiated between older and younger Diné generations: "If you're dealing with the Navajo older generation, be very careful and respect what they say. If they say no, don't say a word, walk off. . . . With the new generation, they don't care. They say, 'Go ahead, learn. Come into the sweathouse. Do this; do that.' They'd probably teach them the peyote way or some other religious way, but it's different."[27] Anthony did not entirely discourage this woman from learning about Diné traditions of spirituality, but he underscored the divergence of "the new generation" from ancestral Diné teachings. According to him, the older Diné generation guards sacred knowledge, which requires respect. On the other hand, he implies that a younger Diné generation might adhere to nontraditional Diné practices while being more inclusive.

Some Diné Latter-day Saints have warned about becoming too involved in Diné ceremonies and cultural identity. Anna Benally, who went on ISPP and then attended BYU, remembered the few active Latter-day Saint men she knew on the Navajo reservation. A Diné member of the stake presidency "started getting into the real Native part of his heritage and just went overboard. Now, he's successful business-wise, but he's totally left the Church." She believes he became consumed by his Diné cultural identity at the expense of his faith in the Church: "They get themselves in trouble when they get too far into the Native heritage and start wearing that as a front plate for their whole body."[28]

Marci Brown shared the same viewpoints as Anna. She saw the members on the reservation as different from the ward in Page, Arizona. She observed that "some of them try to incorporate their traditional beliefs with the Church." Brown does not attend ceremonies, even to mingle socially, since she was raised in the Church and her father did not participate in them. But for many on the reservation, "ceremonies are family oriented. Everybody in the family gets together." For those on the reservation, it was difficult to be not only a Latter-day Saint but merely Christian, because people would confront them with the claim: "You're not a true Navajo if you're a member of the Church or if you're Christian."[29] Individuals from both respective Diné and LDS communities have pressured Diné converts of the Church to choose a side when identities are not such clear-cut dichotomies in reality.

Lillie Pooley, a Diné and Latina woman, and her Hopi and Diné husband both grew up without a focus on Diné ancestral teachings. Rather than going to the ceremonies, they give money to help pay for the food at the gatherings. Lillie adapted, however, the Diné belief that a newborn's umbilical cord, known as nits'ę́ę́', should be safeguarded. Diné have learned that the person who holds onto the nnits'ę́ę́' will become close to the child. Pooley kept her grandson's cord with her until one day when she buried it on the temple grounds. She has sustained a loving relationship with her grandson and wants him to follow the Lord and become worthy and willing to one day enter the temple. She has hoped that he would gravitate toward the temple. Burying his umbilical cord on the temple grounds, she believes, would draw him to the temple. Pooley has redirected this traditional belief toward her faith in the Church and the blessings that temple worship represents to her.[30]

Some Diné Latter-day Saint converts such as Susie T. Kinlacheeny's husband have come from families that continued Diné ceremonies and ancestral practices. Susie was serving as the Tuba City Stake Young Women's President in 1997 when she referred to how her husband faced great sacrifices to join the Church and go to the temple. He was willing to pursue some new directions to follow a pathway as a Latter-day Saint.[31] While reflecting on her work with young women, Susie Kinlacheeny describes gospel teachings that her husband and all Latter-day Saints have received, such as knowing that they are children of God and how the plan of salvation leads them to return to God's presence.

Some oral history narrators drew connections between Diné and Latter-day Saint beliefs and teachings. Irene B. Jones noticed similarities in spiritual songs as a Placement student when she was eight years old. Soon after starting the program, Jones attended a sacrament meeting during which the congregation sang, "To Nephi Seer of Olden Times." The song refers to the Book of Mormon story of Lehi and Nephi's vision about an iron rod leading through clouds of darkness to a tree with brilliant fruit. The chorus includes the line: "Hold to the rod, the iron rod." The words "struck" Jones, reminding her of her grandfather who sang about a "reference to a rod" in ceremonies. In the song, her grandfather would say to "keep this rod in front of us to protect us." When she asked for information, her foster mother showed her the story in the Book of Mormon, and they read a series of Book of Mormon stories. As a child, Jones sensed "there was clearly a connection" between Latter-day Saint and Diné teachings, which reassured her.[32] Jones believes that the Church offers the only true gospel; thus, only the Diné cultural traditions and beliefs that harmonize with this gospel are true.[33] Shauntel Talk identifies Diné and Latter-day Saint conceptualizations of harmony and hózhǫ́ as part of these compatible beliefs: "In order for your life to be in balance and in harmony, all aspects of your life should be filled with beauty. . . . When things are aligned, our lives are a lot more peaceful and happy."[34] Talk evoked hózhǫ́ when referring to life "with beauty."

While some draw similarities between Diné and LDS belief systems,

Dennis and Irene Jones with Farina King, 2007, in Page, Arizona. Courtesy of author.

others have focused on their differences. Oliver Whaley, a former BYU student from Kayenta, Navajo Nation, did not "know that there could be a harmony" between ancestral Diné and Latter-day Saint teachings. While he believes that some "traditional Navajo beliefs at some point could be traced back to the Book of Mormon and the gospel of Jesus Christ," he compares "Navajo tradition" to "drinking downstream rather than going to the source where it's cleaner." For him, ways of butchering sheep and planting crops are traditional practices that Diné Latter-day Saints should keep. He contends that "as far as religious beliefs, some of the religious stories and ceremonies, these are things that you have to do away with when you accept the gospel of Jesus Christ."[35] Yanibaa Collins, Oliver's older sister, agrees: "If a Navajo was really living his Navajo culture, he would be living a very reverent lifestyle," but it would be "missing all the key things" such as "the priesthood and all the other keys that come from the gospel."[36] According to Oliver and Yanibaa, the Church completed the pathway to the true gospel for all people, including Diné.

Shauntel Talk also sensed a need to "draw the line between practices" of ancestral Diné and Latter-day Saint spiritual ways. She refers to "people who have tried to live in both worlds, and it just doesn't work. They go and forget about the covenants they have made in the Church and do things in the Native American culture that they're not supposed to do" as Latter-day Saints.[37] In Native American studies, most references to "two worlds" denote a white world and Native American world, which scholars have challenged by emphasizing the entanglements of multiple worlds.[38] In Talk's use of the two-world phrase, she differentiates between Diné and Latter-day Saint worlds in terms of spirituality. In an oral history with Donald Pine, a Lakota Latter-day Saint and past branch president of a predominantly Diné congregation of the Fort Wingate Branch, he applies a similar adage: "We have to remember that we're members of the Church first, and we are Lamanites second."[39] Talk and Pine speak about identities in terms of binaries, such as two "worlds" and an order of first and second, which represent frameworks and mindsets that Diné Latter-day Saints have faced with difficulty.

The question hovers uneasily and unanswered: to what degree do Diné Latter-day Saints take part in Diné ceremonies? As the oral histories illustrate, views vary. Some have participated in traditional Diné ceremonies for themselves and their children, while others have avoided them. Diné Latter-day Saint Jessica Mills felt that Diné could "practice most of the traditions and still have it be congruent with LDS standards." Mills named healing practices such as meditation, sandpainting, and sweathouses, which could "be good therapeutically": "It's more drawing on powers from different beings instead of being just Heavenly Father and Jesus."[40] Mills recognizes a potential of combining spiritual powers through Diné and Latter-day Saint healing practices.

In their interactions with Diné communities, some Euro-American Latter-day Saints have also acknowledged truth and value in Diné ceremonies and teachings. Lucy Bloomfield, who had requested the Church send some of the first LDS missionaries to the Navajo reservation, served as an intermediary between Latter-day Saints and Diné throughout her life. She befriended and advised many Diné Latter-day Saints in particular. For example, she convinced George P. Lee, who became one of the first known Native American General Authorities of the Church, to go on ISPP. She wrote poetry about her experiences with Diné that encapsulates some contradictions in white settler Latter-day Saints' perspectives of Native Americans. In one of her poems, she writes that the Lord considers "the Lamanites," which she uses to refer to Native Americans, to be the "Chosen Seed." Although she believed that she could learn from Native Americans, she also regarded them as a "fallen people" who needed the message of her religion. She appreciated "Navajo friends [who] drop in for a chat." But in a patronizing view, she assumed: "I can tell them a bit [of] the right way to live."[41]

Bloomfield did not immediately dismiss the value of Diné ceremonies and the possibilities of Diné Latter-day Saint involvement in them. In 1942 she asked the Navajo-Zuni mission president, Ralph William Evans, if Diné Latter-day Saints could "go to sings." She added that the gatherings were social as well as ceremonial occasions. She intended to attend some of the sings to "trace any of it back to the truth they once had." She wondered if she could "find old stories that could have had no other origin but from the knowledge of . . . the Book of Mormon."[42] I am not sure how Evans replied to Bloomfield's questions, but some mission presidents such as J. Edwin Baird, president of SWIM from 1961 to 1965, openly considered Diné spiritual views and practices "superstitions" that were "difficult to eradicate."[43]

For Diné Latter-day Saint Wallace Brown, however, knowledge of Diné ceremonies strengthens his faith in the Church. He explains: "Knowing that what I know about the traditional and cultural teachings of the Diné, if the Diné people knew for sure the ceremonials, the songs, and the prayers for real, they would understand that that was the only way that our people could preserve the teachings and prophecies that were going to come to pass." He then tells of a ceremony where two holy people appear to a young boy, and they give him authority to preside over twelve men. Brown testifies:

We know now the young boy that was the outcast is named Joseph Smith. We know now the two holy beings that appeared to him are the Father and the Son Jesus Christ. We know now that they gave him the authority to make the restoration come about. . . . With the ceremonies that we have, we actually have these teachings preserved in that way. They are the prophecies and teachings. If every Diné understood that and knew that, there is no doubt in my mind that every Diné or every Native American person would be a member of The Church of Jesus Christ of Latter-day Saints.[44]

Wallace sees Diné ceremonies as part of gospel truths that the Church upholds. To him, Diné ceremonies have even foretold the developments of the Church, reinforcing prophecies. He and his son Shane Brown started an educational website and video series, beginning in 2017, that features "Elder Wally Brown" and "Navajo Traditional Teachings." Brown shares Diné ancestral teachings with more than tens of thousands of people through digital storytelling.[45]

Some Diné Latter-day Saints acknowledge great power in Diné ceremonies and ancestral spiritual practices, but they question the source of the power. They talk about the opposition between the power of the priesthood and the "power of priestcraft," and some of them believe that the hataałii or medicine men are associated with priestcraft.[46] While he served as the bishop of the Papago Ward in the Salt River Pima-Maricopa Community, Thomas Tsinnijinnie remembered learning the difference between power of the hataałii and power of the priesthood in the Church. Both of his Diné grandfathers were hataałii. As Tsinnijinnie explained, one grandfather was the "good kind and the other the bad kind." The grandfather of the "bad kind" converted to the Church. His grandfather told him that he had received power through the adversary to perform his medicine before receiving the priesthood through Christ in the Church. When Tsinnijinnie asked if he could learn how to use the herbs for healing, his grandfather told him that he would have to renounce his faith in the Church first. He said that even the "good kind" of hataałii must make some covenant with the adversary. They speak to the spirits of the plants for aid, which is granted through a power and being other than Christ and Heavenly Father.[47]

Jim Dandy shared a similar experience when his father told him after his request to learn traditional Diné medicine that he "should remain with what [he] believed" in the Church: "'You are strong in that faith so better stay with it. There are things that you might otherwise practice that might hurt you.' There were teachings that they were afraid of and did not want to pass on. It is said these teachings cost human lives." Dandy explains that his father and grandfather encouraged him to keep his faith in the Church, because they did not want him "to get involved in" some practices and traditions. They taught him that "to become a very knowledgeable and powerful medicine man, one has to experience evil in order to help others overcome it. There are a lot of things that hold power and must be controlled."[48]

Tsinnijinnie also spoke of an experience when three medicine men came to his branch at Inscription House near Navajo Mountain. When they were in a Sunday school class, they asked the teacher of the class from where the power of their priesthood came. The teacher explained that Christ gave them the priesthood. When the teacher asked the medicine men where they received their power, they responded that the "Son of Morning" gave it to them. The teacher and other Diné Latter-day Saints in attendance were astonished, because Latter-day Saints recognized the "Son of Morning" as Lucifer in the Old Testament reference of Isaiah 14:12. The medicine men all converted to the Church and left "their medicine" behind, giving away their jish, medicine bags or bundles and signs of medicine potency, according to Tsinnijinnie.[49] In Tuba City a Diné Latter-day Saint told me that his father, who was a medicine man, was successful but realized that his powers came from a source of "priestcraft." He noticed that his father did not live righteously and could only understand his power as being granted by an evil source.[50] Ed Tano, the former Tuba City Stake president, also warned against priestcraft, a term denounced in the Book of Mormon.[51]

On the other hand, some Diné Latter-day Saints are not wary of medicine men and believe they can go to medicine men in a certain context without denying their faith in the Church and the power of the priesthood. Ellouise Paredes finds psychological help from medicine men and traditional healers, including women, and considers them psychiatrists.[52] A Diné member of a Latter-day Saint congregation in Gallup, New Mexico, sometimes visited the medicine man for her chronic headaches.[53] She believes that the prayers of local Latter-day Saints would heal her, but she still does not have "pure faith" in the priesthood of the Church, as Tsinnijinnie would say. Tsinnijinnie explained that some Diné go to the priesthood first for a blessing but are not healed because they do not have enough faith; they then go to the hospital. If they do not receive the desired relief, they finally go to the medicine man and are healed, because they have more faith in that power. During interviews to prepare and receive a recommend to enter the temple, Tsinnijinnie would ask the members if they go to the medicine man. He would not grant a temple recommend to members who still turn to the medicine men or hataałii for healing.[54] Such approaches were not an explicit standard for bishops and officials in the Church, which raises questions about whether Tsinnijinnie overextended his authority by withholding temple recommends from Diné and other Native Americans who continued to follow traditional healers.

The difference between priestcraft and priesthood is significant for many Diné Latter-day Saints, but even so, some Diné Latter-day Saints rely on the spiritual examples of their ancestors. Tsinnijinnie gains strength from what he considers the faith of his forebears. He recalled family stories about his ancestors who evaded the roundup of Diné during the Long Walk in the nineteenth century. His ancestors hid in the canyon and had to hunt in what is now considered southern Utah for food, forcing them to cross a river. When the river was too deep and dangerous to cross, his ancestors evoked the power to divide the water so that they could go across it. Tsinnijinnie believes that his ancestors showed great faith and thus obtained the power to survive from a sacred source.[55] Michael Allison, a past bishop of the Franklin Second Ward in Provo, spoke during a fast and testimony meeting about the examples of his parents who were not members of the Church. Both would pray daily, which is how he learned to pray.[56] Diné have long expressed their spirituality through prayer, fasting, and song, all of which the Church also encourages its members to do.

Ruby Whitesinger Benally was baptized when she was eight years old in Tuba City. She later was rebaptized when she lived in the Navajo dorm in Richfield, Utah, as a high school student. At the time of her first baptism, she had just participated in a ceremony where a bead was tied on a shell that she wore. When the missionaries asked her what the bead signified, she told them it was not their business. She felt that the missionaries were being condescending to her tradition so she "shut them out."[57] Benally found power in Diné bizaad and in the ceremonies. She described that saying something such as "Heavenly Father loves us and accepts all of us" meant more to her in Diné bizaad than in the English language. She felt that the ceremonies preserve mental health and cited, as an example, returning war veterans who would participate in a Blessing Way ceremony that treated the trauma and restored harmony.[58] Prayers could remove negative thoughts, and walking with corn pollen when praying led Diné to "walk in that path of righteousness." She agreed with LDS church historian Matthew Heiss when he suggested that the corn pollen path was like the New Testament's reference to the "straight and narrow way."[59]

For those who have walked the pathways of Diné and Latter-day Saint beliefs, there is no clear answer of how they connect. Both offer strong identities that combine in multiple ways for Diné dóó Gáamalii, and some people see a harmony between them. Others say that Diné Latter-day Saints need to select one or the other, questioning the very existence of Diné dóó Gáamalii. In 1997 Heiss, who worked for the Church History Department, interviewed ninety-three-year-old Nanabah Bia Begay in Many Farms, Navajo Nation, with the help of Helena Yellowhair as his Diné interpreter. Begay expressed in her own language, Diné bizaad, her decision to prepare and enter the temple. My father, Phillip Smith, translated parts of Begay's oral history recording, which I include in the following with English translations directly after the quotes in Diné bizaad:

Yellowhair asked Begay: 'Ako.' Háá'nit'é łe, 'akoo ałnanidáágó?
Well, how are you when you go there [referring to the temple]?
Begay answered: 'Ako.' Shijéí 'eíya' yá'át'ééh. Shinits'ikéés nlei' yá'át'ééh.
Well, my heart is good. My mind [or thinking] is good.

When Yellowhair inquired on behalf of Heiss whether she recognized similarities between Diné and Latter-day Saint temple ceremonies, Begay responded:

'Aoo,' jó' eí,' eí' 'ako't'é.' 'Ei' Diné binahghá' 'ado' kwo'dóó. Tá'dídíin da' 'eí' dóó bee nizh'íid da.
Yes, well, it is like that. The Navajo religion and here. The sacred corn pollen and others, I just don't bother with it.[60]

Begay, like many of the Diné Latter-day Saint oral history narrators, recognized commonalities between Diné and LDS pathways, but she articulated a choice to embrace a Latter-day Saint pathway because of such personal confirmations as a "good heart and mind." This choice did not erase her Diné identity but changed it and how she perceived the world and life as Diné dóó Gáamalii. Some critics of the Church might blame missionaries or white settlers for brainwashing and manipulating Diné converts such as Begay and others that I cited and know personally like my father. But any pressure or force, whether from Latter-day Saints or non–Latter-day Saints, on Diné Latter-day Saints to "choose a side" along constructed binary lines is a manifestation of colonialism to control people's rights to define themselves on their own terms. As a Diné woman said, Diné spirituality is "in their heart," and Begay and other Diné Latter-day Saints believe that their "heart is good" when they join the Church. They continue to shape their multifaceted and compounded identities as Diné dóó Gáamalii.

Epilogue

The Fort Wingate Branch in New Mexico has been another home congregation for me, especially since more of my relatives have been attending church there. One Sunday morning in June 2021, I visited the branch and family simultaneously after more than a year of separation because of the COVID-19 pandemic. We lost many Diné to COVID-19, including my beloved aunt Florence. Several of her children and grandchildren came to church that day when branch president Donald Pine invited me to speak at the pulpit during the sacrament meeting. Although the invitation was unexpected, I knew immediately what I would say to the congregation. I told them how I saw Cheii again. Cheii, meaning "grandfather," also refers to horned toads, which Diné respect and view as bearers of good luck. Some of my earliest memories are of caressing horned toads in my hands when I was a child, living in Diné Bikéyah. Since then, I could not remember seeing Cheii very often, if ever.

My dear uncle Albert "selected the name *Na'ashǫ́'ii dich'ízhii* (Grandfather Horned Toad) as his identity."[1] Uncle Albert was the first one in my family to teach me about our clans and what k'é means to Diné. He and his wife, my aunt Helen, took in and raised many children, welcoming them and many others like me to their home. I have missed them since they passed away. When I return to Diné Bikéyah, I think of them every time. I also think of Cheii, and I started to sense how Cheii represents family who have passed on, including Albert, Helen, and Florence. In my travels in the summer of 2021, I prayed to see Cheii again after so many years. I longed to connect with Cheii and to seek his guidance. I even told my children that I was looking for Cheii, as I walked off among the juniper trees and shrubbery around our relatives' homes. Only when we visited the daughters of my aunt Florence, who had recently passed away, did my children then call out to me that they had found Cheii. I rushed outside to hold Cheii, which my

Farina King with her son Wesley, holding Na'ashǫ́'ii dich'ízhii (Grandfather Horned Toad) in Iyanbito, Navajo Nation, 2021. Courtesy of author.

children pointed out to me. I touched the soft scaly, small body of Cheii in the palm of my hand with gentle tears filling my eyes.

As I recounted this experience at the pulpit in church, I drew the connections about what Cheii means to me. Cheii symbolizes divinity to me—a hope that we will be with our families forever and see our loved ones again who have passed on. Cheii represents coming full circle from childhood to adulthood in humility, as we turn to our children for guidance and loved ones for support. After all the years that I had not seen Cheii, I wondered if I would ever see him again. But I finally made a real effort to search for Cheii, and my own children helped me along the way. Many of the predominantly Diné congregation understood this significance and meaning of Cheii. My cousin Flora later told me how she continued to see Cheii by her home, where my aunt Florence used to live with her. She asked if I held Cheii to my chest for good fortune, strength, and the ability to run, referring to an ancestral teaching about horned toads that Diné have passed down through generations.

Navajo Latter-day Saints are Diné dóó Gáamalii. We are Diné who decided to walk a Latter-day Saint pathway, although not always consistently or without reappraising that decision. Romero Brown, who served a mission under George P. Lee, left the Church for three years because of Lee's excommunication; but then he returned to the Church where he has remained ever since, becoming a stake president. When asked what he wanted to teach his children, Brown explained, "I really want them to know who they are. They're Native American and Navajos. They have a clan system that they need to identify themselves with. Most of all, we want them to have strong testimonies of the Church."[2] He pointed with pride to his daughter Monika, who stayed active in the Church during the time that he and her mother followed Lee.

Monika attended BYU where she met Samuel ("Sam") Crowfoot, a Latter-day Saint of the Siksika Nation with Oneida, Saulteaux, and Akwesasne descent who was also a BYU legacy student. They married in the temple, and they raised their children as members of the Church in their early years. Our families crossed paths and became closer friends when we attended the same congregation in Madison, Wisconsin, while pursuing graduate degrees. Before moving to Madison, we both lived in Provo, Utah, where I interviewed Monika in 2007. She then told me how the Church provided her direction in life, offering her a source of hope that she will again see her brother who passed on after an accident.[3] In 2020 Monika and Sam shared with me and a larger public through social media about some troubling experiences and concerns of Latter-day Saints and the Church, especially while living and attending church in the Gallup, New Mexico, area. Monika declared how "we are dismantling white supremacist systems in our home," renouncing her "complicity and support of a religious institution that was inherently racist, oppressive, and prejudiced."[4] She referred to her faith in eternal families while reflecting on her struggles in the Church:

There was a constant battle going on in my head. On the one hand, Mormonism and its doctrines of eternal families and life after death brought me extraordinary comfort. My brother died when he was fourteen and I was fifteen. Believing that I could see him again and forever be sealed to him kept me going on the days I wanted to end it. It was a thousand times more when I looked in each of my babies' black glassy eyes that I knew some of these teachings were good. On the other hand, the most racist situations I've ever experienced were with well-meaning Mormons.[5]

In a guest post for the *Exponent II*, Monika addressed her "Mormon friends and family," including Diné and Native American Latter-day Saint networks, reassuring them that "just because we left, does not mean we've rejected you. We love you just the same, if not even more, because our god is love."[6] Although our lives and paths have followed different directions, Monika and I are sister threads that intertwine often in a tapestry or diyogí, a Diné rug, on our common journeys to walk in beauty—love. Reflecting on Monika, her family, and our relationships also underscores how we all grow and change. This book offers windows into past lives and voices that do not predict or show the present or future.

As a child, I remember playing with Monika's younger brother, Darrell, when our families attended church together in St. Michaels, Navajo Nation. Darrell and I reconnected as friends after we coincidentally registered for the same religion course at BYU. Our religion course instructor, John Livingston, was a former missionary of the Southwest Indian Mission, and he asked if there were any Navajo students in the class. Darrell and I self-identified as Diné, and then we recognized each other and exchanged contact information. As a young adult and college student, Darrell reiterated his father's commitment to the Church. In an interview, he explained, "I respect my tradition just because that's who I am. I am proud to tell everybody I'm Navajo." He also appreciates the Book of Mormon. He claimed that "if every Navajo converted, people would think we'd lose our tradition. I would say that we gain so much more just because of knowing the Book of Mormon and that's our heritage. We would still respect our traditions, but we would also have the total truth in our lives."[7]

Other oral history narrators centered on their identity as Latter-day Saints. For example, Anna Benally explained: "I am more LDS than I am Native, to tell you the truth."[8] Elouise T. Goatson pointed out that "one of the biggest things that we taught our children was that being Native American is not as important as being a child of God."[9] Derik Goatson, her son who also attended BYU at the same time that I did, described his expression of identity that he uses with his associates. If his relatives asked if he was more "Mormon or Native," he noted: "I would answer Native definitely with them, because that is where I felt was my identity. But at the same time if I was among members of the Church . . . I would probably end up saying Mormon, but I wouldn't feel comfortable with that choice either."[10] He saw the forced either/or as a partial answer. Victor Mannie Sr. focused on teaching his children: "Number one . . . we believe the Church is true, the only true church on this earth. . . . Likewise, we also tell them to get a good education." His children see "there are two cultures here, their LDS religion and their [Navajo] culture. It is out there for them that they recognize that's a lot of things they like about the traditional Indian culture. It's a contest between that and the church and school. . . . But they seem to understand, though, that religion is first in my life."[11]

My father, Phillip Smith, exemplifies someone who has tried to reconcile Diné and Latter-day Saint pathways. As I began this book, I emphasized that my father grew up on Diné land in the checkerboard Gallup region and was baptized by missionaries after he turned eight without his family's consent, although he did not remember it. He worked for a farmer, Merle Kunz, in Idaho for several summers, learned about the Church, and attended BYU, where he decided he wanted to join the Church. It was then that he found his name was already on the Church records. He served in the Southwest Indian Mission. After graduating from BYU, he became a medical doctor and lived in the Navajo Nation with my mother and family, where he served as a church leader in Tuba City and Window Rock. He entered BYU to learn and returned to serve his people, as the university motto claims to represent.[12]

My grandfather had hoped to pass on to him Diné traditions, ceremonies, and medicine ways that he cherished. When my father told him of his conversion and commitment to the Church, my grandfather disowned him and outcast him from the family. However, during his mission, he was able to visit his ailing father and reconnect with him before he died in 1971. My father comments candidly about the prejudice he faced at BYU. He wanted to marry a Native American, but many Native American BYU female students refused to date him since he had not gone on the Indian Student Placement Program. A friend arranged a blind date with my mother, an Anglo-American woman, and they fell in love and married at a time when

Church leaders discouraged interracial and intercultural marriage.[13] But my parents, Phil and JoAnn, have had a happy marriage and raised their children to be lawyers, doctors, professors, and leaders. They raised us to always remember we are Diné and children of loving heavenly parents.

My siblings and I have been more a part of a dominant, hegemonic Euro-American society, since my father worked for the Indian Health Service in the Washington, DC, area, where I mostly lived and attended school in my youth. In 2012, after my siblings and I graduated high school, my father retired and returned to Diné Bikéyah in Monument Valley to work for a Utah Navajo Health System clinic there. Soon after moving there, he accepted a calling as a branch president and later a bishop of the Monument Valley Ward on the reservation, which he held for about eight years. When I have asked him about how being Diné affects his faith in the Church, he has asserted that he is Diné, and the Book of Mormon has revealed many truths to him because of his Diné heritage and identity.[14]

In my youth, when living with my father and mother, I convinced my parents to let me visit Diné Bikéyah and our relatives whenever possible—both the few who are Latter-day Saints and the many who are not. I have studied my Diné ancestry and sometimes adapt some Diné traditions. For example, Diné have a special celebration for a baby's first laugh, and I hosted a laughing baby party for each of my children. Luci Tapahonso, a Diné poet, describes how Diné family and friends gather for the First Laugh Ceremony to recognize how an infant has "consciously performed the act of thinking, Ntsékees, which is associated with the beginning of creation, childhood, and sunrise."[15] Ntsékees aligns with the sacred direction of the East and the sacred mountain Sis Naajiní (Blanca Peak). These teachings lead to hózhǫ́. While I have focused on being a Latter-day Saint, I see myself as Diné and respect my people's traditions and knowledge such as the directions of the Four Sacred Mountains, which show us ways to harmony and beauty.

While some Diné see the two identities as separate—even competing—others have found a connection between their Latter-day Saint and Diné beliefs. In Tuba City I attended Sunday school in Diné bizaad. Brother Ray Mitchell, a former bishop of the Tuba City Ward, taught about the Book of Mormon in the Diné language, often stressing that the guidance of the scriptures would bring hózhǫ́. In the same ward I heard the term "nizhóní'íígo," which means "beautiful" (used as an adverb describing an action word, literally "toward beauty") and stems from hózhǫ́. Beauty, in the Diné language and mindset, is conveyed through the concept of hózhǫ́. Mitchell and the Diné class used the terms they inherited from their ancestors who developed the Diné Bisodizin Bee Hadahaazt'i'igii (the Navajo Introductory Prayer), which concludes with the following lines: Si'ah Naagháí Bik'eh Hózhǫ. Hózhǫ nahasdlii' ("I shall be in harmony, walk in beauty, and live in happiness with all things that exist. Beauty has come again").[16]

Liz Nez, who served with the Young Women in the Tuba City Second Ward, stresses to the youth: "You have to know who you are. You are a daughter of God. You're royalty. You're beautiful. You're royal. I think that is the one thing I've always believed in. We need to remember who we are."[17] The Diné prayer evokes the imagery of the journey to return to "beauty" and eternal bliss. Diné Latter-day Saints such as Nez and Mitchell still envision this journey while focusing on remembering their potential as children of heavenly parents and their eternal destiny. Latter-day Saints believe that they attain beauty and happiness by returning to God.

Thomas Tsinnijinnie's grandfather had told him that the mountains used to not be there on the Diné lands. During his mission among his people, Tsinnijinnie met a medicine man who shared that same story, adding that the lands were once tropical. Tsinnijinnie saw this account as parallel to Latter-day Saint beliefs that Christ came to the Americas after his resurrection and shared the gospel with the Lamanites in a tropical environment. He interpreted it as evidence that the Lamanites are the ancestors of Diné.[18] Romero Brown's grandfather told him about the "White Father" who taught Diné ancestors the gospel. Diné have a sacred name for this White Father. Tsinnijinnie also mentioned that the medicine man he encountered on his mission spoke to him about this sacred name. These Diné elders, both Tsinnijinnie and Brown emphasized, were not Christians and did not learn of Christianity before they recounted these stories to them.[19]

Diné Latter-day Saints have continued to express themselves in Diné bizaad, which connects them to a Diné world and epistemology even though new terms have evolved. In Nanabah Begay's interview with Matthew Heiss for which Helena Yellowhair interpreted, Heiss had Yellowhair ask Begay to share her thoughts about a testimony she had shared in church:

'Eí' 'eíya' 'adin, nleí 'áádi' ei' dóóda. Jó bilagáana 'eíya, jó nlei' nahi' di' t'eíya,' dikwííshí nahai' yéédáá' 'akw'éé' hasdzíí'. T'áá' nahi' 'ají,' Chinili. 'Eí' t'eíya taała'ídi 'adi' datsí 'ako'dzá.'

Over there, no. Over there, no! It is all white. But here, several years ago, I spoke. Over here in Chinle. That I did. Just once, I did that.

Begay clarified that she was able to share her testimony in Navajo among a predominantly Diné congregation in Chinle who would understand her.

When Yellowhair continued to inquire about her testimony, Begay asserted:

'Aoo.' 'Ako' t'áá'áníí' yá'át'ééh. 'Íídáá' koji' diné' binahagha' eí,' eí' bits'aniya dinííd.
Yes. It is really good. Back then, I said I left the Navajo religion [or way].

She confirmed that she had spoken about going to the temple and had left certain Diné traditional ways behind since joining the Church.[20] At the same time, she expressed her testimony in Diné bizaad, drawing on concepts such as nizhóní and pathways to express her new direction of life as a Latter-day Saint. The Church of Jesus Christ of Latter-day Saints provided a new pathway of life in a spiritual sense but did not destroy the fabric of traditional Diné life that defined Begay's experience.

Nora Kaibetony of Moenave, Navajo Nation, also lived a traditional Diné lifestyle but joined the Church. She spent most of her day tending to her sheep, other livestock, and plants as well as weaving in her hogan. In her home there was a Book of Mormon in Diné bizaad. She never learned English and would hitchhike to church every Sunday when her children were not able to drive her.[21] Mitchell talked in the Tuba City Sunday school class about the beauty of the gospel—"nizhónígo." He described attending a funeral with some relatives and lamented that his family who were not Latter-day Saints lacked gospel truths that would have strengthened and comforted them during such hard times. Their spirituality, according to him, did not connect them beyond death.[22]

Many Diné members have been drawn to the Church because of the importance of families emphasized in the gospel. Latter-day Saints prioritize family and value it greatly. Diné Latter-day Saints believe in this significant value, desiring to be with their families forever and striving to strengthen their homes. However, many Diné Latter-day Saints must deal with the fact that most of their relatives are not active members of the Church, a condition that ironically separates them from their families. How can they bring their family together? Some take the hopeful position that things will all work out in the end. Latter-day Saints invest much effort in tracing family history and doing proxy temple ordinances that offer deceased relatives the opportunity to accept the gospel after death. In mortality, though, Diné Latter-day Saints differentiate themselves from some of their relatives in many cases, even as they try to share the gospel and unite their families under the covenants of their faith.[23]

Many of the Redd Center and the Church Historical Department oral histories reveal positive outlooks of Diné Latter-day Saints. Interviewers and interviewees often referred to the belief that the "Lamanites," or Native Americans, would "blossom as a rose."[24] In 1873 Apostle and later President Wilford Woodruff paraphrased a scripture from the Doctrine and Covenants: "The Lamanites will blossom as the rose on the mountains." Woodruff wondered if that was possible "when I see the power of the nation destroying them from the face of the earth," and he confessed that "the fulfillment of that prophecy is perhaps harder for me to believe than any revelation of God that I ever read." Yet, Woodruff continued, "Notwithstanding this dark picture, every word that God has ever said of them will have its fulfillment." He was quoted more than one hundred years later in a 1975 special issue of the Church magazine *The Ensign* about "Lamanities."[25]

Matthew Heiss and Michael Landon, the History Department oral historians, frequently asked how their interviewees felt about the phrase "blossoming as a rose." Their answers help explain how the interviewees considered their membership in the Church. Ruby Whitesinger Benally was born in Ganado, Navajo Nation, in 1953. Benally attended both boarding schools and public schools in Richfield, Utah, although she returned to the reservation each summer and as an adult. For her the creation of the Chinle Stake was an opportunity for Diné to blossom as a rose. While she feels "blossoming" was a popular image in the 1970s, that discussion faded in the 1980s. For her, "to blossom" meant helping others, but that goal was hard to complete with everyday concerns.[26] Virginia Morris Tso Tulley was born in 1961 in Winslow, Arizona, and was on ISPP in Orem, Utah. At the time of the interview, she was the Chinle Stake's Relief Society President and saw the stake as part of the "blossoming."[27]

Jerome Wilmer Willie feared that programs like ISPP had taught some Navajos to "jump to conclusions as Lamanite" so they did not expect serious responsibilities in the Church. Willie told Heiss: "But I think it is still up to us as Lamanites. We have to pay our dues as far as living the commandments, going to church, paying our tithing. I think that's where the blossom is. I think the blossom is receiving a testimony."[28] Wilson Yazzie Deschine agreed that "blossoming" meant having an individual testimony of Jesus Christ.[29]

For Dan K. Smith, who is Diné, the Lamanites needed to have a seed develop in them so they could grow and change. While some things were happening on the reservation, the blossoming had to start with individuals, then expand to the group and the nation. He believes: "When the flower blooms, it's to be picked, trimmed and put in the vase for display." He added that "it's coming to that." But first the seed needed to be planted and allowed to grow without cutting.[30]

The Redd Center oral history interviewees were not specifically asked about blossoming as a rose, but some used the phrase since they had heard it throughout their lives. Loren Begay, a former BYU student from Chinle, explained in 2007 that he was "pessimistic" about the future of Native Americans in the Church: "They say in the scriptures that the Lamanites will blossom like a rose. It depends on how you interpret it." At one time, Begay thought it meant that thousands of Native Americans would be baptized and "there would be a strong church" among them. But he continued: "Going back, I don't know if that is the way you interpret it or what. Right now there are a lot of things lacking. For certain there is a lot of work that needs to be done. I'm still kind of skeptical about the whole thing." Despite this negative view, he tried to see "some things to be optimistic about. You can't really lose hope. You always need to be optimistic, think positive about things and have a hope for things in the future. If that scripture hasn't come true, we should have the faith that it will." He told of one family that was investigating the Church and said it gave him hope.[31]

Begay was not alone. Monika Crowfoot admitted in her interview in 2007: "I was wondering about the scriptures where it says that the Lamanites will blossom as a rose. I was wondering how that would all actually play out, because right now it's hard to kind of see it." For example, she mentioned how "back in Arizona it seems like the ward has grown smaller from the time I was there." She considered then whether she should return to help strengthen it, but she added that she was not planning to move "back to my hometown" or to her husband's reservation. While she felt some guilt—"it's really bad on our part"—she reasoned that they were going to school and "still trying to get our careers."[32] But William Numkena explains the blossoming as a rose more literally. To blossom as a rose meant not only the flower but also the thorns on a rose. For him, the thorns represented life's problems.[33]

For many Diné Latter-day Saints, blossoming as a rose connotes a special mission. While the concept of the Lamanites building a New Jerusalem was infrequently discussed, a few interviewees knew and accepted the story. Dennis Little explained: "I used to think about great things when I was younger. We'd build the New Jerusalem, and we'd do this and that because we're descendants of the Lamanites and Nephites." While he saw the promises as more individual now as an adult, he still recognized great things happening with Indigenous people. He continues to notice: "It's a little slow here, but you look south of the border, into South America and Central America and you see how people have really progressed from a very backward state into a better state. For some reason, it seems to be slower here in the United States. But it will come because we're the same people that they are." His wife Marie also felt that the blossoming would come. She asserts that "it will happen. I think it will happen when the people are going through a lot of trials. Now at this time they have a lot of material things holding them back. When it comes time, it will happen. That's one thing I believe."[34]

While my dad and family lived in the Washington, DC, area, many local members of the Church were fascinated by our Diné background. Family friends in our ward asked my dad to sing a Diné song for their sons' Eagle Scout ceremonies, especially since the Boy Scouts have historically appropriated Native American cultures.[35] His children, including me, learned of their Diné heritage and culture from these public performances of "Indianness" in church settings. We did not recognize at the time, however, the layers of our father's singing, which he had learned from his father and ancestors. Diné elders such as Andrew Natonabah have urged Diné to know even one song, because the songs preserve the oral traditions, knowledge, and rationale that have defined Diné collective identity through generations.[36] My father teaches me to "always wear the songs [our ancestors] gave us," as Luci Tapahonso stresses in her poetry.[37]

My father's displays of Indianness, his singing, conveyed and taught Diné philosophy and worldview through the codes of the song. Only those who receive instruction in the meanings of the symbols and Diné ancestral teachings understand the significance of these performances and songs. My father was trying to pass on certain teachings and worldviews from his upbringing as Diné to his audiences, including his own children, but most of his listeners could not fully grasp them. Kenneth Roemer explains in his article "It's Not a Poem. It's My Life: Navajo Singing Identities" that Diné shape and internalize their identity by singing certain songs.[38] The audiences of my father's performances often romanticized his singing and did not understand the songs as Diné ancestral teachings and spirituality. Diné youth also face challenges reconnecting with this singing because of constant attacks on Indigenous peoplehood and existence.

My father often sings what he calls an "honor song," and he rarely translates what he sings in Diné bizaad. He explained this song in more detail for the first time that I can remember in 2012 after my brother, Aaron Smith, married in the Arizona Mesa Temple. He told the audience at the wedding reception that he was singing about the life of his son, the bridegroom. He described how Aaron had grown over time, and he sang about his future family. While he sings of the Four Sacred Directions, he does not sing about the North, which aligns with Old Age and a new cycle.[39]

My father was singing about the compass of Diné life, the Four Sacred Directions and Mountains, and stages of life. He was describing the laws that guide Diné ways of life and future. He was teaching about the way to walk with hózhǫ́ in our lives. He begins the song by focusing on the East, the Dawn, of life. He then describes the South, the youth and potential of life. He then speaks of the future and hopes to live a long life to see the West and eventually the North, the Old Age and Dusk, of life. His song was a condensed version of Diné teachings, which his ancestors sustained. He did not completely abandon the teachings of his father when he converted to the Latter-day Saint faith. Instead, he passed on his father's songs to his posterity although in a church context. I continue to sing with him and my children, learning these songs along with scriptures, songs, and teachings of Jesus Christ Binahagha' Akée'di Dayoołkáałgo yá Naazínígíí, which guide them on the pathways to happiness as Diné dóó Gáamalii.

This poem stems from the honor song that commemorates the life pathways of Diné generations, past, present, and future:

Pay attention. Listen to the East.
Listen in Beauty.
He was born and raised in Beauty.
Heé ya'ho hwe'yaajineé.
Heé ya'ho ha'aa'a'déé hwe'yaajinée.
Baahozhogo hwe'yaajinéé.

The author with some of her Smith relatives, including her cousin Julie Ann Livingston, 2019, in the Fort Wingate Latter-day Saint church. Courtesy of author.

Listen to the South.
Hear the Voices of the South.
In his youth, He grew well.
He went to school.
Baahozhogo bidiishch'i' dóó biyaaho'a'.
Heé ya ho shadi'ahdéé hwe' yaajinee.
Biniłsi'kee yá'át'ééhgo biyaaho'a.
Ołta'go biyááho'a'.
Listen to the West.
He lived and worked in Strength.
His Home is Good.
Hee ya ho a'a'ááhdeejí hwe' yaajinéé.
Binaanish nizhogo dóó bidzilgo nína'.
Bighan yá'át'ééhgo bił haash'a'.
Listen to the North.
Wait for the Voices of the North.
Hee ya ho, hwe' yaajinéé.
Hee ya ho nahokosdee hwe'yaajinee.
Hee ya ho hwe haa ho—hwei ya héé.[40]

In the summer of 2021, news spread of mass unmarked graves of Native American and First Nations' children who were sent to boarding schools, known as residential schools in Canada. In this context, I was talking with a friend from another tribal nation who has dedicated her life's work to finding the voices of the stolen generation. When I mentioned family history work at some point in our conversation, she asked me directly if I was "Mormon." As soon as I responded affirmatively that I was raised in the Latter-day Saint faith, she started exclaiming expletives. For this very reason, I have hesitated to tell people that I am a Latter-day Saint. A wave of prejudgments, assumptions, and suspicions flooded my friend's mind and comments toward me, although she had known me for several years. She warned me not to try to convert her or her family. I then emphasized to her what I present as my conclusion to this book. I cannot erase that my parents converted and joined the Church of Jesus Christ of Latter-day Saints. I cannot erase how they raised me. I would never want to erase my upbringing and history, but I can always live out and act on my values and ideals that my ancestors have taught me for my children and posterity to learn.

Everyone has their own paths to pave, including me and my family, but all our paths also cross and intertwine over generations. One of my Diné cousins, Julie Ann Livingston, told me what inspired her faith as a Latter-day Saint: "I try to do the best I can. I always feel like Christ helped everybody. He didn't say, 'You are like this,' or 'You are not like that. I can't help you. I can't do this for you.' I'm trying to do my best to be like that to help whoever, whenever."[41] Livingston served her local Diné community, especially working with Diné veterans and different chapter committees of Church Rock.[42] In December 2021 she passed on, joining our uncle Albert, her parents George and Rose Smith, and our ancestors who came before us. I keep looking for Cheii everywhere I go, and I hope that my children and grandchildren continue to remember and find Na'ashǫ́'ii dich'ízhii, Grandfather Horned Toad.

Appendix

Oral History Interviews and Oral History Sources

LATTER-DAY SAINT NATIVE AMERICAN ORAL HISTORY PROJECT, SPECIAL COLLECTIONS, HAROLD B. LEE LIBRARY, BRIGHAM YOUNG UNIVERSITY, PROVO, UTAH

Adison, Shannon, interviewed by Farina King, October 15, 2007, Provo, Utah.

Begay, Loren, interviewed by Farina King, September 16, 2007, Provo, Utah.

Begay, Matthew, interviewed by Farina King, November 10, 2007, Page, Arizona.

Ben, Olivia, interviewed by Corey Smallcanyon, 2008, Orem, Utah.

Benally, Anna, interviewed by Farina King, January 24, 2008, Provo, Utah.

Benally, Jimmy, interviewed by Odessa Newman, 1990, Provo, Utah.

Benally, Ruby Whitesinger, interviewed by Matthew K. Heiss, 1997, Chinle, Navajo Nation, Arizona.

Benally, Thomas, interviewed by Matthew K. Heiss, April 26, 1997, Chinle, Navajo Nation, Arizona.

Beyal, Anthony, and Brenda Allison, interviewed by Corey Smallcanyon, 2008, Mapleton, Utah.

Boone, Audrey, interviewed by Malcolm Pappan, 1990, Provo, Utah.

Bowman, Emery, interviewed by Deborah Lewis, January 27, 1990, Provo, Utah.

Brown, Darrell, interview by Farina King, September 19, 2007, Provo, Utah.

Brown, Laura, interviewed by Farina King, February 17, 2008, St. Michaels, Navajo Nation, Arizona.

Brown, Marci, interviewed by Farina King, November 11, 2007, Page, Arizona.

Brown, Romero, interviewed by Farina King, February 17, 2008, St. Michaels, Navajo Nation, Arizona.

Brown, Wallace (Wally), interviewed by Farina King, November 10, 2007, Page, Arizona.

Butler, Virginia, interviewed by Jessie Embry, 2012, Tuba City, Navajo Nation, Arizona.

Chavez, Julius Ray, interviewed by Odessa Neaman, June 27, 1990, Provo, Utah.

Chun, Miriam, interviewed by Farina King, September 5, 2007, Provo, Utah.

Cinniginnie, Gabriel, interviewed by Malcolm T. Pappan, April 9, 1990, Provo, Utah.

Collins, Yanibaa, interviewed by Farina King, October 4, 2007, Provo, Utah.

Cox, Vickie Washburn, interviewed by Farina King, February 14, 2008, Rio Rancho, New Mexico.

Crowfoot, Monika Nikki, interviewed by Farina King, December 1, 2007, Provo, Utah.

Dandy, James L., interviewed by Jessie L. Embry, October 2, 1990, Blanding, Utah.

Gardner, Benjamin and Anthony Gardner, interviewed by Farina King, September 22, 2007, Provo, Utah.

Garrett, Milli Cody, interviewed by Odessa Newman, June 12, 1990, Provo, Utah.

Goatson, Derik, interviewed by Farina King, January 18, 2008, Provo, Utah.

Goatson, Elouise T., interviewed by Farina King, November 10, 2007, Page, Arizona.

Groves, Alan, interviewed by Corey Smallcanyon, 2008, Provo, Utah.

Groves, Jeanie, interviewed by Farina King, February 12, 2008, Orem, Utah.

Hogue, Helena, interviewed by Ernesteen B. Lynch, August 21, 1990, Fruitland, New Mexico.

Jensen, Celia, interviewed by Jessie L. Embry, 2008, Gunnison, Utah.

Jones, Irene B., interview by Farina King, November 11, 2007, Page, Arizona.

Lane, Rex, interviewed by Farina King, November 10, 2007, Page, Arizona.

Little, Dennis, and Marie Little, interviewed by Farina King, October 8, 2007, Orem, Utah.

Lopez, Alexia, interviewed by Ernesteen B. Lynch, August 10, 1989, Provo, Utah.

Lynch, Ernesteen B., interviewed by Jessie L. Embry, May 17, 1990, Provo, Utah.

Mannie, Victor Sr., interviewed by Farina King, November 11, 2007, Page, Arizona.

Manygoats, Charlene, interviewed by Jessie L. Embry, 2012, Tuba City, Navajo Nation, Arizona.

Mills, Jessica, interviewed by Farina King, September 24, 2007, Provo, Utah.

Mirabal, Shaynalea, interviewed by Farina King, October 30, 2007, Provo, Utah.

Nez, Harlan, interviewed by Jessie L. Embry, 2012, Tuba City, Navajo Nation, Arizona.

Nez, Liz, interviewed by Jessie L. Embry, April 22, 2012, Tuba City, Navajo Nation, Arizona.

Paredes, Ellouise, interviewed by Farina King, March 13, 2008, Salt Lake City, Utah.

Pine, Donald L., interviewed by Farina King, February 17, 2008, Ft. Wingate, New Mexico.

Pooley, Lillie, interviewed by Jessie L. Embry, 2012, Tuba City, Navajo Nation, Arizona.

Pooley, Ray, interviewed by Farina King, 2012, Tuba City, Navajo Nation, Arizona.

Quintana, Eileen, interviewed by Farina King, February 13, 2008, Springville, Utah.

Sekaquaptewa, Ken, interviewed by Odessa Neaman, June 11, 1990, Provo, Utah.

Singer, Lewis, interviewed by Jim M. Dandy, 1990, Blanding, Utah.

Singer, Ronald L., interviewed by Odessa Newman, June 14, 1990, Provo, Utah.

Smith, Phillip L., interviewed by Farina King, January 5, 2008, Kensington, Maryland; September 8, 2008, Kensington, Maryland.

Talk, Shauntel, interviewed by Farina King, January 18, 2008, Provo, Utah.

Tsinnijinnie, Thomas, interviewed by Farina King, September 12, 2012, Salt River Pima-Maricopa Community, Arizona.

Whaley, Aneta, interviewed by Jim M. Dandy, 1990, Monument Valley, Navajo Nation, Utah.

Whaley, Oliver, interviewed by Farina King, September 28, 2007, Provo, Utah.

Willie, Shaela Ann [Avery], interviewed by Farina King, December 14, 2007, Provo, Utah.

CHURCH HISTORY LIBRARY OF THE CHURCH OF JESUS CHRIST OF LATTER-DAY SAINTS, SALT LAKE CITY, UTAH

Buchanan, Golden, interviewed by William G. Hartley, 1974–1975, Salt Lake City, Utah.

Buchanan, Thelma S., interviewed by William G. Hartley, 1976, Salt Lake City, Utah.

Deschine, Wilson Yazzie, interviewed by Matthew K. Heiss, 1992, Window Rock, Navajo Nation, Arizona.

Flake, David Kay, interviewed by Matthew K. Heiss, April 25, 1997, Window Rock, Navajo Nation, Arizona.

Gardner, Harvey Leon, interviewed by Matthew K. Heiss, 1992, Page, Arizona.

Jensen, Miles, interviewed by Gordon Irving, 1983, Salt Lake City, Utah.

John, Dallin J., interviewed by Matthew K. Heiss, 1991, Chinle, Navajo Nation, Arizona.

Kalauli, Mitchell Davis Kapuni, interviewed by Matthew K. Heiss, 1992, Tuba City, Navajo Nation, Arizona.

Kalauli, Winna B., interviewed by Matthew K. Heiss, 1991, Chinle, Navajo Nation, Arizona.

Kinlacheeny, Susie T., interviewed by Matthew K. Heiss, 1997, Kayenta, Navajo Nation, Arizona.

Numkena, William, interviewed by Matthew K. Heiss, April 28, 1992, Tuba City, Navajo Nation, Arizona.

Smith, Dan K., interviewed by Matthew K. Heiss, April 30, 1992, Chinle, Navajo Nation, Arizona.

Tano, Edwin, interviewed by Matthew K. Heiss and Michael Landon, May 2, 1997, Kayenta, Navajo Nation, Arizona; interviewed by Matthew K. Heiss, May 4, 1991, Chinle, Navajo Nation, Ariona.

Tulley, Virginia Morris Tso, interviewed by Matthew K. Heiss, 1997, Window Rock, Navajo Nation, Arizona.

Willie, Jerome Wilmer, interviewed by Matthew K. Heiss, 1997, Window Rock, Navajo Nation, Arizona.

Young, June, and Ernst Clifford, interviewed by Matthew K. Heiss, April 23, 1992, Chinle, Navajo Nation, Arizona.

Whaley, Ollie J., interviewed by Matthew K. Heiss, 1997, Kayenta, Navajo Nation, Arizona.

OTHER ORAL HISTORY COLLECTIONS

James, Damon, oral history interview transcript, January 21, 2012, Brigham City Museum of Art and History, Brigham City, Utah.

Kee-Jansen, Chauma, interviewed by Yadira Veamatahau, February 22, 2019, Provo, Utah, Native BYU Oral History.

Kelly, William Keoniana, interviewed by Rachel Nathan, February 6, 1994, Orem, Utah, Latter-day Saint Polynesian American Oral History Project, Charles Redd Center for Western Studies, L. Tom Perry Special Collections, Harold B. Lee Library, Brigham Young University, Provo, Utah.

King, Randell K., interviewed by Jessie L. Embry, 2009, Provo, Utah, Provo South Stake Oral History Project, Charles Redd Center for Western Studies, L. Tom Perry Special Collections, Harold B. Lee Library, Brigham Young University, Provo, Utah.

Turnblom, Sherry, interviewed by Rebecca Vorimo, 1994, LDS Sister Missionaries Oral History Project, Charles Redd Center for Western Studies, L. Tom Perry Special Collections, Harold B. Lee Library, Brigham Young University, Provo, Utah.

Yazzie, April, interviewed by David Bolingbroke, 2009, Provo, Utah, Provo South Stake Oral History Project, Charles Redd Center for Western Studies, L. Tom Perry Special Collections, Harold B. Lee Library, Brigham Young University, Provo, Utah.

Glossary

ałk'idą́ą́: long ago.

Asdzą́ą́ Nádleehé: Changing Woman, one of the most revered Diné deities, the mother of all the clans and identified as White Shell Woman.

'Awéé' ch'ídeeldlo': First Laugh Ceremony, when Diné celebrate and bless their babies after their first laugh.

Awéétsáál: the Diné cradleboard for infants.

biil: Diné rug dress.

Bilagáanaa: Anglo-American, or what Diné call white Americans.

Bilasáanaa diwozhí: "thorny apple" or pineapple, which Diné called the Kānaka Maoli or Native Hawaiian Latter-day Saint missionaries during the late twentieth century.

branch: a term that refers to a local Latter-day Saint congregation with fewer members than a ward.

chapter: a center of local Diné government in communities of the Navajo Nation.

Cheii Na'ashǫ́'ii Dich'ízhii: Grandfather Horned Toad who blesses Diné.

Ch'ínílį́: Chinle, Navajo Nation, which translates as "where the water flows out," referring to how the water flows from the nearby Tséyi' or Canyon de Chelly.

Ch'óol'į́'í: Gobernador Knob, one of the sacred inner mountains in Diné homelands.

Dibé Nitsaa: the sacred mountain of the North, Hesperus Peak in Colorado.

Diné: "The People," what the Navajos call their nation and people.

Diné Bikéyah: Navajo lands, demarcated by the Four Sacred Mountains in the Four Corners region of the American Southwest.

Diné bizaad: Navajo language.

Diné dóó Gáamalii: Navajo and Latter-day Saint.

Dinéjí na'nitin: traditional Navajo teachings and ways of life.

Diyin Diné: the "Holy People," gods, deities, or supernatural beings.

Dook'o'oosłííd: the sacred mountain of the West, the San Francisco Peaks in northern Arizona.

Dził Ná'oodiłii: Huerfano Mountain, one of the sacred inner mountains of Diné homelands.

'E'e'aah: West, affiliated with Dook'o'oosłííd (San Francisco Peaks), yellow, twilight, abalone shell, autumn, reflection, adulthood, and life.

Gáamalii: Mormon, or what Diné call Latter-day Saints.

Gáamalii Bina'nitiní: Latter-day Saint missionaries.

Ha'a'aah: East, affiliated with Sis Naajiní (Mount Blanca), dawn, white, white shell, spring, preparation, birth, and thinking.

hataałii: traditional Navajo healer, known as a medicine man or woman.

hooghan: hogan, the traditional dwelling and home of Navajos.

hózhǫ́: the Diné ideal of society, a desirable state of being translated as beauty, harmony, and happiness.

Hózhǫ́ǫ́jí: Blessing Way ceremony that maintains hózhǫ́ through blessings.

Hwééłdi: "The Land of Suffering," the Bosque Redondo and Fort Sumner, located in eastern New Mexico, where the US government interned the Navajos.

Hwe'odlą': Diné concept that some Diné Latter-day Saints associate with principles of faith.

Indian Student Placement Program (ISPP): also referred to as Placement, the program that the Church of Jesus Christ of Latter-day Saints organized, which placed Native American youth with Latter-day Saint families off the American Indian reservations for schooling approximately between 1947 and 2000.

Jesus Christ Binahagha' Akée'di Dayoołkáałgo yá Naazínígíí: the Diné translation referring to the Church of Jesus Christ of Latter-day Saints.

Kanaka 'Ōiwi: Native Hawaiian (singular).

Kānaka Maoli: Native Hawaiians.

Kinaaldá: the female puberty ceremony for young Diné women who menstruated for the first time.

K'é: kinship and clan system.

Lamanites: ancient Israelite peoples who came and lived in the Americas according to the Book of Mormon, which became synonymous with Native American and Indigenous peoples among Latter-day Saints in the nineteenth and twentieth centuries since they were considered the descendants of Laman, the son of a prophet called Lehi.

Maoris: Indigenous peoples of New Zealand, which is known as Aotearoa.

nahaghá: Diné rituals.

Náhookǫs: North, affiliated with Dibé Ntsaa (Mount Hesperus), folding darkness, black, obsidian, black jet, winter, conclusion, new beginning, faith prayers, and old age.

Nayee'ijí: Protection Way ceremony that restores hózhǫ́ through protections.

Nephites: ancient peoples who, according to the Book of Mormon, came from Israel to the Americas and descend from a prophet known as Nephi.

Ólta' Gáamalii: "Mormon School," or what Diné call the Indian Student Placement Program of the Church of Jesus Christ of Latter-day Saints.

Shádi'ááh: South, affiliated with Tsoodził (Mount Taylor), blue twilight, blue, turquoise, summer, activity, adolescence, and planning.

shits'ę́ę́': the umbilical cord with the first-person possessive pronoun (compared to nits'ę́ę́', which means "your umbilical cord"), considered sacred to Diné because of its continual connection to its person of origin.

Si'ąh Naagháí Bik'eh Hózhǫ́ (SNBH): the Diné philosophy of "Walk in Beauty," or "live to old age in beauty."

Sis Naajiní: the sacred mountain of the East, Blanca Peak in Colorado.

sodizin bá hooghan: the Diné word for church.

Southwest Indian Mission (SWIM): the Latter-day Saint mission in the Four Corners region of the American Southwest that included the Navajo Nation between 1949 and 1974.

stake: the term that refers to a set of wards, or Latter-day Saint congregations, in a region.

survivance: Gerald Vizenor's concept that stresses how Indigenous cultures and peoples thrive rather than merely survive.

táádidíín: corn pollen, the powder from the top of corn stalks on the tassels, which is sacred to Navajos.

To'Nanees'Dizi: also spelled as Tó'naneesdizí, the Navajo word for Tuba City, Arizona, which the local chapter uses.

ts'aa: Navajo wedding basket.

Tségháhoodzání: the "Perforated Rock," or Window Rock, Navajo Nation.

Tséyaaniichii': "Termination of Red Streak of Rock," part of the "checkerboard" of Diné communities that lies at the eastern edge of the border town of Gallup, New Mexico.

Ts'ithootso: St. Michaels, Navajo Nation, or a place "that extends out in yellow and green" or "green meadow."

tsodizin dóó sin: song and prayer, or what Diné call "religion."

Tsoodził: the sacred mountain of the South, Mount Taylor in New Mexico.

ward: the term for a local congregation of the Church of Jesus Christ of Latter-day Saints.

Yéii' bicheii: Navajo ceremonial dance performed only in winter after the first snowfall.

Yoołgai Asdzą́ą́n: White Shell Woman who is considered the same but in different form of Changing Woman, a Diné deity and mother of all clans.

Notes

INTRODUCTION

1. I use the terms Navajo and Diné interchangeably since they are both common. The Navajo Nation is the official name of the tribal nation, but Navajos, including me and my ancestors, have called themselves Diné ("the People") since time immemorial. Diné have commonly called Latter-day Saints "Gáamalii." I also alternate between Mormon and Latter-day Saint, since members of the Church of Jesus Christ of Latter-day Saints have historically been known by both terms. However, church members question both terms. After a 2018 Church General Conference, the President and Prophet of the Church, Russell M. Nelson, explained that he "released a statement regarding a course correction for the name of the Church. . . . I did this because the Lord impressed upon my mind the importance of the name He decreed for His Church, even The Church of Jesus Christ of Latter-day Saints." See Russell M. Nelson, "The Correct Name of the Church," General Conference, October 2018, https://www.lds.org/general-conference/2018/10/the-correct-name-of-the-church?lang=eng. I try to use "Mormon" in historical context.

2. See Hastiin Biyo' Łání Yéé Biye', Robert W. Young, and William Morgan, *The Ramah Navahos: Tł'ohchiníjí diné kéédahat'ilnii baa hane'* (Washington, DC: US Department of the Interior, 1949), ii.

3. To learn more about autoethnography, see Sarah Wall, "Easier Said than Done: Writing an Autoethnography," *International Journal of Qualitative Methods* 7, no. 1 (2008): 38–53, https://journals.sagepub.com/doi/pdf/10.1177/160940690800700103.

4. Philip of Bethsaida was one of the original apostles who followed Jesus in the New Testament. Refer to Matthew 10:2–4 and John 1:43–45. To learn more about the Rehoboth Christian Reformed Church, see "Celebrating the Past—a History of Rehoboth CRC," Rehoboth Christian Reformed Church website, accessed December 26, 2020, https://rehobothcrc.weebly.com/history.html.

5. Personal conversation with Phillip L. Smith, my father, on March 31, 2017.

6. See, for example, Kimberly Jenkins Marshall, *Upward, not Sunwise: Resonant Rupture in Navajo Neo-Pentecostalism* (Lincoln: University of Nebraska Press, 2016), 18. Marshall's focus on "resonant rupture" in Diné forms of neo-Pentecostalism could apply to various religious experiences. Also see David M. Brugge, *Navajos in the Catholic Church Records of New Mexico, 1694–1875* (Santa Fe: School for Advanced Research Press, 2010); Steve Pavlik, "Navajo Christianity: Historical Origins and Modern Trends," *Wicazo Sa Review* 12, no. 2 (1997): 43; Elizabeth L. Lewton and Victoria Bydone, "Identity

and Healing in Three Navajo Religious Traditions: Sạ'ah Naagháí Bik'eh Hózhǫ́," *Medical Anthropology Quarterly* 14, no. 4 (2000): 476.

7. Anonymous Diné elderly woman to Hal L. Taylor (Southwest Indian Mission president, 1965–1968), cited in James D. Mathews, "A Study of the Cultural and Religious Behavior of the Navaho Indians Which Caused Animosity, Resistance, or Indifference to the Religious Teachings of the Latter-day Saints" (master's thesis, Brigham Young University, 1968), 83.

8. Thomas Benally oral history, interview by Matthew K. Heiss, Chinle, Arizona, April 26, 1997, pp. 7, 10, OH 1628, Church History Library, Church of Jesus Christ of Latter-day Saints, Salt Lake City, Utah (hereafter Church History Library).

9. Ernie Bulow, *Navajo Taboos* (Gallup, NM: Buffalo Medicine Books, 1991), 14.

10. *Diné Cultural Content Standards for Students*, "*T'áá Shá Bik'ehgo Diné Bí Ná nitin dóó íhoo'aah*" (Window Rock, AZ: Office of Diné Culture, Language, and Community Service, Division of Diné Education, 1998), ix. The source does not italicize Diné terms and translates hózhǫ́ as "blessing," although hózhǫ́ has various translations. Anthropologist John R. Farella argues that "Sạ'a Nagháí Bik'e Hózhǫ́ is *the* key concept in Navajo philosophy, the vital requisite for understanding the whole." See Farella, *The Main Stalk: A Synthesis of Navajo Philosophy* (Tucson: University of Arizona Press, 1984), 153. The verses of the Beauty Way (similar to the Blessing Way) prayer vary in different sources, but the main idea remains the same: Diné pray for hózhǫ́ to surround and fill them in order to live well. See also Farina King, *The Earth Memory Compass: Diné Landscapes and Education in the Twentieth Century* (Lawrence: University Press of Kansas, 2018).

11. Joel W. Martin, *The Land Looks After Us: A History of Native American Religion* (New York: Oxford University Press, 2001), ix.

12. For more about the changing conceptualizations of "religion" in Indigenous experiences and struggles with colonialism, see Tisa Wenger, *We Have a Religion: The 1920s Pueblo Indian Dance Controversy and American Religious Freedom* (Chapel Hill: University of North Carolina Press, 2009). To understand various meanings and dynamics of hózhǫ́ and Diné identity in the twentieth century, see Vincent Werito, "Understanding Hózhǫ́ to Achieve Critical Consciousness: A Contemporary Diné Interpretation of Philosophical Principles of Hózhǫ́," in Lloyd L. Lee, ed., *Diné Perspectives: Revitalizing and Reclaiming Navajo Thought* (Tucson: University of Arizona Press, 2014), 25; Larry W. Emerson, "Diné Culture, Decolonization, and the Politics of Hózhǫ́," in *Diné Perspectives*, 49; Kristina M. Jacobsen, *The Sound of Navajo Country: Music, Language, and Diné Belonging* (Chapel Hill: University of North Carolina Press, 2017); Marshall, *Upward, not Sunwise*; Maureen Trudelle Schwarz, *"I Choose Life": Contemporary Medical and Religious Practices in the Navajo World* (Norman: University of Oklahoma Press, 2014), 72; Lloyd L. Lee, *Diné Identity in a Twenty-First-Century World* (Tucson: University of Arizona Press, 2020).

13. See, for example, Robert S. McPherson, Jim Dandy, and Sarah E. Burak, *Navajo Tradition, Mormon Life: The Autobiography and Teachings of Jim Dandy* (Salt Lake City: University of Utah Press, 2012).

14. Jim Dandy's story exemplifies how Diné have embraced Latter-day Saint teachings in addition to their ancestral Diné ways of life. See McPherson et al., *Navajo Tradition,*

Mormon Life, 49. Concerning Diné philosophy, see Gary Witherspoon, *Language and Art in the Navajo Universe* (Ann Arbor: University of Michigan Press, 1977), 24–25. Si'ąh Naagháí Bik'eh Hózhǫ́ and hózhǫ́ have different spellings and diacritical marks depending on the literature. I use the same spelling as the Division of Diné Education in their publications of the late 1990s. See, for example, *Diné Cultural Content Standards for Students*, ix.

15. Ernest Harry Begay, "Navajo Philosophy," lecture, Navajo Lecture Series, Arizona State University, Tempe, Arizona, November 1, 2013. I attended this lecture and kept notes. Begay is a *hataałii*, a traditional Diné healer. Diné have regarded the two entities as concepts and actual beings.

16. Witherspoon, *Language and Art*, 25.

17. A sacred number to Diné, four and the Four Sacred Directions are significant in various ways. There are actually seven principal directions that signify Diné world-views: "east, south, west, north, zenith, nadir, and center." The Four Sacred Mountains and other central landmarks of Diné Bikéyah include Sisnaajiní, or Blanca Peak of the East; Tsoodził, Mount Taylor of the South; Dook'o'oosłííd, San Francisco Peak of the West; Dibé Nitsaa, La Plata Peak of the North; Ch'óol'į́'į́, Gobernador Knob known as the "heart" or "chimney" of Navajo country; and Dziłná'oodiłii, Huerfano Peak, known as the "doorway" at the center. See Maureen Trudelle Schwarz, *Blood and Voice: Navajo Women Ceremonial Practitioners* (Tucson: University of Arizona Press, 2003), 28.

18. Arlene Nofchissey Williams became one of the first Native American women nominated for a Grammy when her album *Proud Earth* was considered for the Spiritual Music award. See "Biography: Arlene Nofchissey Williams," last.fm, accessed December 28, 2020, https://www.last.fm/music/Arlene+Nofchissey+Williams/+wiki.

19. "I Walk in Beauty," B2 on Arlene Nofchissey (Williams) and Carnes Burson, *Go My Son*, Blue Eagle Records BE-6840, 1967, 33⅓ rpm. Arlene Nofchissey Williams also has her own album titled *We Are One with Nature*. She wrote and sang "I Walk in Beauty."

20. Ernesteen B. Lynch, interview by Jessie L. Embry, Provo, Utah, May 17, 1990, MSS OH 1488, LDS Native American Oral History Project (hereafter cited as LDS NAOH), Charles Redd Center for Western Studies, L. Tom Perry Special Collections, Harold B. Lee Library, Brigham Young University, Provo, Utah (hereafter cited as BYU Special Collections). All quotations from Lynch here are from this interview.

21. See the seminal work of Albert Memmi, *The Colonizer and the Colonized* (Boston: Beacon Press, 1965 [originally published 1957]). Common discourse continues to apply these clear-cut terms and categories of "colonizer" and "colonized." Matthew Garrett addresses this "conflict-bound binary of colonizers and the colonized," but he continues to frame a binary of an American Indian world and a white world. See Matthew Garrett, *Making Lamanites: Mormons, Native Americans, and the Indian Student Placement Program, 1947–2000* (Salt Lake City: University of Utah Press, 2016), 5.

22. Monika Brown Crowfoot, "The Lamanite Dilemma: Mormonism and Indigene-ity," *Dialogue: A Journal of Mormon Thought* 54, no. 2 (Summer 2021): 57.

23. See the foundational work of Vine Deloria Jr., "Missionaries and the Religious Vacuum," in *Custer Died for Your Sins: An Indian Manifesto* (Norman: University of Oklahoma Press, 1988 [originally published 1969]), 101. See also the brief reference to

the Church of Jesus Christ of Latter-day Saints in Thomas King, *The Inconvenient Indian: A Curious Account of Native People in North America* (Minneapolis: University of Minnesota Press, 2018 [originally published 2012]), 62–63.

24. For more critiques of these binaries, see James Joseph Buss and C. Joseph Genetin-Pilawa, eds., *Beyond Two Worlds: Critical Conversations on Language and Power in Native North America* (Albany: State University of New York Press, 2014); Bryan C. Rindfleisch, "What We Say Matters: The Power of Words in American and Indigenous Histories," *American Historian*, February 2017, https://www.oah.org/tah/issues/2017 /february/what-we-say-matters-the-power-of-words-in-american-and-indigenous -histories/. These binaries also reinforce erasure of Indigenous histories; see, for example, Jean M. O'Brien, *Firsting and Lasting: Writing Indians Out of Existence in New England* (Minneapolis: University of Minnesota Press, 2010).

25. Homi K. Bhabha has addressed such questions in *The Location of Culture* (New York: Routledge, 2012 [originally published 1994]).

26. Waziyatawin Angela Wilson and Michael Yellow Bird, eds., *For Indigenous Eyes Only: A Decolonization Handbook* (Santa Fe: School of American Research Press, 2007), 2.

27. See Michelene Pesantubbee, "Foreword," in Joel W. Martin and Mark A. Nicholas, eds., *Native Americans, Christianity, and the Reshaping of the American Religious Landscape* (Chapel Hill: University of North Carolina Press, 2010), xi–xii. For more references about histories of settler colonialism in the United States, see such works as Roxanne Dunbar-Ortiz, *An Indigenous Peoples' History of the United States* (Boston: Beacon Press, 2014); Nick Estes, *Our History Is the Future: Standing Rock versus the Dakota Access Pipeline, and the Long Tradition of Indigenous Resistance* (New York: Penguin Random House, 2019); Dina Gilio-Whitaker, *As Long as Grass Grows: The Indigenous Fight for Environmental Justice, from Colonization to Standing Rock* (New York: Penguin Random House, 2019); Jennifer Nez Denetdale, *Reclaiming Diné History: The Legacies of Navajo Chief Manuelito and Juanita* (Tucson: University of Arizona Press, 2015 [originally published 2007]); Nick Estes, Melanie K. Yazzie, Jennifer Nez Denetdale, and David Correia, *Red Nation Rising: From Bordertown Violence to Native Liberation* (Oakland, CA: PM Press, 2021).

28. Linda Tuhiwai Smith, *Decolonizing Methodologies: Research and Indigenous Peoples* (London: Zed Books, 1998), 4.

29. See, for example, Daniel K. Richter, *Facing East from Indian Country: A Native History of Early America* (Cambridge, MA: Harvard University Press, 2009 [originally published 2001]); Denetdale, *Reclaiming Diné History*; Malinda Maynor Lowery, *Lumbee Indians in the Jim Crow South: Race, Identity, and the Making of a Nation* (Chapel Hill: University of North Carolina Press, 2010); Matthew Sakiestewa Gilbert, *Education beyond the Mesas: Hopi Students at Sherman Institute, 1902–1929* (Lincoln: University of Nebraska Press, 2010); Jeffrey P. Shepherd, *We Are an Indian Nation: A History of the Hualapai People* (Tucson: University of Arizona Press, 2010); Jodi A. Byrd, *The Transit of Empire: Indigenous Critiques of Colonialism* (Minneapolis: University of Minnesota Press, 2011); Jean M. O'Brien, Juliana Barr, Nancy Shoemaker, and Scott Manning Stevens, eds., *Why You Can't Teach United States History without American Indians* (Chapel

Hill: University of North Carolina Press, 2015); Julie L. Reed, *Serving the Nation: Chero-kee Sovereignty and Social Welfare, 1800–1907* (Norman: University of Oklahoma Press, 2016); King, *Earth Memory Compass*; Brianna Theobald, *Reproduction on the Reservation: Pregnancy, Childbirth, and Colonialism in the Long Twentieth Century* (Chapel Hill: University of North Carolina Press, 2019); Maurice S. Crandall, *These People Have Always Been a Republic: Indigenous Electorates in the U.S.-Mexico Borderlands, 1598–1912* (Chapel Hill: University of North Carolina Press, 2019).

30. See Jeff Corntassel, Taiaiake Alfred, Noelani Goodyear-Kaōpua, Hokulani Aikau, Noenoe Silva, and Devi Mucina, eds., *Everyday Acts of Resurgence: People, Places, Practices* (Olympia, WA: Daykeeper Press, 2018), 17; Jeff Corntassel, "Re-envisioning Resurgence: Indigenous Pathways to Decolonization and Sustainable Self-Determination," *Decolonization: Indigeneity, Education and Society* 1, no. 1 (2012): 86–101.

31. Many histories use some form of the term "Mormon-Indian." See Farina King, "Indigenizing Mormonisms," *Mormon Studies Review* 6 (2019): 1–16. See also Ned Blackhawk, *Violence over the Land: Indians and Empires in the Early American West* (Cambridge, MA: Harvard University Press, 2006); Elise Boxer, "'To Become White and Delightsome': American Indians and Mormon Identity" (PhD diss., Arizona State University, 2009); Denetdale, *Reclaiming Diné History*; Stanley Thayne, "The Blood of Father Lehi: Indigenous Americans and the Book of Mormon" (PhD diss., University of North Carolina, 2016); Max Perry Mueller, *Race and the Making of the Mormon People* (Chapel Hill: University of North Carolina Press, 2017); Elise Boxer, "'The Lamanites Shall Blossom as the Rose': The Indian Student Placement Program, Mormon Whiteness and Indigenous Identity," *Journal of Mormon History* 41, no. 4 (2015); Gina Colvin and Joanna Brooks, eds., *Decolonizing Mormonism: Approaching a Postcolonial Zion* (Salt Lake City: University of Utah Press, 2018); Moroni Benally, "Decolonizing the Blossoming: Indigenous People's Faith in a Colonizing Church," *Dialogue: A Journal of Mormon Thought* 50, no. 4 (Winter 2017); P. Jane Hafen and Brenden W. Rensink, eds., *Essays on American Indian and Mormon History* (Salt Lake City: University of Utah Press, 2019).

32. See, for example, Christopher C. Smith, "Mormon Conquest: Whites and Natives in the Intermountain West, 1847–1851" (PhD diss., Claremont Graduate University, 2016); W. Paul Reeve, *Making Space on the Western Frontier: Mormons, Miners, and Southern Paiutes* (Urbana: University of Illinois Press, 2006); Will Bagley, ed., *The Whites Want Every Thing: Indian-Mormon Relations, 1847–1877* (Norman: Arthur H. Clark, 2019); Jared Farmer, *On Zion's Mount: Indians, Mormons, and the American Landscape* (Cambridge, MA: Harvard University Press, 2008). See also the early historic text of Frank Jenne Cannon and George Leonard Knapp, *Brigham Young and His Mormon Empire* (Princeton, NJ: Princeton University, 1913). Frank Jenne Cannon was one of the first senators from Utah in the US Congress between 1896 and 1899.

33. Linda T. Smith, *Decolonizing Methodologies*, 24.

34. A major part of this misunderstanding is the lack of Native American history and perspectives in general education and curriculum. See, for example, Sarah B. Shear, Ryan T. Knowles, Gregory J. Soden, and Antonio J. Castro, "Manifesting Destiny: Re/presentations of Indigenous Peoples in K-12 U.S. History Standards," *Theory and Research in Social Education* 43, no. 1 (2015): 68–101; Roxanne Dunbar-Ortiz and Dina

Gilio-Whitaker, *"All the Real Indians Died Off" and 20 Other Myths about Native Americans* (Boston: Beacon Press, 2016).

35. Frederick Cooper, *Colonialism in Question: Theory, Knowledge, History* (Berkeley: University of California Press, 2005), 14.

36. Patricia Nelson Limerick, *The Legacy of Conquest: The Unbroken Past of the American West* (New York: W. W. Norton, 1987), 18.

37. J. Kēhaulani Kauanui, "'A Structure, not an Event': Settler Colonialism and Enduring Indigeneity," *Lateral* 5, no. 1 (2016), https://csalateral.org/issue/5–1/forum-alt-humanities-settler-colonialism-enduring-indigeneity-kauanui/.

38. Cooper, *Colonialism in Question*, 16.

39. Jean Comaroff, *Body of Power, Spirit of Resistance: The Culture and History of a South African People* (Chicago: University of Chicago Press, 1985), 3.

40. John L. Comaroff and Jean Comaroff, *Of Revelation and Revolution*, vol. 1: *Christianity, Colonialism, and Consciousness in South Africa* (Chicago: University of Chicago Press, 1991), 4.

41. Moroni Benally, "Decolonizing the Blossoming: Indigenous People's Faith in a Colonizing Church," *Dialogue: A Journal of Mormon Thought* 50, no. 4 (Winter 2017): 74.

42. See, for example, Darron T. Smith, "These House-Negroes Still Think We're Cursed: Struggling against Racism in the Classroom," *Cultural Studies* 19, no. 4 (July 2005): 440; James C. Jones, *"Mormonism and White Supremacy* as an Explanation of Mormonism's Relationship with White Supremacy," Review Roundtable in *Dialogue* 54, no. 1 (Spring 2021): 155; LaShawn C. Williams, *"Mormonism and White Supremacy* as White Mormon Scholarship," Review Roundtable, 162; Joanna Brooks, *Mormonism and White Supremacy: American Religion and the Problem of Racial Innocence* (New York: Oxford University Press, 2020), 2; David Lee Keiser, "Learners not Widgets: Teacher Education for Social Justice during Transformational Times," in Nicholas M. Michelli and David Lee Keiser, eds., *Teacher Education for Democracy and Social Justice* (New York: Routledge, 2005), 49; Glenn E. Singleton, *More Courageous Conversations about Race* (Thousand Oaks, CA: Corwin, 2013), 131–142.

43. I was present during the Annual American Indian Studies Association Conference, February 8, 2013, in Tempe, Arizona (on the main campus of Arizona State University) for Elise Boxer's presentation "'Go My Son': The Construction and Negotiation of Mormon Native Identity in the Indian Student Placement Program."

44. "The Title Page," *The Book of Mormon* (Salt Lake City: Church of Jesus Christ of Latter-day Saints, 1989).

45. For more about the Papago Ward, see D. L. Turner, "Akimel Au-Authm, Xalychidom Piipaash, and the LDS Papago Ward," *Journal of Mormon History* 39, no. 1 (Winter 2013): 158–180; Jill B. Adair, "Pres. Hinckley Shows 'Great Love for Sons, Daughters of Lehi,'" *Church News*, September 20, 1997, https://www.thechurchnews.com/archives/1997-09-20/pres-hinckley-shows-great-love-for-sons-daughters-of-lehi-129603.

46. Robert L. Scabby quoted in J. Neil Birch and John A. Forster, "Choosing the Good Life: Bob Scabby and Indian Placement," *Ensign*, July 1981, available at https://www.churchofjesuschrist.org/study/ensign/1981/07/choosing-the-good-life-bob-scabby-and-indian-placement?lang=eng.

47. Elise Boxer, "The Book of Mormon as Mormon Settler Colonialism," in Hafen and Rensink, *Essays on American Indian and Mormon History*, 3.

48. Cooper, *Colonialism in Question*, 240.

49. Smith, *Decolonizing Methodologies*, 36.

50. Donald Fixico, *Call for Change: The Medicine Way of American Indian History, Ethos, and Reality* (Lincoln: University of Nebraska Press, 2013), 77.

51. See 2 Nephi 2:25 (Book of Mormon).

52. Latter-day Saints cite this scripture as Moses 7:18 in "One Heart and One Mind," *Ensign*, December 2010, https://www.churchofjesuschrist.org/study/ensign/2010/12/one-heart-and-one-mind.

53. Lee, *Diné Identity*, 37.

54. Lee, 93, 96.

55. Olivia Ben, interview by Corey Smallcanyon, Provo, Utah, 2008, LDS NAOH.

56. Olivia Ben interview.

57. Denetdale, *Reclaiming Diné History*, 179. See also Jennifer Nez Denetdale, "The Value of Oral History on the Path to Diné/Navajo Sovereignty," in Lee, *Diné Perspectives*, 68–82.

58. Regina H. Lynch, *A History of Navajo Clans* (Chinle, AZ: Navajo Curriculum Center at Rough Rock Demonstration School, 1987), 8–9.

59. Annie Ross inspires my use of "homeland" by applying "Home/Land." See Annie Ross, "'Our Mother Earth Is My Purpose': Recollections from Mr. Albert Smith, Na'ashǫ́'ii dich'ízhii," *American Indian Culture and Research Journal* 37, no. 1 (2013): 105. Albert Smith, who passed away in 2013, was my father's older brother—my uncle.

60. Paul Spruhan, "The Origins, Current Status, and Future Prospects of Blood Quantum as the Definition of Membership in the Navajo Nation," *Tribal Law Journal* 8, no. 1 (2007): 7.

CHAPTER 1. DINÉ DÓÓ GÁAMALII: NAVAJO LATTER-DAY SAINTS

1. Edward L. Kimball Jr. and Andrew E. Kimball, *Spencer W. Kimball* (Salt Lake City: Bookcraft, 1977), 252, cited in "The Gospel of Love: Stories about President Spencer W. Kimball," *Ensign*, December 1985, https://www.churchofjesuschrist.org/study/ensign/1985/12/the-gospel-of-love?lang=eng.

2. Ruth Polacca, District Conference, Toadlena, New Mexico, September 9–10, 1950, MS 13266, box 3, folder 22, Church History Library.

3. Roger Begay, "The Cornstalk Philosophy of Learning," Judicial Branch of the Navajo Nation Peacemaking Program (2007), 19, https://courts.navajo-nsn.gov/Peacemaking/corntext.pdf.

4. Terry Teller, daybreakwarrior, "Where Are You From?" (Navajo Language Study), YouTube, September 25, 2012, https://www.youtube.com/watch?v=MYvRKHIE3VY.

5. I went on this trip for the LDS Native American Oral History Project with former associate director of the Charles Redd Center for Western Studies, Jessie Embry, April 21–22, 2012, in Tuba City, Navajo Nation, Arizona.

6. Some scholars have explored syncretism and hybridization of Christianity and Native American traditions in depth. See Ethel Emily Wallis, *God Speaks Navajo* (San Francisco: Harper & Row, 1968). Angela Tarango contends that the "Indigenous principle" enables Native Americans to support their sovereignty as Pentecostals. See Tarango, *Choosing the Jesus Way: American Indian Pentecostals and the Fight for the Indigenous Principle* (Chapel Hill: University of North Carolina Press, 2014), 5. See also Luke Eric Lassiter, Clyde Ellis, and Ralph Kotay, *The Jesus Road: Kiowas, Christianity, and Indian Hymns* (Lincoln: University of Nebraska Press, 2002). Jennifer Graber explains how Indigenous engagement with Christianity also stemmed from strategies to survive and struggles over lands. See Graber, *The Gods of Indian Country: Religion and the Struggle for the American West* (New York: Oxford University Press, 2018).

7. Steve Pavlik, "Of Saints and Lamanites: An Analysis of Navajo Mormonism," *Wicazo Sa Review* 8, no. 1 (Spring 1992): 21.

8. See Marshall, *Upward, not Sunwise*, 8–12; Elizabeth L. Lewton and Victoria Bydone, "Identity and Healing in Three Navajo Religious Traditions: Są'ah Naagháí Bik'eh Hózhǫ́," *Medical Anthropology Quarterly* 14, no. 4 (December 2000): 476–497; Sergei Kan, *Memory Eternal: Tlingit Culture and Russian Orthodox Christianity through Two Centuries* (Seattle: University of Washington Press, 1999), 313. Consider Kan's ideas of "converged agendas." See also Comaroff and Comaroff, *Of Revelation and Revolution*, vol. 1: *Christianity, Colonialism, and Consciousness in South Africa*. For more about Native American appropriations of Christianity, see Jack Maurice Schultz, *The Seminole Baptist Churches of Oklahoma: Maintaining a Traditional Community* (Norman: University of Oklahoma Press, 1999); Lassiter et al., *Jesus Road*; James Treat, ed., *Native and Christian: Indigenous Voices on Religious Identity in the United States and Canada* (New York: Routledge, 1996).

9. Dinétah refers to ancestral Navajo land, whereas Diné Bikéyah could refer to contemporary Navajo land claims and properties.

10. Peter Iverson, *Diné: A History of the Navajos* (Albuquerque: University of New Mexico Press, 2002), 8. See also Paul Zolbrod, *Diné Bahane': The Navajo Creation Story* (Albuquerque: University of New Mexico Press, 1984).

11. See Kenneth M. Roemer, "It's Not a Poem. It's My Life: Navajo Singing Identities," *SAIL* 24, no. 2 (Summer 2012): 84–103; Kenneth M. Roemer, "Whitman's Song Sung the Navajo Way," *Transmotion* 4, no. 1 (2018): 25–39; Larry Evers, ed., "By This Song I Walk," in *Words and Place: Native Literature from the Southwest* (Tucson: University of Arizona Press, July 12, 2010), available at https://parentseyes.arizona.edu/index.php/node/884.

12. This part of the narrative refers to much of my research and writing in King, *Earth Memory Compass*.

13. Klara Kelley and Harris Francis, *A Diné History of Navajoland* (Tucson: University of Arizona Press, 2019), 6.

14. Luci Tapahonso, "This Is How They Were Placed for Us," in *A Radiant Curve* (Tucson: University of Arizona Press, 2008), 42.

15. The viewpoints here come from many Navajo authors, including storytellers and teachers, Claudeen Arthur (Tsé Níjíkiní), [et al.]; seekers who asked and understood, Judy Apachee (Táchii'nii), Rex Lee Jim (Kin Łichíi'nii); artists who looked and drew, Rudy

Begay (Kin Łichíi'nii), Wayne Charlie (Naaneesht'ézhí), Hank Willie (Tsi'naajinii); listeners, learners, and scribes, Sam and Janet Bingham, *Between Sacred Mountains: Navajo Stories and Lessons from the Land* (Chinle, AZ: Rock Point Community School, 1982), v.

16. See Regina H. Lynch, *A History of Navajo Clans* (Rough Rock, AZ: Rough Rock Demonstration School Navajo Curriculum Center, 1987). Some clans also became "extinct" or unknown by the twenty-first century.

17. For more information on Diné history, see Iverson, *Diné*. For Diné language, culture, and history, see Witherspoon, *Language and Art in the Navajo Universe*; and Robert McPherson, *Dinéjí Na'nitin: Navajo Traditional Teachings and History* (Boulder: University Press of Colorado, 2012).

18. Ernie Bulow, *Navajo Taboos* (Gallup, NM: Buffalo Medicine Books, 1991), 59.

19. Bulow, 14. See also Witherspoon, *Language and Art in the Navajo Universe*, 23.

20. This is based on my conversations with Phillip Smith, my father.

21. Ernesteen Lynch interview by Jessie Embry, p. 24, MSS OH 1488, LDS NAOH. R. Warren Metcalf also referred to this part of Lynch's oral history in his article about BYU Native American students. See Metcalf, "'Which Side of the Line': American Indian Students and Programs at Brigham Young University, 1960–1983," in Hafen and Rensink, *Essays on American Indian and Mormon History*, 225.

22. Garrick Bailey and Roberta Glenn Bailey, *A History of the Navajos: The Reservation Years* (Santa Fe: School of American Research Press, 1986), 289.

23. See examples in Lee, *Diné Perspectives*. For Navajo livestock reduction experiences, see Marsha Weisiger, *Dreaming of Sheep in Navajo Country* (Seattle: University of Washington Press, 2009). For a discussion of Indian child removal for assimilationist efforts among Diné, see Margaret D. Jacobs, *White Mother to a Dark Race: Settler Colonialism, Maternalism, and the Removal of Indigenous Children in the American West and Australia, 1880–1940* (Lincoln: University of Nebraska Press, 2011), 131.

24. Olivia Ben interview by Corey Smallcanyon, LDS NAOH, p. 16.

25. Lynch interview.

26. Denetdale, *Reclaiming Dine History*, 7–8, 134–140. Denetdale emphasizes the significance of Diné oral traditions.

27. See Fixico, *Call for Change*; McPherson, *Dinéjí Na'nitin*.

28. "First Vision," *Gospel Topics*, Church of Jesus Christ of Latter-day Saints, accessed January 6, 2021, https://www.churchofjesuschrist.org/study/manual/gospel-topics/first-vision?lang=eng. See also Joseph Smith Jr., "Joseph Smith—History: Extracts from the History of Joseph Smith, the Prophet, *History of the Church, Vol. 1*, Chapters 1–5," in *The Pearl of Great Price* (Salt Lake City: Church of Jesus Christ of Latter-day Saints, 1991 [originally compiled in 1851]), 47–59 (hereafter cited as "Joseph Smith—History").

29. "Joseph Smith—History," 1:19.

30. "Restoration of the Church," *Gospel Topics*, Church of Jesus Christ of Latter-day Saints, accessed January 6, 2021, https://www.churchofjesuschrist.org/study/manual/gospel-topics/restoration-of-the-church?lang=eng.

31. "Joseph Smith—History," 1:11.

32. John L. Brooke extends the discussion of Latter-day Saint origins to Europe and prerevolutionary history in *The Refiner's Fire*, but I do not explore Mormon foundations

extensively in this book. See Brooke, *The Refiner's Fire: The Making of Mormon Cosmology, 1644–1844* (New York: Cambridge University Press, 1994). For more about Church history, see Benjamin E. Park, *Kingdom of Nauvoo: The Rise and Fall of a Religious Empire on the American Frontier* (New York: Liveright, 2020); Mueller, *Race and the Making of the Mormon People*; Bagley, *Whites Want Every Thing*; Richard Lyman Bushman, *Joseph Smith: Rough Stone Rolling* (New York: Alfred A. Knopf, 2005).

33. Most of this information is standard beliefs that Latter-day Saints such as my family learn from their youth. Standard history books such as Leonard J. Arrington and Davis Bitton, *The Mormon Experience: A History of the Latter-day Saints* (Urbana: University of Illinois Press, 1992) cover this material. See also Matthew Bowman, *The Mormon People: The Making of an American Faith* (New York: Random House, 2012).

34. 2 Nephi 5 (Book of Mormon).

35. 3 Nephi 11–26 (Book of Mormon).

36. Gene R. Cook, "Miracles among the Lamanites," October 1980, Official Website of the Church of Jesus Christ of Latter-day Saints, accessed March 2, 2023, https://www.lds.org/general-conference/1980/10/miracles-among-the-lamanites?lang=eng. See also Doctrine and Covenants 49:24.

37. Into the twenty-first century, many have debated whether there is DNA evidence for Latter-day Saints' claims that the Indigenous peoples of the Americas are of the House of Israel. See Thomas W. Murphy, "Simply Implausible: DNA and a Mesoamerican Setting for the Book of Mormon," *Dialogue: A Journal of Mormon Thought* 36, no. 4 (Winter 2003): 109–131; Daniel C. Peterson, ed., *The Book of Mormon and DNA Research: Essays from the FARMS Review and the Journal of Book of Mormon Studies* (Provo: Neal A. Maxwell Institute for Religious Studies, Brigham Young University, 2008). See also Thomas Murphy, "Lamanite Genesis, Genealogy, and Genetics," in Dan Vogel and Brent Metcalfe, eds., *American Apocrypha: Essays on the Book of Mormon* (Salt Lake City: Signature, 2002), 47–77.

38. Boyé Lafayette De Mente, *Cultural Code Words of the Navajo People* (Phoenix: Phoenix Books, 2005), 6.

39. See Donald L. Fixico, *The American Indian Mind in a Linear World: American Indian Studies and Traditional Knowledge* (New York: Routledge, 2003); Thomas N. Norton-Smith, *The Dance of Person and Place: One Interpretation of American Indian Philosophy* (Albany: State University of New York Press, 2010).

40. See works of Pierre Bourdieu for the meaning of "habitus" in this context, such as "Structures, Habitus, Power: Basis for a Theory of Symbolic Power," in Nicholas B. Dirks, Geoff Eley, and Sherry B. Ortner, eds., *Culture/Power/History: A Reader in Contemporary Social Theory* (Princeton, NJ: Princeton University Press, 1994), 163.

41. Diné journalist Jolene Yazzie explains that "there are at least six genders [in Diné bizaad]: *Asdzáán* (woman), *Hastiin* (male), *Náhleeh* (feminine-man), *Dilbaa* (masculine-woman), *Nádleeh Asdzaa* (lesbian), *'Nádleeh Hastii* (gay man)." These different genders stem from the Diné creation story. See Jolene Yazzie, "Why Are Diné LGBTQ+ and Two Spirit People Being Denied Access to Ceremony?," *High Country News*, January 7, 2020, https://www.hcn.org/issues/52.2/indigenous-affairs-why-are-dine-lgbtq-and-two-spirit-people-being-denied-access-to-ceremony. "Náhleeh" is also commonly

spelled as "Nádleehí." For more information about Diné conceptualizations of gender, see Souksavanh Tom Keovorabouth, "Reaching Back to Traditional Teachings: Diné Knowledge and Gender Politics," *Genealogy* 5, no. 4 (October 2021): 95; Lloyd L. Lee, "Gender, Navajo Leadership, and 'Retrospective Falsification,'" *AlterNative: An International Journal of Indigenous Peoples* 8, no. 3 (2012): 277–289.

42. Diné scholar Harry Walters has said that the "Navajo language is only one generation away from becoming extinct." See Charlotte J. Frisbie and Eddie Tso, "The Navajo Ceremonial Practitioners Registry," *Journal of the Southwest* 35, no. 1 (Spring 1993): 53–92. See also Harold Carey Jr., "Harry Walters—Navajo Historian," *Navajo People*, January 23, 2013, https://navajopeople.org/blog/harry-walters-navajo-historian -video/.

43. Gordon B. Hinckley mentioned several times that men should receive the priesthood soon after baptism. One example was a satellite broadcast on February 21, 1999, titled "Find the Lambs, Feed the Sheep" where he told of a new convert who held the Aaronic Priesthood for a short while and then was made an elder. Hinckley said that was a necessary step. See Gordon B. Hinckley, "Find the Lambs, Feed the Sheep," February 21, 1999, Church of Jesus Christ of Latter-day Saints, http://www.lds.org/general -conference/1999/04/find-the-lambs-feed-the-sheep?lang=eng.

44. Balance in ways of life and gender are foundational teachings. See Keovorabouth, "Reaching Back to Traditional Teachings," 97.

45. See Roger Begay, "Empowering Values of the Diné Individual," in "The Cornstalk Philosophy of Learning," Judicial Branch of the Navajo Nation Peacemaking Program (2007), 14, https://courts.navajo-nsn.gov/Peacemaking/corntext.pdf; J. Dale Miller and Russell H. Bishop, *Anglo-Navajo Culture Capsules* (Salt Lake City: Culture Contrasts, 1974), 79.

46. J. Edwin Baird to Mathews, May 9, 1968, quoted in James D. Mathews, "A Study of the Cultural and Religious Behavior of the Navajo Indians Which Caused Animosity, Resistance, or Indifference to the Religious Teachings of the Latter-day Saints" (master's thesis, BYU, 1968), 86.

47. Quoted in Clarence R. Bishop, "Indian Placement: A History of the Indian Student Placement Program of the Church of Jesus Christ of Latter-day Saints" (master's thesis, University of Utah, 1967), 19.

48. Lynch interview, 31.

49. Farina King conversations with Diné family and observations.

50. Robert S. McPherson, *Sacred Land, Sacred View* (Provo: Charles Redd Center for Western Studies, 1992), 1–2. See also *Treaty between the United States of America and the Navajo Tribe of Indians, with a Record of the Discussions That Led to Its Signing* (Las Vegas: K. C. Publications, 1968), 2–3.

51. Rosalie H. Wax and Robert K. Thomas, "American Indians and White People," *Phylon* 22, no. 4 (1961): 306, cited in Bishop, "Indian Placement," 20.

52. Jim Dandy oral history, interview by Jessie L. Embry, 1990, Blanding, Utah, LDS NAOH, p. 6.

53. McPherson, *Sacred Lands, Sacred Views*, 71–72, 129–130. The specific examples are on these pages. The entire book introduces various Diné beliefs.

54. My father, Phillip Smith, and I have had several informal conversations about his upbringing and memories.

55. Phillip Smith conversations with Farina King.

56. See, for example, Boxer, "Book of Mormon as Mormon Settler Colonialism," 3–22; Boxer, " Lamanites Shall Blossom as the Rose"; Hokulani K. Aikau, *A Chosen People, a Promised Land: Mormonism and Race in Hawai'i* (Minneapolis: University of Minnesota Press, 2012); Gina Colvin, "A Maori Mormon Testimony," in Colvin and Brooks, *Decolonizing Mormonism*, 27–46; Gina Colvin, "Introduction: Theorizing Mormon Race Scholarship," *Journal of Mormon History* 41, no. 3 (July 2015): 11–21; Moroni Benally, "Decolonizing the Blossoming"; P. Jane Hafen, "The Being and Place of a Native American Mormon," in Terry Tempest Williams, William B. Smart, and Gibbs M. Smith, eds., *New Genesis: A Mormon Reader on Land and Community* (Salt Lake City: Gibbs Smith, 1998), 35–41; Farina King, "Miss Indian BYU: Contestations over the Crown and Indian Identity," *Journal of the West* 52, no. 3 (Summer 2013): 10–21; Corey Smallcanyon, "Contested Space: Mormons, Navajos, and Hopis in the Colonization of Tuba City" (master's thesis, Brigham Young University, 2010); George P. Lee, *Silent Courage: An Indian Story* (Salt Lake City: Deseret, 1987); Lacee A. Harris, "To Be Native American and Mormon," *Dialogue: A Journal of Mormon Thought* 18, no. 4 (1985); McPherson et al., *Navajo Tradition, Mormon Life*. An example of a podcast includes an episode on *Mormon Stories* titled "Mormonism and Colonization—An Interview with Native American Mormons about Lamanite Myths and Identity," November 21, 2018, https://www.mormonstories .org/podcast/mormonism-and-colonization/.

57. See Sarah Newcomb, *Lamanite Truth* (blog), accessed March 3, 2023, https:// lamanitetruth.com/author/lamanitetruth/.

58. See "The Nephite Project," accessed January 7, 2021, https://www.facebook.com /groups/216417728719502.

59. See "Tribe of Testimonies," accessed January 19, 2021, https://www.facebook .com/tribeoftestimonies/.

60. Andrea Hales, host, "Introduction to Tribe of Testimonies," *Tribe of Testimonies* (podcast), January 9, 2021, https://tribeoftestimonies.buzzsprout.com/1517116 /7213087-introduction-to-tribe-of-testimonies?play=true. As of 2023, Hales continues to post weekly episodes on her podcast, interviewing different Native American Latter-day Saints.

61. Most of the workshop was closed to the public, but there were two open sessions that were recorded. See Ignacio Garcia, "My Search for a Lamanite Identity: The Mexican Revolution, Rama Mexican, Margarito, Eduardo, Aztlan, and the San Antonio 4th Ward," and "Reflections on Discourses about 'Lamanites': A Panel Discussion" with Robert Joseph, Sarah Newcomb, Thomas Murphy, and Amanda Hendrix-Komoto, Workshop on Indigenous Perspectives on the Meanings of "Lamanite," August 5, 2022, University of Utah, Salt Lake City, recording available at https://mormon.utah.edu /conferences.php.

62. Arcia Tecun [Daniel Hernandez], "A Divine Rebellion: Indigenous Sacraments among Global 'Lamanites,'" *Religions* 12, no. 280 (2021): 1.

63. Hemopereki Hōani Simon, "Hoea Te Waka ki Uta: Critical Kaupapa Maori

Research and Mormon Studies Moving Forward," *New Sociology: Journal of Critical Praxis* 3 (2022): 2. See also Hemopereki Hōani Simon, "Mormonism and the White Possessive: Moving Critical Indigenous Studies Theory into the Religious Realm," *Journal for Cultural and Religious Theory* 21, no. 3 (Fall 2022): 331–362.

64. *In Laman's Terms: Looking at Lamanite Identity*, directed by Angelo Baca (2008; Seattle, WA: Native Voices, University of Washington), https://www.cultureunplugged .com/play/1590/In-Laman-s-Terms-Looking-at-Lamanite-Identity.

65. Angelo Baca, "Porter Rockwell and Samuel the Lamanite Fistfight in Heaven: A Mormon Navajo Filmmaker's Perspective," in Colvin and Brooks, *Decolonizing Mormonism*, 70.

66. "Shash Jaa': Bears Ears Official Film Website," accessed August 28, 2021, https:// shashjaa.wordpress.com; Thomas Burr, "San Juan County Seeks to Join Bears Ears Case," *Salt Lake Tribune*, May 1, 2018, https://www.sltrib.com/news/politics/2018/05 /01/san-juan-county-seeks-to-join-bears-ears-case-says-overturning-trumps-changes -would-hurt-its-economy/. See also Farina King, "Walk in Beauty Every Step," in Melissa Wei-Tsing Inouye and Kate Holbrook, eds., *Every Needful Thing: Essays on the Life of the Mind and the Heart* (Provo, UT: Neal A. Maxwell Institute for Religious Scholarship, 2022), 121–123.

67. See Thomas W. Murphy and Angelo Baca, "DNA and the Book of Mormon: Science, Settlers, and Scripture," in Matthew L. Harris and Newell G. Bringhurst, eds., *The LDS Gospel Topics Series: A Scholarly Engagement* (Salt Lake City: Signature, 2020), 69–95.

68. See Jacqueline Keeler, ed., *Edge of Morning: Native Voices Speak for the Bears Ears* (Salt Lake City: Torrey House, 2017); Rebecca M. Robinson, ed., *Voices from Bears Ears: Seeking Common Ground on Sacred Land* (Tucson: University of Arizona Press, 2018); David Roberts, *The Bears Ears: A Human History of America's Most Endangered Wilderness* (New York: W. W. Norton, 2021).

69. Monika Brown Crowfoot, "The Lamanite Dilemma: Mormonism and Indigeneity," *Dialogue: A Journal of Mormon Thought* 54, no. 2 (Summer 2021): 63.

70. Arrington and Bitton, *Mormon Experience*, 146.

71. See, for example, Mueller, *Race and the Making of the Mormon People*, 29; Colvin and Brooks, *Decolonizing Mormonism*; Hafen and Rensink, *Essays on American Indian and Mormon History*.

72. Lane Johnson, "Who and Where Are the Lamanites? Worldwide Distribution of Lamanites," *Ensign*, December 1975, 15, https://www.lds.org/ensign/1975/12/who-and -where-are-the-lamanites.

73. 4 Nephi 1:17 (Book of Mormon).

74. Moroni 9:3–24 (Book of Mormon).

75. The author was present and heard President and Prophet of the Church Russell M. Nelson give this devotional address that was broadcast to Latter-day Saints in Oklahoma and Kansas in October 2021. See references to this devotional broadcast meeting in Jason Swensen, "Church's $2 Million Donation to Oklahoma's First Americans Museum Will Help Reconnect Native American Families," *Church News*, October 18, 2021, https://www.thechurchnews.com/2021/10/18/23217338/first-americans-museum -oklahoma-familysearch-russell-nelson-mckay-native-americans. Nelson said in 2016

that the Book of Mormon "is not a textbook of history, although some history is found within its pages. It is not a definitive work on ancient American agriculture or politics. It is not a record of all former inhabitants of the Western Hemisphere, but only of particular groups of people." See Rachel Sterzer Gibson, "The Book of Mormon Is a 'Miraculous Miracle,' Says President Russell M. Nelson at 2016 Seminar for New Mission Presidents," *Church News*, June 30, 2016, https://www.thechurchnews.com/2016/6/30/23214366/the -book-of-mormon-is-a-miraculous-miracle-says-president-russell-m-nelson-at-2016 -seminar-for-new-m.

76. John-Charles Duffy, "The Use of 'Lamanite' in Official LDS Discourse," *Journal of Mormon History* 34 (Winter 2008): 118–122.

77. Thomas W. Murphy explained that he was not excommunicated from the Church but faced the threat due to his research and publications. Murphy's presentation was titled "Lamanite Genesis, Genealogy, and Genetics: Twenty Years Later," Sunstone 2022 conference ("Many Mansions!"), July 30, 2022, Sandy, Utah. See also Thomas W. Murphy, "Inventing Galileo," *Sunstone* 131 (March 2004): 58.

78. Carrie A. Moore, "Debate Renewed with Change in Book of Mormon Introduction," *Deseret News*, November 8, 2007, https://www.deseret.com/2007/11/8/20052445 /debate-renewed-with-change-in-book-of-mormon-introduction; Peggy Fletcher Stack, "Single Word Change in Book of Mormon Speaks Volumes," *Salt Lake City Tribune*, November 8, 2007, https://archive.sltrib.com/story.php?ref=/lds/ci_7403990.

79. Murphy, "Lamanite Genesis, Genealogy, and Genetics: Twenty Years Later."

80. Duffy, "Use of 'Lamanite,'" 122–131, quotation on 126.

81. Oliver Cowdery cited in Bagley, *Whites Want Every Thing*, 43.

82. Duffy, "Use of 'Lamanite,'" 132–144; Armand L. Mauss, *All Abraham's Children: Changing Mormon Conceptions of Race and Lineage* (Urbana: University of Illinois Press, 2003), 74–80.

83. David Kay Flake oral history, interview by Matthew K. Heiss, 1997, Window Rock, Arizona, Church History Library, quotation on 11. The conference talk that Flake referred to can be found on the Church website. J. Thomas Fyans, "The Lamanites Must Rise in Majesty and Power," April 1976, http://www.lds.org/general-confer ence/1976/04/the-lamanites-must-rise-in-majesty-and-power?lang=eng.

84. Flake oral history, 11.

85. Mueller, *Race and the Making of the Mormon People*, 43.

86. Although it is fiction, Mette Ivie Harrison's *The Book of Laman* seeks to empathize with Laman in the Book of Mormon. See Harrison, *The Book of Laman* (Salt Lake City: BCC Press, 2017).

87. Spencer W. Kimball, "First Presidency Message: Our Paths Have Met Again," *Ensign*, December 1975, 2.

88. Aikau, *A Chosen People, a Promised Land*, 56, 75.

89. Mauss, *All Abraham's Children*, 130.

90. Mauss, 130–134.

91. Shaynalea Mirabal oral history, interview by Farina King, 2007, Provo, Utah, p. 10, LDS NAOH.

92. Olivia Ben oral history, 15.

93. Thomas Benally oral history, interview by Matthew K. Heiss, 1997, Chinle, Arizona, p. 14, Church History Library.

94. Virginia Morris Tso Tulley oral history, interview by Matthew K. Heiss, 1997, Window Rock, Arizona, pp. 11–12, Church History Library.

95. Oliver Whaley oral history, interview by Farina King, 2007, Provo, Utah, p. 8, LDS NAOH.

96. Shannon Adison oral history, interview by Farina King, 2007, Provo, Utah, p. 11, LDS NAOH.

97. Duffy, "Use of 'Lamanite,'" 151, 152 (quotations) and 152–167.

98. Duffy, 150–151.

99. The Church of Jesus Christ of Latter-day Saints, *Church History in the Fullness of Times* (Salt Lake City: Church of Jesus Christ of Latter-day Saints, 2003), 564; Spencer W. Kimball, "Remember the Mission of the Church," *Ensign*, May 1982, 4.

100. These changes affected not only the Lamanite programs but many other Church programs as well. For examples and explanations of the reasons for the changes, see Jessie L. Embry, *Spiritualized Recreation: Mormon All-Church Athletic Tournaments and Dance Festivals* (Provo: Charles Redd Center for Western Studies, 2008), https://reddcenter .byu.edu/Pages/Spiritualized.aspx. These programs are also discussed in James B. Allen and Glen M. Leonard, *Story of the Latter-day Saints* (Salt Lake City: Deseret, 1992).

101. Darren Parry, presentation for BYU Department of History Book of the Year, October 27, 2022, Brigham Young University. See also Darren Parry, *The Bear River Massacre: A Shoshone History* (Salt Lake City: BCC Press, 2019).

102. For another example of Native Americans identifying with "Lamanite" identity, see Rios Pacheco cited in Miacel Spotted Elk, "The Complexities of Teaching Indigenous History," *High Country News*, September 2, 2022, https://www.hcn.org/articles /indigenous-affairs-education-the-complexities-of-teaching-indigenous-history. I attended and listened to Rios Pacheco, a spiritual leader and elder of the Northwestern Band of Shoshone, who asserted his people's Lamanite identity during the excursion featuring Shoshone history at the Railroads in Native America gathering in northern Utah, May 2022. Whether Latter-day Saint Native Americans identify as "Lamanite" or not, Latter-day Saint Native Americans have organized events such as the Gathering of Tribes with the Church's sponsorship. In announcements and social media descriptions of the Gathering of Tribes, attendees are invited to "strengthen our community and faith in Jesus Christ through a temple walk in regalia/traditional wear, traditional dancing at the Mesa Interstake Center, and conference in Mesa, March 10–11, 2023." See "Gathering of Tribes- LDS Conference and Social Powwow," https://www.facebook.com/events /728028525608050?ref=newsfeed, accessed March 7, 2023. There was a similar gathering of "Indigenous members of the Church of Jesus Christ of Latter-day Saints" held in Calgary, Alberta, in 2022. "Gathering of Tribes," https://www.gatheringscatteredisrael .com/?fbclid=IwAR1mxh8PaPTWgjig8RMX4OdvaVIlO5a2cmH5m3K7B92IRrZayRK _Ig-Hmek, accessed March 7, 2023; Annette Reil, "Indigenous Latter-day Saints Participate in a Gathering of Tribes in Calgary, Alberta," *Newsroom*, September 25, 2022, https://news-ca.churchofjesuschrist.org/article/indigenous-latter-day-saints-participate -in-a-gathering-of-tribes-in-calgary-alberta.

1. Phillip L. Smith oral history, interview by Farina King, January 5, 2008, Kensington, Maryland, p. 1, MSS 7752, transcript, LDS NAOH.

2. Kelli Carmean, *Spider Woman Walks This Land: Traditional Cultural Properties and the Navajo Nation* (Walnut Creek, CA: Rowman Altamira, 2002), 27. See also Richard White, *The Roots of Dependency: Subsistence, Environment, and Social Change among the Choctaws, Pawnees, and Navajos* (Lincoln: University of Nebraska Press, 1988), 230.

3. The Red Nation, "The Red Nation: Border Town Justice and Native Liberation," YouTube, April 15, 2015, https://youtu.be/rXRs3M5H_dw. "The Red Nation is a coalition dedicated to the liberation of Native peoples from capitalism and colonialism." See also Amanda Blackhorse, "Blackhorse: Border Town Violence, Injustice, and the Opposition," *Indian Country Today*, October 19, 2015, http://indiancountrytodaymedianetwork.com/2015/10/19/blackhorse-border-town-violence-injustice-and-opposition-162140; Jennifer Nez Denetdale, "'No Explanation, No Resolution, and No Answers': Border Town Violence and Navajo Resistance to Settler Colonialism," *Wicazo Sa Review* 31, no. 1 (Spring 2016): 111–131. See also Estes et al., *Red Nation Rising*.

4. Consider Louise Lamphere, "Migration, Assimilation and the Cultural Construction of Identity: Navajo Perspectives," *Ethnic and Racial Studies* 30, no. 6 (November 2007): 1132–1151. In a study of a New Mexican Navajo family, Lamphere underscores "the processes by which meanings and practices from two cultures are integrated, redesigned, or woven together." She also concentrates "on variability within families, networks and communities" to show "more evidence of overlap among populations" (1134).

5. Phillip L. Smith oral history, 3.

6. Thomas A. Tweed, *Crossings and Dwellings: A Theory of Religion* (Cambridge, MA: Harvard University Press, 2006), 54, 59. He also claims that "religions position women and men in natural terrain and social space," which emphasizes the boundary formations and interconnections (74).

7. See, for example, Manuel A. Vasquez and Marie F. Marquardt, *Globalizing the Sacred: Religion across the Americas* (New Brunswick, NJ: Rutgers University Press, 2003).

8. For translations of "religion," Diné speakers use tsodizin dóó sin, which means "prayer and song"—the most practiced manifestations of spirituality.

9. The Honorable Robert Yazzie, former Navajo Nation chief justice, was one of the people who taught me about the differences between Euro-American institutional concepts and Diné ways of life. See Robert Yazzie, "'Life Comes from It': Navajo Justice Concepts," *New Mexico Law Review* 24, no. 2 (Spring 1994): 175–190. He explains, "Navajos say that 'life comes from *beehaz'aanii* [the Navajo word for 'law'],' because it is the essence of life. The precepts of *beehaz'aanii* are stated in prayers and ceremonies which tell us of *hozho*—'the perfect state'" (175).

10. Phillip L. Smith oral history, 7.

11. Jimmy N. Benally oral history, interview by Odessa Newman, July 18, 1990, Provo, Utah, transcript, MSS 7752, p. 4, LDS NAOH.

12. See Nick Estes's work on border-town colonialism, injustice, and violence that continues into the twenty-first century, for example, "Chamberlain, South Dakota:

A Border Town and Its 'Indian Problem,'" *Indian Country Today*, June 25, 2014, and "Border Town, USA: An Ugly Reality Many Natives Call Home," *Indian Country Today*, August 15, 2014. In "Border Town, USA," focusing on Gallup, New Mexico, Estes notes: "Chronic poverty and historic structural challenges breed widespread violence, unemployment, health issues, and increased criminalization and incarceration rates." For images that capture the dark and violent effects of colonial legacies on Native American populations in border towns, specifically those with major Diné populations, see Marc Gaede, *Bordertowns: Photographs* (Albuquerque: University of New Mexico Press, 1988). See also Bob Sipchen, "Gritty Portraits of Self-Destruction from the Reservation's Edge," *Los Angeles Times*, January 10, 1988.

13. Jimmy Benally oral history, 1.

14. See *Treaty between the United States of America and the Navajo Tribe of Indians.*

15. For a Navajo perspective of hózhǫ́, see Herbert J. Benally, "Hózhǫ́ǫgo Naasháa Doo: Toward a Construct of Balance in Navajo Cosmology" (PhD diss., California Institute of Integral Studies, 2008).

16. John P. Livingstone, *Same Drum, Different Beat: The Story of Dale T. Tingey and American Indian Services* (Provo: Religious Studies Center, Brigham Young University, 2003), 55. I discuss the mission and some of these key points in Farina King, "Aloha in Diné Bikéyah: Mormon Hawaiians and Navajos, 1949–1990," in Hafen and Rensink, *Essays on American Indian and Mormon History*, 161–182.

17. Lamanites are ancient peoples of the Americas in the Book of Mormon that many Latter-day Saints have believed descended from the House of Israel through the family of Lehi. Latter-day Saints have considered Native Americans as descendants of the Lamanites since the establishment of the Church. See Duffy, "Use of 'Lamanite.'" See also Mauss, *All Abraham's Children*, 74–80.

18. Mauss, *All Abraham's Children*, 81. The Northern Indian Mission officially opened in 1964 with Rapid City, South Dakota, as the headquarters, but the Southwest Indian Mission included parts of northern Indian reservations primarily in the Dakotas, Montana, and Wyoming for a couple years before then. See Jay H. Buckley, Kathryn Cochran, Taylor Brooks, and Kristen Hollist, "Grafting Indians and Mormons Together on Great Plains Reservations: A History of the LDS Northern Indian Mission, 1964–1973," in Hafen and Rensink, *Essays on American Indian and Mormon History*, 183–210.

19. Edward Fraughton, "Spencer W. Kimball and the Lamanite Cause," *Brigham Young University Studies* 25, no. 4 (Fall 1985): 72–75.

20. See King, "Aloha in Diné Bikéyah," 163.

21. Richard Dilworth Rust, "A Mission to the Lamanites: D&C 28, 30, 32," February 22, 2013, in "Revelations in Context," *Church History*, Church of Jesus Christ of Latter-day Saints, https://history.lds.org/article/doctrine-and-covenants-lamanite-mission?lang=eng.

22. Mauss, *All Abraham's Children*, 51. See also Bruce A. Chadwick and Stan L. Albrecht, "Mormons and Indians: Beliefs, Policies, Programs, and Practices," in Marie Cornwall, Tim B. Heaton, and Lawrence Alfred Young, eds., *Contemporary Mormonism: Social Science Perspectives* (Urbana: University of Illinois Press, 1994), 287–310. The quote about "nursing fathers and mothers" comes from 1 Nephi 21:23 in the Book of

Mormon. Some Euro-American Latter-day Saints used it to justify their responsibilities to Native Americans.

23. Peggy Fletcher Stack, "Church Removes Racial References in Book of Mormon Headings," *Salt Lake Tribune*, December 20, 2010, https://archive.sltrib.com/article.php ?id=50882900&itype=CMSID. See also Boxer, "To Become White and Delightsome"; Boxer, "Lamanites Shall Blossom as the Rose."

24. Arrington and Bitton, *Mormon Experience*, 145–160. See Will Bagley, "Introduction: A Union with the Indians—Numics, Mormons, and the Frontier," in *Whites Want Every Thing*, 31–63.

25. Bagley, *Whites Want Every Thing*, 58.

26. Arrington and Bitton, *Mormon Experience*, 145–160; see also, for example, Mueller, *Race and the Making of the Mormon People*, 155, 172.

27. See Thomas G. Alexander, *Utah: The Right Place* (Salt Lake City: Gibbs Smith, 2003), 449–450. Alexander summarizes the experiences of the Utahns—especially Latter-day Saints—with the Native Americans of the area. Throughout the book, he explains the cultures of Native Americans and their relationships with Latter-day Saints. Not all LDS settlers were white, but they were mostly non-Native Americans. See, for example, Amy Tanner Thiriot, *Slavery in Zion: A Documentary and Genealogical History of Black Lives and Black Servitude in Utah Territory, 1847–1862* (Salt Lake City: University of Utah Press, 2022).

28. See, for example, Thomas Alexander, *Brigham Young and the Expansion of the Mormon Faith* (Norman: University of Oklahoma Press, 2019), location 1819 [Kindle version]. See also Bagley, *Whites Want Every Thing*. I discussed these points in my paper "Thomas Alexander and Native American History and Future Scholarship" for the session titled "Assessing the Career of Historian Thomas Alexander" at the Western History Association annual conference on October 29, 2021.

29. See Richard Neitzel Holzapfel and Robert F. Schwartz, "A Mysterious Image: Brigham Young with an Unknown Wife," *BYU Studies Quarterly* 41, no. 3 (July 2002): 49–58, https://scholarsarchive.byu.edu/cgi/viewcontent.cgi?referer=https://www.google .com/&httpsredir=1&article=3576&context=byusq. Before it was deleted in June 2020, I also accessed Robert Boyd's "Exclusive: Brigham Young's Secret Wife?" (2012) via the defunct link https://localtvkstu.wordpress.com/2012/09/21/exclusive-brigham -youngs-secret-wife/.

30. Jennifer Hale Pulsipher presented the paper "'To Identify Our Interests with Theirs': The Fort Supply Mission and Indian-White Intermarriage" at the 2019 Mormon History Association in Salt Lake City that I attended.

31. Joshua Bernhard, "The Provo River Battle," *Intermountain Histories*, May 9, 2017, last updated June 22, 2020, https://www.intermountainhistories.org/items/show/44.

32. See Jared Farmer's description of his book *On Zion's Mount* (2008) at https:// jaredfarmer.net/books/on-zions-mount/, accessed January 7, 2021. See also Jared Farmer, "Introduction," in *On Zion's Mount: Mormons, Indians, and the American Landscape* (Cambridge, MA: Harvard University Press, 2008), 1.

33. For more about "the American Indian soul wound," see Eduardo Duran, Bonnie Duran, and Maria Yellow Horse Brave Heart, "Healing the American Indian Soul

Wound," in *International Handbook of Multigenerational Legacies of Trauma* (New York: Springer, 1998), 341–354; Denise K. Lajimodiere, *Stringing Rosaries: The History, the Unforgivable, and the Healing of Northern Plains American Indian Boarding School Survivors* (Fargo: North Dakota State University Press, 2019).

34. Steven Pavlik, "Of Saints and Lamanites: An Analysis of Navajo Mormonism," *Wicazo Sa Review* 8, no. 1 (Spring 1992): 21. See also Smallcanyon, "Contested Space," 13. Latter-day Saints also developed settlements in the Four Corners area of southeastern Utah and northwestern New Mexico. For information about the Mormon settlements on Diné lands, see Robert S. McPherson, *A History of San Juan County: In the Palm of Time* (Salt Lake City: Utah State Historical Society, 1995).

35. David Kay Flake, "History of the Southwest Indian Mission" (n.p., 1965), 84.

36. *Church History in the Fulness of Times: The History of the Church of Jesus Christ of Latter-day Saints* (Salt Lake City: Church of Jesus Christ of Latter-day Saints, 1989), 545. See also *Improvement Era* 47 (Salt Lake City: Young Men's Mutual Improvement Association, 1944), 175.

37. I use the term "American Indian" for specific historic and legal contexts as the official term for such cases.

38. Iverson, *Diné*, 145.

39. See Weisiger, *Dreaming of Sheep*; George Arthur Boyce, *When Navajos Had Too Many Sheep: The 1940's* (San Francisco: Indian Historian Press, 1974); Lawrence C. Kelly, *The Navajo Indians and Federal Indian Policy, 1900–1935* (Tucson: University of Arizona Press, 1968).

40. Iverson, *Diné*, 178. See also Omer Call Stewart, *Peyote Religion: A History* (Norman: University of Oklahoma Press, 1987), 296; Thomas C. Maroukis, *The Peyote Road: Religious Freedom and the Native American Church* (Norman: University of Oklahoma Press, 2012), 52, 116, 188.

41. Iverson, *Diné*, 178.

42. "Ralph William Evans," Obituaries, *Deseret News*, July 4–5, 2002, http://www .legacy.com/obituaries/deseretnews/obituary.aspx?n=ralph-william-evans&pid= 390168.

43. Flake, "History of the Southwest Indian Mission," 93; Ralph William Evans, statement from December 25, 1943, Southwest Indian Mission Manuscript History and Historical Reports, 1942–1977, LR 8571 2, Church History Library (hereafter SWIM Manuscript History). The manuscript histories are quarterly reports that Church units submitted to the Church History Archives until 1972. Some documents provide exact dates; other documents only show the dates of the quarterly report.

44. See W. Paul Reeve, *Making Space on the Western Frontier: Mormons, Miners, and Southern Paiutes* (Urbana: University of Illinois Press, 2007); Ned Blackhawk, *Violence over the Land: Indians and Empires in the Early American West* (Cambridge, MA: Harvard University Press, 2009). Evans sounds similar to Brigham Young, who told Mormons to "feed" instead of "fight" Indians. Lawrence George Coates, "Brigham Young and Mormon Indian Policies: The Formative Period, 1836–1851," *Brigham Young Studies* 18, no. 3 (Spring 1978): 428.

45. Ralph William Evans, April 8, 1944, SWIM Manuscript History.

46. There are different spellings of "Howela" Polacca in the records, including "Havela." See, for example, 1930 US Census, Precinct 14, San Juan, New Mexico, p. 18A, National Archives microfilm 2341133, roll 1398, available at https://www.ancestry.com /discoveryui-content/view/108221948:6224. Other Navajos, who also befriended the Bloomfields and supported Latter-day Saint missions among Navajos, included Clyde Beyal and Harry Turley. See Will Evans, *Along Navajo Trails: Recollections of a Trader, 1898–1948* (Logan: Utah State University Press, 2005), 19; David Kay Flake, "A History of Mormon Missionary Work with the Hopi, Navaho and Zuni Indians" (master's thesis, BYU, 1965), 90.

47. July 23–26, 1946, SWIM Manuscript History.

48. "This Week in Church History," March 8, 2003, *Church News*, Church of Jesus Christ of Latter-day Saints, http://www.ldschurchnewsarchive.com/articles/43337/This -week-in-Church-history.html.

49. Flake, "History of Mormon Missionary Work," 113. The Polaccas lived near Crystal, Navajo Nation, New Mexico, and assisted with missionary work there. See also "Stories about President Spencer W. Kimball," *Gospel of Love*, December 1985, available at https://www.lds.org/ensign/1985/12/the-gospel-of-love?lang=eng. See also Ruth Polacca interview by Spencer Woolley Kimball, Gallup, New Mexico, 1953, MS 3878, Church History Library.

50. See Buckley Jensen, "Albert R. Lyman: Old Settler Albert R. Lyman Was the Father of Blanding Giants of San Juan," *San Juan Record*, June 4, 2008, http://www.sjrnews.com /view/full_story/6745903/article-Albert-R-Lyman?instance=series_giants_sanjuan.

51. August 12, 1946, SWIM Manuscript History.

52. August 12, July 23, 24, 25, 26, 1946; October 29, 30, 1946; December 23, 31, 1946; January 7, 1947, SWIM Manuscript History.

53. October 29, 30, 1946, SWIM Manuscript History.

54. Iverson, *Diné*, 190–191.

55. February 1, 1947, SWIM Manuscript History. I remember seeing a copy of the resolution from the Navajo Nation tribal archival files as well. Council Resolutions, 1922–51 book, J. M. Steward Attest, General Superintendent Navajo Service, Subject Matter—Mormon Church Schools—Permission to Build, etc.—November 1947, Meeting: 64 (Appendix—Item 11); Discussed 66–68; Action Tabled November 5, 1947. The President and Prophet of the Church of Jesus Christ of Latter-day Saints, George Albert Smith, followed issues of Diné education, endorsing one of the largest federal Indian boarding schools known as the Intermountain Indian Boarding School, which opened for Diné students in Brigham City, Utah, by 1949. See Scott C. Esplin, "'You Can Make Your Own Bright Future, Tom Trails': Evaluating the Impact of the LDS Indian Seminary Program," *Journal of Mormon History* 42, no. 4 (October 2016): 176.

56. Flake, "History of Mormon Missionary Work," 117.

57. November 10–11, 20, 1953, SWIM Manuscript History; Spencer W. Kimball Journal, November 10, 11, 1953, journal in private possession, used by permission via Jessie Embry.

58. Sam Gorman, cited in Navajo Indians tribal council meeting, January 14, 1953, Window Rock, Navajo Nation, Arizona, Record Group 75, Bureau of Indian Affairs,

Central Classified Files, Decimal 054, p. 279, National Archives and Records Administration, Washington, DC (hereafter cited as NARA).

59. March 10, 1955, SWIM Manuscript History.

60. Kimball journal, July 12, 1960; September 30, 1960, SWIM Manuscript History.

61. Clifford Beck cited in Navajo Indians tribal council meeting, November 15, 1960, Window Rock, Navajo Nation, Arizona, p. 15, NARA.

62. See David M. Brugge, *The Navajo-Hopi Land Dispute: An American Tragedy* (Albuquerque: University of New Mexico Press, 1994); Malcolm D. Benally, ed. and trans., *Bitter Water: Diné Oral Histories of the Navajo-Hopi Land Dispute* (Tucson: University of Arizona Press, 2011); Jerry Kammer, *The Second Long Walk: The Navajo-Hopi Land Dispute* (Albuquerque: University of New Mexico Press, 1980); Emily Benedek, *The Wind Won't Know Me: A History of the Navajo-Hopi Land Dispute* (New York: Knopf, 1992).

63. Clifford Beck cited in Navajo Indians tribal council meeting, November 15, 1960, 15, 18.

64. Norman M. Littell cited in Navajo Indians tribal council meeting, November 15, 1960, 18.

65. Norman M. Littell citing John Sterling Boyden in Navajo Indians tribal council meeting, November 15, 1960, 18. See also John Dougherty, "A People Betrayed," *Phoenix New Times*, May 1, 1997, https://www.phoenixnewtimes.com/news/a-people-betrayed -6423155.

66. Arizona Holbrook Mission Records, August 29, 1972, Church History Library, used by permission. One proposal designed the "Four Corners Mission" (where the states of Colorado, Utah, New Mexico, and Arizona meet); the other proposal demarcated a New Mexico mission. The Church did not adopt either proposal completely, but church officials eliminated SWIM and reorganized the mission according to some of the suggestions.

67. "Boundaries of Three Missions in Southwestern U.S. Realigned," *Church News*, November 11, 1972, 4; Paul Felt, "I Remember When," p. 115, MSS SC 2983, BYU Special Collections.

68. Arizona Holbrook Mission Records, June 26, 1973.

69. Ken Sekaquaptewa oral history, interview by Odessa Neaman, 1990, p. 6, LDS NAOH.

70. Arizona Holbrook Mission Records, November 16, 1978; March 25, 1979; April 29, 1979.

71. Ronald L. Singer, an informal conversation with and shared by Jessie L. Embry, July 20, 2012.

72. James B. Allen and Glen M. Leonard, *Story of the Latter-day Saints* (Salt Lake City: Deseret, 1992), 549, 568, 610. See also Benjamin H. White, "A Historical Analysis of How Preach My Gospel Came to Be" (master's thesis, BYU, 2010).

73. February 27, 1944, SWIM Manuscript History.

74. February 27, 1944, April 28, 1947, SWIM Manuscript History.

75. Julie Benally oral history, interviewed by Farina King, September 21, 2007, Provo, Utah, transcript, MSS OH 2293, p. 4, LDS NAOH.

76. Julie Benally oral history, 3–5.

77. Mildred (Millie) Cody Garrett oral history, interview by Odessa Newman, June 12, 1990, transcript, MSS 7752, p. 18, LDS NAOH.

78. SWIM boundaries also included Whiteriver, Arizona, and the Fort Apache Indian Reservation.

79. Lane Johnson, "Who and Where Are the Lamanites? Worldwide Distribution of Lamanites," *Ensign*, December 1975, https://www.lds.org/ensign/1975/12/who-and -where-are-the-lamanites?lang=eng.

80. Ian G. Barber, "Matakite, Mormon Conversions, and Māori-Israelite Identity Work in Colonial New Zealand," *Journal of Mormon History* 41, no. 3 (July 2015): 167–220; Marjorie Newton, *Tiki and Temple: The Mormon Mission in New Zealand, 1854–1958* (Draper, Utah: Greg Kofford Books, 2012); Aikau, *A Chosen People, a Promised Land*; Duffy, "Use of 'Lamanite'"; K. W. Baldridge, Laurie F. Maffly-Kipp, and Reid Larkin Neilson, eds., *Proclamation to the People: Nineteenth-Century Mormonism and the Pacific Basin Frontier* (Salt Lake City: University of Utah Press, 2008); Mauss, *All Abraham's Children*, 150.

81. See also R. Lanier Britsch, "Maori Traditions and the Mormon Church," *New Era*, June 1981, https://www.lds.org/new-era/1981/06/maori-traditions-and-the-mormon -church?lang=eng; Amanda Hendrix-Komoto, *Imperial Zions: Religion, Race, and Family in the American West and the Pacific* (Lincoln: University of Nebraska Press, 2022).

82. There is some overlap between this chapter and my previous published chapter, "Aloha in Diné Bikéyah," in Hafen and Rensink, *Essays on American Indian and Mormon History*.

83. *Lamanite Israel*, February 1966; see Southwest Indian Mission publications, 1947–1972, LR 8571 20, Church History Library. SWIM president J. Edwin Baird started this newsletter for the mission, which ran until 1972.

84. Gabriel Cinniginnie oral history, interview by Malcolm T. Pappan, April 9, 1990, Provo, Utah, transcript, MSS OH 1171, p. 5, LDS NAOH.

85. Zenobia Kapahulehua Iese, telephone interview by author, July 6, 2013.

86. SWIM Manuscript History, November 22, 1962.

87. Ronald L. Singer oral history, interview by Odessa Newman, June 14, 1990, Provo, Utah, transcript, MSS OH 1153, p. 11, LDS NAOH.

88. Rex Lane was baptized in 1949.

89. Rex Lane oral history, interview by Farina King, November 10, 2007, Page, Arizona, transcript, MSS OH 2358, p. 5, LDS NAOH.

90. Robert Lowell Brown, *Robert Lowell Brown: A Personal History Plus* (Orem, Utah: R. L. Brown, 2008), 48.

91. Victor Mannie Sr. oral history, interview by Farina King, November 11, 2007, Page, Arizona, transcript, MSS OH 2360, p. 10, LDS NAOH.

92. March 15, 1954; January 1954, SWIM Manuscript History.

93. John Edwin Baird (1908–2003), Southwest Indian Mission Papers, 1961–1965, MS 20569, Church History Library (hereafter Baird Papers).

94. *Gaamalii*, January 1, 1949, p. 3, Church History Library.

95. Phillip L. Smith, conversations with Farina King, January 2, 2016.

96. Jimmy Benally oral history, 4–5.

97. Phillip L. Smith, conversations with Farina King, April 12, 2012, Orem, Utah. Whitehorse is located in the Navajo Nation, New Mexico.

98. Maureen Trudelle Schwarz, *Navajo Lifeways: Contemporary Issues, Ancient Knowledge* (Norman: University of Oklahoma Press, 2001). She notes, "Interment was a private or family matter, and only those few people who were needed to perform the requisite procedures and were willing to expose themselves to the potentially dangerous effects of death were involved in the process" (145). In a sense, Diné traditionally perceived how they risked their own well-being in the burial service. Only certain people, who could withstand such risks, would take them. For more about my father's missionary experiences and impacts on his life, see Farina King, "Diné Doctor: A Latter-day Saint Story of Healing," *Art for Uncertain Times*, Center for Latter-day Saint Arts, https:// www.centerforlatterdaysaintarts.org/king-art-for-uncertain-times; Farina King, "Diné Doctor: A Latter-day Saint Story of Healing," *Dialogue: A Journal of Mormon Thought* 54, no. 2 (Summer 2021): 81–85.

99. Golden R. Buchanan, "Teaching Aids for Lamanite Missionaries prepared under the direction of the Indian Relations Committee," p. 34, M256.1 B918t, Church History Library.

100. Phillip L. Smith, conversations with Farina King, April 14, 2012.

101. Language Training Mission, *Diné Bizaad Naʼnitiníbá* (Provo: The [LDS Church] Mission, 1973). Hardcopy of the textbook in author's possession.

102. Richard Cowan, *Every Man Shall Hear the Gospel in His Own Language* (Provo: Mission Training Center, 1984), 49.

103. Allen and Leonard, *Story of the Latter-day Saints*, 549, 568.

104. Buchanan, "Teaching Aids for Lamanite Missionaries," 5, 6, 10, 11, 12, 15, 16, 17. The lessons included (1) Who the American Indians are and their relationship to the Book of Mormon, (2) the Book of Mormon and Bible support each other, (3) the Book of Mormon belongs to the American Indians and they are "children of promise," (4) the promise to the Lamanites comes through the Gentiles, (5) the story of the gold plates, the restoration, and Joseph Smith, (6) Christ, (7) Christ in America, (8) the Role of Christ, (9) Christ's church, (10) apostasy from truth after Christ's death, (11) why a restoration, (12) Godhead with a suggestion to keep the teachings simple, (13) faith, (14) repentance, (15) baptism, (16) authority in the Church of Jesus Christ of Latter-day Saints, (17) Holy Ghost, (18) summary and acceptance of baptism if a believer, and (19) acceptance of responsibility as a member of the Church. According to the guide, it states: "Now clinch all the above points by getting them to agree with you. This is one discussion, if properly done, that will appeal to most Indians" (21). It also notes that "the Indian people will understand and appreciate this lesson. They are strong for family and tribal authority. Use examples of reservation authority."

105. Buchanan, "Teaching Aids for Lamanite Missionaries," 34.

106. See Robert S. McPherson, "Wind, Hand, and Stars: Reading the Past, Finding the Future through Divination," in *Dinéjí Naʼnitin: Navajo Traditional Teachings and History* (Boulder: University Press of Colorado, 2012). A journalist featured the story of a Diné hand trembler in the *New York Times*. John Noble Wilford, "Medicine Men Successful Where Science Falls Short," *New York Times*, July 7, 1972, 33.

107. Delbert L. Stapley, May 7, 1966, SWIM Manuscript History.

108. "Maori Indian Travels 9,000 Miles to Attend Navajo Language School," *Navajo Times*, March 12, 1964, 6; SWIM Manuscript History, 1964.

109. Phillip L. Smith, conversation with Farina King, April 11, 2012, Orem, Utah.

110. March 15, 1954; January 1954, Southwest Indian Mission Manuscript History.

111. Phillip L. Smith, conversation with King, April 11, 2012, Orem, Utah.

112. "A Systematic Program for Teaching the Gospel to the Navajo People," prepared for the use of missionaries of the Southwest Indian Mission (Church of Jesus Christ of Latter-day Saints, Southwest Indian Mission, 1958); lessons included (1) the Godhead according to Latter-day Saints in comparison to other religions, (2) Jesus, (3) the Holy Ghost is a spirit and not the wind, (4) the purpose of life, (5) the apostasy, (6) the existence of many churches, (7) the origins of many American Indian tribes, (8) the restoration, (9) the history of The Church of Jesus Christ of Latter-day Saints, (10) the first principles of the gospel, (11) the call to repentance, and (12) the commandments.

113. *Lamanite Israel*, January 1966, SWIM publications, Church History Library.

114. Singer oral history, 12–13; Jimmy Benally oral history, 4.

115. Singer oral history, 12–13.

116. Dennis and Marie Little oral history, interview by Farina King, October 8, 2007, Orem, Utah, transcript, MSS OH 2414, p. 10, LDS NAOH.

117. Dennis and Marie Little oral history, 1–2.

118. Baird Papers. Lukachukai is on the Navajo reservation in Arizona.

119. February 4, 1965, SWIM Manuscript History.

120. See Buchanan, "Teaching Aids for Lamanite Missionaries," 6, 10–12, 15.

121. Ernst Clifford and June Young oral history, interview by Matthew K. Heiss, April 23, 1992, Chinle, Navajo Nation, Arizona, transcript, History of Chinle, OH 2269, p. 13, Church History Library.

122. William Keoniana Kelly oral history, interview by Rachel Nathan, February 6, 1994, Orem, Utah, transcript, MSS OH 1880, pp. 3–4, 8–9, Latter-day Saint Polynesian American Oral History Project, Charles Redd Center for Western Studies oral history project records, BYU Special Collections.

123. Delbert L. Stapley report, May 7, 1966, SWIM Manuscript History.

124. *Lamanite Israel*, 1969, Southwest Indian Mission publications, Church History Library; January 28, 1969, SWIM Manuscript History.

125. Jimmy Benally oral history, 5.

126. Kapahulehua Iese interview.

127. William Keoniana Kelly oral history, 3–4, 8–9.

128. See King, "Aloha in Diné Bikéyah." I appreciate the opportunity to refer back to the sources and key points from my previous chapter publication in this book.

129. My father and other Diné language speakers have not shared a knowledge of the origins or meanings of this term, but Diné use it to refer directly to Mormons or Latter-day Saints. The official newsletter of the Southwest Indian Mission was titled "The Gaamalii," beginning in 1949. As mentioned before, linguists Robert W. Young and Morgan William claim that *Gáamalii* came from a Diné adaptation of "Mormon." See foreword in Hastiin Biyo'Łání Yéę Biye', Robert W. Young, and William Morgan, *The*

Ramah Navahos: Tł'ohchiníjí diné kéédahat'ilnii baa hane' (Phoenix: Phoenix Indian School, 1949).

130. Sherry Turnblom oral history, interview by Rebecca Vorimo, 1994, p. 15, LDS Sister Missionaries Oral History Project, Charles Redd Center for Western Studies, BYU Special Collections.

131. Loren Begay oral history, interview by Farina King, 2007, Provo, Utah, p. 2, LDS NAOH.

132. Jessie L. Embry and John H. Braumbaugh, "Preaching through Playing: Using Sports and Recreation in Missionary Work," *Journal of Mormon History* 35, no. 4 (Fall 2009): 82.

133. *Lamanite Israel*, January and February 1970, Baird Papers.

134. Phillip L. Smith conversation with Farina King, April 13, 2012, Orem, Utah.

135. *Servant Sword*, 1976; *Warriors Trump*, May 1977, Arizona Holbrook Mission.

136. Lane oral history, 4.

137. Phillip L. Smith conversation with Farina King, April 13, 2012, Orem, Utah.

138. Lewis Singer oral history, interviewed by Jim M. Dandy, 1990, Blanding, Utah, p. 4, LDS NAOH.

139. Jimmy Benally oral history, 3.

140. Louise Lamphere with Eva Price, Carole Cadman, and Valerie Darwin, *Weaving Women's Lives: Three Generations in a Navajo Family* (Albuquerque: University of New Mexico Press, 2007), 130–132; Joseph D. Calabrese, *A Different Medicine: Postcolonial Healing in the Native American Church* (New York: Oxford University Press, 2013), 94, 103; John F. Garrity, "Jesus, Peyote, and the Holy People: Alcohol Abuse and the Ethos of Power in Navajo Healing," *Medical Anthropology Quarterly* 14, no. 4 (December 2000): 521. In 2003 the Native American Church of Navajoland became known as Azee Bee Nahagha of Diné Nation, Inc. (ABNDN). See "History of ABNDN: A Historical Overview of the Peyote Ceremony," Azee Bee Nahagha of Diné Nation, Inc., accessed November 5, 2022, http://www.abndn.org/history-of-abndn.html.

141. Turnblom oral history, 16–17.

142. Ollie J. Whaley oral history, interview by Matthew K. Heiss, 1997, Kayenta, Arizona, pp. 5, 10, Church History Library; Aneta Whaley oral history, interview by Jim M. Dandy, 1990, Monument Valley, Utah, p. 5, LDS NAOH.

143. Matthew Begay oral history, interview by Farina King, November 2007, Page, Arizona, LDS NAOH.

144. Phillip L. Smith, conversations with Farina King, July 24, 2016.

145. Clyde Kluckhohn, "The Ramah Navaho," *Anthropological Papers* no. 79 in the Bureau of American Ethnology Bulletin (Washington, DC: Smithsonian Institution, Bureau of American Ethnology, 1966), 334, 337.

146. See Farina King, "Diné Doctor: A Latter-day Saint Story of Healing," *Dialogue*.

147. SWIM missionaries also helped recruit Diné for ISPP, which many Latter-day Saints believed would prepare devout converts to sustain Latter-day Saint communities in Diné Bikéyah. The program, however, became controversial since it separated Diné children from their families and became another form of assimilative education. In 2016 some Diné have sued the Church for sexual abuse in ISPP. Jennifer Dobner, "Utah Man

Is Fourth Navajo to Sue Mormon Church, Alleges Sexual Abuse in Foster Program," *Salt Lake Tribune*, June 7, 2016, http://www.sltrib.com/news/3977794-155/utah-man-is -fourth-navajo-to. See also Matthew Garrett, "Mormons, Indians, and Lamanites: The Indian Student Placement Program, 1947–2000" (PhD diss., Arizona State University, 2010); Garrett, *Making Lamanites*.

148. I owe special credit and gratitude to Dee Garceau who guided the articulations of these key points.

CHAPTER 3. ÓLTA' GÁAMALII: "MORMON SCHOOL"

1. Cal Nez, "Post by Cal Nez," March 8, 2017, https://www.facebook.com/Former -LDS-Indian-Placement-Students-150634325016206/.

2. For more background about Cal Nez, see Lane Franklin, "Cal Nez Brings Business Experience to His Effort to Become Tribal President," *Navajo Times*, June 19, 2014, http:// navajotimes.com/politics/2014/0614/061914nez.php; "Former LDS Indian Placement Students," Facebook.com, accessed June 29, 2021, https://www.facebook.com/Former -LDS-Indian-Placement-Students-150634325016206.

3. Tom Harvey, "Abuse Case against Mormon Church to Continue in Navajo Court; Attorneys Want LDS Leader Monson to Testify," *Salt Lake Tribune*, November 16, 2016, http://www.sltrib.com/news/4596141-155/abuse-case-against-mormon-church-to.

4. Dennis Romboy, "Lawsuit Accuses LDS Church of Failing to Protect Navajo Students," *Deseret News*, June 7, 2016, http://www.deseretnews.com/article/865655781 /Lawsuit-accuses-LDS-Church-of-failing-to-protect-Navajo-students.html; Tom Hartsock, "Shattered Dreams: When Faith, Abuse Intersect," *Gallup (New Mexico) Sun*, April 1, 2016, http://www.gallupsun.com/index.php?option=com_content&id=8746 %3Ashattered-dreams-when-faith-abuse-intersect&Itemid=600.

5. Alysa Landry, "Navajo Siblings Claim 'Horrific' Sexual Abuse; Sue Mormons," *Indian Country Today*, April 5, 2016, https://indiancountrymedianetwork.com/news /native-news/navajo-siblings-claim-horrific-sexual-abuse-sue-mormons/.

6. Cal Nez, Facebook post, November 16, 2016, https://www.facebook.com/Former -LDS-Indian-Placement-Students-150634325016206/.

7. Response on Facebook to Cal Nez post on November 16, 2016.

8. For more about Diné lesbian, gay, bisexual, transgender, queer, and Two-Spirit (LGBTQ2) perspectives, see Gabriel Estrada, "Two-Spirits, Nádleeh, and LGBTQ2 Navajo Gaze," *American Indian Culture and Research Journal* 35, no. 4 (January 2011): 167–190.

9. Tyson King, personal statement prepared for the Mormon History Association 2017 conference, September 22, 2016, personal copy in author's possession.

10. Hartsock, "Shattered Dreams."

11. Quoted in Hartsock.

12. Dan Smith cited in Dale Shumway and Margene Shumway, eds., *The Blossoming: Dramatic Accounts in the Lives of Native Americans* (self-published, 2002), 251.

13. Doctrine and Covenants 130:18.

14. Manuelito, c. 1880, cited in J. Neil Birch, "Helen John: The Beginnings of Indian Placement," *Dialogue: A Journal of Mormon Thought* 18, no. 4 (Winter 1985): 119. The quotation was also found online at Harrison Lapahie Jr., *Manuelito*, August 27, 2001, accessed April 15, 2008 (no longer available), http://www.lapahie.com/Manuelito.com. Many Diné accredit Manuelito with this famous phrase.

15. Language Training Mission, *Diné Bizaad Na'nitiníbá* (Provo: The Mission, 1973). Hardcopy of the textbook in private possession.

16. Iverson, *Diné*, 190–191. See also Davida Woerner, "Education among the Navajo: An Historical Study" (PhD diss., Columbia University, 1941).

17. See Jon S. Blackman, "A History of Intermountain, a Federal Indian Boarding School" (master's thesis, Brigham Young University, 1998); Farina King, Michael P. Taylor, and James R. Swensen, *Returning Home: Diné Creative Works of the Intermountain Indian School* (Tucson: University of Arizona Press, 2021).

18. Iverson, *Diné*, 192–195. For historical background, see also Katherine Jensen, "Teachers and Progressives: The Navajo Day-School Experiment, 1935–1945," *Arizona and the West* 25, no. 1 (1983): 49–62; Wendy Shelly Greyeyes, *A History of Navajo Nation Education: Disentangling Our Sovereign Body* (Tucson: University of Arizona Press, 2022).

19. Council Resolutions, 1922–51 book, J. M. Steward Attest, General Superintendent Navajo Service, Subject Matter—Mormon Church Schools—Permission to Build, etc.—November 1947, Meeting: 64 (Appendix—Item 11); Discussed 66–68; Action Tabled November 5, 1947. See also Farina King, "Mormon Navajo Youth at the Intermountain Indian Boarding School," *Juvenile Instructor* (blog), October 11, 2013, https://juvenileinstructor.org/mormon-navajo-youth-at-the-intermountain-indian-boarding-school/; Jessie Embry, "Indian Placement Program Host Families: A Mission to the Lamanites," *Journal of Mormon History* 40, no. 2 (Spring 2014): 243. Jessie and I collaborated on the initial drafts about histories of Latter-day Saint Diné, including on parts that she used for this published article about Placement host families. She consented to allow me to develop this work for this book and respective chapters.

20. Karl R. Lyman, *The Old Settler: A Biography of Albert R. Lyman* (Salt Lake City: Publishers Press, 1980), 123–130, 141.

21. James B. Allen and Glen M. Leonard, *Story of the Latter-day Saints* (Salt Lake City: Deseret Books, 1992), 548.

22. Scott C. Esplin, "'You Can Make Your Own Bright Future, Tom Trails': Evaluating the Impact of the LDS Indian Seminary Program," *Journal of Mormon History* 42, no. 4 (October 2016): 175. The Brigham City Museum started an oral history project with Intermountain Indian School alumni in 2012.

23. Damon James, oral history interview, January 21, 2012, Brigham City Museum of Art and History, Brigham City, Utah, cited in King, "Mormon Navajo Youth at the Intermountain Indian Boarding School." See also "Outside the Homeland: The Intermountain Indian School," Box Elder Museum of Art, History, and Nature, accessed November 7, 2022, http://exhibits.boxeldermuseum.org/exhibits/show/intermoutain-indian-school.

24. This chapter does not give a complete discussion of ISPP to avoid duplicating many other studies that cover this material. The focus of this chapter is to give a brief overview and then concentrate on some Diné experiences and views of the program based on the collaboration I had with the Charles Redd Center for Western Studies. See Elise Boxer's chapter on the program in her dissertation, "To Become White and Delightsome," and "Lamanites Shall Blossom as the Rose." For more information about Placement and its negative impacts, see Martin D. Topper, "Mormon Placement: The Effect of Mormon Missionary Foster Families on Navajo Adolescents," *Ethos* 7 (Summer 1979): 142–160. For a general overview, see James B. Allen, "The Rise and Fall of the LDS Indian Student Placement Program, 1947–1996," in *Mormons, Scripture, and the Ancient World: Studies in Honor of John L. Sorenson*, Davis Bitton and John L. Sorenson, eds. (Provo: Foundation for Ancient Research and Mormon Studies, 1998), 85-119. BYU sociology professors Bruce A. Chadwick, Stan Albrecht, and Howard M. Bahr published one of the most extensive studies based on research they conducted for the Church. Their study of 249 students and their natural and foster families showed that the Placement program "enhanced the educational achievements of participants," but that did not translate into "economic advantages." The program "fostered assimilation of the Indian students into white society," and "the severe psychological trauma alleged to afflict former placement students did not appear." For these scholars, "the long-term consequences of the program was either generally favorable or, at worst, neutral." Bruce A. Chadwick, Stan Albrecht, and Howard M. Bahr, "Evaluation of an Indian Student Placement Program," *Social Casework* 68 (November 1986): 515–525, quotations on 525. Scholars and the public continue debates about Placement. For another comprehensive study of ISPP, see Garrett, "Mormons, Indians, and Lamanites," and *Making Lamanites*. Also see Brandon Morgan, "Educating the Lamanites: A Brief History of the LDS Indian Student Placement Program," *Journal of Mormon History* 35, no. 4 (Fall 2009): 191–217; Megan Stanton, "The Indian Student Placement Program and Native Direction," in Hafen and Rensink, *Essays on American Indians and Mormons*, 211–224.

25. Some Diné writers have also condemned the impacts of ISPP on their families as a form of intergenerational trauma. See, for example, Souksavanh Tom Keovorabouth, "Reaching Back to Traditional Teachings: Diné Knowledge and Gender Politics," *Genealogy* 5, no. 95 (2021): 5; Jacqueline Keeler, *Standoff: Standing Rock, the Bundy Movement, and the American Story of Sacred Lands* (Salt Lake City: Torrey House, 2021), 7. Keeler briefly refers to the Placement program and her family's background with it in this book.

26. Birch, "Helen John," 120.

27. Willie John (Helen John's father) cited in Birch, "Helen John," 121.

28. Helen Rose John Hall cited in Shumway and Shumway, *The Blossoming*, 9. See also Helen John cited in Birch, "Helen John," 124.

29. Helen John letter to Amy Avery cited in Birch, "Helen John," 123.

30. Spencer W. Kimball cited in Birch, "Helen John," 122, 125.

31. Golden Buchanan oral history, interview by William G. Hartley, Salt Lake City, Utah, 1974–1975, Church History Library, 2:1–14; Thelma Buchanan oral history,

interview by William G. Hartley, 1976, Church History Library, 1–19, cited in Embry, "Indian Placement Program Host Families," 244.

32. Miles Jensen oral history, interview by Gordon Irving, 1983, Church History Library; Celia Jensen oral history, interview by Jessie L. Embry, 2008, Gunnison, Utah, LDS NAOH, cited in Embry, "Indian Placement Program Host Families," 245, 248.

33. Helen John cited in Birch, "Helen John," 127.

34. Clarence R. Bishop, "Indian Placement: A History of the Indian Student Placement Program of the Church of Jesus Christ of Latter-day Saints" (PhD diss., University of Utah, 1967), 68, 79–80, 97.

35. See Allen, "Rise and Decline of the LDS Indian Student Placement Program."

36. Mauss, *All Abraham's Children*, 88.

37. David J. Whittaker, "Mormons and Native Americans: A Historical and Bibliographical Introduction," *Dialogue: A Journal of Mormon Thought* 18, no. 4 (Winter 1985): 39; Allen, "The Rise and Decline of the LDS Indian Student Placement Program, 1947–1996," 108.

38. Clarence R. Bishop, "Introduction," in Shumway and Shumway, *The Blossoming*, x.

39. The Charles Redd Center conducted oral history interviews with foster parents in the 2010s. As required by the Institutional Review Board (IRB) then, these interviews are numbered and do not include names. Several of the interviewees had students in California and then said that the change in California law eliminated the program there. These interviews focused primarily on ISPP, unlike the LDS Native American oral histories that recorded family histories and a wide range of life experiences. See Embry, "Indian Placement Program Host Families." To understand ISPP as "Indigenous child removal," see Margaret D. Jacobs, "Entangled Histories: The Mormon Church and Indigenous Child Removal from 1850 to 2000," *Journal of Mormon History* 42, no. 2 (April 2016): 29–30.

40. Dawn House, "Lawsuit Seeking to Open School Doors to 3 Navajo Students," *Salt Lake Tribune*, December 28, 1990, B12; Marianne Funk, "Settlement May Spell End of 2 Programs: Free Utah Education Will Be No More for American Indians from Out of State," *Deseret News*, September 30, 1992, n.p., Church History Library.

41. Mauss, *All Abraham's Children*, 86; Garrett, *Making Lamanites*.

42. See Matthew L. Harris, ed., *Thunder from the Right: Ezra Taft Benson in Mormonism and Politics* (Champaign: University of Illinois Press, 2019).

43. D. Michael Quinn, "Ezra Taft Benson and Mormon Political Conflicts," *Dialogue: A Journal of Mormon Thought* 26, no. 2 (Summer 1993): 3.

44. Ezra Taft Benson knew and communicated with Utah senator Arthur Watkins, who served on the Senate Subcommittee on Indian Affairs and launched termination policies in Utah under the anti-communist and anti-socialist banners of postwar conservativism. See Matthew L. Harris, *Watchman on the Tower: Ezra Taft Benson and the Making of the Mormon Right* (Salt Lake City: University of Utah Press, 2020), 35; R. Warren Metcalf, *Termination's Legacy: The Discarded Indians of Utah* (Lincoln: University of Nebraska Press, 2002), 21–22.

45. Keeler, *Standoff*, 7–8.

46. Bishop, "Introduction," x.

47. See Edward W. Said, *Orientalism* (New York: Pantheon, 1978).

48. Eileen Quintana oral history, interview by Farina King, 2008, Springville, Utah, p. 5, LDS NAOH.

49. Quintana oral history, 5.

50. Quintana oral history, 9.

51. Anthony and Brenda Allison Beyal oral history, interviewed by Corey Smallcanyon, 2008, Mapleton, Utah, p. 4, LDS NAOH.

52. Julius Ray Chavez oral history, interviewed by Odessa Newman, 1990, Provo, Utah, pp. 7–8, LDS NAOH.

53. Chavez oral history, 9.

54. Ellouise Paredes oral history, interview by Farina King, 2008, Salt Lake City, Utah, p. 7, LDS NAOH.

55. Phillip Smith, conversations with Farina King.

56. Paredes oral history.

57. Audrey Boone oral history, interviewed by Malcolm Pappan, 1990, Provo, Utah, p. 5, LDS NAOH.

58. Jimmy Benally oral history, interviewed by Odessa Newman, 1990, Provo, Utah, p. 6, LDS NAOH.

59. See Kliph Nesteroff, *We Had a Little Real Estate Problem: The Unheralded Story of Native Americans and Comedy* (New York: Simon & Schuster, 2021), 86.

60. Jimmy Benally oral history, 6.

61. Boone oral history, 4.

62. Jimmy Benally oral history, 3.

63. Maybell Begay White cited in Shumway and Shumway, *The Blossoming*, 173.

64. Chavez oral history, 9.

65. Helena Hogue oral history, interview by Ernesteen Lynch, 1989, Fruitland, New Mexico, p. 3, LDS NAOH.

66. Irene B. Jones oral history, interview by Farina King, 2007, Page, Arizona, pp. 7–8, LDS NAOH.

67. Benjamin and Anthony Gardner oral history, interview by Farina King, September 22, 2007, Provo, Utah, p. 11, LDS NAOH.

68. Prestine Ann Kelly James cited in Shumway and Shumway, *The Blossoming*, 58.

69. Wallace (Wally) Brown oral history, interview by Farina King, 2007, pp. 6–7, Page, Arizona, LDS NAOH.

70. Hogue oral history, 2–3.

71. Elouise Thinn Goatson oral history, interview by Farina King, 2007, Page, Arizona, pp. 2–3, LDS NAOH.

72. "Foster Parent Guide," April 1965, Church History Library, 3–4. The foster parent interviews explained the same issue. See Embry, "Indian Placement Host Families," based on interviews with host families.

73. For more about the significance of terms and debates in Native American studies and frameworks, see Stephanie Nohelani Teves, Andrea Smith, and Michelle Raheja, eds., *Native Studies Keywords* (Tucson: University of Arizona Press, 2015).

74. Patty Tauchin Etscitty cited in Shumway and Shumway, *The Blossoming*, 25.

75. Victor Mannie Sr. oral history, interview by Farina King, 2007, Page, Arizona, pp. 1–4, LDS NAOH.

76. Emery Bowman oral history, interviewed by Deborah Lewis, January 27, 1990, Provo, Utah, p. 10, LDS NAOH.

77. Bowman oral history, 9–14.

78. Beyal oral history, 5.

79. See Andrew T. Bay, "The Power of Native Arts," *Y Magazine* (Spring 2022), https://magazine.byu.edu/article/the-power-of-native-arts/; "Native American Curriculum Initiative," BYU Arts Reaching and Teaching in Schools (ARTS) Partnership, 2022, http://advancingartsleadership.com/NACI.

80. Hogue oral history, 11.

81. Mannie oral history, 7–8.

82. Mannie, 7–8.

83. My cousins, who attend the Fort Wingate Branch, reminded me that the event took place in their chapel on March 23, 2019 (personal correspondence). Some of them participated in the event, known as a "fireside," by singing a church hymn.

84. "Foster Parent Guide," 3–4.

85. Helen John Hall cited in Shumway and Shumway, *The Blossoming*, 17–18.

86. Emily Benedek, *Beyond the Four Corners of the World: A Navajo Woman's Journey* (New York: Knopf, 1995), 118–131, 229–234. All quotations from Bedonie come from Benedek's book.

87. Bloomfield's song also appeared in *Church News*, October 11, 1952, as "Lamanite Song of Thanks." Lucy Guymon Bloomfield, Correspondence, 1905–1981, MS 13266, Church History Library.

88. Adolph June Jr. cited in Dale Shumway and Margene Shumway, eds., *The Blossoming II: Dramatic Accounts in the Lives of Native Americans* (self-published, 2007), 172.

89. King, "Mormon Navajo Youth at the Intermountain Indian Boarding School."

90. Ida Pauline Olsen Deem, Intermountain Indian School Files, MS 19981, Church History Library.

91. Arlene Nofchissey Williams and Carnes Burson, "Go, My Son," *Go My Son*, Blue Eagle Records BE-6840, 1967, 33⅓ rpm.

92. P. Jane Hafen, "'Great Spirit Listens': The American Indian in Mormon Music," *Dialogue: A Journal of Mormon Thought* 18, no. 4 (Winter 1985): 141.

93. For privacy and confidentiality purposes, I omit the identity of this individual who shared these insights and stories with me during this conversation at my parents' home, but I wrote notes with direct quotations from the meeting, which remain in my personal collection.

94. Yvonne Martin Bigman cited in Shumway and Shumway, *The Blossoming*, 137.

95. Tyson King's statement about his Placement experience, September 22, 2016, personal collection of Farina King.

96. For more background about Sarah Newcomb's work and perspective, see Diana Kruzman, "Indigenous Mormons Struggle to Balance Pride in the Faith with LDS

History," *Religion News Service*, January 11, 2022, https://religionnews.com/2022/01/11
/indigenous-mormons-struggle-to-balance-pride-in-the-faith-with-lds-history/.

CHAPTER 4. SODIZIN BÁ HOOGHAN: CHURCH

1. Laurance D. Linford, *Navajo Places: History, Legend, Landscape* (Salt Lake City:
University of Utah Press, 2000); Cindy Yurth, "More than a Mission: St. Michaels Is
Ready to Claim Its Due," *Navajo Times*, February 20, 2014, https://www.navajotimes
.com/news/chapters/022014stmichaels.php.

2. Romero Brown to Brian King, email correspondence, March 10, 2011, copy in
author's possession.

3. Frankie Gilmore cited in Shumway and Shumway, *The Blossoming*, 198.

4. SWIM Manuscript History, Church History Library. The manuscript histories are
quarterly reports submitted to the Church History Library until 1972. There are sometimes exact dates, but sometimes only the date listed at the top of the quarterly report.
The manuscript history included minutes from the conferences held in the branches and
districts, which makes it possible to count the numbers of congregations. This is based
on Jessie Embry's research in the Church History Library, which she shared with me.

5. *Navajo Times*, September 9, 1974, clipping file, Arizona Holbrook Mission, Church
History Library.

6. Sister Shumway, "Primary," *Gaamalii*, April 3, 1949, 2.

7. Rudy Begay, personal interview with Farina King, June 2011, Chinle, Arizona.

8. SWIM Manuscript History, March 14, 1945; June 1945; July 25, 1945; November
3, 1959, Church History Library.

9. United States Commission on Civil Rights, Carol J. McCabe, Hester Lewis, Paul
Alexander, and Lawrence Bear Glick, *The Navajo Nation: An American Colony: A Re-
port of the United States Commission on Civil Rights* (Washington, DC: US Government
Printing Office, 1975), 123; Diné Policy Institute, "Land Reform in the Navajo Nation:
Possibilities of Renewal for Our People," June 2020, p. 22, https://www.dinecollege.edu
/wp-content/uploads/2020/06/Land-Reform-In-Navajo-Nation.pdf. See also Duane
Champagne, "Is Keeping Communal Land Possible?" *Indian Country Today*, September
13, 2018, https://ictnews.org/archive/is-keeping-communal-land-possible.

10. SWIM Manuscript History, April 1946; July 25, 1945.

11. SWIM Manuscript History, April 11, 1950.

12. SWIM Manuscript History, July 16, 1953.

13. SWIM Manuscript History, November 22, 1950.

14. Ernst Clifford and June Young oral history, interview by Matthew Heiss, April 23,
1992, Chinle, Navajo Nation, Arizona, pp. 1–13, Church History Library.

15. June 1978, Arizona Holbrook Mission, Church History Library. This reference is
the source for all quotations and information in these paragraphs.

16. Golden Buchannan oral history, interview by William G. Hartley, 1974–1975, Salt
Lake City, Utah, 4:132, Church History Library.

17. Winna B. Kalauli oral history, interview by Matthew K. Heiss, Chinle, Navajo Nation, Arizona, 1991, p. 5, Church History Library.

18. Dale Tingey, interview [and notes] with Farina King, Provo, Utah, 2012.

19. Yurth, "More than a Mission."

20. See Cheryl C. D. Hughes, *Katharine Drexel: The Riches-to-Rags Life Story of an American Catholic Saint* (Grand Rapids, MI: William B. Eerdmans, 2014); "Building Our Future, since 1902," St. Michael Indian School, accessed September 18, 2021, https://stmichaelindianschool.org/history/.

21. The US government licensed the trading post system on the reservation "as a necessary aspect of the Reservation barter-economy." The *Navajo Yearbook* explains: "It was not until 1947 that the Tribal Council began to consider, in their capacity as landlords, the question of controlling Reservation trading to demand payment of rental on areas of tribal lands used for trading purposes, and to establish regulations deemed necessary for the protection of the Navajo people." See Robert W. Young, ed., *The Navajo Yearbook of Planning in Action* (Window Rock, Navajo Nation, AZ: Navajo Agency, 1955), 245. Traders received a lease from the Navajo Nation (known formally as the Navajo Tribe) to run a trading post on the reservation, and they then followed the regulations of the tribal nation. Only a few traders had "privately owned reservation land—land that was privately owned before the reservation was established in 1868." See US Federal Trade Commission, *The Trading Post System on the Navajo Reservation: Staff Report to the Federal Trade Commission* (Washington, DC: US Government Printing Office, 1973), 11.

22. SWIM Manuscript History, August 25, 1963.

23. SWIM Manuscript History, August 25, 1963; October 13, 1968.

24. Ernesteen Lynch oral history, interview by Jessie L. Embry, 1990, Provo, Utah, p. 28, LDS NAOH.

25. Farina King family history and personal observations; JoAnn Smith, interview by Farina King, Orem, Utah, 2012.

26. Shaela Ann Willie [Avery], interview by Farina King, 2007, Provo, Utah, p. 12, LDS NAOH.

27. Laura Brown, interview by Farina King, 2008, St. Michaels, Navajo Nation, Arizona, LDS NAOH, 14.

28. Dallin J. John oral history, interview by Matthew K. Heiss, 1991, Chinle, Navajo Nation, Arizona, pp. 2–6, Church History Library.

29. Robert Begay, interview by Farina King, July 9, 2015, Tuba City, Navajo Nation, p. 11, cited in King, *Earth Memory Compass*. There are different spellings for Navajo words depending on the accents. Tó'naneesdizí is another spelling of the word for Tuba City with accents that reflect the pronunciation.

30. Smallcanyon, "Contested Space," 13.

31. See, for example, references about the Navajo-Hopi Land Dispute, including David M. Brugge, *The Navajo-Hopi Land Dispute: An American Tragedy* (Albuquerque: University of New Mexico Press, 1994); Malcolm D. Benally, ed. and trans., *Bitter Water: Diné Oral Histories of the Navajo-Hopi Land Dispute* (Tucson: University of Arizona Press, 2011); Jerry Kammer, *The Second Long Walk: The Navajo-Hopi Land Dispute*

(Albuquerque: University of New Mexico Press, 1980); Emily Benedek, *The Wind Won't Know Me: A History of the Navajo-Hopi Land Dispute* (New York: Knopf, 1992). See also William Michael Havens, "Intercultural Dynamics of the Hopi-Navajo Land Dispute: Concepts of Colonialism and Manifest Destiny in the Southwest" (master's thesis, University of Arizona, 1995); Deborah Lacerenza, "An Historical Overview of the Navajo Relocation," *Cultural Survival*, February 24, 2010, https://www.culturalsurvival.org/publications/cultural-survival-quarterly/historical-overview-navajo-relocation.

32. Walter Wolf cited in Navajo Indians tribal council meeting, May 16, 1961, Window Rock, Navajo Nation, Arizona, p. 36, NARA.

33. Larry Rodgers, *Chapter Images: 1996 Edition* (Window Rock, Navajo Nation: Division of Community Development, Navajo Nation, 1997), 51.

34. Virginia Butler oral history, interview by Jessie Embry, 2012, Tuba City, Navajo Nation, Arizona, p. 2, LDS NAOH.

35. SWIM Manuscript History, June 5, 1949; July 25, 1953; January 16, 1965.

36. Ray Pooley oral history, interview by Farina King, 2012, Tuba City, Navajo Nation, Arizona, pp. 1–10, LDS NAOH.

37. As of 2023, the official name of the tribal nation is the Hopi Tribe.

38. Edwin Tano, the former stake president of the Chinle and Tuba City Stakes, told Jessie Embry and me this story during interviews in Tuba City. Several interviewees repeated the same story. See Ray Pooley oral history, 2; Butler oral history, 3.

39. Phillip L. Smith, interview with Farina King, Orem, Utah, February 2012.

40. Lillie Pooley oral history, interview by Jessie Embry, 2012, Tuba City, Navajo Nation, Arizona, p. 6, LDS NAOH.

41. Butler oral history, 3, 7.

42. Rex Black [pseudonym], interview by Farina King, Tuba City, Navajo Nation, Arizona, April 21, 2012, LDS NAOH. Name changed by request.

43. Home teaching refers specifically to men visiting families and individuals in the same congregation, and visiting teaching refers to women visiting with other women in the congregation.

44. Phillip Smith oral history, interview by Farina King, 2008, Kensington, Maryland, pp. 12–13, LDS NAOH.

45. Liz Nez oral history, interview by Jessie Embry, 2012, Tuba City, Navajo Nation, Arizona, p. 7, LDS NAOH.

46. Charlene Manygoats oral history, interview by Jessie Embry, 2012, Tuba City, Navajo Nation, Arizona, p. 8, LDS NAOH.

47. Manygoats oral history, 2–3; Butler oral history, 4.

48. Liz Nez oral history, 7; Harlan Nez oral history, interview by Jessie Embry, 2012, Tuba City, Navajo Nation, Arizona, p. 7, LDS NAOH.

49. Liz Nez oral history, 6.

50. Ruth Littlefield, conversation with Jessie Embry, 2012, Tuba City, Navajo Nation, Arizona, notes in author's records; Liz Nez oral history, 6. For more information, see Allie Schulte, "Seeds of Self Reliance," *Ensign*, March 2011, http://www.lds.org/ensign/2011/03/seeds-of-self-reliance?lang=eng; Fernanda Santos, "Some Find Path to Navajo Roots through Mormon Church," *New York Times*, October 30, 2013, http://www

.nytimes.com/2013/10/31/us/for-some-the-path-to-navajo-values-weaves-through-the -mormon-church.html?pagewanted=all&_r=0.

51. Santos, "Some Find Path to Navajo Roots."

52. Chinle Chapter, official website, accessed October 8, 2021, https://chinle .navajochapters.org/#:~:text=The%20Navajo%20people%20call%20this,out%20 from%20Canyon%20de%20Chelly.&text=Today%2C%20about%2040%20Navajo %20families,limits%20access%20into%20the%20area.

53. Young oral history, 13–17. The transcript includes a history of the Chinle Branch, information also discussed on p. 8 in that history.

54. Several people mentioned in their oral histories that Spencer W. Kimball had talked about five stakes. See Edwin Tano oral history, interview by Matthew K. Heiss and Michael Landon, 1997, Kayenta, Navajo Nation, Arizona, pp. 1–5, Church History Library. For information on Harvey Gardner's discussion with Boyd K. Packer, see Harvey Leon Gardner oral history, interview by Matthew Heiss, 1992, Page, Arizona, p. 10, Church History Library.

55. Harvey L. Gardner, Francis M. Lyman, Donald L. Jack, Bryson N. Jones, Richard Carlson, Earl Owens, and Dale Patton to H. Burke Peterson, August 12, 1990, Church History Library.

56. 1992 annual report, Church History Library.

57. Gardner oral history, 10.

58. Ruth Ann Brown McCombs, Chinle Stake Annual Report, 1992, Church History Library.

59. Ruby Whitesinger Benally oral history, interview by Matthew K. Heiss, 1997, Window Rock, Navajo Nation, Arizona, p. 20, Church History Library.

60. James Lee Dandy oral history, interview by Jessie Embry, 1990, Blanding, Utah, p. 18, LDS NAOH.

61. William Numkena oral history, interview by Matthew Heiss, 1992, Tuba City, Navajo Nation, Arizona, p. 5, Church History Library.

62. Mitchell Davis Kapuni Kalauli oral history, interview by Matthew Heiss, 1992, Tuba City, Navajo Nation, Arizona, pp. 5, 9, Church History Library.

63. McCombs, Chinle Stake Annual Report, 1992; 1994 Annual Report, Church History Library.

64. Dan K. Smith oral history, interview by Matthew K. Heiss, 1992, Chinle, Navajo Nation, Arizona, p. 7, Church History Library.

65. See Steamboat Branch, Southwest Indian Mission, Steamboat Branch manuscript history and historical reports, 1967–1982, Church History Library.

66. Tano oral history, 5.

67. Romero Brown, conversation with Farina King, September 2022, Norman, Oklahoma.

68. Justine Calma, "The Navajo Nation Faced Water Shortages for Generations— and Then the Pandemic Hit," *Verge*, July 6, 2020, https://www.theverge.com/2020 /7/6/21311211/navajo-nation-covid-19-running-water-access.

69. Eliza Smith-Driggs, "Church Partners with Farmers Feeding Utah Program to Help Navajo Reservation amid COVID-19," *Church News*, June 1, 2020, https://www

.thechurchnews.com/2020/6/1/23216316/church-donates-sheep-navajo-reservation
-covid-19-pandemic; "Church Participates in Sheep Donation on Navajo Reservation,"
Church News, June 2, 2020, https://newsroom.churchofjesuschrist.org/article/navajo
-reservation-receives-food-supplies-bishops-central-storehouse; "Latter-day Saints
Participate in 'Operation Firewood Rescue' to Help Utah's Native Americans," *Church
Newsroom*, September 27, 2020, https://newsroom.churchofjesuschrist.org/article/after
-severe-windstorm-latter-day-saints-participate-in-"operation-firewood-rescue-to
-help-utahs-native-americans; "Latter-day Saint Charities Participate in Donation to Navajo Nation: Hundreds of Volunteers Donate COVID-19 Relief Supplies for Navajo Tribal
Members," *Church News*, December 9, 2020, https://newsroom.churchofjesuschrist
.org/article/latter-day-saint-charities-participate-in-donation-to-navajo-nation.

70. Jason Swensen, "Latter-day Saints on the Navajo Nation in the Thick of the CO-
VID-19 Fight," *Church News*, May 20, 2020, https://www.thechurchnews.com/members
/2020-05-20/covid-19-navajo-nation-latter-day-saints-184664.

71. Ollie Whaley and Romero Brown cited in Swensen.

CHAPTER 5. BEYOND DINÉ BIKÉYAH

1. Farina King, "Indigenizing Mormonisms," 3.

2. Spencer W. Kimball journal, February 3, 1966, in private possession.

3. Golden Buchanan oral history, interview by William G. Hartley, 1974–1975, Salt
Lake City, Utah, Church History Library, 5:24, 122–124. Buchanan even listed General
Authorities who either opposed or supported the language branches: Harold B. Lee, Jo-
seph F. Merrill, Stephen L. Richards, and David O. McKay opposed the branches, and J.
Reuben Clark, Joseph Fielding Smith, Matthew Cowley, Mark Peterson, LeGrand Rich-
ards, and Ezra Taft Benson were supporters of the branches.

4. Robert Larsen and Sharlyn H. Larson, "Refugee Converts: One Stake's Experience,"
Dialogue: A Journal of Mormon Thought 20 (Fall 1987): 55; Chad Orton, *More Faith than
Fear: The Los Angeles Stake Story* (Salt Lake City: Bookcraft, 1987), 262–263.

5. A copy of the Basic Unit Plan is available in the Church History Library.

6. "Aid Minorities, Pres. Kimball Asks Leaders," *Church News*, October 11, 1980, 4.

7. This information is from A. LeGrand Richards, who served as president of the
Provo Utah South Stake in 2012. See Jessie L. Embry and A. LeGrand Richards, "Spe-
cialized Units," *Mapping Mormonism: An Atlas of Latter-day Saint History* (Provo: BYU
Press, 2012), 154–155.

8. US Congress, Senate Committee on Indian Affairs, *Survey of Conditions among
the Indians of the United States: Partial Report*, Document No. 310, 78th Cong., 1st sess.,
1943; *Supplemental Report*, Document No. 310, pt. 2, 78th Cong., 2nd sess., 1944. See US
Commission on Civil Rights, *Indian Tribes: A Continuing Quest for Survival: A Report
of the United States Commission on Civil Rights* (June 1981), "The Termination Period:
1945–1965," 22, and "Termination Policy, 1953–1968," Partnership with Native Americans, accessed November 15, 2022, http://www.nativepartnership.org/site/PageServer
?pagename=PWNA_Native_History_terminationpolicyNP.

9. Arthur V. Watkins, "Termination of Federal Supervision: The Removal of Restrictions over Indian Property and Person," *Annals of the American Academy of Political and Social Science* 311 (May 1957): 47–55.

10. This resolution is known as House Concurrent Resolution 108. See HR Con. Res. 108, 83rd Cong., 1st sess., 67 Stat. B132 (1953) cited in US Commission on Civil Rights, *Indian Tribes*, 35–36.

11. See R. Warren Metcalf, *Termination's Legacy: The Discarded Indians of Utah* (Lincoln: University of Nebraska Press, 2007).

12. Carolyn Grattan-Aiello, "Senator Arthur V. Watkins and the Termination of Utah's Southern Paiute Indians," *Utah Historical Quarterly* 63, no. 3 (1995): 271.

13. President Richard M. Nixon, "Special Message on Indian Affairs," July 8, 1970, in *Public Papers of the Presidents of the United States: Richard Nixon (Containing the Public Messages, Speeches, and Statements of the President, 1969 to August 9, 1974)* (Washington, DC: US Government Publishing Office, 1975), 564–567, 576.

14. Michael C. Walch, "Terminating the Indian Termination Policy," *Stanford Law Review* 35, no. 6 (July 1983): 1185, 1191.

15. The Indian Relocation Act is also known as the Adult Vocational Training Program, Indian Vocational Training Act of 1956, or Public Law 959. See Public Law 84–959, 25 USC 309, 84th Cong., 70 Stat. 986 (August 3, 1956). See also Max Nesterak, "Uprooted: The 1950s Plan to Erase Indian Country," APM Reports, November 1, 2019, https://www.apmreports.org/episode/2019/11/01/uprooted-the-1950s-plan-to-erase -indian-country.

16. Michelle R. Jacobs, *Indigenous Memory, Urban Reality: Stories of American Indian Relocation and Reclamation* (New York: New York University Press, 2023), 15–17; "American Indian Urban Relocation," *National Archives*, accessed March 14, 2023, https://www.archives.gov/education/lessons/indian-relocation.html; Carrie Saldo, "Defunct Relocation Policy Still Impacts American Indians," KUNC, NPR for Northern Colorado, May 6, 2013, https://www.kunc.org/arts-life/2013-05-06/defunct-relocation -policy-still-impacts-american-indians.

17. For more about Native American experiences with relocation, see Nicolas G. Rosenthal, *Reimagining Indian Country: Native American Migration and Identity in Twentieth-Century Los Angeles* (Chapel Hill: University of North Carolina Press, 2012); Douglas Miller, *Indians on the Move: Native American Mobility and Urbanization in the Twentieth Century* (Chapel Hill: University of North Carolina Press, 2019); Donald Lee Fixico, *Termination and Relocation: Federal Indian Policy, 1945–1960* (Albuquerque: University of New Mexico Press, 1986); Donald Lee Fixico, *The Urban Indian Experience in America* (Albuquerque: University of New Mexico Press, 2000); Kent Blansett, Cathleen D. Cahill, and Andrew Needham, eds., *Indian Cities: Histories of Indigenous Urbanization* (Norman: University of Oklahoma Press, 2022); Donna Martinez, Grace Sage, and Azusa Ono, *Urban American Indians: Reclaiming Native Space* (Santa Barbara, CA: Praeger, 2016).

18. Los Angeles Indian Branch, Manuscript History, September 23, 1961, Church History Library.

19. Indian Branch, South Los Angeles Stake, Record of Members Collection,

"Marriages, Divorces, and Excommunications," 1962, Church History Library. The records did not include the tribal affiliation of members, but they show their place of birth and family names, which help identify their connection to a tribal nation. These Church records spanned 1961 to 1970, and other member names and birthplaces indicate that several Diné Latter-day Saints attended this branch during that time.

20. See, for example, Farina King, "Voices of Indigenous Dallas-Fort Worth from Relocation to the Dakota Access Pipeline Controversy," *Family and Community History* 24, no. 2 (Summer 2021): 147–174.

21. Audrey Boone oral history, interview by Malcolm Pappan, 1990, Provo, Utah, p. 11, LDS NAOH.

22. Ernesteen Lynch oral history.

23. Arnold D. Yazzie, interview by Michael Landon, April 26, 1997, Window Rock, Navajo Nation, Arizona, Church History Library, 29; see also Arnold D. Yazzie interview by Michael Landon, May 4, 1991, Chinle, Navajo Nation, Arizona, Church History Library.

24. Native American and Indigenous Latter-day Saints in the area, including Miriam Chun who is Diné, referred to the Franklin Second Ward in Utah Valley as the "Lamanite ward."

25. Miriam Chun, interview by Farina King, Provo, Utah, September 5, 2007, LDS NAOH, 5.

26. Farina King, personal observation during 2011–2012; A. LeGrand Richards, conversation with Jessie L. Embry, August 25, 2013.

27. Chauma Kee-Jansen, interview by Yadira Veamatahau, February 22, 2019, Provo, Utah, Native BYU Oral History, https://cdm15999.contentdm.oclc.org, 10. Chauma Kee-Jansen attended the BYU 144th Ward.

28. April Yazzie oral history, interview by David Bolingbroke, 2009, Provo, Utah, p. 1, in Provo South Stake Oral History Project, Charles Redd Center for Western Studies, BYU Special Collections (hereafter Provo Oral History).

29. Taran K. Chun history of the Franklin Second Ward, copy in possession of Jessie Embry and shared with the author.

30. Alan Groves oral history, interview by Corey Smallcanyon, 2008, Provo, Utah, p. 11, LDS NAOH.

31. Anthony and Brenda Beyal oral history, interview by Corey Smallcanyon, 2008, Provo, Utah, p. 7, LDS NAOH.

32. Chun history.

33. Chun history.

34. Groves oral history.

35. Chun history.

36. Chun history.

37. Beyal oral history, 7.

38. Beyal oral history, 7.

39. Farina King, personal history and memories.

40. Chun history.

41. Randell K. King oral history, interview by Jessie Embry, 2009, p. 12, in Provo Oral History.

42. Beyal oral history, 25.

43. Boxer, "To Become White and Delightsome"; Boxer, "'This is the Place!': Disrupting Mormon Settler Colonialism," in Colvin and Brooks, *Decolonizing Mormonism*, 77.

44. Groves oral history, 25.

45. Chun history.

46. I observed this event during my time in the Franklin Second Ward between 2011 and 2012.

47. I refer to these broad and ambiguous terms of ethnicity because members of the ward and others have historically used these terms in their vernacular. These terms are problematic and more work needs to be done to represent the diversity and what people call themselves. See Seini Taufa cited in Andrea McRae, "'Pacific Islander' an Insulting Umbrella Term, Researcher Says," *Pacific Island Times*, July 28, 2021, https://www.pacificislandtimes.com/post/pacific-islander-an-insulting-umbrella-term-researcher-says.

48. For more about the history of the Papago Ward, see D. L. Turner, "Akimel Au-Authm, Xalychidom Piipaash, and the LDS Papago Ward," *Journal of Mormon History* 39, no. 1 (Winter 2013): 158–180.

49. I lived within the same stake area of the Maricopa North Stake with the Papago Ward, between 2012 and 2015, where I met Bishop Thomas Tsinnijinnie.

50. The Church of Jesus of Latter-day Saints sponsors and operates FamilySearch, and the American Indian Services (AIS) was originally founded at Brigham Young University. FamilySearch supports family history research and connections throughout the world. AIS became an independent nonprofit scholarship organization. I refer more to AIS in the next chapter about Diné experiences with Native American programs at BYU.

51. Hailee Roberts, "Success Story" for American Indian Services, America's Best Charities, accessed November 16, 2022, https://www.best-charities.org/find/charitypage.php?ein=87-0477049.

52. Hailee Roberts cited in Isabel Toa, "Students Make Spiritual and Lifelong Connections while Gathering Native American Oral Histories," *Church News*, October 4, 2019, https://www.churchofjesuschrist.org/church/news/students-make-spiritual-and-lifelong-connections-while-gathering-native-american-oral-histories?lang=eng.

53. Sheiyenne Baloo cited in Toa, "Students Make Spiritual and Lifelong Connections."

54. See, for example, "Native American Oral Histories," Media Library, Church of Jesus Christ of Latter-day Saints, July 1, 2022, https://www.churchofjesuschrist.org/media/video/2019-05-0010-native-american-oral-histories?lang=eng&collectionId=2cf8c727d7a544d0ac1d440d4ea0992e. In October 2021 the Church tried to donate $2 million to the First Americans Museum (FAM) in Oklahoma City to develop family history resources with FAM for Native Americans. See "Church Donates $2 Million to First Americans Museum in Oklahoma," *Church News*, October 17, 2021, available at *Deseret News*, https://www.deseret.com/2021/10/17/22731854/the-church-donates-us-2-million-to-first-americans-museum-in-oklahoma. Although there were numerous

articles about the donation to FAM, it is difficult to know what happened with the donation. I heard from different personal sources that FAM returned the donation to the Church after some concerns from Native Americans in Oklahoma about it.

CHAPTER 6. RED POWER AT BYU

1. For historical reviews of the Red Power movement, see Alvin M. Josephy, *Red Power: The American Indians' Fight for Freedom* (Lincoln: University of Nebraska Press, 1999); Daniel M. Cobb, *Native Activism in Cold War America: The Struggle for Sovereignty* (Lawrence: University Press of Kansas, 2008); Bradley G. Shreve, *Red Power Rising: The National Indian Youth Council and the Origins of Native Activism* (Norman: University of Oklahoma Press, 2012); Sherry L. Smith, *Hippies, Indians, and the Fight for Red Power* (New York: Oxford University Press, 2012); Daniel M. Cobb and Loretta Fowler, eds., *Beyond Red Power: American Indian Politics and Activism since 1900* (Santa Fe: School for Advanced Research Press, 2007).

2. Patricia Mann, "'Red Power' at BYU: Educational," *Daily Universe*, April 17, 1970, 8.

3. Most scholars demarcate the 1950s and 1960s as the civil rights era, tracing African American activism and civil rights movements. In his historical analysis of policies and the federal government, Hugh Davis Graham defines the period between 1960 and 1972 as the "civil rights era." See Hugh Davis Graham, *The Civil Rights Era: Origins and Development of National Policy, 1960–1972* (New York: Oxford University Press, 1990). BYU had the largest enrollment of Native American students during the late 1960s and early 1970s.

4. In 1943 Church president George Albert Smith assigned Kimball to work with American Indians. See Edward L. Kimball and Andrew E. Kimball Jr., *Spencer W. Kimball: Twelfth President of the Church of Jesus Christ of Latter-day Saints* (Salt Lake City: Bookcraft, 1977), 237. See also Petrea Kelly, "Spencer W. Kimball: He Did Not Give Up," *Liahona*, March 1994, https://www.lds.org/liahona/1994/03/spencer-w-kimball-he-did-not-give-up; Shumway and Shumway, *The Blossoming*, xii. The Shumways refer to Kimball's patriarchal blessing that prophesied he would serve American Indians and "Lamanites." Latter-day Saints receive patriarchal blessings one time, which is an ordinance directed personally to the individual through the authority and expression of a patriarch (a designated priesthood holder) when they are deemed worthy and ready.

5. Ernest L. Wilkinson, ed., *Brigham Young University: The First One Hundred Years*, vol. 4 (Provo: Brigham Young University Press, 1976), 418.

6. Jeanie Groves, interview by Farina King, Orem, Utah, February 12, 2008, transcript, p. 9, LDS NAOH. I use the terms Native American, American Indian, Indian, Indigenous, and Native interchangeably. During the 1960s and 1970s, "Indian" was commonly used, and Latter-day Saints also used "Lamanite" to refer to American Indians. For different perspectives of "Native American" and "American Indian," see Amanda Blackhorse, "Blackhorse: Do You Prefer 'Native American' or 'American Indian'? 6 Prominent Voices Respond," *Indian Country Today*, May 22, 2015, https://indiancountrymedianetwork

.com/culture/social-issues/blackhorse-do-you-prefer-native-american-or-american
-indian-6-prominent-voices-respond/. Blackhorse wrote several related articles.

7. Adrian L. Smith, Letter to the Editor, *Eagle's Eye*, March 1971, 2.

8. Indian Committee to Ernest L. Wilkinson, December 2, 1963; Indian Committee to Ernest L. Wilkinson, December 4, 1963, folder 12, box 12, University Archives (UA) 552, BYU Special Collections; Wilkinson, *Brigham Young University*, 3: 508. Ernest L. Wilkinson served as the president of BYU from 1951 to 1971. Wilkinson supported the Indian Committee's efforts to make BYU the "Indian capitol of the world."

9. Due to the limits of a chapter-length manuscript and the focus of this piece on student perspectives (shared through oral histories and the student newspaper, the *Eagle's Eye*), I do not delve into the intricacies of the BYU Indian Education administration, programs, and structure. For a historical background of BYU, see Gary James Bergera and Ronald Priddis, *Brigham Young University: A House of Faith* (Salt Lake City: Signature, 1985).

10. Edwin Butterworth Jr., ed., *1000 Views of 100 Years* (Provo: Brigham Young University, 2005), 272. See also "Lamanite Enrollment Record Set," *Eagle's Eye*, October 1971, 1. This article notes that "550 American Indians had registered for the fall semester" from more than seventy different tribes.

11. For more about the history and context of the Indian Student Placement Program, see Garrett, *Making Lamanites*; Boxer, "Lamanites Shall Blossom as the Rose"; Embry, "Indian Placement Program Host Families"; Morgan, "Educating the Lamanites"; Stanton, "Indian Student Placement Program."

12. Personal conversations with Phillip L. Smith, my father. I refer to my father as "dad," "father," and "shizhééʼ" (the Diné term for "my father"), as well as by his name.

13. Vickie Washburn Cox, interview by Farina King, Rio Rancho, New Mexico, 2008, p. 13, LDS NAOH.

14. See Victor Selam, "Don't Sit under the Apple Tree," *Diné Baa-Hani* 3, no. 3 (October 19, 1971), 10, cited in Megan Falater, "LDS American Indians in Their Tribal Communities," *Juvenile Instructor* (blog), November 6, 2013, http://juvenileinstructor.org/lds -american-indians-in-their-tribal-communities/. For more about mimicry, see Homi Bhabha, *The Location of Culture* (New York: Routledge, 1994), 85–92.

15. In many Indigenous cultures, both men and women grow their hair long to signify honor, life, and spirituality. See Kathleen J. Fitzgerald, *Beyond White Ethnicity: Developing a Sociological Understanding of Native American Identity Reclamation* (Lanham, MD: Lexington, 2007), 178; Anton Treuer, "Religion, Culture, and Identity," in *Everything You Wanted to Know about Indians but Were Afraid to Ask* (St. Paul, MN: Borealis, 2012).

16. Selam, "Don't Sit under the Apple Tree." See also Jennifer Duqué, "'Many Hearts yet Beat with the Hurt of a Wounded Past': Miss Indian BYU, Lamanite Identities, and the Subversive Potential of Pageants," *Thetean* 43 (2014): 91.

17. Stanley Snake cited in "Ways to Solve Indian Problems Decided by Leaders at 'Y' Meet," *Daily Herald* (Provo, Utah), November 12, 1972, 6.

18. This motif was embodied in the song "Go, My Son" that BYU Indian students Arlene Nofchissey Williams and Carnes Burson wrote in the mid-1960s. See P. Jane Hafen,

"'Great Spirit Listens': The American Indian in Mormon Music," *Dialogue: A Journal of Mormon Thought* 18, no. 4 (Winter 1985): 141.

19. Spencer W. Kimball, "To You, Our Kinsmen," *Eagle's Eye*, April 1975, 3.

20. Jansen B. Werner, "Two Strivings: Uplift and Identity in African American Rhetorical Culture, 1900–1943" (PhD diss., University of Wisconsin–Milwaukee, 2016), ii. For more about the background and effects of racial uplift ideology among African Americans, see Kevin K. Gaines, "Racial Uplift Ideology in the Era of 'the Negro Problem,'" *Freedom's Story*, TeacherServe, National Humanities Center, accessed June 15, 2017, http://nationalhumanitiescenter.org/tserve/freedom/1865-1917/essays/racialuplift.htm. Uplift referred to the idea that marginalized and disadvantaged populations such as racial minorities of African Americans needed self-help and that they were responsible for improving their own lives, communities, and race especially through education and schooling.

21. For more about Latter-day Saint forms of racialization involving Native American and Indigenous peoples, see Garrett, *Making Lamanites*; Boxer, "The Book of Mormon as Mormon Settler Colonialism"; Mauss, *All Abraham's Children*; Aikau, *A Chosen People, a Promised Land*; Gina Colvin, "Introduction: Theorizing Mormon Race Scholarship," *Journal of Mormon History* 41, no. 3 (July 2015): 11–21.

22. For more about these conceptualizations and their historical context, see Mauss, *All Abraham's Children*, 74–75.

23. Department of Indian Education, January 23, 1974, box 1, folder 1, UA 670.

24. "Meet the Club Officers Jeff Simmons and Tribe," *Eagle's Eye*, December 1970, 3.

25. See Farina King, "Miss Indian BYU: Contestations over the Crown and Indian Identity," *Journal of the West* 52, no. 3 (Summer 2013): 10–21.

26. Victoria (Vickie) Sanders, interview by Farina King, Provo, Utah, March 27, 2008, transcript, p. 15, LDS NAOH. In 2014 her preferred name was Victoria Comes Out Bird. Her maiden name was Bird. During the interview her legal name was Victoria Sanders. I refer to her as Comes Out Bird or Bird.

27. For examples, see Matthew Garrett, "Rival Ideologies and Rival Indians: Self-Determination in the 1960s and 1970s," in *Making Lamanites*, 170–171; Warren Metcalf, "'Which Side of the Line?': American Indian Students and Programs at Brigham Young University, 1960–1983," in Hafen and Rensink, *Essays on American Indians and Mormons*, 225–245; Mauss, *All Abraham's Children*, 131.

28. I prefer "ways of life" and "ways of being" rather than the term "religion," but I use the latter word to relate to the language that was used in the historical context of the 1960s and 1970s. My approach is influenced by studies and conceptualizations of intersectionality. See Ange-Marie Hancock, *Intersectionality: An Intellectual History* (New York: Oxford University Press, 2016), 4.

29. See Garrett, *Making Lamanites*; Boxer, "The Book of Mormon as Mormon Settler Colonialism"; Colvin, "Introduction," 16; Margaret D. Jacobs, "Entangled Histories: The Mormon Church and Indigenous Child Removal from 1850 to 2000," *Journal of Mormon History* 42, no. 2 (April 2016): 27–60. Jacobs refers to "intimate entanglements" of Navajos and Latter-day Saints to trace Mormon forms of "Indian child removal" over a couple centuries (30). See also McPherson et al., *Navajo Tradition, Mormon Life*.

30. Ned Blackhawk, *Violence over the Land* (Cambridge, MA: Harvard University Press, 2006). See also Christopher C. Smith, "Mormon Conquest: Whites and Natives in the Intermountain West, 1847–1851" (PhD diss., Claremont Graduate University, 2016); W. Paul Reeve, *Making Space on the Western Frontier: Mormons, Miners, and Southern Paiutes* (Urbana: University of Illinois Press, 2006); Jared Farmer, *On Zion's Mount: Mormons, Indians, and the American Landscape* (Cambridge, MA: Harvard University Press, 2008).

31. See R. Warren Metcalf, *Termination's Legacy: The Discarded Indians of Utah* (Lincoln: University of Nebraska Press, 2002); Garrett, *Making Lamanites*; Farina King, *Earth Memory Compass*.

32. Metcalf, "Which Side of the Line?," 238. Edward Valandra refers to the origins of the Oceti Sakowin Oyate and their sovereignty: "The Oceti Sakowin Oyate predates modern states, and our sovereignty flows directly from our origin story: how we came to be and the primary responsibility given us." See Valandra, "Mni Wiconi: Water Is [More Than] Life," in Nick Estes and Jaskiran Dhillon, eds., *Standing with Standing Rock: Voices from the #NoDAPL Movement* (Minneapolis: University of Minnesota Press, 2019), 102–128, quotation on 104.

33. Mauss, *All Abraham's Children*, 91.

34. Sanders interview, 7 (quotation), 4–5.

35. Royce P. Flandro, *Heritage Book of Remembrance*, self-published autobiography, p. 124, box 3, UA 5303.

36. Sanders interview, 9. She did not specify the exact verses of scripture to which Williams referred. In the Book of Mormon, Lehi tells Nephi, "Go, my son," directing him to retrieve plates of brass that contain scriptures and genealogy (see 1 Nephi 3:6). Another prophet in the Book of Mormon, Alma, uses the phrase "Go, my son" when he advises and gives guidance to his sons (Alma 38:15).

37. For more information about Manuelito, see Jennifer Nez Denetdale, "A Biographical Account of Manuelito: Noble Savage, Patriotic Warrior, and American Citizen," in *Reclaiming Diné History*, 51–86.

38. "History," Diné College, 2014, http://www.dinecollege.edu/about/history.php; Ellen McCullough-Brabson and Marilyn Help, *We'll Be in Your Mountains, We'll Be in Your Songs: A Navajo Woman Sings* (Albuquerque: University of New Mexico Press, 2001), 151.

39. Cox interview; Sanders interview.

40. Flandro, *Heritage Book of Remembrance*, 124.

41. See chapter 3 for more about the lyrics of "Go, My Son." Arlene Nofchissey Williams and Carnes Burson, "Go, My Son," 1967. See Flandro, *Heritage Book of Remembrance*, 124. In 1966 Flandro notes that Williams and Burson wrote the song that BYU Native American students performed on tours to Indian reservations. They arranged the song within thirty minutes for a filmstrip shooting on the Provo campus for one of the series that the Church Educational System used to present in seminary and religion classes. They received a short-notice request to cover for someone else who failed to prepare a piece.

42. Non-BYU and non-LDS groups have also sung and popularized "Go, My Son."

43. A BYU Yavapai alumnus, Maurice Crandall, articulated this idea of navigating multiple worlds to me in 2016. Gina Colvin, Maori lecturer at the University of Canterbury, also emphasizes understanding "compound worldviews" when examining Indigenous Latter-day Saint experiences. She spoke at the 2017 Mormon Studies Conference, "Multicultural Mormonism: Religious Cohesion in a New Era of Diversity," March 30, 2017, Utah Valley University, Orem, Utah. Her keynote address was titled "There's No Such Thing as 'A' Gospel Culture."

44. Because of my personal connections, I refer to my father throughout this paper. I do not cite our conversations since they were often informal and spanned over my life. I encouraged the development of a BYU Native American alumni oral history project and website, which Dr. Michael P. Taylor launched with BYU students around 2019. Students interviewed me for the project, and they presented about the oral histories at the 2019 Oral History Association annual meeting in Salt Lake City, in a session titled "Native BYU: Engaging Undergraduates in Indigenous Oral Histories," held on October 17, 2019. I attended the session and viewed some clips from the oral histories about alumni experiences, including a clip from my oral history. See "Native BYU," accessed March 14, 2023, https://native.byu.edu.

45. Metcalf refers to Mel Thom in "Which Side of the Line?," 16. See also Passie Roy, "BYU Indian Graduates Listed since First in '58," Eagle's Eye, 1983.

46. Bradley Glenn Shreve, "Red Power Rising: The National Indian Youth Council and Origins of Intertribal Activism" (PhD diss., University of New Mexico, 2007), 159.

47. Dan Edwards cited in Shreve, Red Power Rising, 99.

48. Melvin Thom cited in Cobb, Native Activism in Cold War America, 59–60.

49. For more about Indigenous futurity, see Laura Harjo, Spiral to the Stars: Mvskoke Tools of Futurity (Tucson: University of Arizona Press, 2019); Alexandra Hauke and Birgit Däwes, eds., Native American Survivance, Memory, and Futurity (New York: Routledge, 2017).

50. Informal conversations with Phillip Smith, my father, in 2017.

51. Paul R. McKenzie-Jones, Clyde Warrior: Tradition, Community, and Red Power (Norman: University of Oklahoma Press, 2015), 177; Mauss, All Abraham's Children, 132. To learn more about the origins of the National Indian Youth Council, see Shreve, Red Power Rising; Sterling Fluharty, "'For a Greater Indian America': The Origins of the National Indian Youth Council" (master's thesis, University of Oklahoma, 2003).

52. Personal conversations with my father, Phillip Smith, in 2016. My father shared memories of these events, but he was not sure of the exact dates. For a reference about the NIYC national meeting held at OU possibly in November 1969, see Boyce Timmons, director of the Indian program and chair of the American Indian Institute at OU, cited in Val Pipps and Connie Burke Ruggles, "Little Red: What Is at Issue?," Sooner Magazine, October 1970, 21. Instead of the fall of 1969, my father could have been referring to the "3-day Indian 'power' conference" held the weekend of September 19, 1970, which the "45-member OU chapter of the National Indian Youth Council" sponsored. See Robert B. Allen, "'Little Red' Debate Slated by Indians," Daily Oklahoman, September 12, 1970.

53. Dave Poolaw, Oklahoma City sophomore and president of the OU chapter of the NIYC, cited in Pipps and Ruggles, "Little Red," 20.

54. Smith, informal conversations, 2016 and 2017.

55. Melvin Thom cited in "Warrior Eulogized," *Oklahoman City Times*, July 9, 1968, p. 19.

56. Sherry L. Smith, *Hippies, Indians, and the Fight for Red Power*, 29; Annelise Orleck, "Introduction: The War on Poverty from the Grass Roots Up," in Annelise Orleck and Lisa Gayle Hazirjian, eds., *The War on Poverty: A New Grassroots History, 1964–1980* (Athens: University of Georgia Press, 2011), 2. For more about Native American activism in the late twentieth century, see Shreve, *Red Power Rising*; Cobb, *Native Activism in Cold War America*; Sherry L. Smith, "Indians, the Counterculture, and the New Left," in Cobb and Fowler, *Beyond Red Power*, 142–160.

57. My dad referred him to Vine Deloria Jr.'s book *Custer Died for Your Sins: An Indian Manifesto*, which was originally published in 1969 by the University of Oklahoma Press.

58. Mauss, *All Abraham's Children*, 90.

59. Flandro, *Heritage Book of Remembrance*, 127. Flandro explains that the missionaries and social service workers acted as "advanced agents for BYU to motivate students to attend BYU, to prepare them to attend, to help them to fill out the appropriate forms and get on their way to BYU where we would pick them up and carry them from there" (127).

60. Mauss, *All Abraham's Children*, 81.

61. Wilkinson, *Brigham Young University*, 3:508–509; Woodruff J. Deem and Glenn V. Bird, *Ernest L. Wilkinson: Indian Advocate and University President* (Alice M. Wilkinson, 1982), 440–441.

62. For more about the interconnections between Mormonism and Termination, see Metcalf, *Termination's Legacy*, 32. ISPP is an example of Church programs that aligned with Termination Era policies and practices. See Garrett, *Making Lamanites*, 58–90.

63. Wilkinson, *Brigham Young University*, 3: 517–520.

64. *Banyan* (Brigham Young University), 1971, 239. See also the work of Grace Soelberg, who researches the histories of BYU students who are Black, Indigenous, and People of Color by using the *Banyan*: Grace Soelberg, "BYU Slavery Project," *Utah Historical Quarterly* 90, no. 1 (Winter 2022): 73–76; Grace Soelberg, "Peculiar Students of a Peculiar Institution: A Historical Analysis of Racial Minority Students and Race Relations at Brigham Young University as Presented in the Banyan from 1911–1985" (undergraduate honors thesis, Brigham Young University, 2021).

65. These figures appear in Wilkinson, *Brigham Young University*, 3:520, and L. Robert Webb, *An Examination of Certain Aspects of the American Indian Education Program at Brigham Young University: A Study* (Provo, Utah: Brigham Young University Press, 1972), 15.

66. Paul Felt to Ernest L. Wilkinson, January 3, 1967, folder 7, box 4, UA 552.

67. James "Jim" Lee Dandy, interview by Jessie Embry, Blanding, Utah, October 2, 1990, 13, LDS NAOH.

68. Jeremy Begay, interview by Farina King, Provo, Utah, April 4, 2008, 5, LDS NAOH.

69. Masthead, *Eagle's Eye*, December 1970, 1.

70. Richard "Dick" Neztsosie, "Thanksgiving the Red Power Way at Plymouth Rock 360 Years Later," *Eagle's Eye*, December 1970, 2.

71. Dick Neztsosie, interview by Jim M. Dandy, Blanding, Utah, January 3, 1991, LDS NAOH.

72. "TMF Forum," *Eagle's Eye*, March 1971, 3.

73. Claralynn West, "'74 Miss Indian BYU Offers Farewell Tribute," *Eagle's Eye*, November 1974. She later married, changing her full name to Claralynn West Merino. See "Miss Indian BYU: Past Winners," *Deseret News*, May 3, 2007, http://www.deseretnews .com/article/660217290/Miss-Indian-BYU-past-winners.html.

74. Doctrine and Covenants 49:24.

75. For a discussion on "Lamanite" identity in the Church, see Mauss, *All Abraham's Children*; Garrett, *Making Lamanites*; Boxer, "To Become White and Delightsome."

76. Robert F. Gwilliam to Antone K. Romney, January 6, 1961, folder 6, box 18, UA 522.

77. Latin Americans of both Indigenous and mestizo ancestry participated in Lamanite Generation.

78. See studies that address definitions and appropriations of Lamanites including Mauss, *All Abraham's Children*, 10; Aikau, *A Chosen People, A Promised Land*; Marjorie Newton, *Tiki and Temple: The Mormon Mission in New Zealand, 1854–1958* (Draper, Utah: Greg Kofford Books, 2012); Stuart Parker, "Queso y gusanos: The Cosmos of Indigenous Mormon Intellectual Margarito Bautista," in *Just South of Zion: The Mormons in Mexico and Its Borderlands*, eds. Jason H. Dormady and Jared M. Tamez (Albuquerque: University of New Mexico Press, 2015); Elisa Eastwood Pulido, *The Spiritual Evolution of Margarito Bautista: Mexican Mormon Evangelizer, Polygamist Dissident, and Utopian Founder, 1878–1961* (New York: Oxford University Press, 2020).

79. Ken Sekaquaptewa, interview by Odessa Neaman, Provo, Utah, June 11, 1990, LDS NAOH.

80. "Our Miss Indian America," *Eagle's Eye*, November 1972, 1.

81. I make this point based on personal anecdotes shared with me from people who had direct interaction with Wilkinson. For an example, see Hugh Nibley, *Brother Brigham Challenges the Saints* (Salt Lake City: Deseret, 1994), 87–90.

82. Flandro, *Heritage Book of Remembrance*, 126.

83. Paul Felt cited in Garrett, *Making Lamanites*, 186.

84. Howard Rainer, interview with Farina King (and informal conversation), Provo, Utah, March 23, 2017.

85. Robert Bennion served a mission among Native Americans in the Southwest between 1947 and 1949 and later supported Indian Education at BYU. See "Obituary: Robert Bennion," *Deseret News*, April 21, 2013, http://www.legacy.com/obituaries /deseretnews/obituary.aspx?pid=164343255.

86. Rainer interview.

87. Flandro, *Heritage Book of Remembrance*, 123.

88. Rainer interview.

89. Flandro, *Heritage Book of Remembrance*, 126.

90. Wilkinson, *Brigham Young University*, 3:514; George P. Lee, *Silent Courage: An*

Indian Story: The Autobiography of George P. Lee, A Navajo (Salt Lake City: Deseret, 1987), 270–274; Flandro, *Heritage Book of Remembrance*, 126. George P. Lee later became the first Native American Latter-day Saint general authority. He was excommunicated "for apostasy and other conduct unbecoming a member of the church," sparking major controversy in 1989. After his excommunication, Lee claimed that he still loved the church, but it became "polluted by pride and racial prejudice." See "Church Explains Excommunication to Navajos as Lee Seeks a Rebirth," *Deseret News*, September 10, 1989, http://www.deseretnews.com/article/62992/CHURCH-EXPLAINS-EXCOMMUNICATION-TO-NAVAJOS-AS-LEE-SEEKS-A-REBIRTH.html; David Grua, "Elder George P. Lee and the New Jerusalem: A Reception History of 3 Nephi 21: 22–23," *Juvenile Instructor* (blog), August 27, 2013, http://juvenileinstructor.org/elder-george-p-lee-and-the-reception-history-of-3-nephi-2122-23/.

91. Phillip Smith, personal conversation, March 2017.

92. Rainer interview.

93. Howard Rainer, "Wounded Knee Where Are You?," *Eagle's Eye*, March 1973. Rainer was referring to Dee Brown, *Bury My Heart at Wounded Knee: An Indian History of the American West* (New York: Holt, Rinehart & Winston, 1970).

94. J. Elliot Cameron to Lyle Curtis, "Indian Student Organizations," Campus Memorandum, Brigham Young University, October 15, 1970, box 30, no. 19, UA 460 c.

95. Phillip L. Smith, interview with Farina King, Orem, Utah, 2012.

96. Jerry Garrett, "Lost Dialogue," *Daily Universe*, October 31, 1969, 2.

97. To learn more about the Black priesthood ban, temple restrictions, and historical context, see Janan Graham-Russell, "Choosing to Stay in the Mormon Church Despite Its Racist Legacy," *Atlantic*, August 28, 2016, https://www.theatlantic.com/politics/archive/2016/08/black-and-mormon/497660/; Matthew L. Harris and Newell G. Bringhurst, eds., *The Mormon Church and Blacks: A Documentary History* (Urbana: University of Illinois Press, 2015); Lester E. Bush and Armand L. Mauss, eds., *Neither White nor Black: Mormon Scholars Confront the Race Issue in a Universal Church* (Salt Lake City: Signature, 1984); Ingrid Britt Bolen, "The Church of Jesus Christ of Latter-day Saints and the Priesthood: An Analysis of Official Church Statements Concerning Black Priesthood Denial" (master's thesis, University of North Texas, 1991), 5; Newell G. Bringhurst and Darron T. Smith, eds., *Black and Mormon* (Urbana: University of Illinois Press, 2004).

98. "BYU Students Plan Their Own Protest," *Independent Record* (Helena, Montana), November 7, 1969, 10.

99. Jay Drew, "BYU Football: Remembering the Black 14 Protest," *Salt Lake Tribune*, November 6, 2009, http://archive.sltrib.com/story.php?ref=/byucougars/ci_13728556. In 2022 BYU journalism students produced and showed a documentary, *The Black 14 Healing Hearts and Feeding Souls*, which features the stories of "the Black 14, University of Wyoming football players who were kicked off of their team in 1969 after requesting to protest racist behavior from BYU's team." The film and event involved two of the Black 14, Mel Hamilton and John Griffin. See Kaylyn Wolf, "'The Black 14: Healing Hearts and Feeding Souls'—Documentary Private Screening Honors Two Black 14 Members," *Daily Universe*, September 22, 2022, https://universe.byu.edu/2022/09/22/black-14-documentary-private-screening-honors-two-black-14-members/. BYU also

honored Hamilton and Griffin by inviting them to "light the huge Y on the mountain" in a pregame ceremony for the BYU football match against the University of Wyoming in September 2022. Tad Walch, "BYU to Honor 'Black 14' Football Players Kicked Off Wyoming's 1969 Team," *Desert News*, September 22, 2022, https://www.deseret.com/sports /2022/9/22/23363986/byu-to-honor-black-14-football-players-kicked-off-wyomings -1969-team. The BYU Office of Belonging spearheaded this tribute as part of their initiatives for "diversity, equity, and belonging."

100. "BYU Students Plan Their Own Protest," 10.

101. Phillip Lee Smith, interview by Farina King, Provo, Utah, February 20, 2012. I referred to this part of the interview in my article "Miss Indian BYU: Contestation over the Crown and Indian Identity," but there was some confusion about which university football team my father remembered. I had initially noted San Diego State University, but my father corrected me to the San Jose State University football team.

102. Ken Sekaquaptewa interview, 5.

103. Sanders interview, 14.

104. Garrett, *Making Lamanites*, 181; Amanda Hendrix-Komoto, "Boycotting General Conference 40 Years Ago: The Lamanite Generation, the American Indian Movement, and Temple Square," *Juvenile Instructor* (blog), April 12, 2013, http:// juvenileinstructor.org/boycotting-general-conference-50-years-ago-the-lamanite -generation-the-american-indian-movement-and-temple-square/. The Church headquarters is located in Salt Lake City, Utah.

105. Sanders interview, 15–16.

106. Cox interview, 11.

107. Cox referred to the version of the hit song by Paul Revere and the Raiders, "Indian Reservation (The Lament of the Cherokee Reservation Indian)," 1971. Don Fardon first popularized the song with his cover of it in 1968. For more about the context of this music, see Craig Harris, *Heartbeat, Warble, and the Electric Powwow: American Indian Music* (Norman: University of Oklahoma Press, 2016), 232.

108. Cox interview, 12.

109. Dustin Tahmahkera, *Tribal Televisions: Viewing Native People in Sitcoms* (Chapel Hill: University of North Carolina Press, 2014), xiv–xv.

110. Groves interview, 9.

111. "Miss Indian America Begay Travels Extensively, Seeks Unity," *Eagle's Eye*, January 1972, 1. See also Farina King, "Miss Indian BYU." In 2013 an undergraduate student at BYU, Jennifer Duqué, met with me to discuss sources about the Miss Indian BYU pageant. She developed a critical essay that assessed Miss Indian BYU's role and "cultural script" in the 1970s and 1980s. She cited Nora Begay and Vickie Bird Sanders among others. See Jennifer Duqué, "'Many Hearts yet Beat with the Hurt of a Wounded Past': Miss Indian BYU, Lamanite Identities, and the Subversive Potential of Pageants," *Thetean* 43 (2014): 85–86, 92–93.

112. "Miss Indian America Begay."

113. "Miss Indian America Begay."

114. Sanders interview, 15.

115. Phillip Smith shared these stories when I asked him if he knew Nora Begay.

116. Phillip Smith interview.

117. For more about Latter-day Saint women's experiences and gender dynamics in the Church, see Joanna Brooks, Rachel Hunt Steenblik, and Hannah Wheelwright, eds., *Mormon Feminism: Essential Writings* (New York: Oxford University Press, 2016); Caroline Kline, *Mormon Women at the Crossroads: Global Narratives and the Power of Connectedness* (Urbana: University of Illinois Press, 2022); Taylor G. Petrey, *Tabernacles of Clay: Sexuality and Gender in Modern Mormonism* (Chapel Hill: University of North Carolina Press, 2020).

118. Nora Begay cited in Chris Lowery, "Past Title Holders Featured: Fireside Opens Miss Indian BYU Pageant Activities," *Eagle's Eye*, April 1976, 1.

119. Sanders interview, 14, 15.

120. Mildred Cody Garrett, interview by Odessa Neaman, Provo, Utah, 1990, 27, LDS NAOH.

121. Groves interview, 14, 15.

122. Janice White Clemmer, "Native American Studies: A Utah Perspective," *Wicazo Sa Review* 2, no. 2 (Autumn 1986): 17.

123. Mauss, *All Abraham's Children*, 99–100, 113, n23.

124. Clemmer, "Native American Studies," 20 (quotation), 18.

125. Duffy, "Use of 'Lamanite,'" 160–161.

126. For criticism on "multiculturalism," see Roxanne Dunbar-Ortiz, *An Indigenous People's History of the United States* (Boston: Beacon Press, 2014), 5.

127. For more details about this sudden decline in Native American programs at BYU, see Clemmer, "Native American Studies."

128. Jeremy Begay interview, 5.

129. Howard Rainer cited Alma 37:19 in the Book of Mormon during the BYU Native American Alumni luncheon that the author attended on March 23, 2017, at Brigham Young University, Provo, Utah.

130. I attended this meeting and took these personal notes of Cynthia Connell's address to the attendees of the BYU Native American Alumni luncheon held on March 23, 2017, at BYU.

131. Larry Echo Hawk, "An Unexpected Gift," August 7, 2007, speech delivered at devotional meeting, Brigham Young University, Provo, Utah, https://speeches.byu.edu /talks/larry-echohawk_unexpected-gift/. I attended one of his "firesides" (speeches) in Flagstaff, Arizona, on July 9, 2013.

132. See Aubrey Eyre, "Native American Professor Joins BYU Committee Examining Race, Inequality," *Deseret News*, July 11, 2020.

CHAPTER 7. DINÉ DÓÓ GÁAMALII PERSPECTIVES

1. Louise Lamphere with Eva Price, Carole Cadman, and Valerie Darwin, *Weaving Women's Lives: Three Generations in a Navajo Family* (Albuquerque: University of New Mexico, 2007), 130–131, 115–116, 230, 97.

2. Syncretism is a complicated term that often refers to how people combine different

cultures. I prefer to think of such internalizations of diverse cultural genealogies as "hy-bridization." However, scholars have primarily discussed such processes as "syncretism," especially concerning Diné, so I will use this term in this case. See, for example, McPherson et al., *Navajo Tradition, Mormon Life*.

3. Dieter F. Uchtdorf, "Heeding the Voice of the Prophets," *Ensign*, July 2008, 4–7.

4. See, for example, Charlotte J. Frisbie, "Temporal Change in Navajo Religion: 1868–1900," *Journal of the Southwest* 34, no. 4 (December 1992): 457–514.

5. Laura Brown oral history, interview by Farina King, 2008, St. Michaels, Navajo Nation, LDS NAOH.

6. Hal L. Taylor cited in James D. Mathews, "A Study of the Cultural and Religious Behavior of the Navajo Indians Which Caused Animosity, Resistance, or Indifference to the Religious Teaching of the Latter-day Saints" (master's thesis, BYU, 1968), 82–83.

7. Taylor cited in Mathews, 82–83.

8. Betty Henderson cited in Mathews, 47. Diné have referred to certain ceremonial dances as "squaw dances" since the twentieth century.

9. Betty Henderson cited in Mathews, 47.

10. Diné sometimes use "sing" and "ceremony" synonymously since most ceremonies involve songs and chants. However, some ceremonies do not involve singing. Phillip L. Smith explained these differences in a personal conversation, February 2, 2015, Monument Valley, Utah.

11. Kenneth Nabahe cited in Mathews, "Study of the Cultural and Religious Behavior of the Navajo Indians," 47.

12. Susie Little cited in Mathews, 48.

13. Helena Hogue oral history, interview by Ernesteen B. Lynch, August 21, 1990, Fruitland, New Mexico, p. 8, LDS NAOH.

14. James L. Dandy oral history, interview by Jessie L. Embry, October 2, 1990, Blanding, Utah, p. 6, LDS NAOH.

15. See McPherson et al., *Navajo Tradition, Mormon Life*, which emphasizes how Dandy found more balance between Diné and LDS beliefs and practices.

16. Julius Ray Chavez oral history, interview by Odessa Neaman, June 27, 1990, p. 18, LDS NAOH.

17. Alexia Lopez oral history, interview by Ernesteen Lynch, August 10, 1989, LDS NAOH.

18. Jimmy N. Benally oral history, interview by Odessa Neaman, July 18, 1990, p. 9, LDS NAOH, 9; Anna Benally oral history, interview by Farina King, January 24, 2008, Provo, Utah, LDS NAOH.

19. Yéii' bicheii is a Diné ceremonial dance held in the winter after the first snowfall. Personal conversations with Anna Benally, 2006. See also "Significance of Diné Moccasins," Grownup Navajo, YouTube, November 3, 2017, https://youtu.be/J5bREb8 Etdc.

20. Ernesteen Lynch oral history, interview by Jessie Embry, May 17, 1990, Provo, Utah, pp. 23–24, LDS NAOH. R. Warren Metcalf also refers to this oral history in his chapter, "'Which Side of the Line?': American Indian Students and Programs at Brigham

Young University, 1960–1983," in Hafen and Rensink, *Essays on American Indian and Mormon History*, 225.

21. Comments at the Navajo Symposium, sponsored by the Charles Redd Center for Western Studies, 1989, shared by Jessie Embry.

22. Olivia Ben oral history, interview by Corey Smallcanyon, 2008, Orem, Utah, LDS Native American Oral History, 13.

23. Dandy oral history, 19.

24. Edwin T. Tano, conversation with Jessie L. Embry and Farina King, 2011, Tuba City, Arizona.

25. Anthony M. and Brenda Beyal oral history, interview by Corey Smallcanyon, August 26, 2008, Mapleton, Utah, pp. 15–16, LDS NAOH.

26. In terms of Diné traditional spirituality, I refer to spiritual and ceremonial practices that originated before European and white American contact, predating introductions to Christianity.

27. Anthony and Brenda Beyal oral history, 15–16.

28. Anna Benally oral history, 17.

29. Marci Brown oral history, interview by Farina King, November 11, 2007, Page, Arizona, p. 6, LDS NAOH.

30. Lillie Pooley, conversations with Jessie L. Embry and Farina King, 2012, Tuba City, Navajo Nation.

31. Susie T. Kinlacheeny oral history, interview by Matthew K. Heiss, 1997, Kayenta, Navajo Nation, Arizona, Church History Library.

32. Irene B. Jones oral history, interview by Farina King, November 11, 2007, Page, Arizona, p. 4, LDS NAOH.

33. I presented about the book manuscript on August 11, 2013, in Page, Arizona, where Irene Jones and other attendees, who were mostly Diné Latter-day Saints, explained this point.

34. Shauntel Talk oral history, interview by Farina King, January 18, 2008, Provo, Utah, p. 8, LDS NAOH.

35. Oliver Whaley oral history, interview by Farina King, September 28, 2007, Provo, Utah, p. 11, LDS NAOH.

36. Yanibaa Collins oral history, interview by Farina King, October 4, 2007, Provo, Utah, p. 10, LDS NAOH.

37. Talk oral history, 9.

38. James Joseph Buss and C. Joseph Genetin-Pilawa, "Introduction: The World Is Not Enough," in *Beyond Two Worlds: Critical Conversations on Language and Power in Native North America*, ed. James Joseph Buss and C. Joseph Genetin-Pilawa (Albany: State University of New York Press, 2014), 5.

39. Donald L. Pine oral history, interview by Farina King, February 17, 2008, Fort Wingate, New Mexico, p. 13, LDS NAOH.

40. Jessica Mills oral history, interview by Farina King, September 24, 2007, Provo, Utah, p. 7, LDS NAOH.

41. Lucy Guymon Bloomfield, Correspondence, 1905–1981, MS 13266, Church History Library.

42. Mrs. George Bloomfield to Ralph William Evans, June 23, 1942, Ralph William Evans Papers, Church History Library. There is no reply to Bloomfield's letter in the Evans Papers.

43. J. Edwin Baird to James D. Mathews, May 9, 1968, quoted in Mathews, "Study of the Cultural and Religious Behavior of the Navajo Indians," 86, 88.

44. Wallace Brown oral history, interview by Farina King, November 10, 2007, Page, Arizona, p. 18, LDS NAOH.

45. See "Navajo Traditional Teachings—Elder Wally Brown Shares Indigenous Ways of Knowing through Digital Stories to Preserve Navajo Culture," Faculty of Education, Indigenous Teacher Education Program (NITEP), February 7, 2022, University of British Columbia, https://nitep.educ.ubc.ca/february-07-2022-navajo-traditional-teachings/; Shane Brown, "Our Story, a Two Man Show," Navajo Traditional Teachings, accessed November 20, 2022, https://navajotraditionalteachings.com/pages/our-story.

46. In Navajo, Diné call their spiritual leaders and healers hataałii. In English, Navajos commonly call them "medicine men," which is the reason for the use of the term in the text.

47. Thomas Tsinnijinnie, interview by Farina King, September 12, 2012, Salt River Pima-Maricopa Community, Arizona.

48. McPherson et al., *Navajo Tradition, Mormon Life*, 122–123.

49. Tsinnijinnie interview. See also Robert S. McPherson, *Dinéjí Na'Nitin: Navajo Traditional Teachings and History* (Boulder: University Press of Colorado, 2012), 86.

50. This interviewee asked to not be identified. Interview with Farina King, 2012, Tuba City, Navajo Nation.

51. For example, see Alma 1:12–16. Ed Tano, conversation with Farina King and Jessie Embry, 2012, Tuba City, Navajo Nation, Arizona.

52. Ellouise Paredes oral history, interview by Farina King, 2008, Salt Lake City, Utah, pp. 2–3, LDS NAOH. There are traditional Diné women healers too. See Wade Davies, *Healing Ways: Navajo Health Care in the Twentieth Century* (Albuquerque: University of New Mexico Press), 5.

53. The interviewee did not want her name used but shared this insight and experience with the author.

54. Tsinnijinnie interview.

55. Tsinnijinnie interview.

56. Farina King, personal observations during the Franklin Second Ward meetings, 2012, Provo, Utah.

57. Ruby Whitesinger Benally oral history, interview by Matthew K. Heiss, 1997, Chinle, Navajo Nation, Arizona, p. 8, Church History Library.

58. See also the famous work of Leslie Marmon Silko, *Ceremony* (New York: Penguin, 1977), which fictionalizes the experiences of a Native American (of Laguna descent) veteran named Tayo who seeks healing through the traditions, histories, and ceremonies of his people.

59. Ruby Whitesinger Benally oral history, 17.

60. Nanabah Bia Begay, interview by Matthew K. Heiss, interpreted by Helena Yellowhair, April 27, 1997, Many Farms, Navajo Nation, Church History Library, tape

recording and transcript. Phillip Smith retranslated the Navajo parts of the interview tape recording in 2013 and provided the Navajo diacritical markings and translations. For more about this oral history and translations, see Farina King, "The Oral History of a LDS Asdzáánsání in Diné Bizaad," *Juvenile Instructor* (blog), November 18, 2013, https://juvenileinstructor.org/the-oral-history-of-a-lds-asdzaansani-in-dine-bizaad/.

EPILOGUE

1. Albert Smith cited in Annie Ross, "'Our Mother Earth Is My Purpose': Recollections from Mr. Albert Smith, Naʼashǫ́ʼii dichʼízhii," *American Indian Culture and Research Journal* 37, no. 1 (2013): 106.

2. Romero Brown oral history, interview by Farina King, February 17, 2008, St. Michaels, Arizona, p. 7, LDS NAOH.

3. Monika Nikki Crowfoot oral history, interview by Farina King, December 1, 2007, Provo, Utah, pp. 4–5, LDS NAOH.

4. Monika Crowfoot, "Guest Post: My Apology for My Complicity," *Exponent II*, July 5, 2020, https://www.the-exponent.com/guest-post-my-apology-for-my-complicity/. Monika Crowfoot is also working on a memoir that addresses her upbringing and affiliation with the Church.

5. Monika Brown Crowfoot, "The Lamanite Dilemma: Mormonism and Indigeneity," *Dialogue: A Journal of Mormon Thought* 54, no. 2 (Summer 2021): 61.

6. Crowfoot, "My Apology for My Complicity."

7. Darrell Brown oral history, interview by Farina King, September 19, 2007, Provo, Utah, p. 9, LDS NAOH.

8. Anna Benally oral history, interview by Farina King, January 24, 2008, Provo, Utah, p. 9, LDS NAOH.

9. Elouise T. Goatson oral history, interview by Farina King, November 10, 2007, Page, Arizona, p. 5, LDS NAOH.

10. Derik Goatson oral history, interview by Farina King, January 18, 2008, Provo, Utah, p. 5, LDS NAOH.

11. Victor Mannie Sr. oral history, interview by Farina King, November 11, 2007, Page, Arizona, p. 5, LDS NAOH.

12. Phillip Smith oral history, interview by Farina King, September 8, 2008, Kensington, Maryland, 4, 7–9, 12. Phillip Smith is my father, and the information not from the interview is personal knowledge.

13. Phillip Smith oral history, interview by Farina King, 2008, Provo, Utah, pp. 4–5, LDS NAOH, and author's personal knowledge.

14. Author's personal knowledge.

15. Tapahonso, *Radiant Curve*, 7.

16. Farina King, personal observation. Navajo translations and concepts were explained by my family, especially my father. "Hózhǫ́ nahasdlii" is repeated.

17. Liz Nez, interviewed by Jessie Embry, 2012, Tuba City, Arizona, LDS Native American, 4.

18. Tsinnijinnie, interview by Farina King, 2012.

19. Romero Brown, email correspondence with Farina King, 2011; Tsinnijinnie interview.

20. Nanabah Bia Begay, interview by Matthew K. Heiss and Helena Yellowhair, 1997, Many Farms, Navajo Nation, Arizona, Church History Library. The Church History Division allowed Phillip Smith to translate parts of the interview that are in Navajo.

21. See Shumway and Shumway, *Blossoming II*; author's personal observations. Her daughter Ellouise Paredes introduced me to her.

22. Author's observations, 2012.

23. Author's personal history and observations.

24. Doctrine and Covenants 49: 24.

25. Spencer W. Kimball, "First Presidency Message: Our Paths Have Met Again," *Ensign*, December 1975, 2; Dean L. Larsen, "Mingled Destinies: The Lamanites and the Latter-day Saints," *Ensign*, December 1975, 8.

26. Ruby Whitesinger Benally oral history, interview by Matthew K. Heiss, 1997, Window Rock, Navajo Nation, Arizona, p. 20, Church History Library.

27. Virginia Morris Tso Tulley oral history, interview by Matthew K. Heiss, 1997, Window Rock, Navajo Nation, Arizona, pp. 11–12, Church History Library.

28. Jerome Wilmer Willie oral history, interview by Matthew K. Heiss, 1997, Window Rock, Navajo Nation, Arizona, p. 11, Church History Library.

29. Wilson Yazzie Deschine oral history, interview by Matthew K. Heiss, 1992, Window Rock, Navajo Nation, Arizona, p. 11, Church History Library.

30. Dan K. Smith oral history, interview by Matthew K. Heiss, 1992, Chinle, Navajo Nation, Arizona, p. 8, Church History Library.

31. Loren Begay oral history, interview by Farina King, September 16, 2007, Provo, Utah, p. 7, LDS NAOH.

32. Crowfoot oral history, 8.

33. William Numkena oral history, interview by Matthew K. Heiss, 1992, Tuba City, Navajo Nation, p. 13, Church History Library.

34. Dennis and Marie Little oral history, interview by Farina King, October 8, 2007, Orem, Utah, p. 12, LDS NAOH.

35. See Philip Deloria, *Playing Indian* (New Haven, CT: Yale University Press, 1998). This part of the epilogue provides more context and draws from one of my previous publications with the University Press of Kansas, *The Earth Memory Compass*, when I referred to my father's honor song. See Farina King, *Earth Memory Compass*, 36–39.

36. Andrew Natonabah, "By This Song I Walk: Navajo Song," *Words and Place: Native Literature from the American Southwest*, accessed August 26, 2013, http://parentseyes.arizona.edu/wordsandplace/natonabah.html (no longer available).

37. Tapahonso, "We Must Remember."

38. See Kenneth M. Roemer, "It's Not a Poem. It's My Life: Navajo Singing Identities," *Studies in American Indian Literatures* 24:2 (Summer 2012): 84–103.

39. See Diné articulations of the Four Sacred Directions and Mountains, including Andrew Natonabah's "By This Song I Walk"; George Blueeyes's "Díí Dził ahéénínilígíí

Nihi Bee Haz'áanii át'é" ("Our Navajo Laws are represented by the Sacred Mountains which surround us"); and Luci Tapahonso's "This Is How They Were Placed for Us."

40. My father, Phillip Smith, wrote and shared the words of this song with me on July 26, 2013. I have the full written song in my personal collection. I wrote this poem for this book based on my father's song. The parts in Diné bizaad (Navajo language) come directly from my father's song, but the English parts are a combination of my poetry and translation of the Diné bizaad. See also Farina King, *Earth Memory Compass*, 38–39.

41. Julie Ann Livingston oral history, interview by Farina King, February 16, 2008, Gallup, New Mexico, LDS Native American Oral History, 19.

42. Livingston oral history; see also Rima Krisst, "Church Rock Matriarchs Fight Age Discrimination," *Navajo Times*, June 13, 2019, https://navajotimes.com/reznews/church -rock-matriarchs-fight-age-discrimination/.

Select Bibliography

ARCHIVES

Charles Redd Center for Western Studies, L. Tom Perry Special Collections,
    Harold B. Lee Library, Brigham Young University, Provo, Utah
    Latter-day Saint Polynesian American Oral History Project
    LDS Native American Oral History Project
    LDS Sister Missionaries Oral History Project
    Provo South Stake Oral History Project
Church History Library, Church of Jesus Christ of Latter-day Saints, Salt Lake City, Utah
    Arizona Holbrook Mission Manuscript History
    Southwest Indian Mission Manuscript History
National Archives, Washington, DC, Record Group 75, Bureau of Indian Affairs,
    Central Classified Files, Decimal 054
    Navajo Tribal Council meeting notes

OTHER SOURCES

Aikau, Hokulani K. *A Chosen People, A Promised Land: Mormonism and Race in Hawai'i.*
    Minneapolis: University of Minnesota Press, 2012.
The Banyan (yearbook). Provo, UT: Brigham Young University Press, 1971.
Benally, Herbert J. "Hózhóǫgo Naasháa Doo: Toward a Construct of Balance in Navajo
    Cosmology." PhD diss., California Institute of Integral Studies, 2008.
Benally, Malcolm D., ed. and trans. *Bitter Water: Diné Oral Histories of the Navajo-Hopi
    Land Dispute.* Tucson: University of Arizona Press, 2011.
Benally, Moroni. "Decolonizing the Blossoming: Indigenous People's Faith in a Coloniz-
    ing Church." *Dialogue: A Journal of Mormon Thought* 50, no. 4 (Winter 2017): 71–78.
Bingham, Sam, and Janet Bingham, eds. *Between Sacred Mountains: Navajo Stories and
    Lessons from the Land.* Chinle, Navajo Nation, AZ: Rock Point Community School,
    1982.
Birch, J. Neil. "Helen John: The Beginnings of Indian Placement." *Dialogue: A Journal of
    Mormon Thought* 18 (Winter 1985): 119–129.
Bishop, Clarence R. "Indian Placement: A History of the Indian Student Placement

Program of the Church of Jesus Christ of Latter-day Saints." MA thesis, University of Utah, 1967.

Bowman, Matthew. *The Mormon People: The Making of an American Faith.* New York: Random House, 2012.

Boxer, Elise. "'To Become White and Delightsome': American Indians and Mormon Identity." PhD diss., Arizona State University, 2009.

———. "'The Lamanites Shall Blossom as the Rose': The Indian Student Placement Program, Mormon Whiteness, and Indigenous Identity." *Journal of Mormon History* 41, no. 4 (October 2015): 132–176.

Buss, James Joseph, and C. Joseph Genetin-Pilawa, eds. *Beyond Two Worlds: Critical Conversations on Language and Power in Native North America.* Albany: State University of New York Press, 2014.

Butterworth, Edwin Jr., ed. *1000 Views of 100 Years.* Provo, UT: Brigham Young University Press, 2005.

Chadwick, Bruce A., Stan Albrecht, and Howard M. Bahr. "Evaluation of an Indian Student Placement Program." *Social Casework* 68 (November 1986): 515–525.

Clemmer, Janice White. "Native American Studies: A Utah Perspective." *Wicazo Sa Review* 2, no. 2 (Autumn 1986): 17–23.

Colvin, Gina. "There's No Such Thing as 'A' Gospel Culture." Speech given at the Mormon Studies Conference, Utah Valley University, Orem, Utah, March 30, 2017.

Colvin, Gina, and Joanna Brooks, eds. *Decolonizing Mormonism: Approaching a Postcolonial Zion.* Salt Lake City: University of Utah Press, 2018.

———. "Introduction: Theorizing Mormon Race Scholarship." *Journal of Mormon History* 41, no. 3 (July 2015): 11–21.

Corntassel, Jeff. "Re-envisioning Resurgence: Indigenous Pathways to Decolonization and Sustainable Self-Determination." *Decolonization: Indigeneity, Education and Society* 1, no. 1 (2012): 86–101.

Crowfoot, Monika Brown. "The Lamanite Dilemma: Mormonism and Indigeneity." *Dialogue: A Journal of Mormon Thought* 54, no. 2 (Summer 2021): 57–63.

Denetdale, Jennifer Nez. "'No Explanation, No Resolution, and No Answers:' Border Town Violence and Navajo Resistance to Settler Colonialism." *Wicazo Sa Review* 31, no. 1 (Spring 2016): 111–131.

———. *Reclaiming Diné History: The Legacies of Navajo Chief Manuelito and Juanita.* Tucson: University of Arizona Press, 2007.

Diné Cultural Content Standards for Students, "T'áá Shá Bik'ehgo Diné Bí Ná nitin dóó íhoo'aah." Window Rock, Navajo Nation, AZ: Office of Diné Culture, Language, and Community Service, Division of Diné Education, 1998.

Duffy, John-Charles. "The Use of 'Lamanite' in Official LDS Discourse." *Journal of Mormon History* 34, no. 1 (Winter 2008): 118–167.

Embry, Jessie L. "Indian Placement Program Host Families: A Mission to the Lamanites." *Journal of Mormon History* 40, no. 2 (Spring 2014): 235–276.

Esplin, Scott C. "'You Can Make Your Own Bright Future, Tom Trails': Evaluating the Impact of the LDS Indian Seminary Program." *Journal of Mormon History* 42, no. 4 (October 2016): 172–207.

Fixico, Donald L. *The Urban Indian Experience in America*. Albuquerque: University of New Mexico Press, 2000.

Flake, David Kay. "A History of Mormon Missionary Work with the Hopi, Navaho and Zuni Indians." MA thesis, Brigham Young University, 1965.

Fraughton, Edward. "Spencer W. Kimball and the Lamanite Cause." *Brigham Young University Studies* 25, no. 4 (Fall 1985): 72–75.

Garrett, Matthew. *Making Lamanites: Mormons, Native Americans, and the Indian Student Placement Program, 1947–2000*. Salt Lake City: University of Utah Press, 2016.

Hafen, P. Jane. "The Being and Place of a Native American Mormon." In *New Genesis: A Mormon Reader on Land and Community*, edited by Terry Tempest Williams, William B. Smart, and Gibbs M. Smith, 35–41. Salt Lake City: Gibbs Smith, 1998.

———. "'Great Spirit Listens': The American Indian in Mormon Music." *Dialogue: A Journal of Mormon Thought* 18, no. 4 (Winter 1985): 133–142.

Hafen, P. Jane, and Brenden W. Rensink, eds. *Essays on American Indian and Mormon History*. Salt Lake City: University of Utah Press, 2019.

Harris, Lacee A. "To Be Native American and Mormon." *Dialogue: A Journal of Mormon Thought* 18, no. 4 (Winter 1985): 87–99.

Harris, Matthew L., and Newell G. Bringhurst, eds. *The Mormon Church and Blacks: A Documentary History*. Urbana: University of Illinois Press, 2015.

Iverson, Peter. *Diné: A History of the Navajos*. Albuquerque: University of New Mexico Press, 2002.

Kelley, Klara, and Harris Francis. *A Diné History of Navajoland*. Tucson: University of Arizona Press, 2019.

Keovorabouth, Souksavanh T. "Reaching Back to Traditional Teachings: Diné Knowledge and Gender Politics." *Genealogy* 5, no. 95 (2021).

King, Farina. "Diné Doctor: A Latter-day Saint Story of Healing." *Dialogue: A Journal of Mormon Thought* 54, no. 2 (Summer 2021): 81–85.

———. *The Earth Memory Compass: Diné Landscapes and Education in the Twentieth Century*. Lawrence: University Press of Kansas, 2018.

———. "Indigenizing Mormonisms." *Mormon Studies Review* 6 (2019): 1–16.

———. "Miss Indian BYU: Contestations over the Crown and Indian Identity." *Journal of the West* 52, no. 3 (Summer 2013): 10–21.

King, Farina, Michael P. Taylor, and James R. Swensen. *Returning Home: Diné Creative Works of the Intermountain Indian School*. Tucson: University of Arizona Press, 2021.

Lamphere, Louise, Eva Price, Carole Cadman, and Valerie Darwin. *Weaving Women's Lives: Three Generations in a Navajo Family*. Albuquerque: University of New Mexico Press, 2007.

Language Training Mission. *Diné Bizaad Na'nitiníbá*. Provo, UT: The [Church of Jesus Christ of Latter-day Saints] Mission, 1973.

Lee, George P. *Silent Courage: An Indian Story: The Autobiography of George P. Lee, a Navajo*. Salt Lake City: Deseret Books, 1987.

Lee, Lloyd L. *Diné Identity in a Twenty-First-Century World*. Tucson: University of Arizona Press, 2020.

————, ed. *Diné Perspectives: Revitalizing and Reclaiming Navajo Thought.* Tucson: University of Arizona Press, 2014.

Linford, Laurance D. *Navajo Places: History, Legend, Landscape.* Salt Lake City: University of Utah Press, 2000.

Livingstone, John P. *Same Drum, Different Beat: The Story of Dale T. Tingey and American Indian Services.* Provo, UT: Religious Studies Center, Brigham Young University, 2003.

Lynch, Regina H. *A History of Navajo Clans.* Rough Rock, Navajo Nation, AZ: Rough Rock Demonstration School Navajo Curriculum Center, 1987.

Mathews, James D. "A Study of the Cultural and Religious Behavior of the Navajo Indians Which Caused Animosity, Resistance, or Indifference to the Religious Teaching of the Latter-day Saints." Master of Religious Education thesis, Brigham Young University, 1968.

Mauss, Armaud. *All Abraham's Children: Changing Mormon Conceptions of Race and Lineage.* Urbana: University of Illinois Press, 2003.

McCullough-Brabson, Ellen, and Marilyn Help. *We'll Be in Your Mountains, We'll Be in Your Songs: A Navajo Woman Sings.* Albuquerque: University of New Mexico Press, 2001.

McPherson, Robert S. *Dinéjí Na'nitin: Navajo Traditional Teachings and History.* Boulder: University Press of Colorado, 2012.

McPherson, Robert S., Jim Dandy, and Sarah E. Burak. *Navajo Tradition, Mormon Life: The Autobiography and Teachings of Jim Dandy.* Salt Lake City: University of Utah Press, 2012.

Morgan, Brandon. "Educating the Lamanites: A Brief History of the LDS Indian Student Placement Program." *Journal of Mormon History* 35, no. 4 (Fall 2009): 191–217.

Murphy, Thomas W., and Angelo Baca. "DNA and the Book of Mormon: Science, Settlers, and Scripture." In *The LDS Gospel Topics Series: A Scholarly Engagement*, edited by Matthew L. Harris and Newell G. Bringhurst, 69–95. Salt Lake City: Signature Books, 2020.

————. "Inventing Galileo." *Sunstone* 131 (March 2004): 58–61.

————. "Lamanite Genesis, Genealogy, and Genetics." In *American Apocrypha: Essays on the Book of Mormon*, edited by Dan Vogel and Brent Metcalfe, 47–77. Salt Lake City: Signature Books, 2002.

Parry, Darren. *The Bear River Massacre: A Shoshone History.* Salt Lake City: By Common Consent Press, 2019.

Pavlik, Steve. "Of Saints and Lamanities: An Analysis of Navajo Mormonism." *Wicazo Sa Review* 8, no. 1 (Spring 1992): 21–30.

Rodgers, Larry. *Chapter Images.* 1996 ed. Window Rock, Navajo Nation, AZ: Division of Community Development, Navajo Nation, 1997.

Roemer, Kenneth M. "It's Not a Poem. It's My Life: Navajo Singing Identities." *Studies in American Indian Literatures* 24, no. 2 (Summer 2012): 84–103.

Ross, Annie. "'Our Mother Earth Is My Purpose': Recollections from Mr. Albert Smith, Na'ashǫ́'ii dich'ízhii." *American Indian Culture and Research Journal* 37, no. 1 (2013): 105–124.

Schwarz, Maureen Trudelle. *Navajo Lifeways: Contemporary Issues, Ancient Knowledge.* Norman: University of Oklahoma Press, 2001.

Shumway, Dale, and Margene Shumway, eds. *The Blossoming: Dramatic Accounts in the Lives of Native Americans.* Granite, UT: self-published, 2002.

Simon, Hemopereki. "Hoea Te Waka ki Uta: Critical Kaupapa Maori Research and Mormon Studies Moving Forward." *New Sociology: Journal of Critical Praxis* 3 (2022).

Smallcanyon, Corey. "Contested Space: Mormons, Navajos, and Hopis in the Colonization of Tuba City." Master's thesis, Brigham Young University, 2010.

Tapahonso, Luci. *A Radiant Curve.* Tucson: University of Arizona, 2008.

Thayne, Stanley. "The Blood of Father Lehi: Indigenous Americans and the Book of Mormon." PhD diss., University of North Carolina, 2016.

Tecun, Arcia. "A Divine Rebellion: Indigenous Sacraments among Global 'Lamanites.'" *Religions* 12, no. 280 (2021).

Topper, Martin D. "'Mormon Placement': The Effect of Mormon Missionary Foster Families on Navajo Adolescents." *Ethos* 7 (Summer 1979): 142–160.

Turner, D. L. "Akimel Au-Authm, Xalychidom Piipaash, and the LDS Papago Ward." *Journal of Mormon History* 39, no. 1 (Winter 2013): 158–180.

Webb, L. Robert. *An Examination of Certain Aspects of the American Indian Education Program at Brigham Young University: A Study.* Provo, UT: Brigham Young University Press, 1972.

Williams, LaShawn C. "*Mormonism and White Supremacy* as White Mormon Scholarship." *Dialogue* 54, no. 1 (Spring 2021): 162–166.

Witherspoon, Gary. *Language and Art in the Navajo Universe.* Ann Arbor: University of Michigan Press, 1977.

Yazzie, Robert. "'Life Comes from It': Navajo Justice Concepts." *New Mexico Law Review* 24, no. 2 (Spring 1994): 175–190.

Young, Robert W., ed. *The Navajo Yearbook of Planning in Action.* Window Rock, Navajo Nation, AZ: Navajo Agency, 1955.

Index

Aaronic Priesthood, 32, 229n43

Abraham, 28, 157

activism, 156–157, 158, 163, 168, 177, 178, 258n3

Adison, Shannon, 46

Adult Vocational Training Program, 255n15

"Aid Minorities" (Kimball), 139

Aikau, Hokulani, 43

AIM. *See* American Indian Movement

AIS. *See* American Indian Services

Akheah, Sam, 58, 59, 60

Akwesasne, 39, 40

Alaskans, 66, 74

Albrecht, Stan, 246n24

alcoholism, 99, 104, 163, 164, 180, 181

Alexander, Thomas G., 54, 236n27

Allison, Michael, 194

Alma Ward, 142

'Altsé 'Asdzáá (First Woman), 22

'Altsé Hastiin (First Man), 22

American Indian, term, 237n37

"American Indian and Polynesian" performance show, 74

American Indian Institute and Studies (BYU), 62

American Indian Movement (AIM), 156, 158, 164, 168, 169, 170, 172, 174

American Indian Services (AIS), 153, 257n50

American Indian Studies Association (AISA), 13

American Sign Language, 149

"America's War on Poverty," 164

ancestry, 11, 32–33, 123; Diné, 15, 201; Indigenous, 60, 145, 176, 264n77

Ancient Ones, 16

Anishinaabe, 39

Apachee, Judy, 226n15

Apaches, 64, 74

apostasy, 18, 43, 241n104, 242n112, 265n90

Arizona Holbrook Mission, 62, 79

Arizona Phoenix Mission, 63

Arizona State University (ASU), 152, 172

Arrington, Leonard, 40

Arthur, Claudeen, 226n15

Articles of Faith, 30

Asdzáá Nádleehé (Changing Woman), 16, 24

assimilation, 6, 27, 63, 140; child removal and, 227n23; education programs and, 93

Assiniboine-Sioux Tribe, 145

Associated Press, 171

Associated Students of BYU, 169

Atlantic, 85

auxiliary programs, 47, 63–64

Avery, Amy, 90, 91

Avery, Shaela Willie, 123–124

Azee Bee Nahagha of Diné Nation, Inc. (ABNDN), 243n140

Babbitt brothers, 116, 127

Babbitt trading post, 126

Baca, Angelo, 37

Bahr, Howard M., 246n24

Bailey, Garrick, 25

Bailey, Roberta Glenn, 25

Baird, John Edwin, 33, 62, 68, 122, 191, 240n83

Baloo, Sheiyenne, 153

baptism, 3, 5, 22, 70, 78–80, 96, 114, 181, 182, 194; baseball, 78; for the dead, 115; Indigenous, 78–79; missions and, 81–83; priesthood and, 32, 229n43; quotas of, 79–80; term, 72

Barboncito, 34

Barolong, Tshidi, 12

Basic Unit Plan, 139

Bateman, Merrill J., 147

Bear River Massacre: A Shoshone History (Parry), 48

Bears Ears, 38–39
Bears Ears Inter-Tribal Coalition, 37
Bears Ears National Monument, 37, 38
Beauty Way Prayer, 8, 25, 220n10
Bedonie, Ella, 106, 107
Begay, Ernest Harry, 221n15
Begay, Jeremy, 165
Begay, Loren, 77–78, 205
Begay, Matt, 81
Begay, Nanabah, 194, 195, 202, 203
Begay, Nora Mae, 119, 266n115; ISPP and, 174;
    photo of, 175; warning from, 176
Begay, Ralph, 135
Begay, Robert, 125
Begay, Roger, 20
Begay, Rudy, 116, 226–227n15
belief systems: Diné, 181, 189; LDS, 181, 189
Ben, Olivia, 15, 16, 44, 185, 186; Diné identity
    and, 26
Benally, Anna, 81, 184, 187, 199; photo of, 185
Benally, Jimmy N., 51, 53, 68–69, 73, 74, 75, 79,
    81, 184; challenges for, 98–99
Benally, Julia, 64
Benally, Moroni, 12
Benally, Ruby Whitesinger, 133, 194, 204
Benally, Thomas, 4–5, 44
Benedek, Emily, 106
Bennion, Robert, 169, 264n85
Benson, Ezra Taft, 92, 93, 247n44, 254n3
Between Sacred Mountains, 23
Beyal, Anthony, 147, 148, 186, 187
Beyal, Brenda, 95–96, 104, 146, 147, 149; on
    Placement Program, 103
Beyal, Clyde, 63, 69, 89, 238n46
Beyond the Four Corners of the World: A
    Navajo Woman's Journal (Benedek), 106
biculturalism, 21, 26
Bigman, Yvonne Martin, 110
Bik'eh Hózhǫ́ ("Road of Beauty"), 7
Bilagáana (whites), 1, 21, 97
Billison, Sam, 61
Billy, Bahe, 119
Bishop, Clarence R., 91, 92, 93
Bitter Water clan, 153
Bitton, Davis, 40
Black, Rex, 128
Black Power, 166
Black-Streaked Woods clan, 1

Black World, 22
Blanca Peak, 201, 221n17
Blessing Way ceremony, 26, 108
Blessing Way Prayer, 25, 35, 194, 220n10
Bloomfield, George, 56, 116, 126
Bloomfield, Lucy, 56, 116, 126, 190; lyrics by,
    107–108
Blue World, 22
boarding schools, 88, 90, 94, 111, 152; religion
    classes at, 89; unmarked graves at, 209.
    See also education
Body of Power, Spirit of Resistance: The
    Culture of History of a South African People
    (Comaroff), 12
Book of Laman, The (Harrison), 232n86
Book of Mormon, 2, 4, 20, 29–30, 43, 44,
    54, 86, 88; analyses of, 40; Diné and, 63,
    64–65, 189; interpretations of, 75–76, 140;
    Lamanites and, 6, 45, 46, 53, 65, 103, 155;
    learning about, 90; misuse of, 13; questions
    about, 64; as tool of colonialism, 13; as tool
    of invasion/replacement, 12; translation of,
    29; truthfulness of, 40–41
Boone, Audrey, 97, 98, 141, 142
border towns, 49, 50, 51, 52, 81, 138
Bosque Redondo, 33, 160
Bourdieu, Pierre, 228n40
Bowman, Emery, 103
Box Elder County, Utah, 34
Boxer, Elise, 13, 85, 149
Boyden, John Sterling, 61
Boy Scouts, 64, 68, 120, 129, 206
brainwashing, 13, 107, 195
Bread Springs, 49
Brigham City, Utah, 88, 89, 152
Brigham Young and the Expansion of the
    Mormon Faith (Alexander), 54
Brigham Young University (BYU), 38, 145,
    154; attending, 2, 64, 155; "multicultural,"
    176–179; Native American students at, 16,
    155–176; racism at, 170–171
Brooke, John L., 227n32
Brown, Anna, 187
Brown, Darrell, 113, 199
Brown, Laura, 113, 123, 181–182
Brown, Marci, 187
Brown, Robert Lowell, 68
Brown, Romero, 113, 123, 124, 135, 137, 198, 202

Brown, Shane, 191–192

Brown, Wallace, 100, 191

Buchanan, Golden R., 49, 61, 74, 139; Avery and, 90, 91; Indian Relations Committee and, 71; mission challenges and, 60, 72; Shadow Leadership and, 120; SWIM and, 62

Buchanan, Thelma, 91

Bulow, Ernie, 24

Bureau of Indian Affairs (BIA), 56, 118, 140

Bureau of Land Management, 50

Burson, Carnes, 7, 108, 109, 159, 160, 259n18, 261n41; photo of, 108

Butler, Virginia, 126, 128, 129

BYU. *See* Brigham Young University

BYU 144th Ward, 145

BYU ARTS Partnership, 104

BYU Lamanite Ward, 138

Cadman, Carole, 180–181

Cameron, J. Elliot, 170

Canyon de Chelly, 132

Cashner, Frances: photo of, 167

Central Navajo District, 132

ceremonies: culture and, 183–195; Diné, 25, 50, 97, 182, 184, 187, 190; sing and, 268n10

Chaco Canyon, 16

Chadwick, Bruce A., 246n24

Charles Redd Center for Western Studies (BYU), 17, 43, 44, 93, 204, 205; interviews by, 102; Native American oral history and, 87, 94, 183–184; Placement students and, 95

Charlie, Wayne, 227n15

Chavez, Julius Ray, 96–97, 99, 184

Cheii, 196, 197, 198

child removal, 227n23, 247n39, 260n29

Chinle (Ch'ínílį), 80, 118, 132–137, 202, 203, 205

Chinle Branch, 118, 119, 253n53

Chinle Church, 119

Chinle District, 132

Chinle Stake, 120, 124, 130, 133, 134–135, 137, 204

Chinle Stake Center, photo of, 45

Chinle Stake Gardens, photo of, 131

Chinle Ward, 118

Christianity, 5, 9–10, 12; devotion to, 182; Indigenous engagement with, 226n6; spreading, 9–10

Christian Reform church, 2, 4950

Chun, Jarrett, 143, 144; photo of, 143

Chun, Miriam, 143, 144; photo of, 143

Chun, Taran K., 146, 147, 148, 150

Church Historical Department, 45, 204

Church History Archives, 237n43

Church History Department, 17, 181, 194, 204

Church History Library, 250n4

Church Indian Committee, 156

Church Rock, 309

Cinniginnie, Gabriel, 66

civil rights, 179; Black, 171; movement, 164, 174, 258n3; Native American, 155–176

clans, 16, 24, 35, 124, 198

Clark, J. Reuben, 254n3

Clemmer, Janice White, 177

Cody, Millie: photo of, 161

Cole, Nat King, 49

Collier, John, 56–57

Collins, Yanibaa, 189

colonialism, 11–12, 13, 57, 63, 82, 94, 95, 138; experiences/struggles with, 220n12; legacy of, 164, 235n12; liberation from, 234n3; structures/frameworks for, 10; violent, 159. *See also* settler colonialism

Colonialism in Question (Cooper), 11

colonization, 10, 12, 13, 19, 90

colonized, colonizer and, 10, 14, 19, 221n21

Columbus, Christopher, 39

Colvin, Gina, 262n43

Comaroff, Jean, 12

Comes Out Bird, Vickie, 158, 159, 160, 172, 174, 176, 260n26

communication, 30, 31; nonverbal, 34

community, 14–17, 19, 26, 155; building, 124, 141; Diné, 15, 17, 18, 38, 70, 71, 82, 116, 142, 144, 154, 180; Indigenous, 42, 167, 175; Lamanite, 154

congregations, 1–2, 119; Native American, 129, 138, 141–144, 146, 152–154

Connell, Cynthia, 177, 267n130

Cook, Gene R., 29

Cooper, Frederick, 11, 12, 13

Corntassel, Jeffrey, 11

Corporation of the President of the Church of Jesus Christ of Latter-day Saints, 84

Corporation of the Presiding Bishop of the Church of Jesus Christ of Latter-day Saints, 84

"Cougar Song, The," 160

Council of Fifty, 54

COVID-19, 136, 137, 196

Cowdery, Oliver, 42, 78
Cowley, Matthew, 254n3
Cox, Vickie Washburn, 156, 173, 266n107
Coyote, 34, 35
Crandall, Maurice, 262n43
Crockett, Earl C., 165
Crowfoot, Monika Brown, 9, 39, 198, 199, 205, 271n4
Crowfoot, Samuel "Sam," 198
Crystal, Navajo Nation, 20, 116
Cub Scouts, 64
cultural differences, 30, 33, 186
cultural exchange, 71, 74, 82
culture, 10, 27, 31, 39, 101, 145, 167–168, 176; alien, 12; ancestral, 82; Anglo-American, 26, 97; ceremonies and, 183–195; Diné, 15, 24, 25, 26, 52, 67, 68, 97, 104, 111, 115, 125, 151, 184, 185, 186, 189, 200; Diné LDS and, 180–195; European-American, 184; excluding, 144; Indigenous, 48, 74, 75, 96–97, 104, 157, 167, 168, 185, 190, 200, 259n15; Lamanite, 167–168; recognizing, 90; white settler, 112
Custer Died for Your Sins (Deloria), 2, 164, 263n57
Cutler, Alpheus, 54

Daily Universe (BYU newspaper), 155, 170
dances, 184; ceremonial, 268n19; Native American, 75, 167; Pacific Islander, 75; Yeii' bicheii, 184
Dandy, James Lee, 34, 165, 184, 186, 192, 220n14; Lamanites and, 133
Darwin, Valerie, 180–181
dating, interracial, 4, 5
decolonization, 10, 11, 13, 37
Decolonizing Methodologies (Smith), 10
Deloria, Vine, Jr., 2, 263n57
De Mente, Boyé Lafayette, 30–31
Denetdale, Jennifer Nez, 16, 27
Deschine, Wilson Yazzie, 123, 204–205
Dialogue: A Journal of Mormon Thought, 39
Dibé Nitsaa, 23, 221n17
Diné, 39, 55, 77, 83, 96; exile for, 33–34; foundations of, 6–14; influence of, 125; Lamanites and, 42, 43–46; LDS, 9, 26–27, 30–35, 68–69, 89, 110, 137; LDS and, 9, 26–27, 30–35, 55; legacy of, 7; pathway of, 195; as religion, 4, 5; relocation of, 141; term, 219n1

Diné Bikéyah (Navajo country), 2, 3, 6, 12, 14, 15, 16, 17, 18, 20, 21, 25, 26, 37, 51, 52, 53, 55, 56, 58, 60, 61, 72, 74, 79; connections to, 124; demarcation of, 152; Kānaka Maoli/ Māori missionaries in, 64–65; landmarks of, 221n17; LDS presence in, 66, 73, 80, 81; mission in, 64, 67, 68, 77; term, 226n9; valuing, 22; wards in, 121
Diné Bisodizin Bee Hadahaazt'i'gii (Navajo Introductory Prayer), 202
Diné bizaad (Navajo language), 1, 15, 25, 52, 62, 80, 97, 99, 111, 113, 124, 130, 141, 150–152, 201, 229n42, 242n129; English and, 73; learning, 71, 77–78; missionary messages in, 69; philosophy and, 30–31; quotes in, 194–195; religion and, 7; studying, 72; teaching in, 123, 130; using, 70, 73, 133
Diné Bizaad Na'nitiníbá, 70
Diné College, 23, 135
Diné History of Navajoland, A (Kelley and Francis), 23
Dinéjí Na'nitin (ancestral teachings), 14, 15
Dinétah, 16, 22; term, 226n9
discrimination, 3, 89, 170, 172; racial, 4
displacement/dispossession, 66, 158–159
Diyin Dine'é, 6
Diyin, term, 72
Doctrine and Covenants, 29, 53, 165, 204
Dodge, Chee, 58
Dook'o'oosłííd, 23, 99, 221n17
Drexel, Mother Katherine, 121
Duffy, John-Charles, 41, 46, 47

Eagle's Eye, 165, 169
Echo Hawk, Larry: armbands and, 171; Native American rights and, 177–178
Edge Water clan, 153
Edmo, Louise, 168
education, 27, 58, 85, 91, 96, 104, 178, 179; assimilation and, 93, 243n147; Bilagaanas', 90; controlling, 87; Diné, 88–89; institutionalized, 47; Native American, 107, 168; poor quality, 88; respectable, 102. *See also* boarding schools
Edwards, Dan, 163
"Elder Wally Brown" (Brown), 191–192
Embry, Jessie, 27, 85, 123, 127, 130, 184, 250n4, 252n38

Enemy Way, 25
Ensign, The, 40, 204
epistemology, 10, 30, 35, 73
"Era of Lamanites," 46
Estes, Nick: colonialism/injustice/violence and, 234n12; on poverty/structural challenges, 235n12
Etcitty, Patty Tauchin, 102
ethnic branches, eliminating, 139
ethnicity, 52, 75, 139, 140, 164, 181; broad/ ambiguous terms of, 257n47; social construct of, 158
Evans, Ralph William, 57–58, 117, 126, 191, 327n44
Executive Order Area, 61
Exponent II, Crowfoot and, 199

family: Diné, 93; importance of, 175, 203–204
FamilySearch, 153, 257n49
Farella, John R., 220n10
Farmer, Jared, 55
Farmington, New Mexico, 49, 142
federal government, relocation policy and, 140–141
Felt, Paul E., 62, 165, 168
firesides, described, 249n83
First Laugh Ceremony, 201
First Nation, 36, 112
First Peoples, 22, 57, 83
First Presidency, 62, 140, 146, 181, 185
First Quorum of the Seventy, 18, 29
First Vision, 27, 28, 73
Fixico, Donald, 14
Flagstaff, Arizona, 49, 99, 178
Flake, David Kay, 42, 59, 124
Flake, S. Eugene, 59, 118
Flandro, Royce, 160, 169, 261n41, 263n59
Flora (cousin), 198; baptism of, 114–115
For Indigenous Eyes Only: A Decolonization Handbook (Wilson and Yellowbird), 10
Fort Apache Indian Reservation, 240n78
Fort Defiance hospital, 122
Fort Sumner, 33, 160
Fort Wingate Boarding School, 50
Fort Wingate Branch, 105, 114, 190, 196, 249n83
Fort Wingate Latter-day Saint church, 208
Four Sacred Directions, 20, 114, 207, 221n17
Four Sacred Mountains, 23, 52, 152, 201, 207, 221n17

Fowler, Lilly, 85
Francis, Harris, 23
Franklin Second Ward, 138, 141, 142, 144, 145, 148, 149, 153, 186, 194; attendance at, 151; Diné members of, 150; Native Americans and, 152
Frazier, Gilbert, 155
Fyans, J. Thomas, 42

Gáamalii (Mormons), 1; term, 219n1
"Gaamalii, The" (SWIM), 242n129
Gáamalii Bina'nitiní, 81
Gallup, New Mexico, 3, 49, 50, 79, 81, 133, 193, 198, 200
Gallup Indian Center, 163
Gallup Sun, 86
Ganado, Navajo Nation, 133, 204
Gardner, Anthony, 99
Gardner, Benjamin, 99
Gardner, Harvey, 127, 132, 133, 253n54
Garrett, Matthew, 85, 92
Garrett, Mildred Cody, 64, 176
Gathering of Tribes, 233n102
gender, 158, 176; Diné conceptualization of, 228–229n41
General Authorities, 46, 58, 59, 65, 115, 133, 147, 254n3; Native American, 110, 190
General Church Lamanite Committee, 59
General Conference, 42
Geronimo, 166
Gilmore, Frankie, 114
Gishi, Leroy, 122
Glittering World, 22
"Go, My Son" (Williams and Burson), 7, 109, 159, 160, 162, 173, 174–175, 259n18, 261n41, 261n42; photo of, 161
Goatson, Derik, 200
Goatson, Elouise Thinn, 101, 199–200
Gobernador Knob, 211n17
God: Diné conceptualizations of, 9; term for, 72
Goldtooth, Mr., 59, 60, 81
Good, the Bad, and the Ugly, The, 127
Gorman, Sam, 60
Goshutes, 54, 55
Graber, Jennifer, 226n6
Graham, Hugh Davis, 258n3
Grandfather Horned Toad, 196; photo of, 197
Grant, Heber J., 56

graves, Native American/First Nation
   children's, 209
Great Eternal Father, 9
Great Eternal Mother, 9
Green Meadow, 121
Griffin, John, 265–266n99
Groves, Alan, 146, 149, 150
Groves, Jeanie Sekaquaptewa, 155–156,
   173–174, 176
Gwilliam, Robert F., 167

Hafen, P. Jane, 109
Hales, Andrea, 36
Hall, Helen Rose John, 90–91, 106
Hamblin, Jacob, 125
Hamilton, Mel, 265–266n99
Harrison, Mette Ivie, 232n86
Hartsock, Tom, 86
Hartvigsen, Milton, 170–171
hataałii (traditional healer), 81, 185, 192, 221n15
Hawaiians, 66, 74, 75, 148, 151
healers: ancestral, 32, 71, 185, 193, 270n45;
   traditional, 81, 85, 192, 221n15
health issues, 47, 88, 136, 235n12
Heavenly Father, 130, 183, 190, 192
Heiss, Matthew, 46, 194, 202, 204
Henderson, Betty, 183; photo of, 175
heritage, 27, 39; Diné, 21–26, 124, 125, 176, 201;
   Indigenous, 18, 153, 187
Hinckley, Gordon B., 32, 185, 229n43
history, 12, 15, 66; decolonization of, 11; erasure
   of, 222n24; family, 151, 152; Native American,
   14, 160, 222n24, 223n34, 245n19. *See also* oral
   history
Hogue, Helena, 100, 101, 104, 184
Holbrook, Arizona, 55, 75, 133
Holti (school), 88
Holy Ghost, 30, 71
Holy People, 6, 23, 24, 25, 97
Holy Spirit, 40, 77
Homestead Act, 50
homosexuality, 85
Hopi-Navajo Long Range Rehabilitation Act
   (1953), 88
Hopis, 55, 74; baptism of, 126; influence of, 125
Horned Toads, 196, 197, 198, 209
House of Israel, 21, 28, 29, 151, 235n17; DNA
   evidence for, 228n37

hózhǫ́, 6, 8, 17, 25, 130, 188, 201, 207, 220n12,
   221n14, 234n9; interpretation of, 7, 220n10;
   teachings of, 102
Hózhǫ́ójí, 108
Huerfano Peak, 221n17
Hunsaker, Don C., 62
Hwééłdi ("The Land of Suffering"), 33, 160

identity, 16, 19, 77, 90, 187; collective, 14, 17, 26,
   166; common, 150–152; compound, 15, 17, 18;
   cultural, 187; Diné, 4, 23, 26, 27, 33, 142, 183,
   195, 201, 206; expression of, 200; Indigenous,
   9, 13, 159, 166, 176; Lamanite, 39–40,
   43–46, 46–48, 65, 75, 162, 166, 167; LDS, 81;
   markers of, 15; multilayered, 21, 27, 44; songs
   and, 207; speaking about, 190; split, 26;
   transnational, 83; tribal, 169, 173
Iese, Tavita, 66
Iese, Zenobia Kapahulehua, 66
imperialism, 11, 19
In Laman's Terms: Looking at Lamanite Identity
   (Baca), 37
Indian Child Welfare Act (ICWA) (1978), 92
Indian Country Today, 85
Indian Education Department (BYU),
   160, 176
Indian Education Program, 8, 47, 93, 156,
   164, 167, 169, 177
Indian Health Service, 201
Indianness, displays of, 206
Indian New Deal, livestock reduction and, 56
Indian Relations Committee, 70, 71
Indian Relocation Act (1956), 151, 255n15
Indian Removal Act (1830), 54
Indian Reorganization Act (1934), 56, 140
Indian Seminary programs, 14, 99
Indian Student Placement Program (ISPP), 8,
   12, 14, 13, 15, 18, 34, 35, 43, 44, 47, 77, 79, 84–
   85, 87, 123, 126, 134, 157, 158, 160, 164, 172, 174,
   185, 187, 190; advantage of, 103; assessment
   of, 104–105; assumptions/interpretations of,
   86; baptisms and, 80; beginnings of, 90–91,
   94; condemnation of, 106, 112, 246n25;
   described, 90–105; Diné bizaad and, 52; end
   of, 86, 92; family sacrifices for, 95–96; foster
   homes and, 156; guidelines for, 105; learning
   about, 93; mixed reactions to, 94; Native
   American empowerment and, 106; as official

church program, 91–93; participation in, 92, 95, 99, 100, 105–112, 114, 180; recruiting for, 165; student views of, 93–104

Indian Vocational Training Act (1956), 255n15

Indian Week, 168

"Indigenous and 'Lamanite' Identities in the Twentieth Century" (Ing), 36–37

Indigenous peoples, 11, 14, 21, 29, 36, 37, 39, 52, 54, 59, 82, 150, 151, 159, 168, 206; presence of, 38; reorientation by, 12; revitalization of, 162; stories of, 18; subjugation/ dispossession of, 112

Ing, Michael David Kaulana, 36

injustice, 14, 112, 163, 164, 170, 234n12

Inscription House, 192

Institutional Review Board (IRB), 247n39

Intermountain Indian Boarding School, 88, 89, 108, 152, 238n55

ISPP. *See* Indian Student Placement Program

Israelites, 3, 28, 36

Iverson, Peter, 56

"I Walk in Beauty" (Williams), 7

Jackson, Cleo: photo of, 167

Jacobs, Margaret D., 260n29

James, Damon, 89

Jensen, Celia, 91

Jensen, Miles, 91

Jesus Christ, 28, 190; redemption and, 30

Jim, Rex Lee, 226n15

John Birch Society, 92

John Paul II, Pope, 121

Johnson, Lane, 40

John the Baptist, 30, 78

Jones, Dennis: photo of, 189

Jones, Helen: photo of, 167

Jones, Irene B., 99, 188; photo of, 189

Jones, Paul, 60

Jumbo, George, 56

Jumbo, Mary, 56, 63

June, Adolph, Jr., 108

Justice, Larry, 130

Kaibetony, Kee, 60

Kaibetony, Nora, 203

Kalauli, Mitchell Davis Kapuni, 134

Kalauli, Winna B., 120

Kan, Sergei, 226n8

Kānaka Maoli, 11, 43, 53, 64, 66, 76–77, 83

Kanaka ʻŌiwi, 36, 66, 75, 143

Kapahulehua, Cynthia, 66

Kauanui, K. Kehaulani, 12

Kayenta, Navajo Nation, 132, 189

k'é (kinship and clan system), 16, 17, 31, 35, 96, 124; traditional teachings of, 15

Kee-Jansen, Chauma, 145

Keeler, Bill, 84

Keeler, Jacqueline, 93

K'é Hwiindzin, 35

Kelley, Klara, 23

Kelly, Prestine Ann, 100

Kelly, William Keoniana, 75, 77

Ketcher, Beverly: photo of, 175

Kim, Kaleiwahine, 151–152

Kimball, Spencer W., 47, 59, 61, 67, 117, 132, 151, 164; assignment for, 258n4; Avery and, 91; blessing from, 258n4; death of, 46; dedication by, 126; Diné/Church functions and, 121; on ethnic branches, 139; Indigenous communities and, 42; influence of, 178; Lamanite Cause and, 6, 52, 166; Lamanites and, 43, 155, 157; leadership of, 8, 156; legacy of, 8; medical issues for, 57; Native Americans and, 18; photo of, 161; plan by, 139; shadow leadership and, 120; vision of, 8, 178; whiteness/delightsomeness and, 86; Wilkinson and, 169

Kinaaldá, 186

King, Brian, 39, 113; photo of, 111

King, Farina Smith, 113; photo of, 111, 185, 189, 197, 208

King, Randy, 148

King, Tyson, 85, 110, 112; photo of, 111

King, Wesley: photo of, 197

Kinlacheeny, Susie T., 188

kinship, 6, 16, 35, 90, 124

Kin Yaʼa, 16

Kinyaaʼáanii, 16, 24

Kunz, Merle, 2, 4, 36, 164, 200

Laman, 29, 40, 43, 44, 232n86

Lamanite, term, 44

Lamanite and Minority Committee, 46

Lamanite Cause, 19, 151; Kimball and, 6, 52, 166; termination of, 92

Lamanite Era, 6

Lamanite Generation, 75, 160, 167, 172–173, 264n77; performance of, 76 (photo)
Lamanite Israel, 78
Lamanite question, 35–43
Lamanites, 3, 18, 29, 36, 37, 39–40, 52, 62, 86, 90, 92, 103, 120, 133, 136, 141, 142, 148, 151, 154, 157, 160, 166, 167–168, 177, 178, 190, 204, 205; appropriations of, 264n78; avoiding, 46–48; Book of Mormon and, 6, 45, 46, 53, 65, 155; Christians and, 108–109; descendants of, 53; Diné and, 42–46, 202; DNA research on, 41; First Peoples and, 57; gospel/membership and, 43; LDS, 174; New Jerusalem and, 206; Oneida, 54; Pacific Islands and, 42, 64–65; performances by, 75; programs/services for, 155; shift from, 48; SWIM and, 64; term, 37, 40, 258n6
Lamanite Singers, 75
"Lamanite Song of Thanks" (Bloomfield), 107
Lamanite Truth, 36
Lamanitettes, 172, 173
Lamoni, King, 43
Lamphere, Louise, 180, 234n4
Landon, Michael, 204
Lane, Rex, 67, 79, 81
Language Training Center, 70, 77
Language Training Mission, 73
La Plata Peak, 221n17
Latin Americans, 64, 151; Lamanites and, 42
LDS Family Services, 84
Lee, George P., 18, 46, 62, 110, 190; Brown and, 198; excommunication of, 123, 133, 178, 264n90; Flake and, 42; ISPP and, 86; newsletter by, 79; photo of, 19; as TMF president, 169
Lee, Harold B., 47, 254n3
Lee, Lester, 121
Lee, Lloyd L., 15
Lee Branch, 121–125
Legacy of Conquest: The Unbroken Past of the American West, The (Limerick), 11
Lehi, 28, 60, 144, 157, 235n17, 261n36; vision of, 188
Lemuel, 29, 43, 44
Lesser, Alexander, 33
Lewis, Hazel, 67
LGBTQ+2S, 85
lifeways, Diné, 23, 182, 220–221n14

Limerick, Patricia Nelson, 11–12
Linton, John G., 73
Littell, Norman M., 59, 61
Little, Dennis, 81, 206
Little, Marie, 73, 81, 206
Little, Susie, 67, 74, 183
Littlefield, Ruth, 130
Living Legends, 75
Livingston, John, 199
Livingston, Julie Ann, 209; photo of, 208
Longenecker, Emmalani Smith: photo of, 111
Long Life in Beauty, 20
Long Walk, 33, 132, 160, 193
Lopez, Alexia, 184
Los Angeles Indian Branch, 141
Lukachukai Ward, 135
Lyman, Albert R., 57, 88, 117, 126
Lyman, Gladys Perkins, 57, 88, 126
Lynch, Ernesteen B., 8, 10, 25, 142, 221n20; baptism of, 122; as bicultural, 26; emotional illness for, 185; missionaries and, 9; oral history of, 227n21; on reservation, 33; split identity for, 26

Máamalii (reservation), 1
Mannie, Victor, Sr., 68, 102, 104, 105, 200
Manuelito, Chief (Hastiin Ch'ilhaajiní, "Man of the Black Weeds Place"), 87, 88, 108–109, 160
Manuscript History of the Indian Branch, 141
Manygoats, Charlene, 128, 129
Māoris, 53, 65, 66, 71–72, 74, 75, 83
marriages, 175; interracial/intercultural, 55, 142, 200
Marshall, Kimberly Jenkins, 219n6
Martin, Joel W., 6
maternalism, paternalism and, 108–109
Mathews, James D., 182
Mauss, Armand L., 41–42, 43, 44, 46, 91
McCabe, Rose, 123
McKay, David O., 254n3
McNeely, Charlyne Kaulukukui, 66; photo of, 67
medicine men, 51, 81, 185, 192, 270n46
meeting places, 116–120
Melchizedek Priesthood, 32, 133, 139
Merrill, Joseph F., 254n3
Methodist church, 8
Mills, Jessica, 190

Minority Group Committee, 139
Mirabel, Shaynalea, 44
Miss Indian America Pageant, 119, 174, 176
Miss Indian BYU, 160, 166, 172, 173–174; candidates/warning for, 176; photo of, 161, 175
Miss Indian BYU Pageant, 158, 174
missionaries, 54, 57, 82, 95, 110, 116, 135; Christian, 72; dialogue/engagement by, 68; Diné, 53, 67, 68, 72, 73, 74, 82, 119; Indigenous, 53, 65–66, 72, 75, 83; Lamanite, 64, 65, 66, 71; Māori, 71–72; Pacific Islander, 75; photo of, 51, 67; Polynesian, 75, 77; service, 120; SWIM, 63, 69, 70, 72, 81–82; True Israel, 66; welfare/health, 47
missionary work, 8, 9, 20, 47, 75, 78, 79
misunderstandings, 31, 34, 80, 96, 150, 223n34; cultural, 33, 35, 97
Mitchell, Ray, 130, 201, 202, 203
Moenkopi Wash, 55, 56, 126
Monson, Thomas S., 185
Monument Valley, Navajo Nation, 110, 130, 201
Monument Valley Ward, 136, 201
Mormon, term, 219n1
Mormon History Association, 36–37
Mormon-Indian, term, 223n31
Mormonism, 17, 18, 199; condemnation of, 14; decolonizing, 37; history of, 12; introducing, 10; lived experiences of, 77; reimagining, 37; status in, 44
Mount Blanca, 23
Mount Hesperus, 23
Mount Taylor, 23, 221n17
Mueller, Max Perry, 43
Multicultural Education Department, 176
multiculturalism, 176–179, 267n126
Murphy, Thomas W., 37, 41, 232n77
music, Indigenous, 74, 75

Naʼashǫ́ʼii dichʼizhii (Grandfather Horned Toad), 209
Nabahe, Kenneth, 183
National Indian Youth Council (NIYC), 156, 157, 158, 166, 170; banning of, 164; purpose of, 163
Native American Church, 80, 119, 180, 181, 243n140
Native American Curriculum Initiative, 104
Native American Oral History Project, 17, 181

Native Americans, 10, 14, 18, 31, 39, 40, 43, 51, 64, 66, 92, 140, 148; addressing, 70; colonization of, 90; derision from, 98; displaced/dispossessed, 158–159; hope/ optimism of, 106–107; ISPP and, 95; Pioneer Day and, 150; relocation of, 141
Native American students, 3, 101, 155–156, 175, 177; armbands for, 170; BYU and, 157, 159, 163, 165, 166–167, 171, 174, 178; prohibitions for, 4; TMF and, 170
Native American studies, 10, 155, 159, 177, 190
Natonabah, Andrew, 23, 206
nature, 6, 33, 38; views of, 24, 25
Navajo, 51, 105, 106, 122, 135, 136, 191, 251n21; entanglements with, 260n29; reaffirming, 6; self-identifying as, 183; term, 219n1; traditional ways and, 5; true, 182. See also Diné
Navajo-Hopi Land Dispute, 61, 125
Navajo House, 192
Navajo Nation, 4, 16, 21, 49, 52, 80, 104, 105, 121, 130, 133, 140, 142, 153; LDS Church and, 115, 117, 125; mission to, 18–19; oral history interviews in, 17; recruiting students from, 91; stakes in, 132, 136; SWIM and, 61; wards in, 136
Navajo Nation District Court, 84
Navajo reservation, 49, 56, 116, 136, 151, 187; congregations on, 115, 119, 135; missions on, 14, 120
Navajo Times, 67, 71
Navajo Tradition, Mormon Life (Dandy), 184
Navajo Tribal Advisory Board, 118
Navajo Tribal Council, 58, 59, 60–61, 79, 88, 125, 135, 251n21; building plans and, 117–118; challenge from, 92; Collier and, 56–57
Navajo-Zuni Mission, 57, 59, 191
Nazarene Church, 81
Nelson, Russell M., 40, 219n1, 231n75
Nephi, 29, 40, 60, 86, 113, 261n36; vision of, 188
Nephite Project, 36
Nephites, 40, 43, 86, 206; genocide of, 29
Newcomb, Sarah, 36, 112, 249n96
New Jerusalem, 36, 206
New Mexico-Arizona Mission, 62
New Testament, 2, 28, 194
New Western History, 11
New York Times, 130, 241n106

Nez, Cal, 84, 85
Nez, Harlan, 129
Nez, Liz, 84, 128, 129, 130, 202
Nez Perce, 157
Neztsosie, Richard "Dick," 165, 166, 168
Nihi Kéyah (Diné land), 15
Ni'hookaa Diyan Diné (Holy Earth People), 22
Nixon, Richard, 140, 141
NIYC. *See* National Indian Youth Council
Norcross, Walker, 118
Northern Indian Mission, 52, 66, 164, 235n18
North Park Fifth Ward, 145, 146, 147, 148–149
North Park Stake, 145
Northwestern Band of Shoshone, 48
Ntsékees, 201
Numkena, William, 133–134, 205

Oceti Sakowin Oyate, 159, 261n32
Office of Belonging (BYU), 266n99
Office of Indian Affairs (BYU), 165
Ólta' Gáamalii ("Mormon School"), 83, 87
Oneida, 39, 198
On Zion's Mount (Farmer), 55
Operation Firewood Rescue, 136
oral history, 17–19, 35, 106, 121, 123, 153, 188, 194, 204, 205, 227n21; LDS, 87; Native American, 14, 23, 87, 94, 161, 183–184
Orientalism (Said), 94
Othering, 94

Pacific Islanders, 53, 65, 71, 75
Pacific Islands, 29, 41; Lamanites and, 42, 64–65
Packer, Boyd K., 32, 253n54
Page, Arizona, 127, 132, 133, 187
Paiutes, 54, 55, 74
Papago Ward, 13, 152–153, 192, 257n49
Paredes, Ellouise, 97, 193
Parry, Darren, 48
paternalism, maternalism and, 108–109
Patton, Dale, 133
Paul Revere and the Raiders, 266n107
Pentecostals, 57
People of the Seven Fires, 159
peoplehood, 15, 22, 28, 109, 121; Indigenous, 173, 207; legacy of, 25–26
Perforated Rock, 121
Petersen, Mark E., 254n3

Peterson, H. Burke, 133
peyote, 57, 80, 99, 187
philosophy, 102; Diné language and, 30–31
Pine, Donald, 190, 196
Pioneer Day, 149, 150
pioneer treks, Native American youth and, 129
Placement families, 84, 91, 92, 102, 107, 165; Diné and, 100; lottery and, 100–101; stereotypes and, 98
Placement program. *See* Indian Student Placement Program
Placement students, 84, 85, 87, 108–109, 110, 111, 112, 188; education of, 103–105; experiences of, 95, 96, 101, 104, 106; lottery and, 100–101; Native American culture and, 96–97; recollection of, 94, 95; religious life of, 103; struggles of, 103; testimony of, 101–102, 119
Plan of Salvation, 30, 48, 70, 72
Plymouth Rock, protests at, 165
Polacca, "Howela," 20, 57, 238n46
Polacca, Ruth Arviso, 20, 57
Polacca Stake, 132
Polynesians, 43, 64, 66, 77, 151, 170
Pooley, Lillie, 127, 187–188
Pooley, Ray, 126
Poor People's Campaign, 164
Potawatomi, 54
poverty, 105, 235n12; race and, 164
prayer, meaning of, 7
Preston, Scott, 60
Price, Eva, 80, 180, 181
priesthood, 30, 47, 183, 192, 193; ban on, 172; baptism and, 32, 229n43; Black, 171; ordination for, 32; power of, 193
Priesthood Executive Committee (PEC), 146
Primary Presidency, 123
proselytization, 6, 48, 54, 61, 63, 65, 68, 74, 126; methods for, 70
Protestants, 57
Proud Earth (Williams), 221n18
"Proudly We Stand" (TMF), 158
Provo, Utah, 138, 144, 184, 198
Provo River Battle (1850), 55
Provo South Stake, 144, 149
puberty ceremony, Diné, 186
Public Law 959, 255n15
public schools, 85, 88. *See also* boarding schools; education

Pueblos, 27
Pulsipher, Jennifer Hale, 55

Quintana, Eileen, 95
Quorum of the Twelve, 139

race, 140, 172, 176, 181; committee of, 179;
   poverty and, 164; social construct of, 158
racial uplift, ideologies of, 157, 260n20
racism, 52, 89, 92, 164, 172, 178, 199; charges of,
   170–171; history of, 12
Rainer, Howard, 168–169, 177, 267n129
Red Power, 155, 157, 158, 159, 161–162, 164, 165,
   166, 174, 178, 258n1
Red Rock 10 movie theater, 49
Reed People, 16
Rehoboth Christian Reformed Church, 2,
   49–50
Relief Society, 62, 63, 91, 118, 120, 124, 129, 133,
   144, 204
religion, 9–10, 27, 74, 84, 158, 176, 182, 200;
   classes, 89; conceptualization of, 220n12;
   freedom of, 60, 119; institutionalized, 7, 180;
   term, 260n28; translations of, 234n8
relocation policy, federal government and,
   140–141
Restoration of the Church, 28
Richards, A. LeGrand, 144, 145, 147, 148–149
Richards, Stephen L., 254n3
Richfield, Utah, 91, 152, 194, 204; ISPP and, 90
Roberts, Hailee, 153
Rock Point Community School, 23
Roe, Doug, 134
Roemer, Kenneth, 206–207
Rohner, Alfred Eugene, 62
Romero, Sandy: photo of, 167
Ross, Annie: homeland and, 225n59

Sacred Mountain, 23, 25, 99
sacred symbols, Diné, 114
Said, Edward, 94
Salina Trading Post, 60
Salt Lake City, Utah, 56, 61, 85, 153, 172
Salt Lake Tribune, 84
Salt Lake Valley, 64, 100
Salt River Pima-Maricopa Indian Community,
   13, 152, 192
Samoan Fire Dance, 75

Samoans, 45, 66, 74, 75, 122
Sanders, Victoria (Vickie), 260n26
sandpaintings, 183, 190
San Francisco Peak, 23, 99, 221n17
San Jose State University football players,
   266n101; boycott by, 170, 171
San Juan County, Utah, 37–38, 55
schools. See boarding schools; education
Secody, Loretta, 67
Second Coming of Jesus Christ, 28
segregation, 138; racial/ethnic, 142
Sekaquaptewa, Ken, 62, 167, 172
Selam, Victor, 157
self-identity, 18, 26, 98, 140–141
seminary program, Native American, 89
Senate Subcommittee on Indian Affairs,
   247n44
Servant Sword, 79
settler colonialism, 13, 53, 149, 173; history of,
   222n27; violence of, 112. See also colonialism
Sevier County, Utah, 152
sexual abuse, 110, 112, 243n47
shadow leadership, described, 120–121
Shash Jaa' (Baca), 37
Sherman, William Tecumseh, 34
Shiprock, New Mexico, 116; chapel in, 118;
   Navajos in, 142
Shiprock Indian School, 63
Shiprock Trading Post, 57
Shoshones, 54, 55, 74, 75, 159
Si'ah Naagháí ("Forever Lasting Life of Old
   Age"), 7
Si'ah Naagháí Bik'eh Hózhǫ (SNBH), 7, 8, 15, 17,
   21, 23, 48, 52, 202, 221n14; defining, 20
sign language, 149
Siksika Nation, 39, 198
Simon, Hemopereki Hōani, 37
sing: ceremony and, 268n10; gathering for, 69
Singer, Amos, 59
Singer, Lewis, 79
Singer, Ronald L., 63, 67, 73
Sis Naajiní, 23, 201, 221n17
Sisters of the Blessed Sacrament, 121
Smallcanyon, Corey, 26, 152
Smith, Aaron, 207
Smith, Adrian L., 156
Smith, Albert, 24, 196, 209, 225n59
Smith, Dan K., 87, 134, 205

Smith, Florence, 137, 196, 198

Smith, George Albert, 58, 209, 238n55, 258n4

Smith, Helen, 196

Smith, JoAnn, 4, 201; photo of, 5, 19

Smith, Johanna Haskeltsie: photo of, 5, 51

Smith, Joseph, 27, 29, 78, 191; death of, 54; Potawatomi and, 54; priesthood and, 30; as prophet, 71; story of, 73; translation by, 53

Smith, Joseph, Jr., 28

Smith, Joseph F., 47

Smith, Joseph Fielding, 254n3

Smith, Linda Tuhiwai, 10, 13–14

Smith, Lot: death of, 56

Smith, Phillip L., 49, 131, 169, 174–175, 194, 200, 201; civil rights movement and, 164; identity of, 5–6; NIYC and, 164; photo of, 5, 19, 51, 162; Placement and, 156; sing/ceremony and, 268n10; Snake and, 163; Sunday School and, 123; Wilkinson and, 170, 171; youth/education of, 2, 3, 4

Smith, Phyllis: photo of, 111

Smith, Rose, 209

Smouse, Donald, 116

Snake, Stanley, 157, 158, 163

SNBH. See Si'ah Naagháí Bik'eh Hózhǫ́

Snowflake Temple, 129

socioeconomic issues, 99, 136, 164, 165, 178

"Son of Morning," 192–193

songs: honor, 207; identity and, 207; meaning of, 7; Native American, 23, 150

Southern Paiutes, 140

Southwest Indian Mission (SWIM), 4, 7, 8, 18, 33, 42, 51, 52, 53, 59, 82–83, 98, 115, 117, 118, 119, 120, 122, 126, 164; approaches of, 63, 80; baptisms and, 78, 79; beginnings of, 57; boundaries of, 240n78; contacts for, 63–78; disbanding, 79; as geographical mission, 132; history of, 66; impacts of, 80–81; Indigenous ancestry and, 60; ISPP and, 94–95; Lamanites and, 64; leadership of, 62–63; missionary practices of, 63–78; Navajo Nation and, 61; newsletter of, 242n129; photo of, 76; sign, 82 (photo)

Southwest Regional Indian Youth Council, 163

sovereignty, 26, 92, 140, 173

Spanish Sign Language, 149

"Special Navajo Program," 88

spirituality, 10, 39, 48, 71, 87, 102, 194, 203, 207;

concepts of, 21–26; Diné, 23, 26–27, 70, 151, 182, 184, 186, 190, 195, 269n26

stakes, 132, 133, 136; Lamanite, 46

Stapley, Delbert L., 71, 156

Steamboat Branch, 134

stereotypes, Native American, 3–4, 38, 71, 74, 98, 156, 173

Stewart, James M., 57, 58

St. George, Washington County, School District, 92

St. Michael Indian School, 121

St. Michaels, Navajo Nation, 113, 121, 199

Sunday School, 123, 130, 151

Sunrise Trading Post, 116

SWIM. See Southwest Indian Mission

Tahmahkera, Dustin, 173

Tahu, Hector, 72

Talk, Shauntel, 188, 189–190

Tano, Edwin L., 124, 130, 186, 193, 252n38; Chinle Stake and, 133, 135

Tapahonso, Luci, 23, 201, 206

Tarango, Angela, 226n6

Taylor, Hal L., 62, 72–73, 118, 182; Chinle chapel and, 119; Diné and, 4

Taylor, Michael P., 262n44

teachings, 70, 102, 181, 207; ancestral, 23, 25, 100, 107; LDS, 27–30; points for, 79

Tecun, Arcia, 37

Teller, Terry, 21

temple ban, condemnation of, 172

temple work, 115, 129

Termination Era, 165

Termination of Red Streak Rock, 49

testimony, 14, 46, 71, 73–74, 76, 81, 101–103, 124, 127, 130–131, 151, 94, 202–205; sharing, 1–2

Teton Valley, 2, 35

"This Is My Vision" (Kimball), 178

Thom, Melvin "Mel" Daris, 163, 164

Thomas, Richard, 116

Thomas, Robert K., 34

Thompson, Janie, 173

Timpanogos Utes, 55

Tingey, Dale, 62, 120; photo of, 108

TMF. See Tribe of Many Feathers

Toadlena, Navajo Nation, 56, 58, 63, 116

Tohatchi, Navajo Nation, school in, 89

Tom Trails (filmstrip series), 109

To'Nanees'Dizí, 21, 113, 125–137, 251n29; chapel in, 127; LDS presence in, 126. *See also* Tuba City, Arizona

"To Nephi Seer of Olden Times," singing, 188

Tongans, 45, 66, 74

Towering House People, 1, 16, 24

trading posts, 57, 60, 116, 126, 251n21

traditions, 48, 108–109; Diné, 20, 100, 183, 184, 187, 189, 190, 200; Native American, 184, 226n6; oral, 16, 23, 206

Trail of Tears, 173

Treaty of 1868, 52, 55, 88

tribal government: Diné, 126; land use and, 117

Tribal Television, 173

Tribe of Many Feathers (TMF), 3, 143, 163, 165, 166, 168, 169, 170, 174; BYU and, 157; membership in, 158; photo of, 167

"Tribe of Testimonies" (Facebook), 36

Tsaile chapel, 135

Tségháhoodzání, 121

Tséyi, 132

Ts'ihootso, 121

Tsinaajinii clan, 153

Tsinnijinnie, Thomas, 153, 192, 193, 194, 202, 257n49

Ts'ithootso, 113

tsodizin dóó sin (prayer and song), 6, 7, 234n8

Tsoodził, 23, 221n17

Tswana, 12

Tuba City, Arizona, 21, 55, 56, 59, 69, 116, 125, 127, 129, 130, 132, 134, 193, 194; proselytizing in, 126

Tuba City Boarding School, 90, 106

Tuba City First Ward, 127, 128

Tuba City Second Ward, 127, 130, 202

Tuba City Stake, 21, 130, 135, 136, 137, 193, 252n38

Tuba City Ward, 121, 127, 128, 130, 134, 201

Tulley, Virginia Morris Tso, 45, 204

Turley, Fred A., 62

Turley, Harry, 238n46

Turnblom, Sherry L., 77, 80

Tuttle, Theodore, 120, 122

Tweed, Thomas A., 50

Two-Spirit issues, 85

Uchtdorf, Dieter F., 181

umbilical cords, burial of, 20–21, 188

University of Oklahoma (OU), NIYC and, 163, 164

University of Wyoming football players: barring of, 171; protest by, 265–266n99

Upon Their Shoulders, 60, 61

Utah County, Utah, 15, 145, 151

Utah Division of Arts and Museums, 104

Utah Navajo Health System, 201

Utes, 38, 54, 55, 74, 159

Vernon, Craig, 84

Walker River Paiute, 163

Walk of Beauty, 7, 48

Walters, Harry, 229n42

wards: Diné, 115–116; Lamanite, 136, 143; Native American, 138, 141–144, 145

Warm Springs, 157

Warrior, Clyde, 163, 164

Warriors Trump, 79

Watchman, Alvin, 146

Watkins, Arthur V., 140, 247n44

Wax, Rosalie H., 34

Weaving Women's Lives: Three Generations in a Navajo Family (Lamphere), 180

wedding basket, photo of, 5

West, Claralynn, 166

Western Athletic Conference, 170, 171

Whaley, Aneta, 80

Whaley, Oliver (Ollie), 45, 46, 80, 137, 189

Whetten, Lester, 3, 164, 170

White Father, 202

Whitehorse Branch, 69

white man way, 25

White Mesa Utes, 38

White Mountain Apaches, 64

whiteness, 86, 90

white settlers, 27, 32, 112

Wilkinson, Ernest L., 168; Indian Committee and, 259n8; Kimball and, 169; Smith and, 170, 171

William, Morgan, 1, 242n129

William, Thornton: photo of, 167

Williams, Arlene Nofchissey, 7, 8, 109, 159, 160, 221n18, 259n18, 261n36, 261n41; photo of, 108

Willie, David J., 141

Willie, Hank, 227n15

Willie, Jerome Wilmer, 124, 204

Willie, Patrick, 159
Willie, Shelby, 123, 124
Wilson, Waziyatawin Angela, 10
Window Rock, Navajo Nation, 58, 61, 113, 123, 124, 200
Window Rock Ward, 113, 121–125
Winslow, Arizona, 55, 133, 204
Winslow Stake, 133
Wolf, Walter, 125
Wolfe, Patrick: on colonialism, 12
Woodruff, Wilford, 204
Wounded Knee, 169–170

Yakamas, 157
Yazhi, Ashkii, 18–19
Yazzi, Grace: photo of, 167
Yazzie, April, 145
Yazzie, Arnold, 142

Yazzie, Chester: photo of, 167
Yazzie, Jolene: genders and, 228n41
Yazzie, Peter Lee, 134
Yazzie, Robert, 234n9
Yazzie, Shirley Hastine, 141
Ye'ii, 6, 24
Yéii' bicheii, 184; described, 268n19
Yellowbird, Michael, 10
Yellowhair, Helena, 194, 195, 202, 203
Yellow World, 22
Young, Brigham, 54, 55, 327n44
Young, Ernst Clifford, 74–75, 118, 132
Young, Robert W., 1, 242n129
Young Men, 146, 149
Young Women, 101, 128–129, 149, 188, 202

Zion, establishment of, 53, 100, 136
Zunis, 74